General Sir Ralph Abercromby and the French Revolutionary Wars 1792–1801

John Divall
In memoriam

General Sir Ralph Abercromby and the French Revolutionary Wars 1792–1801

Carole Divall

Pen & Sword
MILITARY

AN IMPRINT OF PEN & SWORD BOOKS LTD.
YORKSHIRE – PHILADELPHIA

First published in Great Britain in 2018 by
PEN & SWORD MILITARY
An imprint of
Pen & Sword Books Ltd
Yorkshire – Philadelphia

Copyright © Carole Divall 2018

ISBN 9781526741462

A CIP catalogue record for this book is available from the British Library

Typeset in India by Vman Infotech Private Limited

Printed and bound by TJ International, Padstow, Cornwall

Pen & Sword Books Ltd incorporates the Imprints of Aviation, Atlas, Family
History, Fiction, Maritime, Military, Discovery, Politics, History, Archaeology,
Select, Wharncliffe Local History, Wharncliffe True Crime, Military Classics,
Wharncliffe Transport, Leo Cooper, The Praetorian Press, Remember When,
White Owl, Seaforth Publishing and Frontline Publishing.

For a complete list of Pen & Sword titles please contact

PEN & SWORD BOOKS LTD
47 Church Street, Barnsley, South Yorkshire, S70 2AS, England
E-mail: enquiries@pen-and-sword.co.uk
Website: www.pen-and-sword.co.uk

Or

PEN & SWORD BOOKS
1950 Lawrence Rd, Havertown, PA 19083, USA
E-mail: Uspen-and-sword@casematepublishers.com
Website: www.penandswordbooks.com

Contents

List of Illustrations

1. Sir Ralph Abercromby after Hoppner. (*Author's collection*)
2. Sir John Moore from *The Royal Military Chronicle*. (*Author's collection*)
3. William Pitt the Younger. (*National Portrait Gallery*)
4. Henry Dundas. (*National Portrait Gallery*)
5. William Wyndham Grenville, 1st Lord Grenville. (*National Portrait Gallery*)
6. The Duke of York at the Siege of Valenciennes, 1793. (*Anne S.K. Brown Collection*)
7. The Battle of Tourcoing, 1794. (*Alamy*)
8. The Winter Retreat, 1795. (*Alamy*)
9. The 27th (Inniskillings) take Morne Fortuné, 24 May 1796. (*The Inniskillings Museum*)
10. The Capture of Trinidad, 18 February 1797 by Nicholas Pocock. (*Public domain*)
11. John Jeffreys Pratt, 1st Marquis Camden, by William Salter. (*Public domain*)
12. British troops under General Abercromby landing in North Holland, 27 August 1799. (*Courtesy of Michael Crumplin*)
13. The Battle of Egmont, 2 October 1799, after Jan Langendyk. (*Public domain*)
14. The departure of the Anglo–Russian Expedition from North Holland, November 1799. (*Author's collection*)
15. Aboukir Bay, March 1801. (*Author's collection*)
16. British troops landing at Aboukir, 8 March 1801 by Philip James de Loutherbourg. (*Anne S.K. Brown collection*)
17. The Death of General Sir Ralph Abercromby K.B., after Thomas Stothard. (*Anne S.K. Brown Collection*)

Introduction

A NATIONAL REVOLUTION brought about in a period so short, has had no parallel in the history of the World: and though fatal to some, the lives that have been lost in this great accomplishment, are in point of numbers, inconsiderable . . .

The *popular tumult* spreads far and wide: but the triumph of the PARTY is now complete.

Three hundred thousand men are in arms.

After committing various acts of violence, the Party attacked the *Bastile*, which they soon broke open; and similar to the *Riots* in the year 1780 with us, all the prisoners were set at liberty. *Here*, at this moment, scenes as novel and as interesting took place, as ever history recorded. *Here*, Friends long lost again met each other! Here CAPTIVITY regained its *freedom* – and DESPAIR found instant *consolation*! . . .

As soon as the PARTY had destroyed the *Bastile,* they seized the GOVERNOR Monsieur DE LAUNET, and carrying him forth, beheaded him in the sight of the people, and parting the head, all bleeding as it was, upon a pole, bore it before them . . .

Thus *The World* summed up the events in Paris in the summer of 1789, events which were to have a cataclysmic effect on France, on the rest of Europe and on the world beyond.

Whether Ralph Abercromby, a Scottish half-pay officer, read the news in the hyperbolic style of *The World* or in a more sober form, it would certainly have given him pause for thought. France had been in a state of tension for some time. As a man of liberal sympathies, he could not but welcome the news of an attack on the monolithic power of the French crown; but he must have been well aware of the dangerous power of King Mob, memorably witnessed on the streets of London nine years before during the Gordon Riots. He also possessed a pragmatic understanding that liberty was a dangerous weapon and needed to be handled with discretion. Consequently, he feared that 'the French people were not sufficiently instructed to submit to the sober guidance of a Washington, and that they required to be controlled by a firm and energetic hand . . . until they could be gradually trained to the exercise of freedom; since, if they were not restrained, the result might be perilous to them, might obstruct the progress of freedom, and involve the rest of Europe in serious embarrassments.'[1] What he could not have known was the part he would be called upon to play in the convulsions that followed the events of 14 July 1789.

Major General Ralph Abercromby (as he was in 1789) had been born in October 1734, when the French-backed adherents to the Stuart cause were still the biggest threat to Scotland, and to Britain. He was the first surviving son of George Abercromby of Tullibody, who was the largest landowner in the, admittedly small, county of Clackmannan. Through his mother, Mary Dundas, he was connected to an ambitious family that would come to dominate Scottish politics by the end of the eighteenth century. The Abercrombys were by profession lawyers or soldiers. The former was the profession chosen by George Abercromby for his eldest son. After being privately educated at home, he attended Mr Moir's school in Alloa and then Rugby, before entering Edinburgh University in 1752 to study moral and natural philosophy and civil law. According to a fellow student, he 'punctually performed those tasks that were required of him, and he gave much satisfaction to the professors, who regarded him as a youth of sound rather than brilliant parts, and who bid fair to obtain distinction in the pursuits of active life'.[2]

If 'active' is the key word here, then there is the suggestion that a lawyer's life might not be an ideal choice. So it proved. In 1754 he was sent to Leipzig to study civil law. He returned with a determined wish for a career not as a lawyer but as a soldier; and was eventually able to persuade his reluctant father to purchase for him a commission in the 3rd Dragoon Guards. Two years later, upon the outbreak of the Seven Years War (1756–63), he went with his regiment to Germany and was appointed aide-de-camp to Sir William Pitt, a position which gave him a better appreciation of the business of war than he would have acquired as merely a junior officer. As a result he returned to Britain not only as captain, by purchase, but also as a disciple of Prince Ferdinand of Brunswick, from whom he had learnt the importance of balancing strict discipline with concern for the welfare of his men.

There followed twelve quiet years during which he was promoted first to major in 1770, then to lieutenant colonel in 1773, the year that saw the outbreak of war with the North American Colonists. This confronted Abercromby with a crisis of conscience. As a soldier it was his duty to serve his country: as a man of principle he recognized the validity of the Colonists' arguments. He was not alone in coming to the conclusion that in this instance, when Britain herself was not under threat, principle must win over duty, even at the cost of his career. He let it be known that he would refuse any appointment to serve in North America, unlike his younger brother, Robert, colonel of the 37th Foot, who played an active part in the war.

In the same year he was persuaded to stand for Clackmannanshire in the Whig interest under the patronage of Sir Lawrence Dundas, himself Member of Parliament for Edinburgh and a man who had amassed a fortune through speculation and as an army contractor. There ensued a bitter campaign during which Abercromby fought a duel with his opponent, Colonel Erskine. The cause was a defamatory pamphlet that Erskine had written about Lord Kennet, who was married to Abercromby's sister. Kennet could not fight a duel because he was a Lord of the Judiciary and needed someone else to uphold his honour. (Both combatants survived.) Abercromby was duly elected in 1774 but was unwilling to vote at his patron's bidding. According to his son, 'he was not prepared to surrender his judgement to the guidance of a party leader'.[3] He chose not to seek re-election and was replaced by his brother, Burnet, who had made a fortune through dealings with the East India Company and was undoubtedly more at ease with the jobbery of the political world. As Henry Dundas wrote to Robert Abercromby, Burnet 'gave a steady and cordial support in all our late struggles'.[4]

Despite his stand on the American War, in 1781 Abercromby was made colonel of the newly-formed 103rd Foot, the King's Irish Infantry. Three years later the regiment was disbanded and its colonel, now on half-pay, returned to Scotland with his wife, whom he had married in 1767, and six children. He settled into a tranquil existence, supporting his elderly father, looking to the education of his children and involving himself in the welfare of tenants and dependants. He also had a house in Edinburgh and when staying there often attended lectures at the university. (Indeed, it is recorded that on the day he received the offer of an appointment that would resurrect his military career he had been attending a lecture by a Dr Hardy on Church History.) Such might have been his existence for the rest of his life had not the events of 14 July 1789 brought about the complete overthrow of the French political system with repercussions that few anticipated.

*

On 16 May 1801 the Duke of York, as Commander-in-Chief of the Army, issued a general order in response to events in Egypt. Of Abercromby he wrote: 'His steady observance of discipline – his ever watchful attention to the health and wants of his troops – the persevering and unconquerable spirit which marked his military career – are worthy of the imitation of all, who desire, like him, a life of honour and a death of glory.'[5]

Ironically, perhaps, it was York's biographer, Colonel Alfred Burne, who presented a diametrically opposed view when he said of Abercromby:

> All through his life he had been in the habit of giving up. He early gave up his practice at the bar; he gave up the chance of fighting in America; he gave up the West Indies Command; he gave up the Army; he gave up the Irish command; he thankfully gave up the command to the Duke of York [at Den Helder]; he gave up nearly every operation in the field of which he held the command. He might be described as 'the give up' general.

He then expressed an even more damning opinion. 'The universally loved Sir Ralph was one of the most lion-hearted (physically) and most chicken-hearted (morally) generals who ever led a British army to failure and defeat.'[6]

James, Lord Dunfermline, introduced his memoir of his father by explaining that he had been motivated to write it because 'So many lives of those officers who distinguished themselves in the Army and Navy during the protracted war with France have been written, that it has repeatedly been remarked as an omission that no authoritative account of the character and services of Sir Ralph Abercromby had ever been given to the public.'[7] He was writing in 1861. Since then there has been no further study of the man York so admired and Burne so castigated. His reputation has been overwhelmed by the achievements of later heroes, just as the French Revolutionary Wars have been eclipsed by the Napoleonic Wars. The purpose of this study is to examine the last eight years of Sir Ralph Abercromby's military career, most of it spent in active soldiering, in the context of the political and social upheavals of the final decade of the eighteenth century. Much happened in which he was not directly involved, or merely played a minor role. This is particularly true of the War of the First Coalition; yet it was during those first, generally unsuccessful, years of British involvement that Abercromby both became familiar with the form of war as practised by Revolutionary France and laid the foundations of the reputation that would make him 'the commander to whom the government resorted in all its difficulties'.[8]

Furthermore, the policies of a Pitt, a Robespierre, a Catherine the Great; the political manoeuvring of men like William, Lord Grenville, Jacques Pierre Brissot, Baron Johann Amadeus Thugut; the military triumphs and failures of Dumouriez, the Archduke Charles, Moreau; and, most significantly of all, the rise to power of a certain Napoleone Buonaparte, all created the drama in which Abercromby would act out the last years of his life. For this reason, the following study does not seek to be a biography of an overlooked Scottish general. Instead, Abercromby serves as a focal, and increasingly significant participant player in what is essentially a record of British involvement in the first half of what contemporaries would refer to the as The Great War.

[Author's note: quotations are reproduced exactly as written or printed, with bracketed emendation only where spelling makes the meaning unclear. It should be noted that Abercromby consistently spelt his name as written here, but it will frequently be found in source material as Abercrombie.]

Acknowledgements

My thanks are due to the many friends who have supported me through a difficult period and helped me to bring to fruition a long-held wish to do justice to a general, a hero in his own day, who has been almost forgotten in our time. Their willingness to listen and give advice as I formulated my thoughts on General Abercromby provided invaluable encouragement. Michael Crumplin FRCS has once again shared his vast medical and surgical knowledge with me, particularly when discussing Abercromby's fatal wound. Lieutenant Colonel John Downham has been as generous as ever in making available unpublished material, including his own work on the 40th Foot, whose experiences encapsulate the campaigns of the 1790s. Discussion with Garry Wills enabled me to challenge Colonel Burne's interpretation of Boxtel. And I have also enjoyed discussing with Dr Andrew Bamford the travesty of Burne's judgement on Abercromby. Nor must I neglect to give sincere thanks to David Beckford, who has made sense of my less than precise requirements for the maps.

Finally, Rupert Harding of Pen & Sword has, as ever, been both helpful and patient in his efforts to keep the whole enterprise under control.

Maps

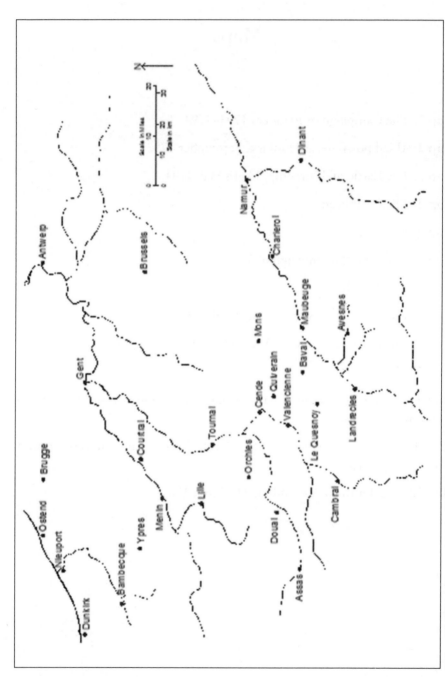

Map 1: The Campaign in Flanders 1793–1794.

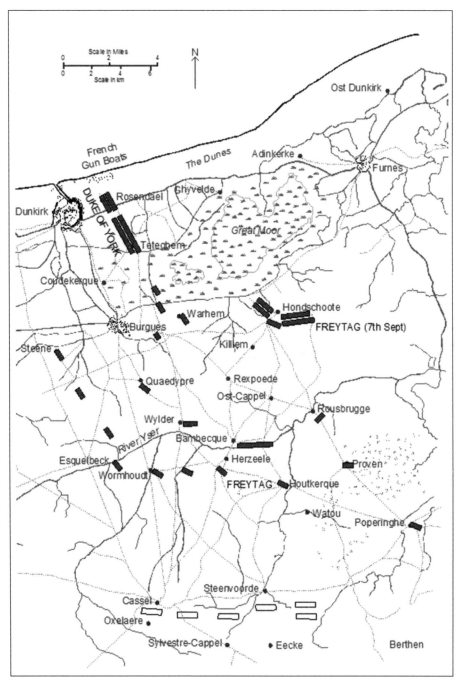

Map 2: Allied positions at Dunkirk, September 1793.

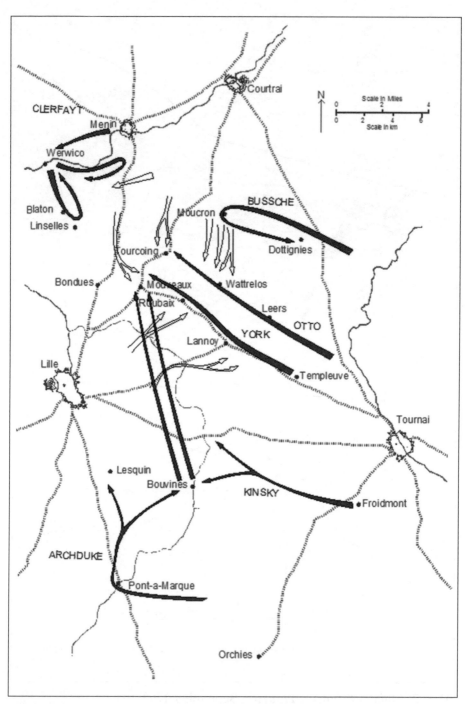

Map 3: The Battle of Tourcoing, 17–18 May 1794.

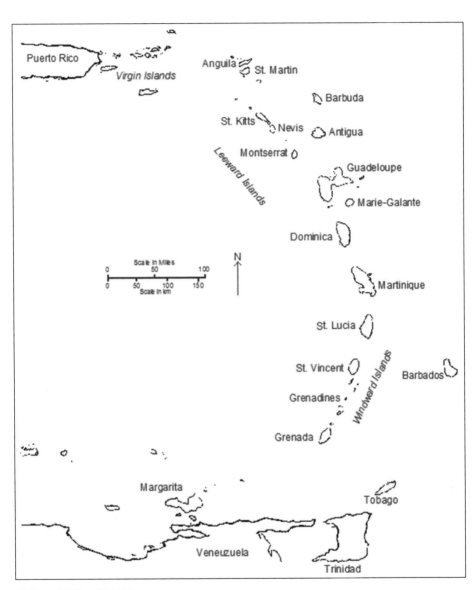

Map 4: The Caribbean.

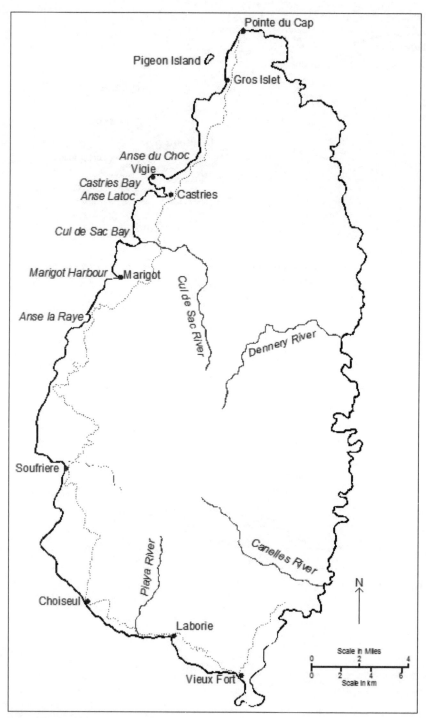

Pointe du Cap

Pigeon Island

Gros Islet

Anse du Choc
Vigie
Castries Bay
Anse Latoc
Castries

Cul de Sac Bay

Marigot Harbour
Marigot

Cul de Sac River

Anse la Raye

Dennery River

Soufriere

Canelles River

Playa River

N

Choiseul

Laborie

Scale in Miles
0   2   4

Scale in km
0   2   4   6

Vieux Fort

Map 5: St Lucia.

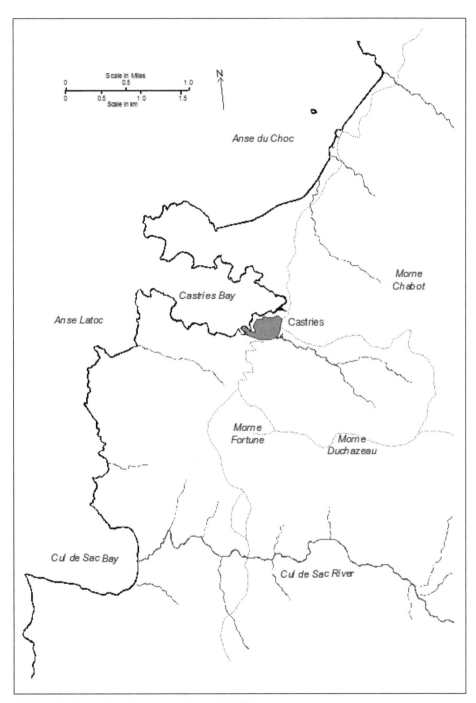

Map 6: St Lucia: the campaign of 1795.

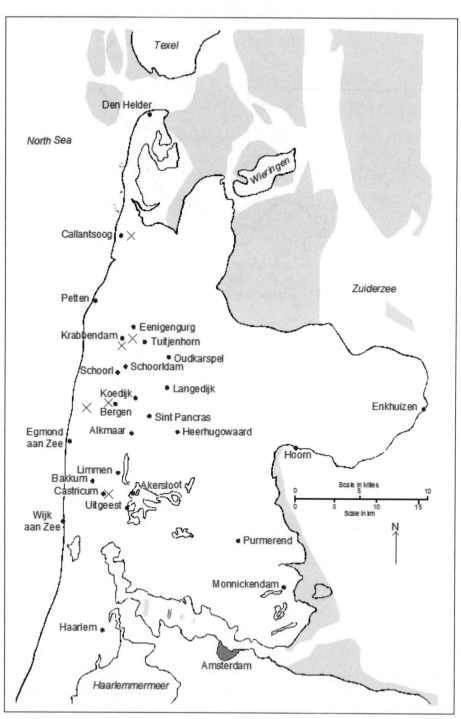

Map 7: North Holland.

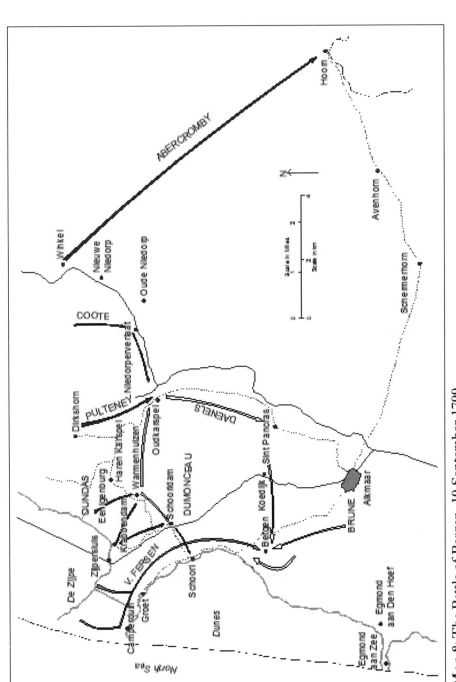

Map 8: The Battle of Bergen, 19 September 1799.

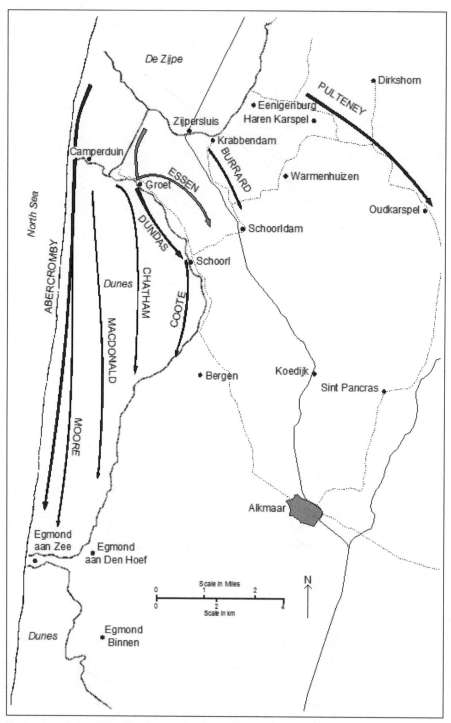

Map 9: The Battle of Egmont, Allied movements, 2 October 1799.

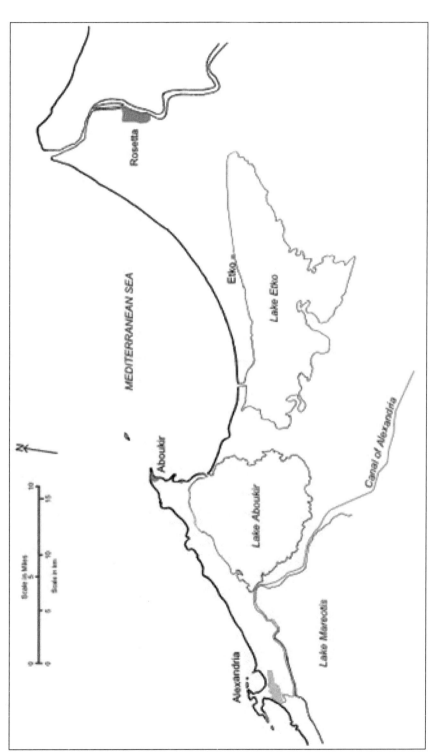

Map 10: Aboukir Bay.

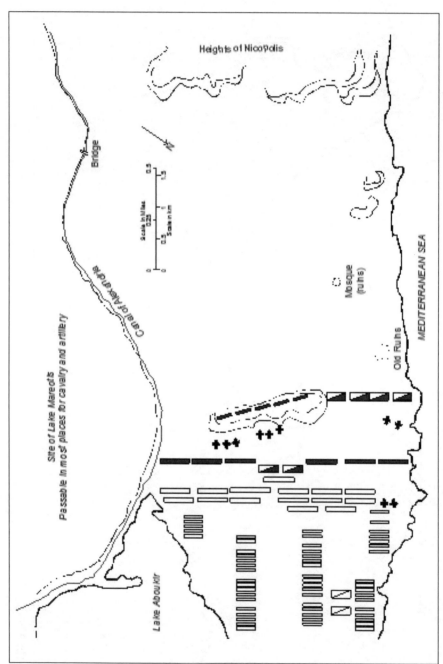

Map 11: Action at Mandorah, 13 March 1801: opening positions (from a contemporary map).

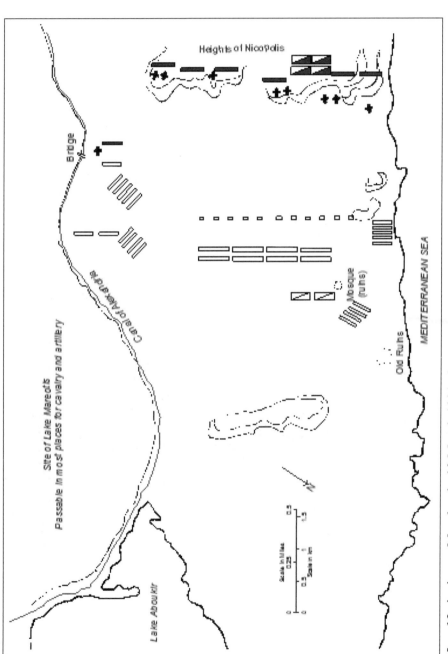

Map 12: Action at Mandorah, 13 March 1801: final positions (from a contemporary map).

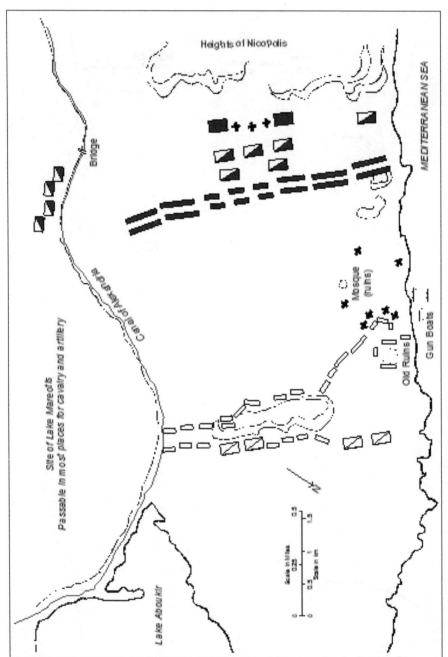

Map 13: The Battle of Alexandria, 21 March 1801.

Chapter 1

The War of the First Coalition

From Revolution to War

On 1 February 1793, and after weeks of sabre-rattling, France, already at war with Austria and Prussia, declared war on Great Britain. War, however, had been a regular occurrence in Europe for most of the eighteenth century. There had been sixteen conflicts between 1700 and 1790, six involving Britain, and one of which, the Seven Years War, had become a world war when it spread to French and British colonies. In the European theatre, though, the nature of eighteenth-century war, the form of war Abercromby had known in his younger days, was essentially limited and defensive. Highly-trained soldiers were expensive commodities, not to be wasted in unregulated conflict. For this reason, sieges were often preferred to pitched battles; the primary strategic aim was often the acquisition of territory and sieges secured possession of territory. Furthermore, the soldiers were the ruler's personal possessions. They fought at his (or her) wish to secure his (or her) objectives. Britain was now about to fight a very different kind of war.[1] Few could have anticipated, therefore, that this new conflict would rage for twenty-three years, with only one short period of peace, and would develop into total war.

Among the causes of the French Revolution French involvement in the American War of Independence must be cited. It beggared the French treasury. This necessitated changes to taxation laws so that money could be extracted from the wealthiest sections of society. There was an inevitable outcry. Louis XVI sought to pacify the objectors when in May 1789 he summoned the Estates-General for the first time since 1614. Instead, he took the lid off a simmering stew of discontent: the bourgeoisie, wealthy but politically powerless, chafed against their lack of influence; the urban poor wanted bread. The result was a rise in violence that would eventually destroy the monarchy, and the *Déclaration des droits de l'homme et du citoyen*, which engendered the desire to enjoy liberty at home and preach it abroad.[2]

What was happening in France inevitably affected the rest of Europe. Britain was not alone in witnessing a rising tide of radical activity, particularly in the most politically-alienated sections of the population. The desire for reform was already an issue before the storming of the Bastille. The American struggle for independence, the popular writings of Thomas Paine, particularly *Common Sense*, the growing frustration with a situation where too much power rested in too few hands, the failure of all attempts to repeal the Test Act, which excluded thousands from the official life of the country, and the failure of several Reform Bills all fed the popular dissatisfaction. The events of 1789 and 1790 in France stimulated this frustration into action. Across the Channel, political clubs and working men's political associations, previously unknown in Britain, were soon forming in increasing numbers. Inevitably, such radicalism was balanced by equally intransigent reaction.

It is interesting to note Abercromby's response to the events which were convulsing France. As Fortescue noted, he was a man whose judgements were based on careful thought. As a liberal he praised George Washington for his moderation, and admired how the American Colonists had acted on principles of religious toleration and civic freedom when framing their constitution. He questioned whether the French would show the same restraint after so long a period of despotism: '. . . he knew that freedom could not be suddenly and safely conceded to people who had been long oppressed, and that they could only be trained to the use and enjoyment of it by experience, and under the influence and control of energetic and wise leaders. He never was for a moment dazzled by the professions of the leaders of the French Revolution, whose conduct he condemned as rash and dangerous in conceding to the people liberties which they were unprepared to understand or use with discretion.' From the beginning he suspected that, without restraint, the result of the Revolution 'might be perilous to themselves, might obstruct the progress of freedom, and involve the rest of Europe in serious embarrassments'.[3]

Others were less aware of this danger, focusing more on internal dissent than external threats. William Pitt, First Lord of the Treasury since 1783 although still in his early thirties, was fixated on strengthening Britain's financial situation after the catastrophe of North America. Lord Rosebery accurately summed up Pitt's problem: 'The task he had set himself was to raise the nation from the exhaustion of the American war; to repair her finances; to strengthen by reform the foundation of the constitution, and by a liberal Irish policy the bonds of Empire.' Once Britain was at war, 'he was doomed to drag out the remainder of his life in darkness and dismay, in wrecking his whole financial edifice to find funds for incapable generals and for foreign statesman more capable than honest, in postponing and indeed repressing all his projected reforms'.[4] Pitt knew that Britain must remain neutral if he were to achieve his objectives, a view that he shared with his cousin, William Wyndham Grenville, first Baron Grenville, the newly-appointed Foreign Secretary.

Grenville was a rigid character, often at odds with his colleagues.

'Old Lord Liverpool once described him as the most extraordinary character he had ever known; for with all his talents and industry he could never see a subject in all its bearings – and consequently his judgement could never be right. Nor could he handle people. Though not ill-tempered, said Liverpool, he had no feelings for anyone. Rapacious of public money for his own family, he was a great economiser where others were concerned; and his outward manner was offensive to the last degree'.[5]

A later judgement described him as 'Uninspiring, prolix and somewhat tactless, both as a speaker and a writer, he chilled his friends and irritated his enemies.'[6] He had an instinctive antipathy for war, contempt for all things military, and limited sympathy for the plight of others. Inevitably, such a man alienated domestic politicians and foreign diplomats alike.

The third member of the triumvirate at the heart of government was Henry Dundas, Home Office Minister with responsibility for the Colonies. He would also be responsible for the war effort, should hostilities be declared. Dundas was an older man than Pitt and Grenville, a member of a dynasty that enjoyed near-despotic power in Scotland (he was popularly known as 'King Harry the Ninth'), a friend of Pitt, with whom he often drank deeply, and sometimes the butt of Grenville's sarcasm. He was an efficient administrator, as he had proved in his management of Indian affairs, but he was popularly believed to be 'so profoundly ignorant of war that he was not even conscious of his own ignorance'.[7] On the other hand, he was a close friend and maternal kinsman of Abercromby. It is difficult to imagine that the two men did not discuss the implications of events in France.

These three ministers were agreed that internal dissent was the greatest threat to British security and could best be alleviated by peace and a flourishing economy. Royalists who had fled France were seeking foreign aid to overthrow the revolution but Grenville was determined to avoid a Royalist crusade. Elsewhere, the Emperor Leopold II was equally disinclined for war with France, despite being the brother of the French queen. His concerns lay to the east with the Polish uprising against

Russia, which had broken out in May 1791, and the Russo–Turkish war. In contrast, Frederick William II of Prussia, with an eye on French territory, had adopted a more bellicose tone.

As the situation in France became increasingly unstable, Louis XVI decided on flight for himself and his family. He intended to put himself at the head of an émigré army which was already assembled at Montmédy on the border and lead a counter-revolution. His arrest at Varennes on 21 June led to the royal family's confinement in the Tuileries Palace. The monarchy itself was now under threat. In response, on 6 July the Emperor issued the Padua Circular, which urged the monarchs of Europe to join him in demanding Louis' release. Then on 27 August, during a conference to discuss the problem of Poland, the two German monarchs issued the Declaration of Pillnitz. They jointly declared that they viewed

> the situation in which the king of France currently finds himself as a subject of interest for all of Europe's sovereigns. They hope that this interest cannot fail to be recognized by the powers from which assistance is being requested. Consequently, jointly with their respective Majesties, they will use the most efficient means in relation to their strength to place the King of France in a position to be totally free to consolidate the basis of monarchical government that shall be amenable to the rights of sovereigns as it is to the wellbeing of the French nation. In this case then, their said Majesties, the Emperor and the King of Prussia are resolved to act quickly, in mutual agreement, and with the forces necessary to achieve the proposed and common goal. Meanwhile, they shall issue their troops the necessary orders to prepare for action.

Not surprisingly, the French, particularly the Girondin faction in the Legislative Assembly, understood the Declaration to threaten them with war. The Girondin deputy Jacques-Pierre Brissot now used his demagogic gifts to foster the belief that war could not be avoided. Yet Leopold almost certainly had no such intention. He was an advocate of enlightened despotism, as he had demonstrated when Grand Duke of Tuscany. His State Chancellor, Wenzel Anton von Kaunitz, was firmly convinced that inciting civil war was the surest way to destroy the Revolution. Even more significantly, the Declaration implied that all the major European powers would have to act together. Leopold certainly did not expect George III to respond to his call.

Instead, it was generally suspected that Britain was standing aloof in the hope of gaining from the French situation.

On 13 September Louis reluctantly swore to uphold a new constitution, which had been a work in progress since 1789. Since it recognized the monarchy and gave the King a limited role, the two German monarchs could choose to believe that Pillnitz had stabilized the situation in France. In France, though, many believed that the King had no intention of respecting a constitution that deprived the monarchy of its powers. Political opinion polarized as opposing groups formed within the Legislative Assembly. The followers of the Marquis de Lafayette were thinking in terms of a political system that borrowed from both Britain and the new United States of America, the course that Abercromby hoped France would adopt. Extremists, however, were agitating for the end of the monarchy. Furthermore, the upheavals of the Revolution had done nothing to solve the economic weakness that was one of its causes. Many posited that war was the solution to all the country's problems.

Brissot's oratory eventually achieved its desired effect; the Legislative Assembly decided that attack was the best means of defence and armies were posted on the borders, ready for action. In response, Leopold sent a despatch to Paris that criticized this provocation and instructed the French to withdraw their troops. With the pro-war party in the ascendant, it was agreed by decree that Austria had violated the treaty which had held the two countries in uneasy alliance since 1756. On 24 January 1792 Louis was instructed to demand an undertaking from the Emperor that he had no warlike intentions. If no reply were received by 1 March, the French would assume that they were at war with Austria. By a quirk of history, Leopold died suddenly on that very day. Since no reply was received in Paris, either by the stipulated date or later, the French fulfilled their threat. On 19 April the Legislative Assembly, undeterred by the defensive alliance that Austria and Prussia had signed on 7 February, issued a formal declaration of war in the name of Louis XVI. France was indeed about to 'involve the rest of Europe in serious embarrassments'.

The new Foreign Minister, General Charles-François Dumouriez, was already thinking in terms of a short war in the Austrian Netherlands (which for convenience will henceforth be referred to as Belgium). This was considered fertile revolutionary territory, as Dumouriez, who identified himself as a Walloon, fully appreciated. In 1787 the estates of Brabant and Flanders, Catholic and conservative, had risen against the Emperor Joseph II's liberalizing church reforms and removal of noble privileges. Although the rebels were initially driven into exile, they returned two years later, defeated an Austrian force at the Battle of Turnhout, and established the United Belgian States. Since only Prussia had offered support, the rebel government was short-lived. It could be surmised, however, that the rebellious instinct still flourished.

Nine days after the declaration of war, the Army of the North invaded Belgium under the command of Generals Rochambeau and Lafayette. The two French heroes of the American War of Independence failed to achieve anything because the inhabitants did not rise in revolutionary fervour. In the face of an Austrian counter-attack, one French force even fled en masse to Lille, where they murdered their Irish commander, General Dillon. The message to Austria was clear, however. The French intended to export revolution through aggressive action. Aggression was inevitably countered by aggression. When that aggression came in the form of the Austrians and the Prussians, there began a war in which a new and challenging ideology was countered by armies fighting in the limited fashion of the eighteenth century to preserve the status quo. The ideology might be lost over the years as it metamorphosed into dictatorship, but its consequences would prove bloody and protracted.

The new emperor, Francis II, untutored in official imperial business, was seduced by the loud voices in Vienna, Berlin and St Petersburg urging action. King Frederick William offered the tempting prize of Alsace and Lorraine. (He expected Jülich and Berg in return.) The Empress Catherine II hoped that with Austria engaged in a war to the west, she would have a freer hand in central Europe, particularly in Poland. Potentially, Poland was a stress point between Russia, Prussia and Austria, and a possible distraction from France, but for the moment France was of greater concern to the two German powers.

Having mustered an army at Coblenz, Prussia formally declared war on France on 24 July. An army under the Duke of Brunswick-Lüneburg crossed the frontier. Brunswick, under instruction, issued a proclamation that Austria and Prussian intended to restore the monarchy and treat all those who opposed their intervention as traitors. This challenge stiffened French resistance. It suggested that Louis had been in collusion with the foreign powers all along. On 10 August a mob attacked the Tuileries Palace, overwhelming the Swiss Guard and forcing the royal family to flee to the protection of the Legislative Assembly. Three days later the King was arrested and sent to the Temple Prison. By early September Brunswick was on French territory. Longwy had fallen and Verdun was ready to surrender.

There was panic in Paris, where rumours quickly spread that Royalist prisoners intended to break free and join the invaders. The result was the September Massacres when gangs of vigilantes attacked the prisons and slaughtered more than 12,000 of the inmates. The Revolution now had very bloody hands.

With a well-trained army encountering a force of distinctly mixed quality, regulars from the old royal army serving alongside enthusiastic volunteers, the outcome should have been a certain German victory. But Brunswick slowed the pace of his advance on Paris and allowed the French to assemble 36,000 men under Generals Dumouriez and François Christophe de Kellermann. At Valmy on 20 September a spirited French attack persuaded Brunswick to retreat. Not only did this seriously dent the reputation of the Prussians, it also boosted the prestige and confidence of the newly-formed National Convention. The day after Valmy the monarchy was abolished and the French Republic, established. Now on the offensive, in September the Convention sent another French army under General Adam Philippe Custine to occupy Nice and Savoy. By October the Papal States were under French control and Dumouriez had launched a second invasion of Belgium. On 6 November he defeated the Austrians at Jemappes and by the end of the month French forces were in control of the whole of the Austrian Netherlands.

Revelling in these military victories, the Convention issued an Edict of Fraternity. Governments (despotic by definition) were enemies: the people were friends. Support was offered to all in the fight for liberty. The contentious Scheldt estuary was declared free water. This swept away the Treaty of Münster, signed in 1648 at the end of the Thirty Years War and confirmed by the French on four further occasions. Using the argument of natural law, the National Convention had taken from the Dutch their right by treaty to control the Scheldt waterway. Furthermore, the French now had possession of Mainz and were aiming to establish a frontier on the Rhine. On 27 November they incorporated Nice and Savoy into France.

The response of the British government was crucial. Dumouriez, as foreign minister, had made it his policy to keep Britain out of the inevitable war. When Charles Maurice de Talleyrand-Périgord arrived in London in January 1792, ostensibly on private affairs but in reality as an advisor to the official French emissary, the Duke of Biron, he was primed to extract a declaration of neutrality from the British government. Talleyrand reported that Britain was disinclined for war. Early in 1792, Pitt had presented a positive economic situation to Parliament and announced that he intended to reduce spending on the Army by £50,000 and on the Navy by £104,000. He also ended Britain's subsidy to those most useful of mercenaries, the Hessians. He further declared: 'We must not count with certainty on a continuance of our present prosperity during such an interval; but unquestionably there never was a time in the history of this country, when, from the situation in Europe, we might more reasonably expect fifteen years of peace, than we may at the present moment.'[8] This was not a government anticipating war.

When Rochambeau attacked the Austrian Netherlands, a new French emissary was sent to London, Bernard-François, Marquis de Chauvelin, young and self-important. Yet although he might be insulted by Grenville's hauteur, he readily believed that a policy of neutrality had been decided in Cabinet. Grenville certainly believed that negotiations would follow the arrival of the first foreign troops into France. Indeed, Britain had reacted to Rochambeau's attack merely with a diplomatic gesture by withdrawing her ambassador, Lord Gower. After the declaration of the French Republic, however, the government refused to recognize Chauvelin's official status since his accreditation had come from the King. Furthermore, Chauvelin had been expressing Jacobin opinions, which were echoed by the more extreme British radicals, who saw in the overthrow of the French monarchy a pattern for Britain. Chauvelin interpreted the establishment of clubs like the London Corresponding Society and the Sheffield Society for Constitutional Information as evidence that Britain was ready for revolution. He ignored the many liberals who believed in a constitutional monarchy and now accepted that they had been deceived by what they had perceived as the dawn of a new age. He might also have noted that failed harvests and rising prices, rather than political ideas, were at the root of such violence as there was.

Grenville still hoped to preserve British neutrality even after Valmy and Jemappes. He blamed Austria and Prussia for initiating a war that had only encouraged extremist activity. Dundas, believing Britain should stand aside from continental events, wrote to his under-secretary, Evan Nepean: 'I think the strength of our cause consists in maintaining that we have nothing to do with the internal politics of Foreign Nations, that we have already undergone all the consequences of Civil disturbances which were terminated by a Revolution which has rendered us happy for more than a century, and we will not submit to or countenance any other revolution in this Country.'[9] Abercromby shared his friend's trust in British institutions, believing that 'a more familiar and instructed acquaintance with the merits of our institutions, and the principles on which they were founded, would give them a stronger hold on the attachment of the people, that many of those who had been seduced by popular fallacies would be restrained, and that if some were still incorrigible, and might be led to acts of violence, they would easily be repressed by the ordinary laws, and with the general approbation of all classes'.[10] He joined an Edinburgh association which sought to spread such knowledge to the general population.

Yet the implications of the French presence in Belgium could not be ignored. French possession of both Antwerp and the Scheldt raised the possibility of an attack on the east coast and the Thames estuary. Indeed, such plans were under discussion in Paris by the end of the year. Furthermore, the Dutch Republic was also under threat, particularly as the French were pushing towards one of their claimed natural frontiers, the Rhine, beyond which lay the wealth of Amsterdam. The independence of the Dutch had been a fixed point in British foreign policy for most of the eighteenth century. The most recent treaty, a triple alliance between Britain, Prussia and the Dutch Republic, had been signed in 1788.

At War with France

In December 1792 the Convention had declared that all their conquered territory would have to accept a revolutionary government and pay the costs of the conquering French army. Any nation that failed to acknowledge the ideology of the Revolution was henceforth to be regarded as an enemy. This was provocation indeed, yet Pitt needed peace to pursue his economic policies and Grenville, although alarmed by French expansionism, was reluctant to interfere in French internal affairs. Both ministers preferred to believe that the most dangerous French weapon was subversion. Yet Grenville also acknowledged that by threatening the Dutch the French were manoeuvring Britain into war. This was confirmed when a letter of 10 January came into British hands. Written by Dumouriez, it instructed General Francisco de Miranda to invade the Dutch Republic within twelve days.

The French were not afraid of war with Britain but Chauvelin's information convinced them that a declaration alone would suit their purposes. They believed his reports that the country was alive with radical activists who would rise in response to such a declaration. There was evidence of widespread radicalism, as already noted, but Chauvelin might have taken heed of a passage in Edmund Burke's *Reflections on the Revolution in France*, published in Britain in November 1790, and quickly translated into French. Like Abercromby, Burke had sympathized with the American rebels and their liberal instincts. He saw the French Revolution as negative and destructive, and confidently believed the British would reject its ideology, a view Abercromby also shared. As Burke observed,

> Because half a dozen grasshoppers under a fern make the field ring with their importunate chink, while thousands of great cattle, reposed beneath the shadow of the British oak, chew the cud and are silent, pray do not imagine, that those who make the noise are the only inhabitants of the field; that of course, they are many in number; or that, after all, they are other than the little shrivelled, meagre, hopping, though loud and troublesome insects of the hour.[11]

By 1792 loyal associations were forming in opposition to the more radical clubs and societies.

The Dutch certainly appreciated the French threat. The Patriot Rebellion of 1780 had been crushed seven years later only with Prussian assistance. The Patriots now constituted a prominent pro-French party both within and outside the Republic. When the Convention proclaimed the right to follow enemy troops wherever they fled, and demanded passage through Maastricht in order to send the Austrians beyond the Rhine, the Stadtholder, William V, Prince of Orange, interpreted it as a declaration of war and called in the promise of British support in the event of a French attack.

As for the Belgians, Dumouriez's policy of conciliation initially persuaded them to accept French occupation, despite some limited pillaging. He held elections for a Belgian Convention and tried to raise a Belgian army, but this offered the Belgians too much independence. The Convention promptly announced that all French armies would be accompanied by revolutionary commissioners whose purpose was to keep the generals under control and enforce the Convention's policy of exploiting the profits of conquest. Thanks to mismanagement and nest-feathering in Paris, the army lacked supplies and the Belgians soon found themselves the victims of systematic, officially-sanctioned pillage. Winning hearts and minds was sacrificed to necessity.

French expansion suffered a setback in December when Prussia regained Frankfurt am Main, which had been taken by the French in October. The Austrians, eager to take back their lost territory so that they could fulfil a long-held ambition to exchange it for Bavaria, were ready to develop a friendlier relationship with Britain. (The two countries had been at odds since the Austro-French alliance of 1756.) Grenville did not trust the Austrians, an attitude that was to harden as the war progressed, but he was prepared to give them a hearing. He was also discussing the possibility of alliances with the Prussians and Russians, and with the Spanish, who had joined the two German powers in August but had quickly reverted to neutrality after Valmy. Grenville was still averse to war but the Convention's December decree with its insistence on the acceptance of revolutionary principles convinced him Britain was in as much danger as the Dutch Republic. As Allison suggested, 'it was not foreign subjugation so much as domestic revolution which was dreaded, if a pacific intercourse were any longer maintained with France'.[12]

The British reaction to the execution of Louis XVI on 21 January 1793 gave the Convention diplomatic justification for declaring war on Britain. Three days after the execution of the King, Pitt used the Aliens Act to expel Chauvelin. On 1 February the Convention responded with a declaration of war against both Britain and the Dutch Republic. The Austrian Netherlands were annexed, to popular fury as the Belgians realized their liberators were actually conquerors. They would not be the last to suffer this fate.

The French were playing a double game. The Foreign Minister, Lebrun, had sent orders of recall to Chauvelin two days before he was expelled, while the Executive Council had decided on war on 10 January. Dumouriez, whose loyalty to the Convention had been severely tested by events in Paris, was ordered to invade the Dutch Republic as soon as possible. He was to take Walcheren in order to prevent a junction of the British and Dutch fleets. This was despite both the ice that that made navigation in the mouth of the Scheldt a serious challenge, and the strong defences of Flushing (Vlissingen) and Bergen-op-Zoom. Dumouriez demurred to conduct a campaign that was likely to fail. The Convention was impatient, however. The wealth of Amsterdam would prove life-giving to a bankrupt French government. Furthermore, the Dutch Republic looked an easy target. The Stadtholder was popularly reputed to be the worst prince in Europe and the Dutch army was under-strength. Dutch Patriots and French agents were busily stirring up revolutionary sentiment, while even the less radical French sympathizers, a longstanding fixture in Dutch politics, were equally assiduous in warning that the British were colonial rivals and untrustworthy allies. Yet while the Patriot exiles in Paris dreamt of an independent Batavian republic, the Convention was thinking of a satellite state that would enrich France and improve French security.

Neither Prussia nor Austria was ready to watch the French swallow up yet more territory. France might have lost its king, but it did not seem to have lost its taste for establishing a universal monarchy, except that it now took the form of a universal revolutionary republic. Yet Prussia and Austria were rivals rather than natural allies, evinced by Prussia's insistence that the two armies should operate separately. How they would operate was also a concern. Brunswick was 67, and Prince Josias von Saxe-Coburg-Saalfeld, in command of the Austrians, was 65. They were both firmly wedded to the form of war learnt from Frederick the Great and might well prove too old to learn new lessons. Nevertheless plans were already being made for a campaign against the French. Brunswick would operate on the Rhine and Coburg, in Belgium. Separately but in conjunction they would overwhelm the French.

The Stadtholder was waiting for the British to take action according to the terms of the 1788 treaty. This guaranteed 'each other mutually in the possession of all their Dominions, Territories, Towns, Places, Franchises and Liberties', including Dutch control of the Scheldt estuary. The British government, however, faced a similar problem to the Dutch, an inadequate army and disaffected troops. A contemporary later wrote: 'Our army was lax in its discipline, entirely without system, and very weak in numbers. Each colonel of a regiment managed it according to his own notions, or neglected it altogether. There was no uniformity of drill or movement; professional pride was rare; professional knowledge still more so. Never was a kingdom less prepared for a stern and arduous conflict.' Furthermore, 'Every department of the staff was more or less deficient, particularly the commissariat and medical branches. The regimental officers in those days were, as well as their men, hard drinkers; and the latter, under a loose discipline, were much addicted to marauding, and to acts of licentious violence . . .'[13]

Nor was quality the only problem. When the French declared war Britain had fewer than 14,000 troops at home with about twice that number in India and the West Indies. There were too many skeleton regiments, with officers of doubtful quality. In response to these shortages, the government held, and won, an emergency vote allowing for an increase in manpower of 25,000 troops against a worsening economic situation. It was easy enough to set a total but finding the men was a challenge. Although the number was partially realized by forming companies a hundred strong which were then drafted into existing units, the shortfall would continue to dog the British war effort for years to come. As Britain prepared to fight against Revolutionary France, it was necessary to look to the Continent for troops; 14,000 Hanoverians and 8,000 Hessians were hired to supplement Britain's inadequate resources.

Britain and the Dutch Republic now entered into formal coalition with Austria and Prussia, a coalition that presented Grenville with several diplomatic complications. Crucially, while he was focusing on restoring the status quo ante bellum in terms of territory, combined with a legitimate and stable French government, Austria and Prussia were both demanding a Royalist restoration. There were further differences that needed to be resolved. Prussia had interests in Poland, where Russia was involved in the War of the Second Partition against the liberals of the Polish-Lithuanian Commonwealth. Having gained Polish territory in the First Partition, Prussia was anxious to protect its interests in the area. At the same time, Austria was keeping an anxious eye on over-mighty Russia. For Britain, France was the rival: for the Central European powers France and Russia were equal threats. This misjudgement on the part of the British government would lead to consistent misunderstanding of the priorities of the principal Prussian minister, Christian, Count Haugwitz, and the Austrian, Baron Johann Amadeus von Thugut. The former served at a court where pro-French sentiments were often voiced while the latter, although he nursed an inveterate hatred of the Jacobins, also had to balance his imperial master's conflicting political concerns. Grenville would frequently be wrong-footed because, unlike Haugwitz and Thugut, 'he preferred to construct policy slowly and systematically rather than in any opportunistic or visionary fashion. The probability, therefore, was that he would find it difficult to devise policies that could support an ever-changing military scenario.'[14]

Pitt believed that Prussia was the more reliable power, and should be Britain's principal ally in conjunction with the Dutch. He also opposed Austria's long-proposed Belgium-Bavaria exchange because Bavaria lacked the resources to prevent French encroachment upon both the Dutch Republic and the northern German states. He suggested instead that the Belgian lands should be strengthened by the annexation of territory in northern France, implicitly with British assistance. Furthermore, since everyone else seemed to be demanding indemnities in the usual eighteenth-century fashion, he decided that Britain should claim Dunkirk, briefly a British possession in the seventeenth century, now a stronghold of privateers who preyed on merchant shipping. Pitt was confident that Dunkirk could be taken in April by a British force augmented by the Hanoverians and Hessians. Then an attack could be launched on France from Dunkirk, which would also serve as an excellent depot for supplies. Needless to say, there was no consultation with the military to establish the viability of this plan.

Grenville was now thinking of war in pan-European terms. He hoped to draw Russia, Sweden and Denmark into an alliance against the French but was frustrated when Catherine II imposed unacceptable conditions and the two Scandinavian kingdoms preferred to continue trading with France.

Spain, however, became a de facto member of the coalition in March when France declared war on her. Portugal, an ally since the fourteenth century, willingly joined while the King of Sardinia, having already lost Nice and Savoy, offered men in return for subsidies and a British naval presence in the Mediterranean. Naples also joined. Thus Grenville had created a web of alliances, although their durability was open to question. Furthermore, Britain was expected to foot the bill. Austria and Prussia both expected subsidies, as well as requiring Britain to provide 75,000 troops, British, Hanoverian and Hessian. Nor had Grenville yet considered what was to be the strategy of the coalition.

It is a truism that politicians cause wars and soldiers fight them. Such would be the case for the British Army for the next twenty-two years, during which only one short period of peace offered a brief respite.

The War in Flanders 1793

According to Abercromby's son, 'there was no doubt that after the French declaration [of war], it was the duty of every loyal subject to support the interest and honour of his country. Sir Ralph accordingly felt that the time had at length arrived when he could heartily embark in the active duties of his profession. Although then about to enter the sixtieth year of his age, he did not hesitate to recommence his active professional life, which had been so long suspended.'[15] The question remains, though, what was it about the French Revolution that persuaded Abercromby to volunteer for active service when he had avoided becoming involved in the war against the American Colonists.

The simplest answer is that the Colonists, unlike the Revolutionaries across the Channel, did not pose a threat to Britain's security. Furthermore, he saw the American conflict as a civil war, while the complaints of the Colonists, in his view, were justified and their objectives were moderate and reasonable. He certainly believed that 'opinions, however delusive or erroneous, could not be controlled or put down by legislative or physical force',[16] as the Colonists had proved. Liberty was a watchword shared by the Revolutionaries on both sides of the Atlantic, and was a concept that was precious to Abercromby. The difference lay in the conduct of the Revolutionaries. By the spring of 1793 events in France were fulfilling his fear 'that those who had so long groaned under the iron hand of despotism, must be ill qualified to reconstruct their government with prudence and wisdom'.[17] Whatever he felt about the intervention of the German sovereigns or the conduct of British ministers, he understood that Revolutionary France posed an existential threat to Britain.

By the time Abercromby's offer of service was accepted and he became involved, the campaign in Flanders was already under way. Following the French declaration of war, the Stadtholder made a specific request for the King's second son, Frederick, Duke of York, and a cadre of experienced officers to assume command of the Dutch army. The government was reluctant to agree since Britain had few enough experienced officers for its own army. Before a decision could be made, both the Stadtholder and the British ministers were overtaken by events. Dumouriez took part of his army and on 16 February launched an attack from Antwerp, forcing the Dutch back to the Meuse. The surrender of Breda was followed by the capitulation of several other Dutch towns. By 9 March Dumouriez had taken up a position at the Hollands Diep in the Rhine-Meuse-Scheldt delta that threatened Amsterdam.

The government was already making plans for an expeditionary force. On 20 February the Duke of York reviewed seven Guards battalions, three of which were destined for service abroad. When they embarked three days later they comprised a force of less than 2,000 men. This ill-prepared little force lacked transport, medical services or even reserve ammunition, and sailed under the command of Colonel Gerald Lake of the 1st Guards in dangerously small colliers that had happened to be moored on the Thames. Fortunately, conditions at sea were benign and the small force landed safely at Helvoetsluys. Lake was charged with preventing Dumouriez from crossing the Hollands Diep but he also had orders not to move further than a 24-hour march from his landing place. He advanced to Dordrecht (Dort), accompanied by Dutch gunboats, and took up a position on the Meuse.

York, meanwhile, had travelled to The Hague to consult with the Stadtholder and the British ambassador, Lord Auckland, before assuming overall command. What he found there was not encouraging. He informed his father that he had failed even to discover the strength of the Dutch forces. He also noted the irresolution of the Stadtholder, who attempted to maintain complete control by sending written orders in all directions, and the general sense of panic. Furthermore, the 20-year-old Hereditary Prince, in command of the Dutch troops, 'lived entirely on board his yacht, very seldom came on shore, and never visited the batteries erected for the defence of the island [Walcheren]. This conduct appeared very extraordinary, when his presence was particularly necessary to animate and encourage his friends and adherents.'[18]

At this point the Allies outnumbered the French overall. Britain's force might be small but the Austrians had 58,000 men on the Rhine, plus 11,000 of their own troops and 13,000 Hanoverians who were destined for Guelderland. The Prussian had a reserve force of 33,000. There were 100,000 German troops further east, and beyond them were the Russians, who might still be persuaded to play an active part. In Belgium, though, the Allies had less than 65,000 troops against the 100,000 Dumouriez could call on. Yet this force was 'in the most deplorable state of insubordination, and miserably deficient in every species of equipment. The artillery horses had in great part perished during the severity of the winter campaign; the clothing of the soldiers was worn out; their spirit had disappeared during the license of Republican conquest.'[19] Now was the moment to strike hard. Instead, Dumouriez had been allowed to seize the initiative.

The Austrians finally crossed the Rhine on 26 February, and the Meuse on 1 March. Coburg was a veteran of the Seven Years War and hero of the more recent Russo-Austro-Turkish Wars. He brought with him an army that enjoyed a good reputation, apart from some irregular units who were regarded as dangerous to friend and foe alike. Coburg's advance might have shown a lack of panache, but he was an honourable man and popular with his troops. If he and his chief of staff, Colonel Karl Leiberich Mack, could adapt to war as fought by Revolutionary France, there was every hope of success.

Coburg now prepared to attack that part of the French army, under General Miranda, which was besieging Maastricht. His second-in-command, the Emperor's 21-year-old brother the Archduke Charles, brought a detachment into position to attack from the west. The French were forced to raise the siege and further attacks drove them back to Louvain in considerable disorder. Their situation was critical. Dumouriez was struggling to collect his forces as his enemies gathered against him. Having reached Helvoetsluys, the Guards and some Dutch troops were advancing on Breda, the loss of which would cut Dumouriez off from the troops still on the Hollands Diep. Brunswick and the Prussians had laid siege to Mainz. Coburg could now have harried them back to France, but instead, in the usual eighteenth-century fashion, he focused on the border fortresses.

On 18 March Dumouriez decided to take the offensive, but his attack at Neerwinden failed completely. He fell back on Louvain with those survivors who did not desert. A slow Austrian advance forced him to abandon first Louvain, then Brussels and Namur. By this time he was implacably opposed to the Convention (and probably realized that he would lose his head if he returned to Paris). He opened negotiations with the Austrians, offering to lead his army into France and restore the monarchy if the Austrians would advance to the border in support. Once again, the Austrian reaction was too slow. Dumouriez could not wait. In early April he deserted to them, bringing with him about a thousand cavalry and twice that number of infantry whose personal loyalty he enjoyed. The rest of the French army either went home or took refuge in the border fortresses.[20] In France a compulsory *levée* had provoked widespread unrest, most seriously in the Vendée, socially the most egalitarian and conservative area of France. Even as the Vendeans resorted to violence against the forces sent to suppress them, the long-anticipated attack on the Girondins by the Jacobin Montagnards led to risings in Lyons, Marseilles and Toulon.

The British government had decided to reinforce the Guards with a line brigade even before the news of Austrian successes at Maastricht and Neerwinden reached them. Abercromby was in Edinburgh when he learnt that he was to command this brigade, which comprised the 14th, 37th and 53rd Regiments of the Line. On 15 March he acknowledged the letter he had received from Henry Dundas: 'I shall endeavour to fulfil his Majesty's intentions by a faithful & pointed compliance with the orders & instructions, which you have communicated to me. I shall not fail to transmit to you from time to time, an account of the proceedings of the troops under my command, and of such other as may appear fitted for his Majesty's information.'[21] On 21 March he sailed from Leith with the 37th and the 53rd Regiments. Six days later he reported from Yarmouth Roads: 'The Troops all well. We have had coarse weather, and anchored here on the 25th, and till this day no Boat could go on shore. Should the wind prove favourable, we shall be able to proceed to Helvoet tomorrow. All this day will be employed in repairing some damage we have sustained on our rigging.'[22]

On 1 April Abercromby again wrote to Dundas, to report that 'the troops from Leith anchored here [Helvoet] last night at five o'clock. I found no orders or instructions, except a duplicate of those I received previous to my sailing from Leith. I have reported my arrival to the Duke of York, and to Lord Auckland. I found here the 14th Regt in garrison at Helvoet. The 37th and 53rd Regiments will remain on board till further orders.'[23]

A further letter, written on 10 April, informed Dundas that the brigade had for some days been under York's immediate command. Abercromby's estimation of the troops is not recorded, but it is unlikely to have been very different from the opinion of the Adjutant General, Sir William Fawcett, who apologised to York for the poor quality of 'the brigade of the Line just sent over to you, as so considerable a part of it is comprised of nothing but undisciplined and raw recruits; and how they are to be disposed of until they can be taught their business I am at a loss to imagine.'[24]

Henry Calvert, aide-de-camp to York, wrote in his journal of the disembarking troops: 'we remarked with concern that the recruits . . . lately received were in general totally unfit for service, and inadequate to the fatigues of a campaign, being mostly either old men or quite boys, extremely weak and short.'[25] He later explained in a letter to his uncle, John Calvert:

> I am sorry to say that our small force is much diminished, by two of the regiments in the second brigade being totally unfit for service. So much so, that the Duke of York has left the 37th and the 53rd at Bruges and Ostend. The recruits that were sent to complete them, immediately before their embarkation, are worse than any I ever saw, even at the close of the American War, and I sincerely hope the representation of the Duke of York may awaken the resentment of the King against whatever person or persons the fault lies with. In the meantime, it is a most cruel circumstance upon the officers who command these regiments, and upon General Abercromby, whose brigade is for the present placed quite *hors de combat*.[26]

This was a frustrating start for a man who 'was animated by the hope that he might still achieve distinction by his military skill, and by his zealous devotion to the services of his country'.[27]

York was restricted by orders that kept him within reach of the coast, so that he had yet to enter into consultation with Coburg. Nor was his situation made any easier by Grenville's distrust of the Austrians. For the Foreign Secretary, the new Emperor would remain suspect for as long as he was distracted by events in Poland or insisted on the Bavarian exchange. At his side was his evil genius, Baron Thugut, whom Fortescue regarded as 'an absolutely unprincipled politician who cared for nothing but power and believed in nothing but success'.[28] Grenville wrote to his brother that 'If he [Thugut] were paid to thwart all our measures and to favour those of France, he could not do it more effectually.'[29] Thugut's own communications reveal a cynical politician for whom the end justified the means, but also a man fully committed to the defeat of France. Yet he was also sufficiently unscrupulous to believe that Britain should pay for much of Austria's war effort in the form of subsidies and low-interest loans. And then there was the expectation of territorial gain.

Sir Morton Eden, British Minister to Austria, had a different impression of the man, however. On a later occasion he wrote: 'I live on the best footing with Baron Thugut. He is communicative, and has never deceived me. He is undoubtedly the ablest man in the country, and perhaps the only one equal to the business of the moment.'[30] This corrective view from an experienced diplomat reminds us that British ministers were seeing Thugut from a distorted perspective and forgetting where his first loyalties lay.

On 25 March Brunswick had successfully attacked Custine near the crucial stronghold of Mainz before driving the French out of Lauter, where he then halted. His failure to follow up his success suggested that, like Coburg, he was locked into the conventions of an earlier time and intended to fight a limited war. Nor was he likely to receive orders to the contrary. Frederick William II was an indolent man with no interest in military matters. Prussia certainly wanted to prevent the French from achieving their long-held ambition of establishing a frontier on the Rhine but there were rich pickings elsewhere to distract the King's attention. Furthermore, he was reluctant to commit himself fully until he had secured a British subsidy. When the first instalment of the subsidy was delayed Francophiles in Berlin were able to persuade the King against campaigning beyond the Rhine.

Yet the Prussian army was as vital as the Austrian to success in the field. Britain might be the paymaster but, as Abercromby had already discovered, British troops were inadequate. As for the Germans in British pay, the Hanoverians were fine soldiers but lacked experience. The Hessians had at least learnt to manoeuvre and operate in loose order during the American War, and there were veterans in the ranks who remembered the lesson. The commander of this force, the Duke of York, was enjoying his first experience of active service and command at the age of 30. As a 16-year-old he had studied Prussian methods of war in Berlin. Like the other Allied commanders, though, he was ill-equipped to deal with a French army that had of necessity abandoned the old methods. Their untrained troops could not be deployed in the style of small, professional and highly trained armies. York might possess 'the cool personal bravery which belongs to his race, but not the higher moral courage which gives constancy and patience in difficulty or misfortune; and hence he was at once sanguine and easily discouraged'.[31] Although this view may be too harsh, the government definitely had reservations. They had appointed him at the King's express wish but were now relying on Sir James Murray, his Adjutant General, to make good the Duke's inexperience. As for York himself, Harry Calvert's journal suggests that he soon came to rely on Abercromby's support.

On 5 April the Allies finally met at Antwerp and it soon became clear that Coburg was focused on containment. He had issued a proclamation assuring the French that there would be no conquest of their territory. Under pressure, he withdrew this declaration, although he still wished to open negotiations with the National Convention. In the meantime, he intended to attack the frontier fortresses with British, Hanoverian and Dutch assistance. This went against the intentions of Pitt, Grenville and Dundas, however. The British public might be happy enough with colonial wars, but they were instinctively opposed to European ones. Under government instruction, York finally thrashed out an agreement by which he would support the Austrians at Condé and Valenciennes, and then Lille; in return the Austrians would lend him troops to take Dunkirk, a limited objective that might well win public approval.

On 8 April, the Austrians blockaded Condé with 25,000 men. It was not until 1 May, however, that Coburg produced his plan of campaign, which presumed that by the middle of the month he would have 92,000 men at his disposal, including all the troops in British pay, the Dutch and 9,000 Prussians. A further 13,000 Austrians were expected early in June. This force would enable him to take Condé before marching on to Valenciennes with 52,000 men while leaving a further 40,000 to cover the line from Maubeuge to Ostend. He anticipated that Valenciennes would fall by the end of July, after which he would post 10,000 men to cover Lille and send 50,000 to the siege of Dunkirk. Thus he would be operating on an extended line using the cordon system, as was the norm in Austrian operations. Although it would enable him to control a wide extent of territory by means of a connected line of positions, the obvious disadvantage was that it would disperse the Allied forces, which precluded a march on Paris. When the government received the Austrian plan, they granted York permission to co-operate with Coburg, but with the proviso that he could withdraw at any time.

The French had been forced out of Belgium after Neerwinden but by the end of April they had reorganized themselves and were ready to continue the campaign under a new commander, General August Marie Henri Dampierre, a former Royalist officer now elected to command the Armies of the North and the Ardennes. The French held a line of frontier fortresses from Dunkirk to Quesnoy, and had other troops posted between Maubeuge and Philippeville, Lille and Dunkirk, and Lille and Famars, a few miles south of Valenciennes, where their main army, 30,000 strong, occupied an entrenched position protected by a series of fortified outposts.

The Allies had 9,000 Dutch and Austrians at Furnes, Ypres and Menin. York was still awaiting the arrival of some promised cavalry squadrons as well as the Hanoverians and Hessians, which limited any assistance he could give. More Austrians, 17,500 strong, covered Condé to the north and south, while the main Austrian army lay further south of the town. In addition, 6,000 men were observing Maubeuge. To the east, 30,000 Austrians were occupying Namur, Treves and Luxembourg, and a Prussian army was operating on the Rhine. Although the Allies had more men, superior in quality to the enemy, there were problems implicit in the geography of their dispositions. The length of the front was problematic of itself, and the fact that it was bisected by the Scheldt made cohesive action difficult.

On 1 May the French attacked Allied positions from St Saulve to St Armand but were driven back at all points, losing men and guns. Dampierre was under specific orders to prevent the loss of Condé, so a week later he attacked again, this time merely demonstrating on the Allied flanks while focusing his main attack against the centre, where the Belgian-born Austrian general, François Sebastien de Croix, Count Clerfayt, was in command. Dampierre's attack overwhelmed the Austrians, although Dampierre himself received a fatal wound. When General Lamalière established himself in position to threaten a Prussian force at Saint Amand and Vicoigne, York sent three Guards battalions forward to support the Prussians and their appearance caused the French to draw back from the position they were entrenching. The Coldstreamers, however, suffered heavy casualties when they advanced against French batteries hidden by dense undergrowth. It might have been expected that there would have been recriminations against the Prussian commander, General Alexander von Knobelsdorf, who had given the order to advance without any intimation of what lay ahead. Yet letters home blamed York for the losses because he had sent the Guards to relieve the Prussians in the first place. Such was the unhappy state of the British army.

More British reinforcements were now arriving in Flanders: a cavalry brigade comprising the 7th, 11th, 15th and 16th Light Dragoons, the Hessians, and several detachments of Hanoverians. More Austrians had also arrived, and Coburg decided to make Valenciennes rather than Condé his objective. The first obstacle was Famars. The position was on high ground, protected to the north by Valenciennes and the confluence of the Scheldt and the Rhonelle, and to the east by the Rhonelle. With broken bridges and heavily guarded fords, this river was a challenging barrier.

An advance in two columns was planned for 23 May. York was given command of the left column, which would attack the French right flank.

He had sixteen infantry battalions, including the Guards brigade, eighteen cavalry squadrons, eight of them British, and thirty-eight unattached guns. Abercromby and his line brigade were with the right column, under the command of General Joseph de Ferraris. This column was to assemble north-east of Préseau and then drive the French from positions east of the Rhonelle before crossing the river or making a feint. This was the plan for the main attack, but a further seven columns were to attack a string of French positions should the opportunity arise.

The morning of 23 May was densely foggy, which delayed the onset of the attack until 7 a.m. York's column, which had been marching all night, advanced on Artres, on the Rhonelle, which was heavily defended. Leaving his heavy guns and some of his troops to engage the French batteries, York took the rest of his force to Mareches, where he located a ford. Ferraris' column had made better progress. Soon after eight it 'attacked the enemy's advance works in front of the village of Aulnoit. After some cannonading, the troops advanced to the attack with great spirit; and the cavalry, turning the right flank of the batteries, charged into them. The French cavalry endeavoured to retake their batteries, but were vigorously repulsed by the Hanoverian and Austrian cavalry.'[32] During this action, which is assumed be his first, Abercromby launched an assault and carried the works, taking seven guns and a hundred prisoners. There can be little doubt that he led the attack from the front, since that was to be the hallmark of his command style.

Coburg now halted Ferraris' column while he waited for news of the other column, which had also halted. By sunset York was at the foot of a steep ascent crowned by four redoubts. His troops had already marched much further than had been intended, so he decided to wait until morning before continuing the attack (seemingly on the advice of General Prince Friedrich Wilhelm Hohenlohe). Of the other columns, only the Prince of Orange at Orchies and Clerfayt at Mont Anzin had achieved their objectives. Elsewhere the French still held their positions.

The following morning it soon became clear that the French had decamped and some had been sent into Valenciennes to strengthen the garrison there. The Allied action can be judged a success, therefore, in as far as it had opened up the approaches to Valenciennes and had cost the French seventeen guns and 300 prisoners, with losses in killed and wounded that may have been as high as 3,000. On the other hand, as Murray informed Dundas, more could have been achieved. Since Ferraris' column had attained its immediate objective, the implication has to be that York should have done more.

Coburg now gave York command of siege operations at Valenciennes. He also appointed Ferraris to York's staff with secret instructions to take responsibility for the actual conduct of the siege. It remains unclear to what extent the Austrian general's influence affected the progress of the siege, but Ferraris certainly opposed the opinion of Murray and Colonel Moncrieff RE, who believed that Valenciennes could be taken in twelve days by a bold *coup de main* which would catch the enemy by surprise. Instead, two weeks were spent just bringing up the heavy guns. The siege was undertaken by 25,000 men, including a cohort of British troops. A further 30,000 covered the operations. The town was held by 10,000 men, General Jean Henri Ferrand in command. Entrenchment began on 2 June, and was undertaken by a party of about 300 men from the Guards and Line battalions. The first trenches were opened eleven days later. There now followed the work that all soldiers hated, digging trenches under enemy fire in wet weather. By 18 June, though, the first Allied batteries were able to open fire, and sent more than 800 shells into the town. During the following weeks, hot shot caused widespread fires and when mortars were added to the Allied firepower the situation for the defenders became critical. Deserters brought news of shortages of food and ammunition and reported that the townspeople were urging Ferrand to surrender, but he steadfastly refused.

Progress remained slow despite York's protests. The third parallel was completed on 15 July, thus allowing the Allies to bring their guns closer to the town and silence many of the French guns. Tunnels had been dug under the walls, mines were in position, and the first assault, on the greater and lesser hornworks on the eastern side of the town, finally took place on 25 July. As evening drew on, three columns, including one of British infantry under Abercromby, moved into position.

> Accordingly, in the evening the first mine was sprung, then the second, and third, with the space of eight minutes between each. Immediately on the springing of the third, the troops being ready, rushed in with the utmost impetuosity, jumping over the palisadoes, and through the breaches the mines had made, like the rushing of a flood, and carried all before them at the point of the bayonet. The enemy made a stout resistance, but were forced to leave us in possession of their works.[33]

York later wrote to his father: 'I cannot sufficiently express to your Majesty the courage and gallantry with which the officers and soldiers of your Majesty's troops behaved, but particularly Major-General Abercromby, Colonel Leigh and Lieutenant-Colonel Doyle.'[34] The other two columns were also successful and York now insisted against Ferraris' advice that a lodgement should be made at the greater hornwork, in order to put further pressure on Ferrand. The French commandant refused an invitation to surrender on 26 July, whereupon he was threatened with another assault on his increasingly vulnerable defences. He capitulated two days later, to the general joy of those still in Valenciennes, including his own troops. York, rather than Coburg, who was also present, received the keys of the town.

Further afield, events generally favoured the Allies. The Army of Italy had been routed at Saorgio on 12 June. Spain was in possession of Rousillon. The Vendée remained in a state of insurrection. In Belgium Condé surrendered to the Austrians on 10 July and on the Rhine the Prussians took Mainz on 22 July, bringing to an end the first revolutionary republic on German soil. For French generals, war was now a dangerous game. Custine, who had replaced Dampierre in command of the French Army of the North, was summoned back to Paris and guillotined for his failure to relieve Condé.

The British government expected the fall of Valenciennes to be followed by operations against Dunkirk. Coburg seems to have had doubts about the viability of taking the port, however, and argued that he must first attack the French by marching on Maubeuge, while the Prussians advanced on Sarrelouis. York protested but it was the intervention of Baron Thugut that forced Coburg to abandon his new plan. Quite what Thugut's intentions were beyond the acquisition of compensatory territory for Austria is unclear, but his interference sent Coburg to Quesnoy while York was able to focus on Dunkirk.[35] A more perceptive view might have appreciated that with France in turmoil this was an ideal moment for an advance on Paris.

One more obstacle had to be overcome before either siege could commence. Caesar's Camp was an extensive area of entrenchments on the left bank of the Scheldt two miles south of Bouchain, held by about 25,000 French troops under the Irish-born general Charles Edward Jennings de Kilmaine, the latest commander of the Army of the North. Two attacking columns, under Generals Count Colloredo with 9,000 men and Clerfayt with 12,000, were to make a forced crossing of the river in front of the French position, while York with 14,000 men would create a diversion by crossing the Scheldt at Masnières and Crevecoeur, and advancing towards Bourlon to cut off the French retreat. Murray detected the weakness in this plan; the French would withdraw as soon as they detected York's advance.

He urged Coburg to provide York with cavalry in order to pursue the French but Coburg refused.

On 7 August the heat was excessive and an eleven-hour march to the Scheldt left York's troops in a state of total exhaustion. Only a few, including York, crossed the river. During the night Kilmaine did as Murray expected and abandoned his position, marching westwards towards Arras. (He was subsequently arrested for this dereliction, but escaped the guillotine.) The following morning York was eager to pursue the French, but Hohenlohe, who was with him, initially delayed the crossing of the Scheldt. When York eventually reached higher ground he could see the French rearguard in the distance. Hohenlohe was reluctant to release his cavalry for a harrying pursuit, so York had to rely on his own small force, about 2,000 men, supported by an infantry detachment and some guns. Kilmaine appreciated the danger to his troops and sent his own cavalry to rescue them. This led to hand-to-hand fighting from which the French successfully extricated themselves. Coburg subsequently blamed York for the failure to take the French at Caesar's Camp.

France was now in a state of post-revolutionary chaos as Royalists challenged Republicans in the Vendée, Lyons, Marseilles and Toulon, and Jacobins sought to eliminate Girondins. The country also faced another external threat when at the end of August the British fleet and forces from Spain and Naples became involved at Toulon. In July, under pressure from all sides, the National Convention had restructured the Committee of General Defence, instituted in January 1793, into the Committee of Public Safety, which became the de facto government. Maximilien Robespierre soon established himself as its dominant voice. To solve their military problems, the Committee turned to an engineer officer, Captain Lazare Carnot, a man of exceptional talent as an organizer, administrator and strategist who undertook to save the Revolutionary Army and give it victory. On 23 August he instituted the *levée en masse*. This declared that 'all Frenchmen are in permanent requisition for the service of the armies. The young men shall go to battle; the married men shall forge arms and transport provisions; the women shall make tents and clothing and shall serve in the hospitals; the children shall turn old linen into lint; the aged shall betake themselves to the public places in order to arouse the courage of the warriors and preach the hatred of kings and the unity of the Republic.'[36]

The chaos in France afforded the Allies another chance of marching on Paris, but York was under orders to invest Dunkirk. Whatever his personal feelings about the wisdom of such a move, and there is evidence to suggest that he appreciated the folly of a diversion to Dunkirk at such a moment, he was obedient to government wishes. As a result, while York was engaged at Dunkirk, Coburg besieged Quesnoy, and the chance to invade France was lost.

York had a force of 35,000 troops, Austrian, British, Hanoverian and Hessian, whom he marched to Marchiennes and then towards Menin. On 18 August, before he could advance further, the Dutch created an unwelcome distraction. They had launched a successful attack on French outposts at Linselles but then left an inadequate force to hold the ground they had gained. When the French counter-attacked and overran the positions, the Prince of Orange sent to York for help. York immediately despatched the Guards under Colonel Lake, who launched a bayonet attack. The Guards were relieved in turn by Abercromby with the 14th and 53rd and the Hessians, and successfully held what the Guards had gained.

The following day York organized his troops into two divisions. The first comprised the Hanoverians, Hessians and ten British squadrons, 14,500 strong, under Field Marshal Heinrich Wilhelm von Freytag. They constituted a covering force to protect York's left flank. The remaining troops were divided into two columns, one made up of Austrian troops under General Josef Alvinci and British under Abercromby and General Sir William Erskine, the other of Hessians under General von Buttlar. On 22 August York left Furnes to invest Dunkirk, taking the French by surprise. General Joseph Souham, in command, had only 5,000 men to defend the town's decayed fortifications. He immediately suffered a setback when his advanced posts were driven in and had to abandon their camp at Glyvelde. Further attacks on the French outposts two days later developed into a fierce fight. 'The flank battalion advanced through a large tract of garden ground, and other inclosures, surrounded with deep ditches full of water, and strong double hedges, through which they forced their way with their usual intrepidity, obliging the enemy to retreat back to the town with precipitation.'[37] The next day the French counter-attacked. They were driven in but when the Allies followed them as far as the glacis, they came under heavy fire. York now took position two miles back from the town, with his left at Tetteghem and his right close to the sea. He later expressed particular gratitude of the exertions of Major General Abercromby, Major General Varneck and Lieutenant General Wurmb.

The Hessians with Freytag had proved their worth when on 21 August they drove the French back into Bergues, taking eleven guns. There was more success on the following two days when the French were ousted from

Wormhoudt and Esquelbecque, losing nineteen guns. This enabled Freytag, who had initially established himself at Ypres, to set up a cordon of posts along a twenty-mile front. At this point it would have been safe to assume, as Murray did, that Dunkirk was close to surrender. Carnot, however, had come to Belgium with the intention of saving Dunkirk. General Jean-Nicholas Houchard, the latest commander of the Army of the North, who was a few miles south of Dunkirk with 23,000 men and the promise of reinforcements, was ordered to concentrate on relieving the town. A small force managed to slip into Dunkirk, bringing Souham's strength to nearly 8,000.

York had started to entrench but he was waiting for the promised siege guns and naval support, which meant he was vulnerable to the fire of the French gunboats that swarmed off the coast. On 27 August a frigate and some cutters brought the gun crews but no guns. Admiral John McBride arrived three days later, but without any ships. He stayed long enough to confer with York before sailing back. As for guns, York finally had to take naval guns from a frigate. Nor were the French idle. Souham was under pressure from the commissioners sent by the Convention to save Dunkirk. (He knew the penalty for failure.) He flooded the countryside, which protected Dunkirk, hindered York's movements and disrupted his communications with Freytag. The swampy ground also created a miasma that brought disease to the besieging troops.

The guns finally opened fire early in September, but Houchard was already on the offensive. He had driven the Dutch back from Cysoing and Tourcoing, which left York in a dangerously exposed position. On 6 September, having received reinforcements from the Moselle which brought his numbers up to 40,000, Houchard attacked Freytag's much smaller force. The Hanoverians and Hessians offered stubborn resistance but were forced to retire towards Hondschoote. They reached Rexpoede only to discover that it was held by the French, who immediately attacked. Freytag and Prince Adolphus, York's brother, were taken prisoner and were only rescued when General Wallmoden brought up his Hanoverians and put the French to flight. On the same day, there was also a co-ordinated sortie from the town against York's forces that was driven off with heavy casualties on both sides.

The covering force, now under Wallmoden's command in place of the seriously wounded Freytag, was attacked for a second time on 7 September. The following day they suffered a defeat at the Battle of Hondschoote when, after four hours of fighting and with their ammunition exhausted, they had to retire to Furnes. They were covered by the Hessians who, like the Hanoverians, had lost approaching a third of their strength. On the same day there was also another sortie from Dunkirk that prevented York from coming to Wallmoden's assistance.

York now recognized the danger of his position. On the advice of a council of war, he decided to raise the siege. The heavy baggage was sent back to Furnes, and at midnight the troops retreated in column for what proved a difficult march. The wagons were overloaded and inadequately designed. As a result, tired men were obstructed by fallen horses and toppled wagons. There was also an avoidable delay when the order for the retreat did not reach two battalions posted at Tetteghem and one of the columns had to await their arrival. By 9 September, however, the whole force had reached Furnes, where they joined Wallmoden's troops. The cost of the aborted siege was considerable. The heavy guns were abandoned, and the army itself had suffered severely: 2,000 men killed or wounded and many more lost to Dunkirk fever, possible as many as 10,000 in total.[38] With ironic timing, McBride's long-awaited fleet finally arrived on 11 September.

The army blamed the government for this expensive fiasco. 'That an undertaking strongly recommended from home, received no countenance or naval co-operation, appeared very extraordinary. This remissness on the part of the government excited much indignation in the army, and no small astonishment among our allies.'[39] In Britain, however, York was held responsible for the debacle, even though he had faced problems that were not of his making, and were beyond his ability and resources to resolve. The ministers had insisted that he should attack Dunkirk but had not given him adequate means to do so. He had asked for heavy guns and naval support. They had failed to provide it in time.

Dundas now sent out eight battalions which were intended for an expedition to the West Indies under General Sir Charles Grey and would be available to York only until October, but he also ordered York to detach 5,000 Hessians and send them to Toulon. To compound the absurdity of government thinking, which seemed to take no note of the resources actually available, plans were also being made for an attack on Brittany in support of the rebels there.

Houchard made no attempt to harass the forces retreating from Dunkirk or Wallmoden's troops at Furnes. Instead, he reinforced Dunkirk and Bergues before attacking the Dutch cordon at Poperinghe from Lille. He successfully took Menin, drove the Dutch back to Bruges and Ghent and severed communications between York and Coburg. Then he paused again.

York's initial intention had been to attack Ypres, which was also under threat from Houchard. When Houchard abandoned this objective, however,

York withdrew to a position between Nieuport and Dixmuyde in order to protect a potential retreat to Ostend, where the heavy baggage had already been sent. He left Abercromby with a detachment at Furnes. This concerned Henry Calvert, who wrote to his uncle on 10 September: 'I cannot be free of apprehension for the fate of Furnes, which must expect the attack of all the enemy's force from Dunkirk. General Abercromby, a very able officer, is left for its defence with all the troops we can spare him . . . ' Three days later he wrote: 'In the meantime, I am rather anxious about General Abercromby. He is left at Furnes, with orders to fall back upon Nieuport, if pressed. All was quiet with him yesterday morning, and I sincerely hope that we may be able to occupy the attention of the enemy, and draw them off from Furnes.'[40] Calvert, for one, fully appreciated Abercromby's value to the army, and to York as a dependable subordinate.

When Houchard took Ghent on 13 September, York ordered Abercromby to fall back on Dixmuyde, where he remained until 23 September. York then brought the rest of his force to Thorout, where he found some of the promised reinforcements from England, the 19th, 57th and three companies of the 42nd. Calvert considered them 'a very fine body of men, much too good for the climate of the West Indies'.[41] On 15 September York marched south, the same day that Houchard attacked an Austrian force at Courtrai. Reinforced by some of York's troops, the Austrians put the French to flight and then moved on to Menin, were the enemy was similarly checked. Houchard's fate was sealed. He was summoned back to Paris, accused of incompetence and sent to the guillotine.

Re-taking Menin was one of several Allied successes. Coburg had taken Quesnoy and then achieved a brilliant cavalry triumph at Avesnes-le-Sec, while Brunswick had enjoyed some success in northern Alsace. The Army of the North now had little choice but to retreat, to Lille, Cassel and Maubeuge. Meanwhile, in Paris the Jacobins were creating political chaos as they implemented the Reign of Terror. Senior officers like Houchard were prime targets, leaving the army in disarray. Once more the road to Paris was open, but Coburg chose to take Maubeuge, which was the centre of a large concentration of French troops and an obstacle to Allied lateral movement. Maubeuge was also vital to French communications between Lille and the Ardennes; but Houchard's replacement, General Jean-Baptiste Jourdan, had 45,000 men available to raise a siege, and a further 60,000 supporting troops. Undeterred, Coburg crossed the Sambre with 40,000 men and laid siege to the town.

York was now covering a 45-mile front with inadequate resources. He had received 16,000 Austrians and was granted leave by Dundas to retain the Hessians, although he was required to part with Grey's battalions. He had also suffered heavy losses, mainly to disease, since the spring. At this point Murray played a trump card. He warned Dundas that Ostend was at risk. Since Dundas considered its possession as vital, he instructed the commandant, General Ainslie, to retain the four most recently-arrived of Grey's battalions. To Abercromby, though, he complained in a private letter, 'It would be impossible to restrain the just indignation of the country, if, for the sake of feeding an army under the command of a Prince of the blood, so substantial an interest to this country as that of the French West Indies had been sacrificed.'[42]

Coburg now urged York to advance with 9,000 troops to a position south of Quesnoy. Before York could intervene, however, Jourdan attacked Coburg at Wattignies on 15 October with 45,000 men, twice the number Coburg had under his immediate command. The fighting lasted two days and the outcome was far from decisive. In fact, Jourdan was prepared for the conflict to continue another day but Coburg decided to raise the siege and retreat north of the Sambre. York was left to hold his position covering a line from Solesmes to Berlaimont.

Jourdan was now ordered by Carnot to drive the Austrians into the Sambre but instead he sent some of his troops to attack allied positions between Cysoing and Werwicq. The Allies were forced to abandon Menin and Furnes and on 24 October Nieuport came under attack. The town was held by no more than 1,300 Hessians. Murray had prudently sent most of the stores from Nieuport to Ostend, where Ainslie immediately disembarked the four battalions that were about to sail to England. When the news that Nieuport was under threat reached Dundas, he sent General Grey and the other four battalions who were intended for the West Indies back to Flanders. Grey would then decide whether these reinforcements were actually needed.

In fact, the tide quickly turned in the Allies' favour. The French were ejected from Cysoing on 24 October and were driven out of Orchies three days later, just as the garrison in Nieuport was strengthened by the arrival of more Hessians. A day later Grey reached Ostend and immediately sent the 42nd and four light infantry battalions to Nieuport. This soon persuaded the French to withdraw after four summons to surrender had been defiantly rejected by the Hessian commander, General Ludwig von Wurmb, who had commanded the Hessian Jägers in the American War and was a famously tough character.

York now sent Abercromby to French-held Lannoy with two Austrian battalions, the 3rd Guards, the flank battalion of the Guards and two squadrons from the 7th and the 15th Light Dragoons. The intention was to distract the French, who were threatening Menin. They reached Lannoy on 28 October.

> About eight o'clock, the flank battalions and 3d regiment of guards, with some squadrons of the 15th light dragoons, two howitzers, and four field pieces, were ordered to march immediately, in order to attack the enemy, who were strongly posted in the village of Lannoy, about five miles from our camp: about twelve o'clock we marched, and on arriving there, the artillery advanced, covered by the infantry, and commenced a brisk cannonade on the enemy, which continued upwards of two hours, and was answered by the French; but finding it too hot for them, they abandoned the village, which General Abercrombie, who commanded, perceiving, ordered the light cavalry to pursue them, which they did, with spirit and activity peculiar to themselves; killed about fifty, and brought back near 100 prisoners, among whom were several officers.[43]

The French lost between 200 and 300 killed, with up to 150 taken prisoner. Five guns, along with tumbrils and baggage wagons, fell into Allied hands.

There were further successes. Marchiennes, which had fallen to the French, was retaken by the Austrians on 29 October. The French then withdrew from Menin and Ypres, and as already noted, abandoned their attempt to take Nieuport. At this point York, who was not given to false modesty, claimed that he had saved West Flanders. The Emperor and the Committee of Public Safety were anxious that their commanders should fight a general engagement. Coburg and Jourdan, more realistic than the politicians, realized that their depleted troops were exhausted and ignored the wishes of their masters. There was still fighting further west, though, where Brunswick had defeated the French at Permasin on 14 September and then in conjunction with the Austrians routed them at the Lines of Weissenberg on 13 October. Unfortunately, both Prussia and Austria were looking greedily at Alsace and mutual suspicion hindered any further co-operation. When in November the French attacked Strasbourg, only Wurmser and the Prussians moved to save the town. The French prevailed. Then, while Strasbourg suffered some of the worst excesses of the Reign of Terror, Wurmser withdrew and contented himself with taking Landau.

In Flanders, the men under York's command went into winter quarters between Ghent and Courtrai, while Grey withdrew the eight West India battalions. It was not an end to the conflict, however. Under Carnot's direction the French were in the ascendant. The Dutch Republic was in their sights. The Allies at this stage were as firmly determined to prevent them, although they were now fighting a war which was more about territory than liberation. Coburg's strategy had definitely cost them all chance of marching on Paris. As for Abercromby, who was presently in command of the outposts protecting York's headquarters at Oudenarde, it was clear from the responsibilities he had already been given that he would play an increasingly significant part in the next campaign. A letter York wrote to his father on 12 December provides clear evidence of this. He intended to visit Coburg and discover his plans for the new season; 'and should I have the least difficulty in persuading him to enter into the business, I shall send General Abercrombie to press him still stronger upon the subject. Nobody, I am sure, could be more fit for such a commission than General Abercromby, as there is not in your Majesty's service a better nor a more honourable man, or one whose military abilities are more universally acknowledged.'[44]

Significantly, three days before the King had written to Dundas, in reply to a letter from Dundas: 'I thoroughly approve of Mr Dundas's draft to Sir James Murray, as also of his not having suggested any particular person for being sent to the Prince of Cobourg, as that might occasion jealousy, but I have written to my son and pointed out M.G. Abercrombie as the person I wish employed on this business.'[45]

In November Sir Morton Eden in Vienna wrote an acerbic letter to his brother, Lord Auckland, suggesting that the Allies would have to sort out their own differences before they could hope to defeat the French.

> What say you to your Dutch friends? who will neither consent to garrison the captured towns [Valenciennes. Condé, and Quesnoy], which would put them out of the way of the danger they apprehend, nor remain in the cordon if it be attacked. If I may credit Crauford [Sir Quentin Crauford, gentleman-spy], their repeated losses were owing to their strong-headedness in remaining scattered, against all advice, in small corps . . . As to the conduct of the Prussians, I cannot give it too hard an epithet. They are like the Deal men, who avail themselves of the perilous situation of the passengers in a ship stranded on the Goodwins to drive a most unconscionable bargain.[46]

Events would prove these criticisms well founded. The Dutch were to prove doubtful allies, divided as they were between pro-French patriots and conservatives anxious to retain their privileges. As for the Prussians, they would soon demonstrate that their other interests were more important than defeating the French. Brunswick's resignation on 6 January strongly suggested that the Prussians intended to disengage from the Rhine in order to focus on Poland.

A New Campaign

There could be no further doubts about French intentions. By the end of 1793 they had forced the Prussians to the east of the Rhine, repulsed an attempt by the King of Sardinia to reoccupy Savoy, and confined the Spanish invasion to southern France. They had suppressed internal rebellion by brutally subjugating the Loire Valley and the Vendée and ejecting the foreign troops from Toulon. They needed more territory, however. Carnot's *levée en masse* meant they had troops to spare but lacked the means to feed them; the armies needed to live off the land on foreign territory, as Carnot always intended. Without the restrictions of depots and supply trains an army had greater strategic flexibility and could move more rapidly, but it needed subjugated people to foot the bill.

At the start of 1794, York's prime concern was to make good his shortages in almost all areas. Murray had now been eased out with an appointment to command a Scottish brigade. His replacement was Major General James Craig, who was considered a more effective mentor for York. Craig was a veteran of the American war, where he had won plaudits for his resourcefulness. He was warmly received by York, and was able to report that any 'distance' between the Duke and Sir William Erskine (who had been in command of the army during York's recent absence in England) was no longer apparent. He was also hoping to meet General Abercromby in the near future, another indication that Abercromby's efforts during 1793 had brought him to official notice. Craig also picked up the problems that Murray had faced: the lack of troops, fit horses, artillery drivers and supplies. Some relief was afforded with the arrival of 'new tents of a round form, and superior quality to the old ones, each tent is to contain sixteen men; also new kettles, two to each tent, with a horse per company to carry them . . . '[47] as York had requested. The tents were soon followed by grey cloth greatcoats in the Austrian fashion, again at York's particular request.

The medical services were another area of concern but these were outside Craig's authority. Since this would remain a constant throughout the decade, it is relevant to consider the system then in use. When the French declared war in February 1793, John Hunter was Surgeon General. On him fell the responsibility for making the necessary medical arrangements, which he did by appointing surgeons from regiments and the half-pay list and setting up a general hospital at Bruges. He also drew up regulations for the management of general hospitals which he hoped would curtail the rivalry between physicians and surgeons. When this still surfaced, to the detriment of the service, he appointed Dr Hugh Kennedy, a veteran of the North American War, as Inspector General with ultimate authority.

The list of equipment afforded to the regimental hospitals of the Guards indicates the ideal. 'Hospital cots made of wooden frames with canvas bottoms were carried for the more severe cases on the scale of 2 for every 100 men in the regiment, and the other beds were simply wooden boards. Palisades, sheets, pillow cases, blankets and ward equipment were provided with close stools, bed pans, and urinals, cooking and feeding utensils, and medical comforts such as sugar, sago, etc. A field chest contained a comprehensive list of some 120 different drugs and dressings.' It is safe to assume that other battalions, particularly those hastily augmented and almost immediately dispatched to Flanders, would not be so well supplied. Nor were arrangements made for wagons to carry the equipment required for the general hospital. Transport, of course, was not within the Surgeon General's remit.[48]

After Dunkirk the shortcomings of the arrangements became clear. There was no room for the 1,000 sick and wounded men who arrived at Bruges. They were sent to Ostend, where the hospital could hold only 200 patients and was already full. They were then sent back to Bruges. Eventually another general hospital was established at Menin. Reports were also reaching England that the wounded were receiving inadequate care. Hunter sent Everard Home, assistant surgeon at St George's Hospital, to investigate. He was soon crossing swords with Kennedy, who insisted that he was responsible only to the Commander-in-Chief. Home was saved from what might have been a wasted journey only when he identified the main problem as the difficulty of treating the wounded between the regimental and general hospitals. He recommended using flying hospitals, a suggested which York immediately approved.

Unfortunately, Hunter died in October 1793 and was replaced by a three-man board consisting of the Surgeon General, Physician General and Inspector of Regimental Infirmaries. They were required to dedicate two hours a day to their duties, and were generally at their desks. This did not prevent them from being elusive when any military officer tried to locate them.[49] With regard to overseas expeditions, they had the same three responsibilities as Hunter: to set up general hospitals, select medical officers, and supply medicines and surgical instruments. Kennedy remained independent of their authority as Inspector General, which led to problems with filling vacancies. Since Kennedy refused even to inform the Board where vacancies existed, shortages could not be addressed. This was clearly a matter of prerogative. Eventually, the members of the Board appealed to the aged Lord Amherst, Commander-in-Chief, who confirmed their responsibility in this respect. In all other respects, though, the conflict of authority remained unresolved. This did nothing to reduce an average sick rate of 20 per cent, even though in March the Medical Board supplied staff and supplies irrespective of Kennedy's wishes.

One step Craig did take as he felt his way into his new position was to use Harry Calvert for intelligence purposes. Thus when there was a false alarm early in February, occasioned by a deserter claiming that a large seaborne force was assembling at Dunkirk, Calvert was given the task of testing the story, which turned out to be untrue. He would continue to provide valuable information for the rest of the campaign.

Nor were the Austrians in much better condition than the British. The Archduke Charles reported to his brother that the troops 'lacked uniforms, rations, and decent hospitals'. Morale was low and the officers were as discontented as the rank and file. Too many promotions had gone to the well-connected on the staff of commanders. There was resentment against staff officers who avoided exposure to combat. Officers of the Kinsky Chevaulegers, he wrote, 'have sworn that the first such gentleman who delivers an order to attack will be forced to take part in the charge'.[50] The army, continued the Archduke, was becoming disaffected.

In February the Allies started planning the new campaign. Both York and Major General (formerly Colonel) Mack were in London for discussions with the relevant government ministers. Pitt and Grenville recognized that the coalition was under strain but were also confident that France would break first by sinking into anarchy or running out of money. They met Mack on 13 February, and immediately made clear that they intended to replace York with General Lord Cornwallis, recently returned from India where, as Governor-General, he had led the successful campaign against Tipu Sultan. They seem to have reached this decision because of York's lack of success, coupled with slanderous reports from some disaffected officers. When Mack pointed out that Cornwallis would find fighting the French a very different experience from fighting in India, Pitt and Grenville then insisted that York should act only with the main army and someone else, possibly Cornwallis, should command in Western Flanders. The King reluctantly agreed, but on condition that his son still commanded an army compatible with his rank and position. As a result, York was given some Austrians, while a British contingent was attached to Clerfayt's force. As for Cornwallis, he remained in England.

Mack had already formulated a plan which Coburg had signed off. It required all four allies to augment their forces so that the main army in Flanders could prepare for a concentrated advance on Paris. The British were to protect the Austrian right flank. Other troops would remain on the right bank of the Meuse and also in Luxemburg as insurance against French incursions, while the Austrians and Prussians would guard the Rhine for the same purpose. Mack also insisted that those border fortresses in Allied hands must be strongly garrisoned. He advocated attack at every opportunity, which demonstrated that he had learnt a valuable lesson from the French, but he also dangerously underestimated the fighting qualities of the new French armies, describing men and officers alike as 'miserable'.[51] Pitt agreed with this plan, and somewhat rashly undertook to provide 40,000 more troops. This was against a background of crimping. 'Crimps' offered to supply recruits for cash in hand and used various nefarious methods to obtain men, sometimes offering money which the gullible recruit would never see, sometimes plying men with drink until they were insensible, and even resorting to kidnapping in extreme cases. The result was that desperate recruiters accepted whatever the crimps presented to them. Recruiting for rank had an equally detrimental effect on the officer corps. That a man had managed to produce the required number of recruits did not mean that he himself was suitable officer material. Furthermore, brokers were busily selling commissions, which had a similar effect on the officer cadre. This period also saw the raising of the first volunteer forces, which distracted some men from regular service. Consequently, when the reinforcements arrived 'they most resembled Falstaff's men, and were as lightly clad as any Carmagnole battalion'.[52]

The Dutch Republic remained a concern. Auckland, who was coming to the end of his period as ambassador at The Hague, reported that 'The patriotic party has laid aside all reserves and is becoming noisy and impudent. There is scarce a village or alehouse in this province [Holland] in which the language is not seditious at the clubs and frequently [boasts] the accession of a travelling Jacobin.'[53] More worrying were the observations of a French agent, that the Patriots were in strength in several provinces, and enjoyed support from all except those who owed their position to the Stadtholder, or belonged to the lowest classes.[54] This was the enemy within. At the same time the Patriots who were serving with the French, particularly General Herman Willem Daendels, were agitating for an invasion of the Republic.

The false alarms continued. On 1 March Craig reported to Nepean that he had just visited Freytag at Courtrai. The field marshal feared an imminent French attack, but Craig had more recent intelligence which suggested this was another rumour without any foundation, a view shared by General Abercromby. As for Abercromby himself, Craig wrote on the 11 March: 'General Abercrombie commands at Menin, which is the most exposed quarter we have – his vigilance & courage may be relied on, & he is this day joined by the Austrian hussars and chasseurs, who have been so long in Ostend. I think he will soon get an opportunity of employing these Gentlemen & perhaps of giving the Enemy a severe lesson – at least they offer a fair opportunity for it if they continue the conduct which they have followed for some days past.'[55] Craig may well be referring to the forward movement which had been planned for 15 and 20 March.

Although Abercromby might be establishing an impressive reputation for himself, the same cannot be said of one of his battalions, the 14th. As York himself reported to Thomas Pelham, an MP had had visited the army the previous year to investigate concerns about discipline, 'one unfortunate peasant was robbed and murdered by a man of the 14th Regiment of Foot. I had him tried by general court martial, who found him guilty but sentenced him only to corporal punishment.' This leniency seemed to make the soldiers more daring because 'On Tuesday [10 April] after the regiment was ordered to march the next morning, two men of the same regiment went to a farmhouse, forced the door open, robbed the poor unfortunate woman of everything she possessed, and since she had only two crowns in money they shot her and likewise her child, who was about four years old, They were immediately taken and confessed their crime. General Abercromby was immediately here and reported the circumstance himself.'

Abercromby had an uncompromising approach to discipline and readily implemented the order he received to 'give immediate directions for assembling such part of your brigade as you can conveniently get together in the time, particularly the 14th Regiment, and that you do cause both the persons to be executed by hanging them till dead, before sunset this evening, if this order arrive in time, for that purpose, if not before your brigade marches tomorrow morning.'[56] Summary justice, but effective. 'This order was of the greatest importance to the army, and the immediate execution of these unfortunate men put a total stop to plundering.'[57]

The Emperor's Intervention

Although Coburg remained in command, the Archduke Charles had persuaded the Emperor to assume personal control of the campaign. He arrived in Brussels on 9 April, bringing with him Baron Thugut, a man who shared something of Grenville's contempt for the military. The British government saw him as an obstacle to the unity of the coalition. This had been demonstrated when, in contradiction of the agreement made between the Allies, he refused to pay some of the British subsidy to Prussia. The Prussians responded by withdrawing troops from the Rhine. For Coburg this defection was a disaster but even with York's support he could not persuade Francis to overrule his minister. Nor could he persuade the Prussian general, von Möllendorf, to delay the withdrawal. Money talks, though, and a British threat not to pay the Austrian subsidy resolved the situation. Satisfied, the Prussian king undertook to provide 62,000 men who would be paid for and utilized by the British. Dundas intended these troops for Flanders as part of an assault that would knock the French out of the war. Frederick William had no such intention.

Coburg now concentrated his position. Clerfayt, in command of 24,000 Austrians, Hanoverians and Hessians, had his headquarters at Tournai. York was in the centre, at St Amand with 22,000 men, Coburg was at Valenciennes with 43,000, and the Hereditary Prince of Orange, at Bavai with 19,000. A further 5,000 men under the Hanoverian General Wurmb were posted on the Scheldt. On the left, an Austro-Dutch force, commanded by General Kaunitz, held a line on the Meuse from Bettigues to Dinant, while a further 15,000 men were in cantonments between Namur and Tréves. This gave the allies a total strength of 120,000 men.

Against them, Carnot had a quarter of a million men at his disposal and was determined to defeat the Allies within the year. He planned to take the coastal region and disrupt the British line of retreat by advancing one part of his force to Ypres and Ghent before swinging inland to Brussels. A second force would distract the Austrians by threatening Namur and Liège, and a reserve would defend a line from Bouchain to Maubeuge. On 11 March General Jean-Charles Pichegru, the present commander of the Army of the North, was ordered to advance on Ypres. Pichegru delayed until 29 March, when he attacked Austrian outposts at Le Cateau. He was repulsed with heavy losses. Yet Coburg did not follow up because he was awaiting the arrival of the Emperor, who was travelling slowly from Vienna.

On 16 April Francis reviewed the main army on the Cateau Heights. According to Calvert, this was an excuse to assemble troops for an attack on the entrenched French positions from Landrecies to Prémont. The following day the Allies advanced in eight columns with three objectives, Cambrai, the Sambre crossing and Wassigny. York had command of two columns to the right. General Erskine was to drive the French out of their entrenchments at Prémont. York, with the other column, led by the advance guard under Abercromby, was to do the same at Vaux. Then both columns would march on Le Catelet.

The advance was across difficult terrain intersected by sunken roads and steep declivities that gave the advantage of surprise. Although under heavy fire, Abercromby stormed the Star Fort and quickly overwhelmed the enemy. As the French fled, they were harried on their way by the 16th Light Dragoons and Austrian hussars. Once again York publically thanked Abercromby for his zeal and gallantry.

General Allied success enabled Coburg to concentrate on Landrecies, which the Dutch entrenched on 20 April. Pichegru was aware of the potential danger to Paris if Landrecies fell, but his desultory efforts to dislodge the Allies from the ground they had gained on 17 April failed to disrupt the siege. York's force was entrenched on a chain of hills from near Le Catelet to the Le Cateau–Cambrai road as part of a semicircle lying to the south of the town.

Having received reinforcements that raised his strength to 200,000 men, Pichegru decided to attack Clerfayt at Lille and then raise the siege of Landrecies. As one of several diversionary attacks, 30,000 men were sent to threaten York's position. On 26 April the French advanced in two columns, one along the Cambrai-Le Cateau road towards Beaumont, the other on a parallel course via Ligny. They drove in York's advance posts under cover of fog and formed up behind a ridge as the fog cleared. York turned his guns on them and sent his light troops against their right. His cavalry, hidden in a fold of ground and formed in three lines, then fell on the unengaged part of the French line from the north. The French guns came into action but the charge was maintained. Panic ensued, and the fleeing French were driven in. At this point a second column also came under cavalry attack and was driven back on its fellows. With Otto and the Archduke Charles also successful, Pichegru had suffered a serious setback.

There followed several weeks of manoeuvring and desultory fighting as the French tried to take control of littoral Flanders. Nieuport and Ypres were under threat and on the 30 April Menin was lost when the garrison abandoned the town, fighting their way out in order to protect the large number of émigrés who had been serving there. On the Allied left, Kaunitz was forced back across the Sambre. Only the surrender of Landrecies bolstered the Allied position.

Fortunately, Pichegru failed to follow up his successes, and on 5 May the Allies went on the offensive to regain Courtrai, which had been lost shortly before. Five days later Clerfayt, as dilatory as Pichegru, finally attacked the suburbs of the town. He quickly came under pressure from a force commanded by General Jean Moreau, while another force under Souham moved to prevent York coming to Clerfayt's assistance. York sent sixteen squadrons of dragoons and two of hussars towards a gap he had noticed in the French line. They encountered the French in square. As the French retreated they pursued the squares, but then came under fire from the French guns. York then sent a British infantry brigade forward, presumably Abercromby's advance guard, while four further battalions followed the route taken by the cavalry. The French infantry began to retreat, covered by their cavalry. The Allied cavalry pounced, and overwhelmed the enemy cavalry. The Allied guns opened fire, targeting the squares. First one broke, then others, as panic spread. The final outcome was a debacle: 1,000 men killed or wounded, 400 taken prisoner, thirteen guns lost.[58] Calvert made an interesting observation in a letter to his friend, Sir Hew Dalrymple, regarding this limited action at Courtrai. 'Poor Winheim, approaching too near a battery, was killed by a cannon-shot. I looked upon him as the Abercromby of the Austrian army. I leave you to judge how great a misfortune I conceive his loss to be at this moment.'[59]

On 1 May Pichegru transferred his attentions back to Clerfayt, who was forced from his position north of Courtrai with the loss of about 1,500 men and two guns. York was now vulnerable and needed reinforcements but the Emperor could not decide whether to send the main army to strengthen the left flank, where Kaunitz was being driven back by the Army of the Ardennes, or to support the forces on his right. Coburg sent Wurmb to join York at Tournai as a temporary measure. He also pointed out to the Emperor that the choice lay between Flanders and the Sambre, and Francis needed to decide which was more important to Austrian interests. The news that Kaunitz had fought a successful action inclined Francis towards Flanders. Nevertheless, he still insisted that the Hereditary Prince should be left at Landrecies with 8,000 men. On 14 May the main army moved west and the Emperor joined York at Tournai while his brother, the Archduke, was only eleven miles to the south with the bulk of the Austrian forces. The Allies were in position for a general attack.

The French had 82,000 men dispersed between Pont à Marque, Sainghin, Mouscron and Turcoing, and along a line from Courtrai to Aelbeke. They also had possession of most of the bridges across the Marque. The Allies had 62,000 men, of which 12,000 were cavalry. This was a disadvantage in country unsuited to cavalry action, particularly along the Marque, where the ground was swampy. York and Clerfayt now intended to isolate those French forces holding a position between the Lys and the Scheldt but on 16 May the Emperor issued an order that extended the purpose of the attack. The intention now was 'to act upon the enemy's communications between Lille and Courtrai, to defeat the armies he has advanced upon the Lys and to drive him out of Flanders'.[60] The plan was Mack's. Predictably it involved a six-column attack. York was in command of the third column, comprised of twelve infantry battalions and ten squadrons of cavalry, plus a reserve of sixteen British squadrons under Erskine's command. His targets were Lannoy, Roubaix and Mouveau and he was to advance in parallel with General Rudolf von Otto.

The columns were to be in position ready for an attack at daybreak on 16 May, but insufficient allowance had been made for the varying distances the columns had to march. Clerfayt, in command of the sixth column, should have been behind the enemy at Mouscron and Tourcoing by daybreak, but received his orders late. He commenced his march in the evening, hampered by the sandy terrain, and when he finally reached the Lys, which he needed to cross, discovered that the necessary pontoons had been forgotten. As another foggy morning dawned, only General Georg Wilhelm von dem Busshe's weak column, Otto's and then York's on Otto's left were in position. There was no news of General Count Kinsky, who should have been on York's left.

York marched to his first objective, Lannoy, where 'the brave General Abercrombie, with four battalions of the guards, seconded by the 7th and 15th Light Dragoons, under Lieutenant Colonel Churchill, attacked the French and compelled them to retire, with the loss of three pieces of cannon'.[61] Leaving two Hessian battalions at Lannoy, York them moved on to Roubaix, which was strongly entrenched and held by a sizeable force, 'but by the judicious conduct of General Abercromby, and the valour of the troops under his command, the entrenchment was forced and the enemy totally routed'.[62] According to Corporal Brown, 'the enemy made a stout opposition . . . and after their out-posts were drove in, answered our cannon for some time with great spirit, and then retreated, getting clear off with all their guns. We then entered the town in triumph . . . Many of the inhabitants had fled, and left their houses shut up, and those who remained, eyed us either with a kind of vacant look, hardly knowing whether to esteem us as friends or foes.'[63]

There was still no news of Kinsky, who should have crossed the Marque in support of York. York decided to leave a detachment at Roubaix and return to Lannoy with his main force, whereupon the Emperor ordered him to attack his main objective, Mouveau. It was after 5 p.m. and York knew that he had insufficient troops but his protest was overruled. He sent in the Guards while Abercromby directed the 7th and 15th Light Dragoons to circle the village, which was strongly defended by palisades, entrenchments and flanking redoubts.

> We accordingly advanced to the attack, with great vigour and alacrity, from the refreshment we had received at Roubaix, and after some time spent in cannonading, the flank battalion which had been in front all day, having formed the line and advancing towards the enemy, eagerly catched the word 'charge', and rushed with the utmost impetuosity into the enemy's works, upon which they fled with the greatest precipitation, leaving behind them three pieces of cannon. In the mean time the light cavalry wheeling round the village, overtook them in their flight, and pursued them about three miles with great slaughter.[64]

Some of the 15th were even able to ride on to Bondues and scatter the French troops there. Having secured Mouveau, York ordered his troops to bivouac, although they were in a dangerously exposed position. He knew Otto had taken Tourcoing but he still had no news of Kinsky, whose support would have secured his position.

The French now needed to re-align before the Allies followed up their attack the next day. In Pichegru's absence, Souham organized a double echelon south of the Lys with salient points at Mouscron, Menin, Courtrai and a position two miles east of Lille. The force posted near Lille, however, subsequently received orders to march on Lannoy and Roubaix. The Allies also held a council of war at which it was recognized that Mack's plan had failed. A new plan, formulated in the early hours, had two columns marching to Lannoy, and a further two, including York's, attacking Mouscron at noon. York's troops were still dispersed: Abercromby in command of the Guards and the 7th and 15th Light Dragoons was at Mouveau; four Austrian battalions and the 16th Light Dragoons were at Roubaix; two Hessian battalions were still at Lannoy; and four Austrian squadrons were on patrol. Although the right was covered, the left was vulnerable to attack from Lille.

By 3 a.m. the French were bringing up 60,000 men against the second and third columns. The former, at Tourcoing and Wattrelos, was the first to be attacked. Otto immediately sent to York for reinforcements and received two Austrian battalions. York had given them strict orders to return if Tourcoing was already lost but instead of returning, they joined the withdrawal. The French then fell on York's column some time between 6 and 7 a.m. General Bonnaud advanced on Lannoy, Roubaix and Mouveau while some of the French who had been successful at Tourcoing appeared north of Roubaix. York had positioned his troops at Mouveau as two sides of a square, with the guns placed at the angle. Abercromby's instructions were to hold the town to the last. General Henry Fox's British brigade, the 14th, 37th and 53rd, were formed up to prevent an advance from Lille. This left York with just three Austrian battalions. He posted half a battalion in Roubaix, and the remainder to the right and rear of Fox's brigade. There was no sign of Austrian relief from the south.

Fox's force was the first to buckle under severe French pressure. This allowed a French brigade to advance between Mouveau and Robaix, which isolated Abercromby and the Guards. York responded by ordering Abercromby to retire to the high ground near Roubaix, and then by riding to Wattrelos with two squadrons of the 16th Light Dragoons to seek help from Otto. It was obvious by now that nothing could be expected from Kinsky or the Archduke.

Lacking specific orders from York, Fox decided to withdraw. At first, the brigade preserved good order, despite being under constant French attack, but when the troops realized that the road was barred by an abattis which concealed a French battery there were the first signs of panic. Fortunately, a Frenchman serving in the 14th happened to know the country well and led them to safety at Leers. Losses were considerable, though, including all but one of their guns.

Abercromby began his own retreat at about 9 a.m, slowed by the large number of guns, which he was anxious not to abandon. The troops

> marched back towards Roubaix, with the artillery and the main body of the brigade, while the skirmishing parties all around us made it appear like a kind of running fight. On coming near the town we found the enemy assembled in great numbers in the wood

to the right of the town, from whence they would have annoyed us greatly on our entrance; we therefore made a halt, and with four twelve pounders being drawn up, gave them such a salute as made them sheer off. We then proceeded through the town, which the front of the column cleared very well, but before the rear got clear of the gate, the enemy pressed very hard upon them, both with grape shot and musketry, and killed and wounded a great many.[65]

As Brown's account makes clear, the suburbs of the town were in French hands. A dismounted squadron of the 16th Light Dragoons held the centre, which was essentially one long street. Although the Guards and the guns reached the far side unmolested, the Austrian hussars and the 15th Light Dragoons in the rear came under fire. Chaos quickly ensued. The hussars dismounted, hoping to escape through the houses. When they found there was no way out, they quickly remounted and galloped desperately through some French infantry posted to stop them. Almost immediately they were confronted by another obstacle, their own horseless guns. The gunners had abandoned the position when the French enfiladed the position. The situation became a mêlée of struggling men and horses, made even worse when loose horses careered into the Guards. At the same time, enemy sharpshooters, concealed in the nearby woods, were picking off their targets. The Guards quickly recovered. They opened their ranks so that the cavalry could pass through and re-form. Once order had been restored, the retreat continued to Lannoy, which was now surrounded by the French.

Abercromby needed to determine whether the Hessians were still in possession of Lannoy. He ordered Colonel Congreve to bring up his guns. Then some blue-coated cavalry appeared and were assumed to be Hessians. The misidentification was recognized when the 'Hessians' began to cut the traces of the guns. Abercromby realized that he could neither make a stand at Lannoy nor advance along the road towards Tournai. Like Fox, he decided on a cross-country route which brought his troops to safety. His total British losses for the day were 196 all ranks from the Guards as well as 52 men and 92 horses from the dragoons. The Austrian hussars had also taken casualties at Robaix. Nevertheless, both his brigade and Fox's, along with their commanders, had proved their worth on this second day of the Battle of Tourcoing.

As for York, he finally made contact with Otto after a desperate cross-country ride. Together the two commanders were able to rally the remnants of their troops at Lees and Nechin. The French made no move against them, and by about 4.30 p.m. the battle had petered out.

Coburg's plan had been frustrated in part by the speed and determination of the French attack, which had overwhelmed York and Otto. The commanders of the other columns had all failed. Busshe's small force had been repulsed. Clerfayt had finally crossed the Lys at 7 a.m. He then encountered a French force of about half his strength and easily overwhelmed it, taking eight guns, whereupon he sat still until news of a French advance drove him back across the Lys. Kinsky, when asked for orders, claimed to be sick and no longer in command. The Archduke had suffered an epileptic fit, which he needed to sleep off. His staff officers were reluctant to act on their own initiative and delayed implementing an order received at 5 a.m. for a march on Lannoy until midday. His column reached the main Tournai-Lille road three hours later and was then ordered to withdraw.

The forces in British pay certainly believed that the Austrians had left all the fighting to them. York had informed the Emperor of his dangerous situation but Francis had sent no urgent message to either Kinsky or the Archduke. Fortescue blamed his chosen villain, Thugut, for Austrian inaction, as a means to bring the war in Flanders to an end.[66] Thugut certainly understood the Allies' situation. He later wrote to a trusted friend: 'Reduced to the defensive, we are continually harassed on two flanks of our position in Flanders and on the Sambre by innumerable hordes who are in fact constantly defeated and repulsed, but our army is vastly weakened by these partial victories while the enemy repairs its losses with the greatest ease.'[67] He understood that the old system was powerless against the limitless resources of the *levée en masse*.

Calvert also realized that the old system was no longer fit for purpose. In another letter to Dalrymple which gave an account of the two–day action he concluded: 'I most sincerely hope that the heavy disaster which has fallen so undeservedly on us will be a warning to our allies; for while the same loose, unconnected, unmilitary system is persevered in, while such rashness and such childish obstinacy are the striking characteristics of their councils, nothing but loss and disgrace can attend the arms of his Imperial Majesty.' The Emperor publically acknowledged that York's was the only column to achieve its objective, which led Calvert to comment: 'I believe the conduct of the British troops has excited the admiration, and perhaps jealousy, of the whole Austrian army.'[68] Captain Jones of the 14th later wrote: 'The abilities and coolness with which Lieutenant General Abercromby and Major General Fox, conducted their corps, under such trying circumstances, has done them immortal honour',[69] honour that both commanders would undoubtedly have shared with their troops.

Despite the festering resentment, the Allies still needed to act together. Coburg brought his whole force to Tournai and took position in a semi-circle to the west of the town. Pichegru, who was now back with his troops, decided to attack the Allied left and right flanks while distracting the centre with a demonstration further south. As a result, on 22 May the Allies were driven from three of their positions. The most significant of these was Pont-à-Chin, which commanded both the road to Courtrai and navigation on the Scheldt. Such was its strategic importance that Coburg launched an immediate counter-attack. York's troops were held in reserve, perhaps in acknowledgement of their efforts at Tourcoing, but it was Fox's depleted line battalion that finally regained the position with the bayonet.

The Austrians were now discussing the possibility of withdrawing beyond the Scheldt to Ath. York, choosing to speak with his father's voice, pointed out that his government had rendered every assistance in the defence of Flanders. He reminded the Emperor that the protection of Holland was the primary British objective. If the Emperor now intended to abandon Flanders, then the British and the Dutch would feel free to act in their own interests without reference to Austria. This seemed to have the desired effect. Francis decided to stand fast at Tournai. Yet a few days later he announced his intention to return to Vienna, offering as an excuse his wife's advanced pregnancy. He left behind a dispirited army.

The French Offensive

The Emperor's departure strongly suggested that Belgium was

> to be relinquished, partly because the inhabitants do not evince attachment to the Emperor; partly because the country is so distant from Austria, and difficult to retain against the enterprising and increasing armies of the French Republic; partly, perhaps, because it is hoped that acquisitions nearer home may compensate the loss of provinces so distant and so little affected.
>
> Those, therefore, of the inhabitants who have remained faithful to their Imperial Sovereign are to be abandoned to their merciless foes. The Emperor's engagements with Holland and Great Britain are to be violated. The British army, inconsiderable in numbers

when compared with the Republican hosts, are now to sustain the conflict alone, unaided by those in dependence on whom they engaged in and hitherto maintained it.[70]

The news was not uniformly bad, however: the Prussians had achieved a notable victory at Kaiserslautern on 23 May; and Kaunitz had crushed the French at Erquelinnes on the Sambre on 24 May. In Paris the political situation was descending into anarchy. Robespierre was determined to control everything. This put him at odds with Carnot, who was under threat of death if he failed to deliver victory. Robespierre had also sent his trusted ally, Louis Antoine de Saint-Just, and five extra commissioners to the Army of the North in order to extend the influence of the Reign of Terror. Saint-Just took immediate control on the Sambre, which undoubtedly enabled Kaunitz to achieve his crushing victory. Robespierre also issued through the National Convention a proclamation that identified England as the enemy of humanity and liberty, a country that was capable of every imaginable crime. 'Republican soldiers, therefore, when victory shall put in your power either English or Hanoverians, strike: not one of them must return to the traitorous land of England, or be brought into France. Let the British slaves perish, and Europe be free.'[71]

It would have been easy for York to descend to the same depths of barbarism. Instead, he issued his own proclamation. This enjoined them to remember 'that mercy to the vanquished is the brightest gem in a soldier's character . . .' and exhorted them 'not to suffer their resentment to lead them to any precipitate act of cruelty on their part, which may sully the reputation they have acquired in the world'. He was scathing in his view of men who themselves would not be facing the dangers of war but who were 'so base and cowardly as to seek to aggravate the calamities of it upon unfortunate people who are subject to their orders. It was indeed reserved for the present times, to produce to the world the proof of the possibility of the existence of such atrocity and infamy.'[72] York also ensured that copies of his order should be found by French patrols. In justice to the French soldiers, unless Allied prisoners insulted them, they 'refused to kill prisoners in cold blood. "Send the prisoners to the representatives of the people," they said, "and let them kill them and eat them, too, if they like; that is not our affair."'[73] Of course, this did not apply to émigrés.

The Prussians now became as recalcitrant as the Austrians. Despite Kaiserslautern, Friedrich Wilhelm was increasingly distracted by Poland and refused to aid the campaign beyond the Rhine. The Emperor's defection merely added to the uncertainty. There was a vocal peace movement in Vienna for whom Thugut was the warmonger, implacably opposed to peace. Thugut, however, recognized that it would be a mistake to offer overtures of peace in the midst of defeat, and managed to convince the Emperor that the struggle must continue.

Meanwhile, under Saint-Just's direction the French re-crossed the Sambre. This forced Coburg to send reinforcements to Kaunitz, which weakened the right centre of his own position. To compound an unhappy situation, Coburg also chose to placate the Dutch by giving the inept Hereditary Prince nominal authority over Kaunitz. Fortunately, Saint-Just, who was no more a soldier than Robespierre, soon demonstrated his incompetence.

Pichegru now returned to littoral Flanders, which the French needed to occupy in preparation for the invasion of England which lay at the heart of Carnot's strategy. At the beginning of June he blockaded Ypres. The Emperor, who was lingering at Brussels, ordered Coburg to send reinforcements to Clerfayt so that he could break the blockade, which he initially achieved. Then a counter-attack by Souham sent him back to Tielt.

The French were in the ascendant. They threatened the Allied right at Orchies and the vital Scheldt crossing at Mortagne, which protected communication between Coburg and Kaunitz. They now had 75,000 men on the Sambre under Jourdan's able command. Elsewhere, they were enjoying success in northern Italy and had forced the Spanish back across the Pyrenees. Their only setback was at sea, when Admiral Howe destroyed the Brest fleet on 'The Glorious 1st of June'. This disrupted Carnot's plan for an invasion of England, although it did not prevent a convoy carrying vital food supplies from safely reaching port. It is no wonder, therefore, that Calvert wrote to Dalrymple:

> I am no croaker, but believe me, dear Sir Hew, our affairs are become very critical, and will be more and more so every day: should the enemy carry their point to the Sambre, and avail themselves of their success with judgement, there will be little time for deliberation, and it will then be too late to be convinced, of what I have long been persuaded, that the safety of all Europe, but particularly of England and Holland, demands that the security of West Flanders should have been the first object of all the Allies, and the French should never be allowed to establish themselves on one foot of Flemish ground.[74]

Ypres surrendered on 20 June, the day after news arrived that Jourdan had finally crossed the Sambre and invested Charleroi. Coburg now made the relief of Charleroi his objective. He expected York to hold an extended position from Tournai to Condé, for which he did not have sufficient troops, even when 5,000 Austrians were placed to strengthen his position. At the same time Coburg was withdrawing supplies north to Antwerp and Brussels, which deepened British suspicions and fed the growing resentment of the Austrians. York had previously written to the King:

> Knowing of how much consequence it was to keep up a good harmony among the different troops I have done everything in my power to smooth and to keep everything quiet, but really the behaviour of the Austrians is such that it is my duty to represent it. They despise everything which is not their own, they are continually throwing every blame upon Your Majesty's Troops and accusing them of slackness when God knows they are infinitely braver than they are, and at the same time wantonly exposing them upon every occasion. Wherever I am they dare not do it, but I have received the strongest complaints on that account from the British, the Hanoverians and the Darmstadters [i.e. Hessians] who are now serving under General Clerfayt.[75]

Coburg marched east on 21 June and York, with a force now only about 7,000 strong, immediately drew in his troops around Tournai. His situation seemed desperate. Fortunately, Dundas was aware that French operations in littoral Flanders threatened Ostend and had gathered an ad hoc force of 10,000 men under Lord Moira. He did not inform York of this, though. The reinforcements arrived on 21 and 25 June, and included among their number a certain Arthur Wesley, Colonel of the 33rd. Moira himself arrived on 26 June, made contact with York, and immediately prepared to attack a French force that was threatening the poorly fortified town

On the same day Richard Hussey Vivian, captain in the 28th, wrote to his father: 'I have just time to tell you that Ypres and Bruges are both taken, and that the French are advancing with all possible speed to take this place [Ostend]; but I hope it will be the lot of Lord Moira's army to give them a good drubbing. Our army are all in the highest possible spirits, anxious to meet them, and, I may say, pretty confident of victory.'[76] This positive spirit was in marked contrast to the mood among York's forces.

Under pressure from Pichegru, Clerfayt was forced to march north, which obliged York to do the same. At Renaix he learnt that on 26 June Coburg had been checked by Jourdan at Fleurus and was now retreating to Brussels. This suggested that he had suffered a heavy defeat but the outcome of the battle was actually rather more problematic and raised questions about Coburg's intentions. After fifteen hours of fighting, with the outcome undecided, Coburg chose to withdraw. It is impossible to know whether this decision was occasioned by loss of nerve, poor military judgement or because he was already thinking in terms of a retreat beyond the Rhine. If the last, then the implications were serious for the British forces. Indeed, Fleurus proved the death knell of the coalition and Austria's possession of Belgium.

York was outnumbered three to one by the nearest French force, which was in position to cross the Scheldt and prevent a safe retreat towards Grammont. Nor would he be safe there if Coburg was making for Namur as the first stage of a retreat across the Rhine. York ordered Moira to join Clerfayt and then await the next French move. Instead of crossing the Scheldt, Pichegru moved towards the coast, having received orders to take Nieuport, Ostend and Walcheren in order to secure the whole of littoral Flanders. (Robespierre was still thinking in terms of an invasion of England, although how it was to be achieved without the Brest fleet seems not to have concerned him.) Moira was ready to join Clerfayt for a joint attack on the French left but Clerfayt had also received news of Fleurus and Coburg's subsequent retreat. He now abandoned any idea of co-operating with either York or Moira, which endangered both British forces. Moira immediately sent his baggage to Sluys and marched beyond Ghent before the French could intercept him, thus saving his own force and strengthening York's position.

According to Major Edward Paget, also of the 28th:

> Lord Moira has as completely saved the Duke of York and his army as – you'll excuse a simile. From what I *know* the Duke of York was in a most critical situation when we arrived at Ostend. It became so great an object of the enemy to impede our progress into Flanders that the whole force opposed to the Duke of York and Clerfayt were immediately sent to prevent our advancing: but, all glory to our commander-in-chief, he out-generaled them and joined the Duke of York this morning at Malines; and this, I may say, he performed, advancing in the front of an enemy, without firing a shot.[77]

At this point York and Clerfayt changed position so that their lines of retreat no longer crossed, as they had since the beginning of the year. The Austrians also abandoned Tournai and the Scheldt, although they continued to hold Condé, Valenciennes, Landrecies and Quesnoy. York had withdrawn his garrisons from everywhere except Nieuport, which was already under attack and fell on 16 July. The French promptly used their artillery to massacre the 500 émigrés who had been in the garrison there. Despite Robespierre's order, the British did not suffer the same fate.

On 5 July the Allies met at Waterloo and decided to hold a line from Antwerp to Namur, but were quickly overtaken by events. On 6 July Jourdan attacked Austrian positions from Braine-le-Conte to Gembloux, forcing the Austrian back to Waterloo. Then Coburg announced the decision that the British had long anticipated. The Austrians had decided to abandon Belgium. Three days later Brussels was in French hands.

York drew back, establishing his headquarters eight miles north of Malines. The Allied line now extended from Antwerp on the right to the Meuse on the left. To York's left were the Dutch and 2,000 Austrians who extended the line to Louvain. The remaining Austrians, something over 45,000 men, were posted from Louvain to the Meuse. From this position they could cross the Rhine whenever the Emperor finally chose to recall them. Calvert wrote to Lord Dalhousie: 'So many concurring circumstances exist, that I can hardly help adopting the idea universally credited throughout this country, and pretty generally in the army, that some foul play, and some very dark designs, exist in a certain quarter.'[78]

On 12 July Pichegru advanced to Malines and Jourdan threatened the Allied left. Three days later both generals achieved their objectives. Pichegru took Malines and Jourdan, Louvain, followed by Jodoigny on 16 July and Namur a day later. Coburg responded by announcing that he intended to withdraw even further east. In fact, the Austrians were already on the march. By 24 July they had crossed the Meuse and were beyond Maastricht. This forced York and the Dutch to abandon Antwerp and withdraw from Belgium.

The attitude of the Prussians had been crucial even before the Austrian defection. The British government believed their subsidy to Berlin was paying for 60,000 troops but the actual total was 40,000 men, deficient in supplies and transport and with no agreed purpose. The Dutch, with memories of Prussian aggression in 1787, wanted them to operate on the Rhine whereas the British saw them as the means to regain West Flanders. Austria intended that they should protect the German lands. In other words, all three members of the alliance saw Prussian support in terms of their own self-interest. While the allies wrangled, the French were enjoying success on the Rhine. Early in July the Prussians had been forced to retire from Mainz, which caused the nearest Austrian troops to cross to the east bank.

Under Robespierre, the French generals had been constrained by the whims of a man who neither understood military matters nor trusted military men. His fall and execution on 28 July, along with Saint-Just and other leading Jacobins, changed the situation. When the Directory gained power a month later it became clear that Carnot, the organizer of recent French achievements, enjoyed its full support. He was ready to make good his claim that he would defeat the coalition by the end of the year.

York had received reinforcements but they were mainly untrained recruits whom Craig dismissed out of hand as men who would struggle to know one end of a musket from the other. Calvert wrote to Dalhousie, 'Explain to me the reason of the recruits joining the army without arms or any appointments necessary for soldiers. I am often asked the question and can't resolve it.'[79] These useless additions had come a price. York had to surrender the flank companies of six of his battalions to reinforce Grey in the West Indies. He also lost Lord Moira over an issue of seniority. Moira had been enjoying an independent command against protocol. Abercromby, with local rank of lieutenant general, and Major General David Dundas, who had recently arrived, were senior to him.

The Dutch under the Hereditary Prince now wanted to adopt the Austrian cordon system to hold back the French. The Prince also wanted British troops to garrison the Dutch border fortresses. York refused both suggestions. He knew the fortresses in question were decayed, so he urged the Dutch to strengthen their defences, particularly Breda, Bergen-op-Zoom, Grave and Nijmegen, which were crucial to the security of the Dutch Republic.

The situation of the Anglo-German forces was becoming increasingly difficult. When Moreau besieged Sluys, the Hereditary Prince decided to abandon all the Dutch fortresses south of the Scheldt and concentrate on the relief of Sluys, York sent a detachment to protect communications between Breda and Bergen so that the garrisons at those two places could be transferred to the relief of Sluys. As had happened before, he then found his own situation complicated by a decision taken in England. Dundas heard the news that the French were threatening Sluys and Flushing in terms of an attack on the English east coast. He sent Lord Mulgrave with five battalions and naval support to defend them. Mulgrave arrived ahead of his troops and undertook a reconnaissance. He concluded that French operations were merely designed to facilitate the shipping of desperately-needed grain to France. Unfortunately, his presence was enough to convince the Dutch that they need no longer worry about Sluys because Mulgrave would obviously relieve it on their behalf. The French, however, brought up another 25,000 men, which meant that Sluys was as good as lost. Mulgrave's battalions finally arrived on 26 August, the same day that Sluys fell to the French.

On 9 August Coburg had issued a proclamation blaming the calamities of the campaign on the Belgians. As Calvert commented with sharp irony: 'The inexhaustible resources of France, its innumerable cohorts, the inactivity of a blinded people who would not listen to the paternal voice of their good Prince, and the secret practices of some of their ambitious representatives, are the causes which have forced the Imperial armies to retreat.'[80] The Archduke Charles was later to ask himself 'How was it possible that a well-equipped, balanced and disciplined army had been defeated by an enemy with raw troops, lacking cavalry and with inexperienced generals?' He answered his own question. 'Ignorance, indolence and egotism are to blame for our misfortunes.'[81] Neither Calvert nor the Archduke held the Belgians responsible. Coburg, though, was held in contempt by both the army and the public. He was described as a mere cipher capable only of retreat and who would be better replaced, even by a corporal.[82] Exhausted by failure, Coburg resigned his command.

His replacement, Clerfayt, was ordered to restore discipline and spirit to the army. He was also instructed to focus on securing Luxembourg, Mainz and Mannheim, which meant abandoning the Low Countries. This exposed the border fortresses to renewed French attack. By 15 August they were in possession of Quesnoy and Landrecies. Clerfayt proposed a general advance to relieve Valenciennes and Condé but it was too late. Valenciennes was already in French hands, and Condé was on the point of surrender. The last chance of concerted Allied action had been lost.

Pichegru marched from Antwerp towards Hoogstraten, threatening York's left flank and forcing him to withdraw to a position between the Peel, an extensive swamp, and 's-Hertogenbosch. Pichegru then advanced to Merle, thus threatening Breda. Leaving a detachment at Merle, he reached Oosterwyk on 12 September and then attacked York's outposts at Boxtel the following day. The place fell on 14 September with the loss of two Hessian battalions. The Hessians blamed York for failing to support them and York blamed the Hessians for panicking. Whatever the rights and wrongs of these accusations, York decided that Boxtel was too important to be lost without a fight. He sent Abercromby with ten battalions and ten squadrons to regain the surrendered ground.

Calvert wrote in his journal on 15 September:

> At midnight General Abercromby marched with the reserve of the army, for the purpose of proving the real force of the enemy, and of re-establishing the outposts if possible. The General approached to within half a league of both the posts of Boxtel and Michel Gister [Sint-Michielsgestel]; but finding the enemy advancing in great force, he retreated with his corps by Middelrode to camp. The accounts we received from deserters and prisoners, made the enemy's numbers amount to about 80,000 men; and stated that Pichegru was moving his columns towards our left, under cover of the attacks made on our outposts. Upon the assurance of this intelligence, his Royal Highness resolved on breaking up his camp, and gave the necessary orders for effecting a retreat upon Grave during the night. The army began to move in two columns, at four in the afternoon, and at nine the rearguard, under General Abercromby, with the reserve and outposts, left the camp.[83]

According to Jones:

> [York] therefore, on the 15th, ordered Lieutenant General Abercromby to march with the reserve to regain the position; but on his arrival there, he found the enemy in so great force, that he could not attack them, and he was obliged to retire; for General Pichegru had not laid siege to Breda, as was supposed, but made a forced march with his whole army, and intended on the next day, to attack the left of the British with 80,000 men. The Duke did not think it prudent to hazard an action with so great a disparity of numbers, for at that time he could not muster 20,000 fighting men.[84]

Neither Calvert nor Jones was with Abercromby as he marched towards Boxtel with a force comprising Major General Samuel Hulse's Brigade of Guards, the line brigade (33rd, 42nd and 44th) of Colonel Arthur Wesley, who was yet to adopt the surname Wellesley, and Colonel Richard Vyse's cavalry brigade (squadrons from 1st Dragoon Guards, and 8th, 14th, 16th Light Dragoons), just under 5,000 men in total. Having left the main Allied encampment at

Berlicom, he marched to Heeswyck to cross the Aa, and then marched on to Schyndel. The advance troops left this village on the road to Boxtel at about 6.15 a.m. They could see a French picket line between themselves and their objective. This suggested the French were in a different position from that anticipated. Abercromby sent to York for further orders and was told to act prudently, whereupon he took the decision to attack. He sent the light dragoons forward, followed by the Guards brigade and the 33rd and 44th, with the 42nd held in reserve. A body of French hussars (the 8th) retreated to the woods where the light infantry and artillery were already posted. As the British light dragoons advanced, the French guns opened fire. Abercromby sensed that he was opposed by a stronger force than he had expected and decided to call off the attack. The 8th Light Dragoons covered the withdrawal as the infantry made for more sheltered ground. When the cavalry ran out of ammunition, however, the pursuing French cavalry were halted by the 33rd, who fired in line at their colonel's order. (Wesley subsequently received York's thanks, which Abercromby personally conveyed to him.) The intervention of the 33rd allowed the 3rd Guards to retreat. About 9 a.m. the troops marched back through Schyndel, covered by the 16th Light Dragoons, while the crossing of the Aa was defended by the 42nd and their battalion guns. The whole force was back at Berlicom by 2 p.m.[85]

The attempt on Boxtel could have been a disaster because Pichegru was on the march east and in a position to overwhelm both Abercromby's detachment and the main army. Although Abercromby perceived the danger and withdrew in good order, there were ninety men lost, two-thirds of them as prisoners. Four officers were subsequently court-martialled for cowardice.[86]

York's subsequent dispatch, written on 17 September, first described how the Hessians were overwhelmed, and then continued:

> As the line of my outposts upon the Dommel could not be maintained while the enemy were in possession of Boxtel, I therefore ordered Lieut.-General Abercrombie to march with the Reserve during the night, with directions to reconnoitre the post at daylight, and to act as he should judge best, from what he could discover from the force of the enemy. Lieut.-General Abercrombie having advanced as directed, found the enemy in such strength as left little room to doubt of the proximity of their army, and he accordingly retired, but in such good order as prevented the enemy from making any impression, although they followed him for some distance.

About this time I received private information, upon which I could rely, and which was confirmed by the observation of my patrols and the reports of deserters, that the enemy had been reinforced by the troops which had hitherto been acting in West Flanders, as well as by a column of the army which had hitherto been employed before Valenciennes and Condé. The same information assured me also that the column which had been marching towards Maastricht had suddenly returned towards us.[87]

Burne chose not to accept this version of events. Instead, he implied that York had lied to Dundas because Abercromby had been specifically ordered to regain Boxtel. Burne also claimed that Abercromby had 'the pick of the English troops'. Abercromby had the Reserve, which may well have been the best troops, but the Reserve was his command. In Burne's version, 'The Guards were ordered to attack, but Abercromby, impressed by the apparent strength of the position, held up the attack whilst he referred back to the Commander-in-Chief for instructions. The Duke replied that he was to persist in the attack, but not to proceed farther than he thought prudent. Abercromby, by some curious reasoning, interpreted this to mean that he need not attack at all, promptly called off the Guards, after about thirty casualties had been suffered, and returned to camp, unmolested by the enemy.' Nor did Burne accept that Pichegru posed a threat. He offered no explanation as to why York should have lied, and dismissed the information on French numbers, obtained most reliably from York's own patrols, as French troops that were lost! For Burne, though, Abercromby was a defeatist and York's evil genius.[88]

York had been uncertain of French intentions until he learnt that Pichegru, reportedly 80,000 strong (actually 56,000), planned to turn his left. He decided to cross the Maas (Meuse), even though he would then be holding a 75-mile front with too few troops. He called in all the men in British pay and instructed the Dutch to repair and hold Crevecoeur and Bommel. He was depending upon joint action with the Austrians for his safety, a hope that was disappointed when an Austrian detachment on the Ourthe was overwhelmed. Clerfayt responded by withdrawing beyond the Roer. He promised to remain in communication with York, but with the proviso that he also reserved the right to cross the Rhine should the situation demand it. Pichegru now sent two divisions to line the Maas, and on 22 September they invested 's-Hertogenbosch. Two days later Crevecoeur came under French bombardment. Although held by a strong Dutch garrison, the place surrendered on 28 September. This disaster seriously weakened York's position. In addition, there was clear evidence of anti-British feeling among the Dutch, provoked by the increasing ill-discipline of the British troops. There were also rumours of a pro-French rising.

At this point Abercromby and Wallmoden urged York to send Craig to Clerfayt in a last attempt to galvanize him into offensive action, but even Craig did not possess the persuasive powers to influence the Austrian commander. When he came under further attack from Jourdan on 2 October, he seized the moment to retreat back to the Rhine, which forced the British and Dutch to move north of the Waal. The alliance was dead in all but name and York's situation was untenable. On 3 October he accepted the inevitable and prepared to occupy a new position that extended from the Bommelerwaard to the confluence of the Waal and the Leck. The reserve under Abercromby crossed the Waal at Nijmegen on 7 October. The following day part of the army occupied an entrenched position before the town, which lies to the south of the river, while Abercromby took command of the troops in the Bommelerwaard. From there on 11 September he was sent to re-occupy Sint-Andreis, about twenty miles from Nijmegen, which had been abandoned by mistake. The following day Calvert wrote to Dalhousie: 'You will have heard that, by some mistake, Fort St André was abandoned. The Duke directed Abercromby, who commands in that quarter (having with him the infantry of the Reserve, together with the five new regiments lately arrived), to re-occupy it, which he did yesterday morning under the cover of a very heavy cannonade, without any loss.' He later added: 'I am very sorry to tell you that Abercromby was yesterday wounded in the arm on the attack made on Fort St André. I know no particulars, but the fort was carried when we last heard from them.' In the final sentence of the letter, however, he was able to report that the wound was slight.[89]

The British ministers now realized, somewhat belatedly, that the subsidies to the Austrians and Prussians represented money wasted. Indeed, subsidies were problematic because they were 'irritating to the donor and humiliating to the receiver. [They] promoted exacting capriciousness on one side and slack performance on the other. Not until both parties could unite frankly and enthusiastically under the stimulus of a great cause could great deeds be accomplished. The story of the year 1794 is the story of the wreck of an imposing Coalition, partly through divergences of aim, but also through a demoralizing reliance on the cash-nexus.'[90] The government did not yet consider abandoning the Low Countries, but York was instructed to inform Clerfayt that there would be no further money unless he showed some initiative. On 10 October 's-Hertogenbosch finally surrendered under suspicious circumstances, which led to another massacre of émigrés. On the same day the government threatened that all British troops would be withdrawn from the Low Countries unless the Dutch showed some resolution. Eight days later, however, without any sign of increased Dutch activity, Dundas authorized a payment of £100,000 to the Hereditary Prince, even though it was clear by now that his father saw the British troops as the means to crush his own rebellious subjects rather than to defeat the French.

Elsewhere, the French continued their victorious progress. Cologne had fallen on 6 October, which left Moreau free to threaten York's left. Twelve days later he sent some of his troops across the Maas on a bridge of boats, and on 19 October took two Allied positions and a large number of prisoners. At the same time, another column advanced on Cleve, which also threatened York's left. The following day the pontoon bridge across the Meuse was replaced by a more permanent structure and the rest of Moreau's force crossed the river and moved on the British outposts in the Bommelerwaard. On 27 October the troops covering Nijmegen were driven into the town and from his headquarters at Arnhem York gave orders for all but fourteen of his battalions to move north of the Waal. This enabled the French to threaten both Nijmegen and Grave. If they fell, North Brabant was lost. The following day, no doubt to York's considerable surprise, Clerfayt paid a visit to British headquarters. Although his main force had crossed the Rhine, he brought the promise of 7,000 Austrian troops to help in the defence of Nijmegen, although they would not arrive until 3 November.

In Vienna, the peace party was making its opinion heard, and enjoyed support from other parts of the Holy Roman Empire. On 24 October the Elector of Mainz proposed the opening of peace negotiations. Thugut urged the Emperor to resist the idea until 'there exists in France an authority or a power with which one can enter into negotiations', rather than 'criminals, who replaced each other with such speed that a peace concluded on one day would mean nothing by the next'.[91] Thugut, however, was becoming increasingly isolated.

The French began digging their trenches at Nijmegen on 1 November. On the same day York learnt that the promised Austrians would not arrive for another week. Wallmoden, in command at Nijmegen, withdrew to the north of the Waal as a precaution after a French bombardment seriously damaged the vital bridge of boats across the river. On 4 November he made a sortie with his Hanoverians, six British battalions and a British squadron. The French were driven out of their trenches and cut down by the pursuing cavalry, although the Anglo-Germans also took heavy losses. The sortie provided only a brief respite. By 7 November the French were back in position, with an extra battery that covered the pontoon bridge. That night the garrison abandoned Nijmegen across the bridge under cover of darkness. The Dutch were the last to leave, by which time the French were awake to what was happening and took 1,100 prisoners. Interestingly, the word spread throughout the Republic that the defenders had departed only after an orgy of pillage and violence, which seems somewhat inconsistent with a night flight from a besieged town, particularly as the fortifications were close to the river. By this time, though, the Dutch were prepared to believe the worst of their allies.

York was thinking about winter quarters in response to the deteriorating weather conditions, which made the inadequacies of government provision for an extended campaign all too obvious. Even such basic necessities as greatcoats and flannel waistcoats had been overlooked. Craig was demanding 20,000 pairs of good shoes; and flannel shirts had to be bought by public subscription. The medical services had deteriorated from inadequate to scandalous. Epidemic numbers of soldiers were falling victim to typhus fever, a situation exacerbated by the lice-ridden rags of their uniforms. By the end of the month 31 per cent of the British troops were returned 'sick absent' and the hospitals could not accommodate them. (This rose to 38 per cent the following month as the weather became ever colder.) Not only were the Dutch refusing to establish more general hospitals; it was also clear that many of them favoured and were aiding the French against both the British and their own troops.

Winter Withdrawal

On 17 November, York was summoned back to England; as the war had spiralled out of British control. Even the Stadtholder claimed that victory was impossible while York remained in command. The government were looking for a scapegoat but they might have done better to think about extricating themselves from the mess of their own making. The present French rulers were determined to protract the war as a means of taking control of the Dutch Republic, which they saw as a crucial player in the defeat of Britain. The Prussians wanted money but there could be no dependence on their promises of aid. (By the end of December they were in negotiation with the French.) The war-weary Austrians had abandoned Belgium. The Russians had merely offered empty promises. Auckland was not alone in his despair when he declared: 'I feel quite glad to be rid of 1794. It has been the most calamitous year of the century; its successor cannot easily be worse . . .'[92]

York was the chosen scapegoat. (He would be compensated with the position of Commander-in-Chief in place of the reputedly senile General Lord Amherst, one of the few wise military decisions made at this time.) Yet to an officer serving under York, the Duke's removal from command meant that 'the British army lost a father and a friend, who had endeared himself to them by his humanity, justice, and benevolence'.[93] As Commander-in-Chief he would demonstrate all these qualities.

Depriving York of command was difficult for Pitt to manage. When he wrote to the King to justify the decision, he praised York's 'zealous and meritorious exertions' before expressing his reservations: '. . . the general impression is formed on other grounds, and even those who know in how many respects he is entitled to praise, are not without apprehension that the want of experience and habits of detail may have render'd it impossible for his Royal [Highness] to discharge all the complicated duties of his situation, and effectively to prevent or to remedy the abuses and evils which have crept into the service . . .' Having presented the need to replace York as tactfully as he could, he then addressed the issue of who should assume command. 'The command of the Hanoverians would probably in that case devolve on Genl. Walmoden, and perhaps it might not be difficult to manage that the British should be under the command of Genl. Abercromby, who seems to stand higher than any other Officer in general opinion.'[94]

Rather than being difficult for Abercromby to assume command, it proved impossible. Lieutenant General William Harcourt was senior to Abercromby and took command of the British troops, even though hitherto his command had been confined to cavalry operations. General Wallmoden, who actually outranked Harcourt, was placed in command of the Hanoverians and Hessians. This unhappy situation seems to have been York's decision, stemming from his reluctance to place British troops under a Hanoverian general.

The French, as exhausted as their opponents by the exigencies of the campaign, had gone into temporary cantonments in position from 's-Hertogenbosch and Grave in the west to the left bank of the Rhine in the east. Against them, the allies held a line beyond the Waal from Tiel westwards to the Pannarden Canal. A force of 30,000 Austrians was notionally covering the Allied left. Harcourt realized that further retreat was inevitable and was anxious to build a second bridge across the Rhine but was frustrated by the Dutch, who refused to supply the means. This was his first setback in a command that would become increasingly onerous. Once again, the excuse was British pillaging, but according to Mrs Harcourt, 'I fear our infantry do pillage a little, and are not as regular as they should be, owing to their having been recruited in so many strange places, and it being necessary to get men at any rate; the very dregs of London were taken, but none of them have behaved so ill as the Dutch.'[95]

The government now sent Dr Jerome Fitzgerald to supervise the evacuation of the sick and wounded, but also to make sure the men had adequate shelter. He was answerable only to Dundas, which inevitably led to conflict with local commanders. Despite this, he persisted in his task. He transferred soldiers from freezing barns and similarly inappropriate accommodation into the more comfortable billets that officers tended to claim for themselves. He preceded the hospital wagons to make sure that quarters were ready for the sick. And he drew on Treasury funds to purchase blankets and other supplies. That he needed to do all these things demonstrates the failure of the medical services.

Paris under the Directory now sensed that complete victory lay within reach and put the local commanders under pressure to continue the campaign. On 11 December Moreau launched a boat attack across the Waal. Although this was repulsed, it was an ominous warning of French intentions. By 18 December the Dutch winter was showing its fangs. (Even Mrs Harcourt's ink froze.) Under these conditions, Harcourt prepared for a fighting retreat. Inevitably, this was the moment Dundas chose to demand that three British battalions should march to Helvoetsluys, with four to follow, because they were needed elsewhere. Somewhat unrealistically, he expected the Austrians to make up the shortfall. To make matters worse for Harcourt, who was struggling with the pressure that he found himself under, the ice on the Waal was thick enough to allow the French free passage. Somewhat helplessly, he sought guidance from Dundas on his future action.

Before any reply could be received, the French pre-empted whatever advice Dundas might have offered by crossing the Waal. The Dutch forces were taken by surprise and fled. The Hessians near Tiel stood firm, however, because reconnaissance had convinced their commander that the French force numbered no more than 2,000 men. Wallmoden then sent ten battalions and six squadrons of British and emigrant troops under the command of David Dundas to Geldermalsen to deal with them. They were formed in three columns and at 1 a.m. on 30 December two of the columns marched in a southerly direction towards Tuil while the third, under Lord Cathcart, who was using a compass to guide him, advanced from the east. He finally brought his column to a halt because of the impossible state of the roads but General Dundas was able to drive the French back over the Waal.

On 4 January 1795 the French took advantage of the frozen conditions to re-cross the Waal. They attacked the following day, whereupon the Dutch gunners abandoned their position. As the French moved on to Geldermalsen, however, they came into contact with Dundas and the 33rd, 42nd and 78th. Despite this opportunity to halt the French advance, Wallmoden recognized that his present position was untenable. He recalled Dundas' force to the north bank of the Leck, which was accomplished with an effective rearguard action. A new front line was established from Arnhem to Honswyck. Almost immediately this retrograde movement seemed unnecessary because a thaw set in, but just as the troops began a forward movement the freezing conditions returned. On 10 January Pichegru attacked at three points between Tiel and the Pannarden Canal. He was beaten back on the right but on the left he drove off some Austrians troops, who had arrived too late to save Nijmegen.

Wallmoden was now thinking in terms of a retreat east, although his plans were initially frustrated by protests from the British envoy at The Hague, and a further thaw. Both Lord St Helens, who operated in political terms, and the vagaries of the weather seemed designed to thwart the Hanoverian general's sensible intentions. On 14 January there was another general attack by the French which was beaten off with heavy losses. It was enough to decide Wallmoden, though, and the next day he ordered a retreat in the worst of conditions:

> . . . the wind was excessive high, and drifted the snow and sand together so strong, that we could hardly wrestle against it; to which was added, a severity of cold almost insufferable. The frost was so intense, that the water which came from our eyes, freezing as it fell, hung in icicles to our eyelashes, and our breath freezing as soon as emitted, lodged in heaps of ice about our faces, and on the blankets or coats that were wrapped around our heads. Inevitably, the weakest failed to maintain the pace of the strongest, and if they lost sight of the column of march, though but a few minutes, it being dark, and no tract [track] to follow, there was no chance of finding it again. Thus many perished.[96]

James McGrigor, newly appointed surgeon of the 88th, had already been horrified by what he had witnessed in hospitals where 'disease, particularly typhus fever, became general. Our hospitals were filled to overflowing and the mortality among medical officers was particularly great.' Furthermore, 'the want of system at this time, and the inexperience of the medical officers were striking.' On the retreat, things were even worse. 'Our troops, raw and composed in great measure of new levies gave way under the harassing marches, bad quarters, and the toil to which they were exposed.' By early February, 'The youngest men, worn down by harassing fatigue succumbed daily, and thinned our ranks. In the extreme cold, the soldiers lay down in the snow by the road-side, overpowered with drowsiness and all the entreaties of the officers could not make them move on.'[97]

Hussey Vivian gave precise numbers for his regiment. 'It is impossible for me to express the wretched state our unfortunate army is reduced to. I will satisfy myself by telling you what alone has been our loss since we left Thiel; and other regiments much more. We marched from Thiel 403 privates besides non-commissioned officers; and our utmost strength on this morning's parade was 157.' In terms of the past few months, he claimed that 'the British army, from being 34,000 men before Breda, are now reduced to less than 7,000.'[98]

Not for the last time, there was a complete breakdown in discipline under the pressure of retreat and the shortcomings of many officers. Men struggled desperately for scarce supplies, which inevitably led to plundering, and a veritable battle between the Guards and the Hessians, hitherto the best disciplined of the troops in British pay. This was, however, the culmination of months of ill-feeling between them. On this occasion the Hessians had the upper hand, having reached Bickborge before the Guards. 'In several houses they positively refused us entrance, and in every one refused us admittance to the fire; at the same time they posted sentries by the cellar doors to prevent the inhabitants selling us liquors; even their commanding officer pushed with his own hands a number of our men neck and heels out of quarters.'[99] On 17 January the temperature plunged far below freezing. The following morning there was a scene of desolation that those who witnessed it were never to forget: men, women, children, horses, all frozen to death.

Most of the army had reached the Yssel by 19 January and went into cantonments from Zutphen to the sea. This could provide only temporary respite for troops weakened by the battle to survive the Dutch winter, lacking supplies, and surrounded by a hostile population ripe for rebellion. Harcourt decided that retreat to the Weser and embarkation for England was the only way to save the army. It became necessary, despite Harcourt's resolve to the contrary, to abandon 600 seriously sick men. It is notable that the conduct of the Dutch to the British 'was cruel and vindictive, to a degree scarcely to be credited; in many instances they were so barbarous as to let them die at their doors, sooner than afford them shelter; they were greater enemies than the French, as the latter always took care of such sick or wounded as came within their power.'[100]

So embittered were the British recollections of this Dutch indifference that Edward Walsh, attached to the medical services and writing from the perspective of a later campaign, remembered how 'The Dutch fight sturdily when actuated by emotions of interest or dislike. But in the present instance (1793), the nominal assistance to the forces, to their allies, was worse than negative. On the first disaster at Dunkirk, the Dutch troops ran off, in a body, and never halted until they got within their own frontier; and, on the subsequent reverses of the allied armies, the conduct of the Dutch was not merely disaffected to the common cause – it was openly hostile.'[101]

The final stages of the retreat commenced on 27 January. Abercromby remained in command of the rearguard:

> . . . the sick and wounded of the army, as also the Guards, were entrusted to his command; in a melancholy march through an inhospitable country, and in a season of great severity, the active and humane mind of General Abercrombie had ample scope for exertion; he conducted the harassed army from Deventer to Oldensaal, through roads almost impassable, inclement weather, and surrounded by an infuriated enemy . . . It was in the course of this arduous retreat that the unbounded philanthropy of the veteran General was so strongly evinced . . .[102]

The British troops marched towards Osnabrück, and the German contingent to Münster. Cathcart, still using his compass, took a detachment along a different route, apparently to ascertain whether there was any loyalty to the House of Orange in West Friesland and Groningen. If this was the purpose, the findings were negative. Once the British reached the Ems they went into cantonments, while the Hanoverians continued their march to Münster

The French had been harassing Cathcart on his march to the east. On 27 February he had to beat off a more determined attack by General Macdonald. This renewed activity suggested an accord between France and Prussia which was confirmed when the Prussians declared North Germany neutral. Meanwhile, the French took possession of West Friesland and

Groningen. As for the Dutch, the Patriots were now fully in the ascendant. The Stadtholder had left for exile in Britain on 18 January. There were still some troops loyal to the cause of the House of Orange but they had little hope of mounting an effective resistance to the French advance. Yet the Patriots were soon to discover that French intentions were rather different from their promises. There would be demands for an indemnity of at least a hundred million florins, a 3 per cent loan for the same amount and confiscation of some territory in Dutch Flanders and that part of Zeeland which bordered the Scheldt. Furthermore, if it had been British pillaging, rumoured or real, which turned the Dutch against their defenders, they were soon to discover that their liberators were cut from the same cloth.[103]

Attacked again on 1 March, Cathcart retreated to the Ems. Two days later the whole British force crossed the river and headquarters were established at Osnabrück. Finally and belatedly, on 8 March the British ministers took the decision to withdraw the army. Harcourt was informed that transport would be provided for 23,000 men. This meant abandoning the Germans who had fought so stoutly throughout the whole campaign, but this was of no concern to the government. No doubt they saw them only as a sum of money on a balance sheet.

On 22 March the British marched to Bremen, surrendering their position on the Ems to the Prussians. The first troops were embarked on 14 April, bringing to an end a European misadventure which hindsight suggests had been doomed from the beginning. One can criticise the temporising of the Austrians, the failure of the House of Orange to rally the Dutch, and the weak commitment of the Prussians, but ultimately until the politicians learnt to trust their own generals the mistakes of the British government would merely be repeated. It is difficult to argue with the view that 'The allies had undertaken to arrest the wild rush of Revolutionary France on Europe, and to restore the old order in France. They failed when success was apparently in their grasp; and they failed, not because their forces were inadequate but because their purposes were divided and their motives selfish. Their greed, in a word, defeated their own policy.'[104] It would take the states opposed to France a long time to learn the necessary lessons.

The colonel of the 33rd famously declared of the Dutch campaign: 'Why – I learnt what one ought not to do, and that is always something.'[105] It could be argued that Abercromby learnt the same lesson, a point which became apparent as the war progressed and he was able to exercise the authority of command. The last word on this whole sorry affair, however, must be given to his son:

Under the circumstances, the duty of protecting the Army during its retreat through Holland devolved on Sir Ralph, and he was so commonly regarded as the chief commander, that some of his friends in England, not foreseeing that in the midst of these disasters, he was earning an European reputation, remonstrated with the government for allowing him to be considered as exercising a responsibility which in fact belonged to another . . .

The judgement with which the retreat was effected, attracted general attention, and commanded respect for the constancy and ability which were displayed by those who conducted it. Infinitely the largest share of the public approbation was by common consent assigned to Sir Ralph, and his character as a commander was established.[106]

This judgement might be interpreted as a son's desire to burnish his father's reputation, but even at the time there was recognition of, and reward for, his achievements. On 28 June, Lord Portland, the Home Secretary, informed the King that 'the proper notice has been given to the Secretary of the Order of the Bath, that it is your Majesty's intention to hold a chapter of that order on Wednesday next for the purpose of conferring the ensigns of it on Sir Joseph Banks and Major General Abercrombie.'[107]

Chapter 2

War in the West Indies

An Economic War

Failure in Flanders required the triumvirate to rethink their war policy. Voices like that of the Duke of Richmond, Master-General of the Ordnance, were advocating naval attacks on the French coast and colonies in preference to land campaigns. The army had failed; only the navy could damage France. Yet there was another approach in which both army and navy could play their part. Since the Seven Years War the European colonial powers had extended their rivalries and conflicts to their colonial territories, particularly India, North America and the West Indies. After the Revolution, France also exported radical and revolutionary doctrines, with inevitably spread like a contagion to neighbouring territories. Such was the situation in the West Indies in the final decade of the eighteenth century. The most powerful competing colonial powers in the Caribbean were the British and the French. The principal possessions of the former were the three Leeward islands, Jamaica, Antigua and St Kitts, the three Windward Islands, Barbados, St Vincent and Grenada, and Dominica; and of the latter, Guadeloupe, St Domingue, St Lucia, Martinique and Tobago. The Spanish and the Dutch also held territory. Both had declined from the height of their power in the seventeenth century; both were now enemies; their territory was fair game. There were also some Danish possessions, but Denmark was neutral.

All the colonial powers were economically dependent on their West Indian trade, particularly the mutual trade of slaves and sugar. The most prosperous in this respect was France. Pitt, ever the pragmatist, recognized the strategic advantage of weakening the French economy by taking territory in the Caribbean and thus destroying her overseas trade. This strategy had the added advantage of utilizing Britain's naval strength rather than being wholly dependent upon an inadequate army. It was now clear that Britain did not have the resources to challenge the French on the Continent, so an alternative argument was fashioned. Success in the West Indies would weaken the French economically; beggaring France would bring her to her knees. The policy was contentious at the time, however, and has been criticized by later historians. Yet Britain was 'a maritime power whose strength was as an economic colossus rather than a military giant, and the limitations and tenuous advantages that this imposed in a struggle against a neighbour which had three times its population and which had been revitalized into a nation in arms by the dynamism released by the French Revolution'.[1] On such terms, exporting the war to the Caribbean made sense to Pitt and Dundas.

Even before the new strategy was implemented, news of the *Declaration of the Rights of Man* by the National Assembly in 1789 had lit a tinderbox in the French Caribbean. The *Rights of Man* implied an end to political inferiority and slavery. This set up a conflict between the white planters and the other peoples of the area. In 1791 there was a mulatto rising in St Domingue (modern Haiti). Although the revolt was eventually suppressed, the mulattos achieved their objective and received full French citizenship. A decree of April 1792 proclaimed equality for whites, mulattos and free blacks. (Although slaves had to wait nearly two more years for formal enfranchisement, the three civil commissioners on St Domingue freed slaves on their own authority in 1793.) Seriously unsettled by this development, the planters declared their opposition to the Revolution, thus provoking a situation where blacks and mulattos rose against whites and the regular army, a conflict distinguished by the horrendous barbarity on both sides. The loss of St Domingue would have been disastrous for the French because it was their largest source of income from the Caribbean. A financial crisis had been one of the triggers for the revolution. Now the Revolutionaries' need for ready money was now as desperate as the old regime's. Issuing *assignats*, paper money based on the value of confiscated church lands, would not hold the problem at bay forever.

Jacobin agents were sent to enforce the 1792 decree throughout the French Caribbean. They openly sided with blacks against whites, particularly after the enfranchisement declaration of 1794; and they assumed power over the established white-dominated institutions of government. British Jamaica was only twenty-four hours sailing time from St Domingue, while the British Windward Islands were certain to be infected by the troubles of their French-owned neighbours. British garrisons were reinforced, which was both a drain on scarce resources and a death sentence for many of the soldiers who served there. At the same time, French planters were seeking British help against the power of the commissioners and their black supporters. In January 1793 a delegation came to London to offer Britain sovereignty of

St Domingue in return for protection. This offer appealed to Dundas, who had a conservative attachment to the idea that the war could be won in the colonies. Even though Britain was not yet officially at war with France, war was known to be imminent, and it was obviously in Britain's interests 'to extend the protection of His Majesty's arms to the French West Indies, and to secure to them the advantage of being subject to the Crown of Britain'.[2] It is unlikely that Dundas considered the practical implications of giving such protection to a small minority against the wishes of the oppressed majority. Nor did he recognize as over-ambitious his intention, fostered by similar requests from the planters of Martinique, Guadeloupe and Tobago, that Britain should take possession of all French territories. He failed to look beyond the popularity that such a policy would enjoy at home.

The French declaration of war on Britain and the Netherlands was a cue for British action against French Caribbean territories. Vice-Admiral Sir John Lahore and the American Loyalist Major-General Cornelius Cuyler were instructed to take Tobago. There were secret orders for action against Martinique, Guadeloupe, St Lucia and Marie-Galante. Success came easily at first. Tobago was in British hands by April, and St Pierre and Migueton followed in May. The next month an expedition was launched against Martinique, but was aborted when the promised Royalist rising failed to materialize. At the same time, news that the French Jacobin agents were stirring up trouble throughout the West Indies was causing Pitt to reconsider this strategy of seizing French territory. He recognized that it might be more advisable to deal with the contagion in existing British territory.

St Domingue, however, where the bloody struggle was ongoing, remained a tempting target. By September 1793 the French half of the island was in a state of total anarchy, but the British forces that had been sent there in response to the planters' requests earlier in the year were too thinly stretched to have any effect on the situation. They were supported by an impotent clique of self-interested whites who proved ineffectual when put to the test. The strength of their enemies lay in the character of their commanders. André Rigaud, the son of a white planter and black slave and commander of the mulattos, was not only ruthless but also had the support of the Jacobin commissioner, Étienne Polverel. Toussaint l'Ouverture, the leader of the blacks, was to prove a man of exceptional ability. These were the visible opponents; even more deadly were the diseases which ravaged the British troops.

On 26 November General Sir Charles Grey finally set sail with the battalions that had briefly served in Flanders. They totalled 7,000 men, less than half the planned number. Vice Admiral Sir John Jervis commanded the naval contingent. There was some initial success: after the surrender of Martinique on 22 March, St Lucia, Marie Galante and the Saintes all capitulated. The biggest prize, Guadeloupe, surrendered on 21 April. The success proved hollow, however. There were simply not enough men to hold all these islands, a weakness demonstrated when the French sent relieving forces. Guadeloupe fell after a bloody struggle, which included the massacre of sick British soldiers and French Royalists. Revolutionary fervour now spread to St Lucia and Grenada, and there were stirrings of unrest in British-held St Vincent and Antigua.

At the same time as the overall situation was becoming increasingly unstable, Grey's army was falling victim to the diseases endemic in the Caribbean during the rainy mosquito season which lasted from May to October. The French forces, which comprised more blacks and mulattos than white regulars, enjoyed considerable immunity, while the British soldiers died by the hundred. The Physician General, Sir Lucas Pepys, had adopted a policy of promoting only Oxbridge graduates who were licentiates, members or fellows of the Royal College of Physicians. Since most military physicians did not fit this requirement, the men sent to the West Indies tended to be young, with no experience of tropical diseases, a factor that undoubtedly increased the mortality rate. By a cruel coincidence, yellow fever, the most lethal of the endemic diseases, which had previously appeared intermittently, became an annual and widespread visitor after 1793.

Grey needed reinforcements to fight against the spreading revolutionary fervour but the inadequate numbers who did finally arrive were of poor quality and made little difference. With the army in Flanders also requiring reinforcements and the government still toying with the idea of an invasion of French territory, there were no more men available. It has been suggested that Grey lost 5,000 men, nearly all of them to disease. To add a sour footnote, Grey and Jervis returned home to accusations of nepotism and dishonesty. Abercromby would subsequently receive a specific order not to imitate their behaviour. His response is not recorded although, as a man famed for his integrity, he was probably less than impressed by such an instruction.

The simplest solution to the appalling death rate was the enlistment of black troops who enjoyed more immunity to the prevalent diseases but this was fiercely opposed by the planters. To make the situation worse, when the Dutch declared war in 1795 the government reacted by planning attacks on Dutch possessions. As the year progressed, St Lucia was lost and British possession of Grenada and St Vincent was limited to the two key points of

St George and Kingston. On St Domingue British troops were struggling to hold their own against a fierce French offensive. Everywhere revolutionary activity was fostered by the subversive activities of agents sent from France, particularly Victor Hugues from his base on Guadeloupe. Only now did the government ignore the protests of merchants and planters and give the local commander in Martinique permission to raise black regiments. As a result, the 1st West India Regiment was embodied in Martinique and the 2nd in St Vincent, on the clear understanding that the men would return to their masters at the end of their period of service.

Yet as one problem was dealt with, another quickly arose. In Jamaica, where the planters' opposition to black soldiers still persisted, the authorities had to confront a rising by the Maroons. These descendants of slaves who had escaped and established independent communities in the mountainous interior during Spanish possession of the island now posed a threat to British rule. They were dealt with fairly quickly, but only by using reinforcements intended for St Domingue, where trouble had spread from the French western half of the island to Spanish Santo Domingo. Toussaint l'Ouverture, who had been lying low for some time, now re-emerged as a unifying leader with whom the Spanish were prepared to negotiate. As for the wider picture, with both Spain and the Dutch Republic at peace with France, the Bahamas and Barbados, so far undisturbed, were potentially under threat. This was a danger that could not be ignored. As Pitt wrote to his brother, the Earl of Chatham, at this point still First Lord of the Admiralty, additional enemies meant the question had to be asked 'whether any British force can, without too great a risk, be hazarded on the Continent of France. I incline to think that our plan must now be changed, and that the only great push must be in the West Indies where I trust enough may yet be gained to counterbalance the French successes in Europe.'[3] Pitt thus identified the conflict at the heart of his government. Grenville believed in Continental intervention: Dundas favoured colonial war.

Yet so far in the West Indies failure outweighed success. Nor was it difficult to establish the reasons. Insufficient troops had been too thinly spread to contain the conflagration of revolutionary enthusiasm and the subsequent uprisings. If the troops were concentrated in one area, though, territory and the goodwill of the inhabitants elsewhere would be lost. It was also impossible to depend upon local support. This had been tried and found wanting in St Domingue. Most serious of all was the attritional loss of men to disease. Thus it was not enough for the government to send one large detachment of reinforcements. They had two choices. They could send a constant supply of new troops, although the only practical way to raise them would be through conscription, a step that no British government was prepared to take; or they could enlist more black soldiers, with or without the consent of their owners. As Grey's replacement, General John Vaughan, wrote, 'I am of opinion that a corps of one thousand men, composed of Blacks and Mulattoes and commanded by British officers, would render more essential service in the Country than treble the number of Europeans who are unaccustomed to the climate.' Victory would only be possible by 'opposing Blacks to Blacks'.[4] Consequently, Pitt's 'great push' must either send more men than ever before, with the inevitable loss, or override the objections of the slave-owners.

A Second Expedition

Dundas, who was responsible for the Colonies, was under severe pressure from the merchants who depended upon the West Indian trade. As early as February 1795 he acknowledged that if Britain were to retain her Caribbean possessions he would have to send a sizeable body of reinforcements, variously described as a 'commanding' or a 'powerful' force. He had been warned that 20,000 men would be needed to restore the situation and was already thinking in terms of setting up an Irish brigade, as well as removing regiments from the Irish establishment so that they could be used in the West Indies. Since it was generally recognized that regiments which had been in garrison in Gibraltar fared better in the Caribbean, he also proposed some shuffling of resources to make these acclimatized troops available. In April four light cavalry regiments were instructed to be ready to sail to the West Indies by August, and as the Flanders regiments returned from north Germany they were ordered to recruit for the same purpose.

Guadeloupe was now the main objective since it was from this island that Hugues was effectively exporting revolution. St Domingue also needed troops to reinforce the British presence and by July Dundas was warning the Transport Board that they would have to provide conveyance to the West Indies for between 25,000 and 30,000 men. Even as the Board struggled to find the necessary tonnage, St Lucia was added to the primary objectives.

A further challenge was to find a military commander determined enough to overrule local objections and deal with local obstructions. Dundas turned to his old friend. In July Abercromby was nominated to lead the expedition, undoubtedly a compliment to his conduct in the Low Countries. His lack of experience of independent command and combined (*conjunct,* to use the contemporary term) operations was not considered significant. He was, however, believed to excel 'in difficult situations in which his independent judgement and stubborn determination could be exercised to the full'.[5] These were certainly requirements in the West Indies. In a private letter to Dundas he had written, in response to the failures in the Low Countries, that 'A General who means to succeed, must follow his own ideas, command his army himself, and choose his own assistants. Official men ought not on all occasions to act the general, and sometimes the politician; they ought to attend to their own business, and things would go better on.'[6] He also pointed out that a successful campaign would depend upon a force possessed of order, discipline and confidence, qualities been had been demonstrated only intermittently in the Low Countries.

There is some suggestion that Abercromby was bribed by the government to accept the command. He had been made a Knight of the Bath in July and the following month was appointed Lieutenant Governor of the Isle of Wight, a post that provided a comfortable income, but both are more likely rewards for his service. His appointment as Commander-in-Chief of the Leeward and Windward Islands was officially announced on 5 August. He was also required to supervise British activity on St Domingue through a deputy, although when the search for a deputy failed to produce anyone suitable the serving commander, General Forbes, was left in place. On his own initiative and aware of his ignorance of the area, Abercromby requested Brigadier General John Whyte as an advisor since he had recently been in command on St Domingue.

On 14 August Dundas wrote to the King outlining the advantages of the expedition. 'Under these circumstances his majesty's confidential servants think it their indispensible duty unanimously to state to his Majesty their opinion that a body of Guards amounting to three thousand men to serve under General Abercrombie is essentially necessary to give a fair chance of prosecuting the war with vigour, or of bringing it to an honourable conclusion.' The King refused. The Guards were his personal troops and he was well aware that if he sanctioned their departure for the West Indies, less than half of them would be mustered on their return. The reason he gave, however, was that the Guards were needed to preserve peace at home, a reminder of the fear of radical unrest.[7]

The Guards, who had frequently performed with distinction in the Netherlands, would certainly have improved the quality of Abercromby's troops, which eventually comprised six brigades of infantry, the 26th Light Dragoons, and the Royal Irish Artillery (see Table 1). The total strength all ranks was 18,433. This constituted the largest overseas expedition ever sent beyond Europe, although the original complement of 30,000 men could not be realized when there were only 31,154 men in 79 battalions actually fit for service in Britain. Such an expedition would also have needed 100,000 tons of shipping, something like 200 ships. As already noted, the nucleus of the planned force was the regiments recently returned from North Germany, although these needed reinforcements to replace their recent losses. Even when recruits could be found (a poor harvest and a harsh winter the previous year helped in this respect), they were often too old or too young for active service, particularly in the harsh conditions of the West Indies. Yet if those who were obviously unfit were rejected, which was Abercromby's intention, there would be a shortage of manpower.

Dundas's solution was to use not only the troops acclimatized at Gibraltar, but also any German mercenary forces he could scrape together. This was frustrated by the reluctance of Germans to serve in the West Indies, although one such unit, Löwenstein's Chasseurs, was to prove its worth. The Duke of York, in his role as Commander-in-Chief, offered a different solution; all regiments numbered over 100 were to be drafted into the West India battalions. The plan had to be abandoned when it caused riots in Dublin, Cork, Newcastle and Essex. York then ordered that all soldier servants should return to the ranks once they reached the West Indies, and be replaced by black servants.

The planned departure dates were 14, 15 and 16 August, and Abercromby made his way to Portsmouth and Southampton to oversee preparations. He also instituted regular roll calls at Netley and Nursling, where the troops were assembling, in order to prevent desertion. At the same time, General Whyte was sent to Cork, where another force was being assembled for St Domingue.

Admiral Hugh Cleobury Christian had been chosen to command the naval element of the expedition. Christian enjoyed a good reputation and had also been chairman of the Transport Board since its inception in July 1794. Previously, any overseas expedition had needed input from the War Department, the Ordnance, the Secretary of State, the Treasury and the Admiralty. This last, through its two sub-divisions, the Navy Board and the Victualling Board, was crucial since it was responsible for the provision of ships and supplies. In 1785 a commission had established that both boards were disorganized, wasteful and fraudulent, but it was not until the outbreak of war in 1793 and the need to transport armies to fight in mainland Europe and the West Indies, that these deficiencies had become obvious. The newly constituted Transport Board was an attempt to establish a body that could oversee and direct the activities of all the other departments except the Treasury, thus creating a more efficient chain of command. Under Christian the Transport Board quickly demonstrated a working method in which the various transport agents, on land and at sea, played a vital role in the speedy delivery of the orders of the Board. Thanks to the work of Christian and his two fellow commissioners, 'After little more than a year in office the Transport Board displayed signs of precision and organization and its methods achieved a degree of efficiency.'[8]

The first task was to hire merchant ships for the transport of troops and supplies. This was no easy operation, however. Just as finding troops for the expedition had become a desperate scraping of the barrel, so hiring transports proved equally challenging. For the shipowner, commercial activities were more profitable than contracting his vessels to the government. Only by raising the freight rate paid to the owners were transports acquired and even then not enough to carry the proposed force of 30,000 men. As a result, it became necessary to await the arrival of convoys of East and West India merchantmen, just one factor of the many that would fatally delay the departure of the expedition.

The appointment of Christian to co-command the expedition proved contentious. He had served in the West Indies during the American War, which might have been thought pertinent. He had also recently been promoted to Rear Admiral of the Blue and earned the following encomium from *The Times*: 'Admiral Christian is universally esteemed as one of the most intelligent officers in the British Navy; for to a thorough knowledge of his profession, he possesses a very clear and sound judgement.'[9] Problematically, he was junior to Admiral Laforey, and Laforey was still in the West Indies. To overcome the issue of seniority, Laforey was posted to Jamaica in nominal command of the Caribbean. Christian could then command the expedition to the Windward and Leeward Islands. There was an immediate protest, on grounds of protocol, from Vice Admiral Charles Middleton, a loud (and well-informed) voice at the Admiralty. The new First Lord of the Admiralty, Earl Spencer, promptly reinstated Laforey. This placed Christian in a subordinate position and would allow Laforey to decide naval policy during the campaign.

Neither Dundas nor Abercromby was initially aware of this change. When Dundas heard about it, he insisted that Laforey must be recalled. Spencer agreed, only to change his mind under Middleton's urging. Abercromby had already recognized that the expedition would require a clear understanding between army and navy. He wrote to William Huskisson, the Under-Secretary at War, to express his reservations about accepting such a paradoxical command, particularly as Laforey was famously disputatious and also reported to be in poor health. Finally Spencer yielded, agreeing to recall Laforey and appoint in his place Admiral Cornwallis, who was fully engaged elsewhere, thus allowing Christian to exercise command. This still did not satisfy Middleton; but he was silenced by being forced to resign.

It has been suggested, by those inclined to denigrate him, that Dundas had thus clearly demonstrated his belief in the primacy of the army over the navy. It would seem, however, that he actually could not understand the problem which was forcing Spencer into such vacillation. Abercromby was junior to many other generals, but there had been no challenge to his appointment. Why should matters be different in the navy, providing there was no-one in the Caribbean actually senior to Christian? As for Abercromby, he was aware of the difficulties that often caused conjunct operations to fail. Better to share command with Christian, with whom he had quickly established a positive relationship, than the notoriously irascible Laforey. Furthermore, he had other priorities which he regarded as more crucial than naval protocol.

Bearing in mind the unhealthy conditions of the West Indies and also of shipboard conditions on a long voyage, he required the Transport Board to act on the advice of medical men who had experience of the West Indies and frame *Regulations for the better Preservation of the Health of troops at Sea and on Service in hot Climates*. These were produced by a conference that included among others the surgeons Mr Thomas Young, who had been in the West Indies in 1792 and was to serve as Inspector General of Hospitals for the expedition, and Mr Weir from Jamaica, now promoted to Inspector General for St Domingue.

The resultant regulations satisfied Abercromby's demands as far as was feasible. It would be impossible to man an expedition of the planned magnitude only with soldiers who had already served in the West Indies or at Gibraltar, thus excluding young, raw troops. Nor would the expedition, already delayed, be ready to set sail in time to benefit from the healthiest season in the Caribbean. He could insist that regulations for troops at sea, covering diet, cleaning, ventilation, fumigation, and the strong recommendation of five men per 10 tons of shipping, should be strictly adhered to. Only this last proved impossible to implement.

The doctors' further recommendations for troops on land included advice on clothing, which had been a particular concern for Abercromby.

The thick European uniform led to excessive sweating which in turn caused men to collapse, exhausted. Instead, the troops would wear short coats, loose cotton trousers and cloth gaiters that would protect against insect bites (for which there should be careful inspection). The universally-detested leather stock was replaced with a black cloth one. Shirts and drawers were to be of flannel. A good supply of medicines, equipment and hospital furniture was also crucial. Camps should be on high ground, away from the disease-ridden coastal plains, and men should be encouraged to bathe in the sea and change and wash their clothes regularly. In order to provide sufficient medical manpower, four physicians, six staff surgeons, four apothecaries, thirty hospital mates, one purveyor and eight deputy purveyors were attached to the expedition. There was also a call for fit, unemployed army surgeons to volunteer. Abercromby added to this request for extra manpower by applying for more junior officers to replace the inevitable losses at that level.[10]

Another expert whom Abercromby consulted was General Grey, whose tactics had initially proved so successful. At the same time, Christian tapped the experience of Admiral Jervis. As a result, the expedition was furnished with charts and valuable advice. Abercromby also took with him a portable telegraph, which represented the latest technology. (Presumably, this was Lord George Murray's innovation, adopted by the Admiralty in 1795.) Whatever the failings of the official preparations, and both Christian and Abercromby crossed swords with officialdom more than once, their own preparations were as thorough as possible. There was also mutual good feeling between them. Christian wrote to Huskisson on 2 November: 'Abercromby is here and every hour makes me more satisfied with and attached to him. He is a truly sensible, honest man.'[11]

It was generally agreed that a large expedition about to undertake a protracted voyage to a distant location needed three months 'to hire, fit, prepare and collect tonnage required by the different departments . . . including the time the troops took in getting ready even after tonnage was allotted to them'.[12] In this respect, the planned sailing dates could never have been realized. The Ordnance Department caused particular problems. The facilities at Woolwich allowed for only two ships to be loaded at a time, and not even the Transport Board could improve the situation. Consequently, planned departure dates came and went: 15 August, 20 August, 1 October.

On 9 October Abercromby received specific orders to set sail for Barbados, preparatory to dealing with the situation in Guadeloupe. Then he was to attack St Lucia. On the presumption that these two islands would quickly fall into British hands, the government required him to consider attacking the Dutch possessions of Surinam, Berbice and Demerara. Since part of the force was destined for St Domingue, and possibly Santo Domingo if the Spanish actively sided with the French, Abercromby would also have to communicate with General Thomas Maitland, now in command there. Not surprisingly, the government had ignored the practical difficulty of maintaining communications against the trade winds.

Even when Abercromby had his orders, departure was still delayed by problems of supply, which allowed the troops to become increasingly demoralized. Expeditions to the West Indies were unpopular with officers and men alike. Delay exacerbated this, particularly as the assembled troops had not initially realized where they were being sent. As Grenville's brother, Buckingham, commented: 'Among a thousand horrid consequences, it is not the least important that the officers and men have had leisure to frame to themselves every mischievous apprehension that can arise from disaffection to this service.'[13] Abercromby was in command of troops who had no enthusiasm for the campaign.

Nor were the winds favourable; and Abercromby was well aware of the practical dangers of delay. Sailing weather was unlikely to improve; consequently, the later the troops reached the West Indies, the sooner they would start to suffer from disease; and the summer rainy season would also hamper military activities. On the other hand, he was equally aware of the disadvantages of undertaking an expedition with an ill-equipped and under-prepared army. Dundas's facile suggestion that he should sail only with those troops that were ready would have left him seriously undermanned. There had also been difficulty assembling the 25,000 stands of arms required,[14] while the ordnance ships destined for St Domingue did not leave the Thames for Cork until 18 October, followed a week later by those intended for the Leeward and Windward Islands, whose immediate destination was Portsmouth. These last sailed into gales, not reaching Spithead until 9 November. Add to all these setbacks the belated realization that no provision had been made for hospital ships and any impression of a thoroughly prepared expedition quickly disappears. Abercromby was famed for his even temper (unlike Admiral Christian, who was known for his volatility) but even he was given to rare moments of irritation. This was undoubtedly one of them.

By early November eight ships of the line including the 118-gun *Commerce de Marseilles*, taken at Toulon in 1793, three frigates, a bomb vessel and six or seven smaller vessels had been assembled to provide the naval escort, while press gangs had been active in order to find the much-needed manpower. Returning convoys from the Indies, East and West, and even the ships in the Channel Fleet were raided for sailors. It had proved yet more challenging to find transports for men, horses, guns, ammunition and provisions. An attempt to hire foreign tonnage failed. As planned, East and West India merchantmen were commandeered, and eventually naval ships were converted into transports. Just to complicate matters further, there was fierce competition for manpower between the navy and the Transport Board. In the meantime, Abercromby had sent strict orders to regimental commanders that they must limit baggage and the number of women who would accompany the troops. In the event, just 808 women sailed, a ratio of one woman to twenty men.

Eventually Abercromby was able to write to Dundas:

> The Number of Troops required for the Windward and Leeward Island Service, has been furnished; in general, they are well equipped and are healthy. The Transports on which the Troops are embarked are, in general, unexceptional. The Hospital Staff is nearly complete. Regulations for the Care of Men on Ship Board, and on their arrival in the West Indies, have been framed by Military and Medical Men of Judgement and Experience, and no pains or Experience have been spared to furnish the Troops with every Article for their Accommodation and Comfort, in Health and in Sickness. The Artillery and Military Stores now embarked will prove Sufficient for the Service. I have the fullest Confidence in the Temper and Professional Abilities of the Naval commander with whom I am to act.[15]

Nevertheless, he felt the need to point out that although everything suggested a successful expedition, it was important to remember the mischances that had befallen previous expeditions.

Abercromby might feel reasonably confident but on the naval side there were strong voices of doom. Admiral Middleton, for all his concerns about protocol, also possessed an acute understanding of the reality of the situation. In his view, it was 'this system of unlimited conquest that cripples us everywhere, and diverts the fleet from its natural use. It is like a farmer wishing to occupy a large farm without money to manage it. The consequence is, that he begins a beggar and ends a ruined man.'[16] In his view, naval blockades were more effective than supporting the army in its vain adventures.

St Lucia, St Vincent and Grenada

The transports were ordered to start assembling at St Helens on 10 November 1795. Yet even now there were problems. The *Prince George,* a 90-gun Second Rate and Christian's flagship, ran aground. Then part of the convoy followed Admiral Cornwallis, who was sailing for the Mediterranean, and Christian had to send an urgent recall. Some of the transports were overcrowded, despite the doctors' advice. And the ordnance transports had still not arrived. As for the foreign troops expected from Germany, there was no news of them. At this season of the year, however, it was important to take advantage of good sailing weather. November 15th was bright and clear with a north north-east wind. This was the moment to weigh anchor and set sail, and the transports finally left Portsmouth, carrying 18,742 all ranks and accompanied by a strong naval escort.

Dr George Pinckard, who was aboard the hospital ship *Ulysses*, destined for the St Domingue expedition, watched the departure:

> . . . the picture was beautiful, as it was grand and animated. On passing round, or, to use the sailor's term, on doubling the point of the Isle of Wight, all the ships seemed to fall into regular succession, forming a lie of numberless extent . . . It was a pleasing spectacle to every beholder and those who felt as Englishmen ought, derived from it sensations peculiarly grateful, To witness such a fleet full-swelling from our little island into the broad ocean to fight our battles in a far distant country, conveyed ideas of greatness and power, which were calculated to raise a just ambition in every British bosom.[17]

Neither Pinckard nor any of the other spectators could have predicted the disaster that lay ahead.

The following day the fleet sailed along the Dorset coast, benefitting from winds that were still favourable, although Christian already suspected that the fine weather would not last. As a precaution, he signalled to the convoy to keep close. Should the weather deteriorate they were to head for Torbay. Early on 17 November, with the fleet off Weymouth Bay and the leading ships already past Portland Bill, pressure dropped and the wind freshened from the north-west, whipping up the sea. A heavy drizzle limited visibility. At this point Christian gave the order to tack for Torbay. By daybreak a strong west wind was causing some of the transports to wallow in the heavy seas. The naval ships and East Indiamen could cope with the conditions but the transports would never make it safely into the shelter of Torbay. At 4 p.m. Christian gave the order to stand out to the south-west.

The wind was now at gale force and continued to strengthen during the night. By the following day, the seas were mountainous. Fog and the howling of the wind destroyed any sense of position. The only sensible course was to head back to Portsmouth, but this did not help the struggling transports. Some of them were able to run for shelter in Weymouth and Portland but others, unaware of their true position, were driven onto Chesil Beach. The transports *Catherine* and *Piedmont*, carrying troops, *Venus*, carrying invalids, and the storeships *Aeolus* and *Golden Grove*, along with the *Thomas*, a merchant ship heading for Oporto, were all lost with about 300 casualties. The local people, who had come out initially to scavenge, and the men of the South Gloucester Militia did what they could but there were few survivors, probably little more than seventy.[18] Nor were these the only ships lost to the gales. The transports *Commerce* and *Pitt* were both wrecked, although those aboard were saved, and an unnamed troopship was lost off the Isle of Wight with only two survivors. As for the rest of the fleet, which eventually limped back to Portsmouth, it was said that all of them needed repairs. Even Christian's flagship, the *Prince George*, had lost its rudder and struggled to reach safety, finally being towed to St Helens by HMS *Colossus*.

While the ships were being repaired news arrived that a contingent of foreign troops expected in Barbados had not arrived, necessitating a change of plan. These missing troops had been intended for St Domingue. General Whyte, who by this time was in Barbados, was ordered to send only seven light dragoon regiments to St Domingue, retaining the rest until Abercromby arrived. Abercromby also suggested that the troops at Cork should sail to Barbados with him, rather than to St Domingue as planned. It was further assumed that the foreign troops must be making their way to Portsmouth rather than the West Indies, so that they too could sail with the fleet when it finally departed for the second time. This augmentation of Abercromby's force led to a change of orders. He was now to make simultaneous attacks on Guadeloupe and St Lucia, and then give his attention to St Domingue. All this planning remained academic, however, until the shattered expedition was ready to put to sea again.

The Portsmouth transport agent, Captain John Schank, faced with accommodating more men on fewer transports, decided to ignore the men-to-tonnage ratio. Christian had crossed swords with Schank several times already and now took an adamant stand against him. As the Commissioner to

Portsmouth Dockyard reported to Cornwallis, 'the unfortunate & untimely dispute between Adml Christian and Capt Schank, which (I am told) went to very indiscreet lengths (at this moment) on the part of the Admiral, Who Collar'd Schank, and then parted with a challenge from Schank, which they say the Adml Accepted and promised to fulfil at his return from the Expedition'.[19] Fortunately, Dundas had come to Portsmouth along with Lord Spencer to inspect the damage caused by the storm and to supervise repairs. They supported Christian's objections. At the same time, though, the Admiralty was putting Christian under pressure to sail as soon as possible, even if it meant leaving behind any transports still under repair.

The expedition was finally ready to sail again by the end of November but contrary winds delayed departure. The fleet eventually left Portsmouth for the second time on 9 December with the fit men of the original force and the recently-arrived Löwenstein's Chasseurs, nearly 20,000 in total, aboard 218 ships. Christian had opted for a northerly route to pick up the trade winds because, with Cadiz now in French hands, the southerly route might invite a French attack. This decision was later to be criticised because it made the fleet more vulnerable to bad weather. By 12 December the convoy had reached the Scilly Isles where once again the ships were dispersed by gales, with many suffering yet more damage. Christian had raised his flag on the *Glory* 94, where among the officers was Lieutenant Francis Austen, Jane Austen's younger brother. And one of the passengers was Thomas Fowle, her sister Cassandra's fiancé, who would die of yellow fever in the West Indies. The *Glory* proved as unlucky as the *Prince George*. When she began to take on water there was a very real chance that she would be lost. According to Midshipman William Dillon, at the point of greatest danger Abercromby came on deck in his nightshirt. When told that the ship was about to sink he merely remarked, 'If that is the case there is no use in my staying here. I may as well go to bed again and take my chance.' Not surprisingly, this *sang froid* won the respect not only of Admiral Christian, who reported that Abercromby's 'demeanour on this occasion was so calm and composed, that it was an example to be admired and followed by all who witnessed it'.[20] There is a further anecdote which has his servant rushing in to warn the general that they were all about to be drowned, whereupon he was calmly told to go back to bed. In the event, the ship was saved by the use of the pumps and the closing of the middle-deck gunports.

Nor was the *Glory* the only ship to be affected. The following morning, 117 ships were in a fit state to continue but 30 were obliged to return to England. The storms continued. Some vessels fell into French hands;

one finished up in Gibraltar; and a few struggled on to Barbados. By 26 December the fleet comprised only ninety-three ships. On 12 January 1796 the survivors were able to pick up the trade winds, but nine days later just forty-nine ships were still en route for the West Indies, and they were then blown back 200 miles by a violent so'wester. Sickness was rife, and there were even threats of mutiny. On 24 January Christian signalled a return to port for those ships still in contact with him. Five days later seventy-three ships had struggled back to St Helens. No wonder the more superstitious of the sailors regarded Christian as an unlucky admiral.

The return to Portsmouth provided Burne with yet more evidence that Abercromby was a 'give-up' general, although he conflated this second return to port with the events after Christian's storm. 'In September the Duke [of York] was again on the south coast, seeing to the embarkation of Abercromby's expedition to the West Indies. This was one of Abercromby's abortive operations, the sequel of which can be read in the Duke's letter to the King of 30 January, 1796.'[21] This letter merely informed the King that because the men would have to disembark, he meant to travel to Portsmouth. There is no suggestion that Abercromby had abandoned the expedition, as indeed he did not.

On 10 January Dundas had despatched a third set of instructions for Abercromby, who was still at sea. From the government's perspective, troubled as they were by riots, shortage of money and the need to import foreign corn, it made sense to limit the scope of the expedition, while for Abercromby the new orders were an improvement because he was now given more discretion to decide the conduct of the campaign. Dundas realized that if St Domingue was to be taken before the rainy season it must remain the principal focus. Guadeloupe and St Lucia were to be ignored. The first task now was to deal with St Vincent and Grenada, and then move on to St Domingue if the situation allowed. Early in February, though, there was another change of mind; a fourth set of instructions required Abercromby to make the pacification of Grenada and St Vincent his first objective, followed by St Lucia and Demerara. St Domingue was no longer of immediate concern. It is easy to criticise Dundas and the ministry generally for this welter of orders which should have demonstrated that the conduct of a campaign on the other side of the Atlantic was best left to the man on the spot rather than being directed from London. This was a lesson the government had still to learn.

Just under 12,000 troops eventually returned to England, so it was assumed that 7,415 must have reached the West Indies. Unfortunately, the rather less than 6,000 troops who had actually reached Barbados comprised only one complete regiment, while the incomplete units varied in strength from six men to 400. As a result the start of active campaigning would be delayed by the need to reorganize these troops and await the arrival of reinforcements. Meanwhile, the troops that sailed from Cork to St Domingue on 10 February also ran into severe gales and had to return to port, only setting sail again a fortnight later with their destination changed to Barbados, as noted above. Thus the consequences of the postponed early-autumn sailing were now obvious.

Abercromby had transferred to the frigate *Arethusa*, commanded by Captain Thomas Woolley, but bad luck struck again when *Arethusa* collided with *Ramillies*. Two days of hurried repairs enabled *Arethusa* to sail on 14 February, and she reached Barbados thirty days later. At the same time, Cornwallis had returned from the Mediterranean and was in position to take command. Christian was relegated to commanding the reserve force convoy that would sail in March, after which he would be in naval command at St Domingue under Admiral Parker in Jamaica.

The force at Cork set sail for the second time on 23 February. The main force, eighty-seven transports and nearly 8,000 men, with a naval escort of eight ships, did not leave Portsmouth until the end of the month, still in a state of confusion. Even the masters of the transports had not been informed of a point of assembly, should the fleet become dispersed. John Moore wrote in his journal on 26 February: 'The confusion of this place [Portsmouth] is beyond anything that could be believed; everything is in disorder, and the expedition will sail in as bad a state as ever expedition did sail from this country.'[22] He knew he was to proceed with Brigadier Perryn's brigade, of which he had been instructed to take temporary command, along with a foreign corps which would be his actual command. These last, however, were in no fit state for service. In the end he sailed without the foreign corps, with only a portmanteau of possessions, and arrived in the West Indies without a command. Moore's experience certainly illustrates the ramshackle nature of preparations which had seemed to start so efficiently.

There were also problems on the naval front. *Royal Sovereign*, Cornwallis's flagship, ran down a transport, causing heavy losses to Löwenstein's Chasseurs. Cornwallis had to put into port for repairs and then refused to sail when he was transferred to the frigate *Astræa*, which he considered too small and lacking in comfort. He was later court martialled but only censured for not continuing on another ship. The convoy eventually reached Barbados on 14 and 15 March without either Cornwallis or Christian, and two days before the commander-in-chief arrived. Christian finally set sail with 5,500 men in forty-one transports on 20 March. Eleven days later he transferred to *Astræa*, and arrived in Barbados on 21 April. He then took command of the Leeward and Windward station, a position he was to hold until Cornwallis arrived, which did not happen.

When Abercromby reached Barbados he was chaired to the governor's house by cheering crowds. He was also met by Major Thomas Picton, who would later identify himself as one of Abercromby's 'pupils'. Picton had been on half-pay for a protracted period when in 1794 he decided to sail to the West Indies in the hope that Sir John Vaughan, who had recently assumed command in the Leeward Islands, would do something for him. His optimism was rewarded when Vaughan made him Deputy Quartermaster General and brevet lieutenant colonel. Unfortunately, Vaughan died in August 1795. Abercromby's arrival was fortuitous, therefore, particularly as the General was acquainted with Picton's uncle. Again, the Welshman's optimism was not misplaced when he was appointed an extra aide-de-camp.

Abercromby found 5,000 troops on Barbados, while a further 1,800 had been sent to Martinique, Grenada and St Vincent and about 200 were serving on ships. He now decided to deal with Grenada first, at least to stabilize the situation there, by sending 600 of the troops on Barbados to General Nicholls, in command.

There were further issues that needed to be resolved. The Quartermaster General, John Knox, had managed to find 2,400 blacks to act as pioneers. However, they were generally the worst slaves, the only ones their owners were willing to part with. He had failed, though, to persuade the slave-owners to support the new West India regiments. Knox had a temporary unit under the command of Colonel Malcolm, while there were two further units in Martinique and Dominica, but Abercromby had hoped for more. There was a chronic shortage of money, while 10 per cent was added to every bill drawn on Britain. As for the campaign itself, Abercromby still lacked troops, having only 6,708 regulars. If he sent some of those to St Vincent, which was supposed to be his next objective, and where even the small amount of territory under British control was under threat, there was a real risk that the adverse trade winds might prevent their recall. He also realized that any attempt to control events in St Domingue from his present location would prove impossible, and he requested to be relieved of that part of his command. Worst of all, Admiral Christian had yet to arrive. There could be no campaign without naval support.

Fortescue wrote of Abercromby that he was 'naturally a man of the gentlest temper and firmest resolution, but after the seven terrible weeks on board ship in continuous gales he began to feel the weight of his sixty-two years, and was probably never so much out of heart with his work as in this West Indian campaign'.[23] He was certainly to demonstrate moments of spleen.

The troops intended for St Domingue finally arrived at the beginning of April. Having inspected them, Abercromby concluded that they would prove both inefficient and unreliable. He suspected that no more than 500 would still be alive come November. They were obviously unfit for service on St Domingue, so when Admiral Laforey arrived with part of his squadron, the rest having been sent elsewhere, Abercromby provided Whyte with a four-frigate escort and dispatched him and his troops to Demerara, where the white inhabitants, led by the Governor, willingly accepted British protection. This was just as well as the boats bringing the troops ashore were soon stuck in the shallow, muddy water and would have been easy targets for the guns of Demerara. As it was, Essequibo and Berbice soon followed the example of Demarara.

In the middle of April two divisions of Admiral Cornwallis's convoy arrived without the admiral, and this gave Abercromby sufficient ships and men, nearly 8,000 fit for service, to attack St Lucia. He had already decided when he considered the quality of the troops under his command that Guadeloupe was too strong for his resources. He also appreciated that war in the Caribbean depended upon tides, currents and winds, which suggested starting in St Lucia and then moving on to St Vincent and Grenada. He knew from the information Knox had gathered that the force on Saint Lucia was reported to comprise 4,000 black troops and some whites, mainly gunners. They were expected to be well entrenched, but even so they represented less of a threat than the rumoured 8,000 coloured troops, 100 cavalry and 300–400 whites Hugues had on Guadeloupe, where numbers were said to be increasing all the time. What does seem clear is that the Commissioner on St Lucia, Gaspard Goyrand, had anticipated a British attack and reacted accordingly. He had strengthened his defences and requested supplies from Guadeloupe. He also personally kept watch for the British arrival.[24]

It was also at this point that Abercromby made the acquaintance of John Moore, who arrived on 13 April and waited on him the next day. This was the beginning of a friendship which was to last for the rest of Abercromby's life. The two Scots, both of a Whig persuasion, soon discovered that they shared similar attitudes to the business of soldiering. The general offered

Moore the position of second-in-command on St Vincent but Moore was anxious for a brigade and service under Abercromby himself in order to gain experience. As a result, Abercromby 'agreed to it, was happy and always should be to do whatever was agreeable to me . . . The General behaved to me with great politeness and kindness.'[25]

By 20 April the convoy was ready to leave Barbados for Martinique and fortuitously Admiral Christian arrived just before the planned departure. He immediately took command of the naval operations, to general relief. By the following night the whole fleet was at sea, and there was some hope that the Admiral's arrival might redirect its route straight to St Lucia rather than making the detour to Martinique. Moore was certainly of the opinion that both Abercromby and Christian believed stopping at Martinique a waste of time, and he wondered why the Admiral had not changed the orders, since the two men could have made their arrangements just as easily in Barbados. Laforey, however, had insisted on handing over his command to Christian in person, and chose Martinique for the rendezvous. When the fleet did anchor in St Anne's Bay off the southern end of Martinique, an ordnance sloop was lost, some of the ships were carried past the bay and the *Minotaur* was beached, but Laforey had his formal handover.

The next two days were spent finalizing arrangements for the landings,[26] and there seems little doubt that the Admiral and the General quickly re-established their good understanding of how matters should be conducted, which was vital to combined operations. Certainly when Abercromby wrote to Dundas that Laforey would have done nothing and Cornwallis, what he chose, he clearly implied the rapport between himself and Christian.[27]

On the 25th the expedition sailed for St Lucia, although not before Abercromby had issued general orders warning against the danger of standing water and of fast-paced marching except when critically necessary. He had already ordered that drill should only take place early in the morning. There would also be extra rum rations to offset the effects of wet weather (a remedy frequently used in the fens of eastern England). The inexperienced troops were reminded not to waste fire, and to maintain watch when on outpost duties. They were also cautioned against pillaging, which carried a death sentence, and drunkenness, which would also be severely punished. He concluded: 'It is never wise to despise the enemy, at the same time there can be no doubt in the present war, if the British soldier will preserve his presence of mind, will disregard the shouts of savages and will be on his guard against surprises, that he will possess infinite advantages over the enemy and that he is certain of success.'

Abercromby and Christian's plan embraced three landing points: Anse du Cap, a bay between Pigeon Island and Pointe du Cap on the north-west extremity of the island; Anse du Choc, which was a few miles further south; and Anse la Raye, about five miles south of Port Castries. All three landings were to be carried out under naval cover. The first landings would take place under Major General Alexander Campbell at Anse du Cap. Once a position had been secured, Abercromby would land more troops at Anse du Choc, followed by Major General William Morshead further south at Anse le Raye.

The first landing took place before daylight on 26 April, from a position off Anse du Cap, at either side of the Carénage rather than in Castries harbour, which was strongly fortified. Even so, the ships closest inshore came under fire from Pigeon Island, but without suffering any damage. Moore, in command of a brigade in General Campbell's division, came ashore with the 14th and 42nd, the only two British battalions that had arrived, and after some skirmishing with the enemy established a beachhead in a good defensive position. He then sent Löwenstein's Chasseurs to occupy Longueville House as an advance post, but they were checked by determined opposition. The delayed arrival of some of the transports meant that when General Campbell landed he told Moore that the grenadiers, 48th and artillery would not be able to come ashore until evening. Furthermore, Abercromby had informed Campbell that the Admiral was not yet ready to offer the necessary naval support. Since it would be difficult to re-embark and dangerous to stay put now their presence was known, Moore suggested that they should post picquets to create a pretence of staying put, but be ready to march by midnight, by which time the grenadiers and the 48th should have landed. He persuaded Campbell to send Captain Hay with a letter to Abercromby, checking that he approved of this plan for a night march, particularly as Campbell's state of health meant that Moore would be giving the orders.

It may be taken as a sign of Abercromby's willingness to trust the judgement of his commanders on the ground that he gave the required permission and instructed Campbell to march whenever he thought fit. This finally happened at 3 a.m. the following day after the remaining troops of the division had landed. The enemy offered some resistance at Longueville House, but then fled before a superior force. Advancing to the heights of Choc, the invaders discovered that two batteries had been abandoned.

Abercromby and Christian now landed at Anse du Choc with the second division. The enemy was in position at Angiers House, so the General ordered the grenadiers to advance, accompanied by a gun, which persuaded their opponents to retire. That evening Abercromby ordered a further advance on Morne Chabot, which was a dominant position near the fortress-crowned Morne Fortuné. This was to be a two-pronged attack.

> One division, consisting of the 53rd Regiment, 100 of Löwenstein's corps, and 100 of Malcolm's [black troops], under the command of Brigadier-General Moore, to march as soon as they are ready after twelve o'clock. The second division, consisting of the 57th, 50 of Löwenstein's, and 100 of Malcolm's, under the command of Brigadier-General Hope, to march half-an-hour after the first. The object of this attack is to drive the enemy from Morne Chabot, and as any communication between the columns in this country is difficult, the column under Brigadier-General Hope will not begin to act till the attack on the left has commenced; when the troops are masters of Morne Chabot 500 men will be posted there, and the remainder of the force will extend themselves towards the left . . .[28]

Moore informed Hope that he should commence his own attack before dawn, thus giving Hope the signal for his own attack.

As Abercromby had recognized, communication and co-ordination would be a serious problem in this difficult terrain as the two columns followed different routes along narrow, broken paths. They were totally reliant upon local guides, who promised Moore half a mile of easy ground from Morne Chabot at the end of the march. Moore arrived ninety minutes before Hope. As his presence had been detected by an enemy picquet he had no choice but to launch an attack while in ignorance of Hope's position, and well before the intended dawn attack. The troops now advanced in single file up a steep gradient to discover the enemy hastily taking up position. As soon as the ground allowed, Moore reorganized his force to present a front six to eight men wide. He ordered an attack with the bayonet. Unfortunately, raw troops and novice officers lacked the confidence for this. Instead, when the enemy fired on them, they returned fire, as did some of the men in the rear ranks. As a result two companies were broken, although in the dark it is possible that the enemy remained unaware of this confusion. Under Moore's encouragement the troops were persuaded to persist in their attack and the position had already been taken with the bayonet before Hope arrived at daybreak.

Moore's comment on the event is pertinent when considering the problems that Abercromby faced. 'In this attack the men showed no want of spirit; no man ever offered to turn his back, but they showed great want of discipline and confidence in their officers. Against an enemy of experience we must have failed.'[29] Nevertheless, Moore had demonstrated that he was the man to execute his commander's plan, a quality he would demonstrate many times over.

Moore quickly appreciated that Morne Duchazeau (Morne de Chasseur according to Moore) which overlooked Morne Fortuné from the east, was now within reach. Having sent a message to Abercromby explaining his intentions, he left the 53rd (Fortescue says the 57th) under Captain John Abercromby, the General's son and aide-de-camp, to hold Morne Chabot. Then he advanced on Morne Duchazeau accompanied by Hope, who had arrived just as Morne Chabot was carried. It was another challenging march, only three miles but over difficult ground, and progress was initially slow. The new position was quickly established, although not without some British casualties.

Abercromby's response to this double success, which gave direct access to Morne Fortuné and also ensured easy communications with General Morshead's troops of the third division, who were still to land, was predictably positive and generous. 'My best thanks are due to you on the judicious decision you made on falling in with the advanced post of the enemy; any hesitation would probably have defeated your purpose. Your determination has given us success; your loss, however to be regretted on account of individuals, is not more than might have been expected on such an occasion. On the whole the conduct of the troops is commendable, and I beg you will return them publicly my thanks.' He also summoned Goyrand, who was on Morne Fortuné, to surrender. Receiving the predictable refusal, he planned for further action. 'I shall advance part of my force and put it in communication with Morne Chabot by placing it at Grons, and the advanced posts at Chambon. I shall endeavour to open a road to Morne Chabot for a few light field-pieces, and shall take the first opportunity of removing the wounded on board the hospital ship.'[30]

On 2 May Abercromby reported Moore's success to Dundas.

In an action, which took place here on the 28th ult. between Lieutenant General Moore, and the advanced picquet of the enemy, between 40 and 50 of the latter were killed, and 200 stand of arms, with some ammunition, taken. The next day the brigadier occupied Morne Duchasseux, in the rear of Morne Fortuné. The division under the command of Major General Morshead, which was destined to land at Ancéla Ray, did not complete their disembarkation for some days, owing to their ships falling to Leeward. They are now in possession of the bar of the Grand Cul de Sac, and invest Morne Fortuné on the South side. It is impossible to describe the difficulty of communication in this country; and as Morne Fortuné is now in a respectable state of defence, it will require time and much labour to erect the necessary batteries to reduce it. Yesterday the enemy attacked the advanced post of the grenadiers, who are commanded by Lieutenant Colonel Mac Donald [*sic*] of the 55th Regiment, but were repulsed with considerable loss; though I am sorry to add, that we had several officers, and forty or fifty men killed or wounded. – The only officer killed was captain Kerr, of the York Rangers, the rest are slightly wounded, among whom is Major Napier, of the 63rd. From the best information I can obtain, the enemy have a garrison of about 2000 well disciplined black troops, some hundred whites, and a number of black people who have taken refuge in the fortress.[31]

By the time the dispatch was written, Abercromby had come to Chabot and reconnoitred the ground. From Moore's post he could see Morshead's troops on Morne Petit and expressed some irritation at the General's slow progress. He also sent his aide-de-camp, Captain Hay, with an offer of more troops and other assistance to help with the destruction of enemy batteries, which would impede any advance. As he returned, Hay told Moore that he had found Morshead 'wavering and uncertain; the Commander-in-chief has in consequence gone over to him'.[32]

On 4 May Abercromby again wrote to Dundas and the dispatch makes clear that the problems with Morshead's brigade had not been solved by his visit.

Yesterday Brigadier General Hope carried the battery Seche, within a short distance of the works of Morne Fortuné, with an inconsiderable loss, had not the brave Lieutenant Colonel Malcolm unfortunately fallen upon this spot. Colonel Riddle, who commanded the column on the left, got possession of the lower battery, called Chepuis, and remained possessed of it for a considerable time; but the column under the command of Brigadier-General Perryn, never having crossed the river at Coals, Lieutenant Colonel Riddle remained unsupported; and Brigadier General Hope's division also became unconnected, and consequently placed in a critical situation. From these untoward circumstances, the plan failed in the execution, and the troops returned to their former position. The ships, which were destined to enter the Cul de Sac, returned to their anchorage. From the intricate nature of this country, and the difficulty of approaching Morne Fortuné on any side, except by Morne Duchasseaux, I have been obliged to undertake a laborious communication from Choc Bay to that [?] Morne, and to form a road capable of allowing the transportation of heavy artillery.[33]

The plan had been for the third division to mount a two-column attack on the enemy batteries that endangered Hope's troops as they in turn attacked the Seche battery, while Moore created a further diversion. One of Morshead's columns, under Colonel Riddle, did indeed operate as required but the other never crossed the river Cul de Sac. Initially, Abercromby blamed General Morshead for this failure. He then learnt that 'General Morshead had the gout, and had entrusted his column, which was to have supported the other two, to Brigadier-General Perryn. This latter, I understand, found his men fatigued with their march to the river which runs through the Valley de Cul de Sac, had not crossed it, and left Colonel Riffel [*sic*, Riddle] and General Hope in the lurch. The whole retired to General Morshead's camp, with the loss of 100 officers and men killed and wounded. The Commander-in-chief is, I understand, infinitely displeased.'[34]

Abercromby was indeed displeased. He knew John Perryn from Flanders and seems to have considered him little better than a madman. Furthermore, Perryn had shown a certain eccentricity when he had unexpectedly departed for the West Indies without his brigade. There is also evidence to suggest that both Morshead and Perryn felt isolated as two Englishmen in a Scots-dominated command, and also believed that were given the most difficult tasks.[35] Abercromby took the first opportunity to send Perryn to St Domingue, and place Major General Charles Graham in command at Morne Petit with what was now nominated the left wing. As for the right wing, command was shared by Hope and Moore, who had already proved themselves reliable subordinates.

Under Graham's command the third division successfully completed the operation that Perryn's inaction had jeopardized on 3 May. The ten-gun batteries were now brought into position on Morne Duchazeau. Nevertheless, Abercromby still faced several intractable difficulties. Because of the terrain, the road building being undertaken by both soldiers and sailors was difficult and laborious. Supply lines extended ten miles and were blocked by Morne Fortuné, which necessitated long detours. Even more serious was the quality of his human resources. Ill-trained, ill-disciplined soldiers commanded by weak officers meant that even outpost duty was a constant concern for the general. Nor was he impressed by the quality of his three major generals, Graham, Campbell and Morshead, while the demands of the engineers, particularly their insistence on more guns than he judged necessary combined with their evident lack of expertise, was another irritation to try his patience. As a result, he found himself with only three brigadiers he could trust to share the burden of command, Moore, Hope and Knox, and that meant he was obliged to attend to day-to-day responsibilities that he might reasonably have expected to delegate to senior officers. He also faced problems of desertion, particularly among the foreign troops.

Moore saw much of Abercromby in the days spent waiting for the extra troops that would be needed for the attack on Morne Fortuné, and confided his judgement to his journal. 'Sir Ralph came here yesterday morning [7 May]. I reconnoitred with him to my left, and ground was pitched upon, which I am to occupy in that quarter . . . Sir Ralph is very short-sighted. Without a glass he sees nothing, but with it he observes ground quickly and well. He has the zeal and eagerness of youth, and for his age has much activity both of mind and body.'[36]

On 9 May the convoy Christian had outpaced finally reached St Lucia with 5.500 troops comprising the 27th, 31st and 57th, Latour's Royal Foreigners and more of Löwenstein's Chasseurs. These extra troops, with the exception of the 31st, were positioned to support the force on Morne Duchazeau and create a link between Moore and Graham. This completed the encirclement of Morne Fortuné so effectively that some of the enemy were killed when they tried to break out. The navy also added to Abercromby's strength with men and guns. Unfortunately, even with these reinforcements he was not able to prevent the enemy landing provisions.

On 16 May eighteen guns opened fire but had little success, which Abercromby blamed on the poor aim of the gunners, although the range was testing. At this point, though, the general was definitely 'out of humour. He is blind, and, never having been in the plain or crossed the country, he has no conception of the impenetrable stuff that covers it.' Unfortunately, the ill-humour was spreading through the army. General Graham, for instance, 'was discontented and hot and full of arguments not at all applicable to the case against coming lower with his forces. The conversation was public at his table upon subjects which should only be discussed in private; in short, the worst *ton* prevailed.'[37]

The following day Abercromby directed a night attack on Vigie, to the north of Port Castries. This, however, ended in disaster for the 31st Regiment when the commanding officer ignored the General's orders and lost control of his ill-disciplined troops. Instead of a silent advance and an attack with the bayonet, the men were allowed to straggle and fire at will. As a result, they came under fire from enemy guns discharging grape, and the regiment took 200 casualties, killed, missing and wounded.

In response, Abercromby issued a general order on 18 May that was obviously designed to bolster the confidence of troops demoralized by failure.

> Although the attack of last night was not altogether so successful as might have been expected, the Commander in Chief has the fullest confidence in the troops he has the honour to command, he hopes they will always have in view the superiority of the British arms and they may rest assured whenever they assert themselves with the vigour and courage that distinguishes Englishmen, that they will be successful.
>
> He entreats them in an attack with the bayonet that they will not hesitate but to push forward till they have obtained their object. The Commander in Chief will not put them upon any service where there is not the fairest prospect of success, and he trusts that in future he will never be disappointed.

There was a firmer tone for the officers, however.

> The Commander in Chief expects at this moment that every officer under his command will exert himself in his situation in carrying on the public service. It is by their zeal and industry that their present labour can be abridged and by their courage they may be crowned with success. Officers commanding working parties will in a particular manner attend to their duty and not allow the men either to be idle or slovenly.[38]

There can be little doubt, however, that the reverse only served to reinforce his opinion that he had been given what another general would later call 'an infamous army'. Fortescue, choosing to place the blame firmly on the government, particularly Pitt and Dundas, later wrote that the troops 'did not consist of soldiers at all. It was composed simply of groups of men in the dress and appointments of famous regiments; and it represented only too truly the state to which the army had been reduced.'[39]

It is, perhaps, an indication of Abercromby's respect for the men he trusted, who were few enough on this campaign, that he was ready to listen to their advice. When he visited the camp where Moore had been conducting matters with considerable energy, the latter had the confidence to point out that 'When it is determined that a post cannot be assaulted, but must be reduced by cannon, a certain time is required; that time, according to circumstances must be greater or less. In a country so mountainous and difficult as this, it must be long.'[40] Moore based this opinion on experience learnt at the taking of Calvi in Corsica. He then 'took the liberty also of telling him, for I saw that nobody about him would, that his presence at this post, which was become the most important one, would infinitely forward the service. It would inspire zeal, and he would be ready to observe and take advantage of events on the instant.' Abercromby's response makes clear that he had another aspect of the campaign to consider, which Moore was unlikely to have made allowance for. 'He assured me it was not from personal convenience that he had now fixed himself here; it had been to be near the Admiral; he should, however, come immediately to this neighbourhood.'[41] This he did, no doubt agreeing with Moore's view that taking Morne Fortuné was the principal objective and other considerations should take second place. Yet it is notable that in a combined service operation Abercromby appreciated the need to maintain close communication with the other service, which was lending both support and manpower.

There was room for optimism, however. The dry, windy weather was holding the rainy season at bay, thus helping to preserve the health of the troops and keep the roads in a passable condition. It was also noticed that enemy fire was becoming less frequent and less effective. The nominal commander Cottin and Goyrand's resources were running low and ammunition needed to be conserved. To add to their difficulties, Castries was torched on the 17th and a large number of women and children fled to the sanctuary they represented. They also seem not to have realized how seriously they were outnumbered, six or seven to one. This was despite Christian's device of landing sailors, then bringing them back to the ships under cover of darkness, before re-landing them the following morning, which was designed to convince them that their opponents had an inexhaustible reserve of manpower.

Two days later, on 19 May, work began on the construction of a second line of batteries in advance of the first on Morne Duchazeau. Moore now used Captain Hay as a messenger to suggest that Knox should join him. Abercromby's immediate response was concern that Moore was fatigued and needed some rest. Moore immediately made clear that he was far from fatigued; instead, he believed that the planned operation, which involved a lodgement to his left, required a man of sense and a good officer to direct the operation. Since Abercromby shared this opinion of Knox, he agreed to Moore's request, no doubt relieved that one of his senior officers could be trusted to make his own judgement on the situation at hand.

With the new guns in position, 23 May was the chosen day

> to make a lodgement as near the enemy works as possible; this, however, was deferred, from necessity until the 24th. The 27th, 53rd, and 57th regiments had previously been placed near the point of attack. On the morning of the 24th, the 27th regiment lodged themselves upon two different points, the nearest of which was not 500 yards from the fort. The enemy made a vigorous effort to dislodge them; but by the good conduct and spirit of Brigadier General Moore, and the steady and intrepid behaviour of the officers and men of the 27th regiment, the enemy was twice repulsed with considerable loss, and before night the troops were completely under cover. At the same time, the communication to the posts, occupied by the 27th regiment, was carried on with the utmost vigour; and two batteries, for eight pieces of artillery, were begun.

At this point Moore joined Abercromby in one of the batteries. As he was making his report they both noticed that a party of men had left the fort and were advancing towards the post that Moore had established. Their purpose was not aggressive. As Abercromby continued in his dispatch to Dundas:

> Upon the evening of the 24th, the enemy desired a suspension of arms until the next day, which was granted until eight in the morning. A capitulation for the whole island ensued; a copy of which I have the honour to enclose. On the 26th the garrison, to the amount of 2000 men, marched out and laid down their arms, and are become prisoners of war. Pidgeon Island is in our possession. The 55th regiment has been detached to Souffriere and Veux Fort,

to receive the submission of the garrisons of those places. From Souffriere we are informed that peaceable possession has been given; from Veux Fort there is no report. The principal object of the blockade of Morne Fortuné has been obtained. The enemy has been prevented from escaping into the woods; their troops, whom they call regulars, have been made prisoners of war; and the armed negroes have been in a considerable degree disarmed. Our operations have been attended with considerable labour and fatigue; roads were everywhere to be made through a mountainous and rugged country, artillery and ammunition to be carried forward; and the line of investment, extending about ten miles, to be supplied with provisions without the assistance of carriages, and with few horses.

Rear Admiral Sir Hugh Christian, and the royal navy, have never ceased to shew the utmost alacrity in forwarding the public service.[42]

The casualty returns for the campaign were attached to the dispatch and were as follows: 4 officers, 1 sergeant and 62 rank and file killed; 33 officers, 14 sergeants, 1 drummer and 329 rank and file wounded; 6 officers, 2 sergeants, 1 drummer and 112 rank and file missing.

When Representant Goyrand surrendered his sword, Abercromby generously responded by praising his opponent's determination and conduct against heavy odds. Moore described him in his journal as 'a plain, honest man, has always been a military man; I suppose he was a sergeant but he rose to be a lieutenant under the old government. He is a man of humanity, did good, and is much liked by the Colony.' This was in contrast to General Cottin, 'a hot-headed, insolent blackguard'.[43]

In his own dispatch to the Lords of the Admiralty Christian wrote:

In the progress of the siege, great difficulties were to be surmounted, and much service of fatigue undertaken. The more effectually to assist the operations of the army, I directed 800 seamen to land, under the command of Captain Lane, of the Astræa, and Captain Ryves, of the Bull-dog. The merit of their services will be better reported by the Commander in Chief of his Majesty's troops; but I feel it an indispensible duty to acquaint their Lordships, that the conduct of the officers and seamen equalled my most sanguine expectations, and that it has been in every instance, highly meritorious . . .

There was praise for several individual captains before Christian continued:

> More exertion has not been evinced; and I believe there never has
> occurred a more cordial co-operation, than has subsisted between
> the army and navy during this siege. Great have been the services
> of fatigue, considering the nature of the country, and the situation
> of the Morne. And very rapidly have they brought to effect the
> reduction of the island. On the morning of the enemy's attack
> on the 24th instant, with a view to repossess themselves of the
> advanced post from the Morne, it became necessary to detach the
> 14th regiment to the support of the troops employed at that post; in
> consequence of which, 320 marines were landed to take the ground
> occupied by the 14th. The conduct of the marines upon this, as
> upon all other occasions, was perfectly correct . . .[44]

The British had retaken Saint Lucia but Abercromby called it a barren
conquest. Its only value was strategic, so there was no compensation for
the 566 men lost. Furthermore, the dense vegetation of the hinterland
was a natural home to the many brigands still at large who would have to
be dealt with. For this reason he needed someone to hold the island and
chose Moore, who had consistently distinguished himself. Moore had no
option but to accept the position, although his journal makes clear that it
was disagreeable to him.

> Sir Ralph, the day before we took possession, sent Brigadier-
> General Knox to me. He told me the Commander-in-chief
> intended to recommend strongly to his Majesty such officers as
> had exerted themselves on the expedition and me in particular; that
> he was much at a loss for a proper officer to leave in command at St.
> Lucia, and would take it as a particular favour if I would remain:
> to this were added some flattering speeches, and that he would
> give me 3000 troops. I had suspected for some days previously that
> this offer would be made to me, and I had mentioned it to General
> Hope, begging that if it was proposed he would prevent it and state
> how disagreeable it would be to me.

His reluctance was based on his dislike of garrison life and his determination
not to be stranded in the West Indies for the rest of his career. 'I stated all these
things to General Knox. He said he was sure Sir Ralph was so eager for my

remaining, that he would be disappointed if I did not. I took for granted that it was in vain to refuse, and therefore accepted.'[45] Moore's distaste for prolonged service in the West Indies is understandable, but there is no doubt Abercromby was choosing one of the few men he could trust with the command. The position of Hope as Adjutant General and Knox as Quartermaster General meant that the third man in the trusted triumvirate was the natural choice. Moore was left with between 4,000 and 5,000 men to deal with a situation where everything military or civil was in the greatest confusion.

St Vincent and Grenada

Abercromby now embarked to undertake the recovery of St Vincent and Grenada, having long since decided that it was too late to start a campaign in Guadeloupe. Before he left Saint Lucia at the beginning of June, however, he informed the government that the foreign troops, with the exception of Löwenstein's, were not to be trusted. He headed first for Carriacou in the Grenada division, where he and Christian decided how to proceed. By 7 June they were at St Vincent, where some relief troops had already arrived. The remainder soon joined them and disembarked at Kingston, having first been treated to a good dinner. They then marched in column to the insurgent stronghold at Vigie Ridge and halted nearby in position for a morning attack. This was to be an encircling movement; a three-pronged attack on the ridge, and two further columns posted to cut off any retreat. Early on 10 June Knox manoeuvred his troops on the seaward side to cut off an enemy retreat northwards, while Lieutenant Colonel Dickens of the 34th created a diversion on the opposite side. Abercromby's dispatch of 21 June makes clear what then happened.

> Two twelve pounders, two six pounders, and two howitzers were advanced with considerable difficulty within six hundred yards of the enemy's works; but not withstanding our efforts to drive the enemy from their post on the Old Vigie, by means of a well served artillery, they maintained themselves from seven in the morning until two in the afternoon. Major General Morshead had very handsomely, early in the day, offered to carry the redoubt by assault; but being willing to spare the lives of the troops, and observing that the part of the line which he commanded, laboured under disadvantages, the assault was deferred until the decline of the day made it absolutely necessary.

From Major General Hunter's division on the right, a part of Lewinstein's [sic] corps, and two companies of the 42d regiment, with some Island Rangers, availed themselves of the profile of the hill, and lodged themselves within a very short distance of the fort. At two o'clock the two remaining companies of the 42d regiment, from Major General Hunter's column, and the Buffs, supported by the York Rangers, from Major General Morshead's, were ordered to advance to the attack. The enemy, unable to withstand their ardour, retired from the first, second, and third redoubts, but rallied round the New Vigie, their principal post. They were now fully in our power, as Brigadier General Knox had cut off their communication with the Charib [Carib] country, and Lieutenant Colonel Dickens, of the 34th regiment, who had previously been ordered to make a diversion with the remains of his own and the 2d West India regiments upon their right, where the Charibs were posted, had succeeded beyond expectation, having forced the Charibs to retire, and taken their post. The enemy, therefore, in the New Vigie, desired to capitulate, which was granted upon the conditions herewith enclosed.

The number of prisoners about 700. At the first of the attack, the Charibs, and, towards the close of it, near 200 of the insurgents of the Island, made their escape into the woods.

Lieutenant Colonel Spence, with 600 men, was immediately detached to Mount Young, and Lieutenant Colonel Gower, with 300 men, embarked to go by sea to Owia; but being unable to land on account of the surf, he has returned; the troops have been disembarked, and he has marched through the Charib country.

I find myself under great obligations to Major General Hunter, and to the gentlemen of the island, for the local information which they gave me, and for the zeal and intelligence which he shewed in conducting the columns. I have to thank Major General Morshead for his exertions; and I am highly satisfied with the behaviour of the officers and soldiers. The corps of Island Rangers, commanded by Lieutenant Colonel Haffey and Major Jackson, rendered essential service. Captain Douglas, of the Royal Engineers, was among the wounded, and is since dead. He is a real loss to the service in this country, as he was indefatigable in the discharge of his duty, and had acquired a minute knowledge of this island.

There is also praise for Captain Woolley, deputed by Christian to command the ships acting with Abercromby's force. 'I can say, with the greatest truth, he has conducted himself with great judgement and good will.'[46]

The black French commander, Marinier, signed honourable, if stringent, terms of surrender on 11 June and the Caribs did the same four days later, although many of them continued to wage what would now be called a guerrilla war. By the end of October resistance had finally collapsed and the survivors were deported to first one and then another undeveloped island. Their numbers were subsequently decimated by disease. Despite the escape of other fugitives, the rebellion was effectively destroyed, at the cost of 17 officers and 168 men killed or wounded. There was also a haul of seventeen guns with their ammunition.

Matters were going equally well on Grenada. Brigadier General Oliver Nicholls' initial attack, involving the island garrison, 2,000 strong, and the 3,000 troops Abercromby had sent him, had failed, mainly due to the impassable state of the roads. On 11 June a contingent from Saint Lucia launched another attack which led to the surrender of the French commander, Captain Jossey, and 180 men. Julien Fédon, the leader of the revolt that had started in March 1795, and a man who thought nothing of killing hostages, withdrew to the interior, taking with him his most determined supporters. They quickly established themselves on Mount Quoca. This was an attempt to play for time but when Abercromby arrived on the 16 June he made clear that Fédon must either surrender and face trial or be hunted to his death. Two days later he witnessed the attack by the 57th, Löwenstein's and the Royal Foreigners on Mount Quoca. Over 100 brigands were killed, and others fled, including Fédon, although he still found time to kill 30 white prisoners. The two foreign units then proceeded to hunt the fugitives down. As on St Vincent, this was the end of the rebellion, and fortuitously only now did the weather break. Those whites who had supported Fédon surrendered or were taken, and eighteen ringleaders were hanged. As for Fédon, he was finally located in a hut by a precipice. Rather than surrender, he leapt over the cliff, presumably to his death, although according to local rumour he may have survived the fall, tried to escape in a canoe and drowned. He certainly never reappeared and his disappearance signalled the end of any possible resurgence by the rebels.

Since Abercromby did not have the resources for an attack on Guadeloupe, and the rainy season, with its attendant sickness, had arrived, this was the end of the campaign. Grenada was securely in British hands and by November St Vincent had been fully pacified. Guadeloupe may have remained in enemy hands and there had been no progress on St Domingue, but the British position in the Caribbean had been stabilized, although at a cost. By the autumn of 1796 half of Abercromby's force had been lost to death or debility. Furthermore, if the rumours of negotiations for a peace treaty proved true, it was probable that all the British conquests would have to be surrendered.

Moore was struggling to achieve anything on St Lucia, where the number of brigands and the effect of yellow fever hampered his activities. A request for more black troops, whom he considered the most able to hunt down the brigands that infested the dense interior of the island, was turned down. He wrote querulously in his journal on 11 July, before the situation in St Vincent and Grenada had been fully stabilized: 'I am extremely dissatisfied with Sir Ralph, whom I believe to be a worthy but weak man. With the reputation of having taken three islands he has not secured one, and the great force he brought to this country has dwindled without securing one possession. If we keep St. Lucia it must be by the greatest accident . . .'[47]

A month later, however, after he had received 300 black troops, and a kind letter, he turned his annoyance onto the officers and men, whom he now blamed for the fatigue and hardship of his situation. As for Abercromby, by the beginning of the following year Moore was writing, 'The kind and friendly manner in which Sir Ralph has uniformly behaved towards me since the attack on Chabot is such, that, unless to General Stuart, I know no person to whom I am so much obliged.'[48]

Christian was now replaced by Admiral Henry Harvey. (Christian's next posting was the Cape of Good Hope station, but he died before he could take it up.) Abercromby, however, had returned to England by the end of the summer, accompanied by the newly-promoted Lieutenant Colonel Picton of the 56th, a promotion that was probably effected through Abercromby's recommendation. He was also now officially the general's ADC. On 3 October 'the West India planters and merchants gave an elegant entertainment at the London Tavern, to Sir Ralph Abercromby and his staff, at which Mr Pitt, Mr Dundas, Marquis de Bouille, etc. etc. were present'.[49]

Trinidad and Puerto Rico

This return to England proved a brief respite for Abercromby. Even while he recovered from the effects of the climate of the West Indies, he received a sequence of contradictory orders, as well as a warning from Dundas that few men or ships would be available to accompany him back to the Caribbean.

He finally sailed on 15 November, again in the *Arethusa*, even though troops and supplies were not ready. One of the reasons for the change of orders was Spain's declaration of war on Britain on 8 October. Having been defeated in the War of the Pyrenees and forced to sign the Treaty of Basel in July 1795, this former ally of Britain was seduced by the French Directory's promise of support should Spain decide upon the conquest of Gibraltar and Portugal. The price was Louisiana. The planters of Tobago and Grenada feared that war with Spain would lead to an attack on them from Trinidad. The island had welcomed French refugees from elsewhere in the Caribbean as long as they were Catholics, and their numbers were subsequently augmented by Republicans fleeing from British aggression in the region. Abercromby was informed that Trinidad was his next objective. Then Dundas decided with Cabinet agreement that Puerto Rico would be an excellent naval base, whereupon it became the prime target. Since St Domingue was now considered lost, the troops there could be added to Abercromby's force. And once Puerto Rico was in British hands, those wishing to leave St Domingue could transfer to the new possession, provided they recognized George III as their sovereign.

From the distant perspective of London, these plans made perfect sense, particularly as the Spanish had sent their fleet to Toulon rather than to the Caribbean; but Dundas had made no allowance for the poor quality of the troops on St Domingue and the lack of information on the strength of the Spanish in Puerto Rico. As for the last part of the plan, the difficulty of transporting 500 people and their possessions against the trade winds had obviously not occurred to him. Fortunately for Abercromby, he was finally relieved of responsibility for St Domingue when General John Graves Simcoe was given the command, a decision taken not by Dundas but by Lord Portland as head of colonial administration.

As always there were practical difficulties, the most pressing being the shortage of troops. With 12,000 white soldiers needed to hold the Windward Islands, Abercromby would have only 9,000 effectives at most. These would comprised the 2nd, 3rd (flank companies), 14th and 53rd, detachments from the 38th and 60th, and three troops from the 20th Light Dragoons. He would also have Löwenstein's, while the only new troops available where the 2nd Regiment of the Irish Brigade, and Hompesch's Light Infantry, Germans of unknown quality. The Irish Brigade was comprised of Irish Catholics serving under Franco-Irish officers. They had won permission in 1794 to serve with the British army after the Brigade's abolition and re-organization as three line regiments by the French National Assembly three years before.

Whatever the quality of these new troops, Abercromby was too familiar with the government's inability to comprehend military practicalities to waste time making a protest. Ever the realist, he concentrated on making the best use of what was available. He was also given 500 infantry and 130 gunners, all recruits, and the promise that once in the Caribbean he would be able to utilize part of the Leeward and Windward garrisons. He was also promised that in March more German troops would be sent to join him, and more black regiments were to be formed by purchasing newly-arrived slaves. In the event, he would finally come to Trinidad with a smaller force, under 4,000, comprising the 14th, 42nd, 53rd, 3/60th, 87th, the two German units, 150 black soldiers from Tobago, and detachments from the 26th Light Dragoons. He also had some artillery and engineers.

By this time Abercromby was well aware of the problems which were peculiar to the West Indies: '. . . you see perhaps one or two days in the Campaign the Troops you command; the moment you begin to act you are obliged to parcel out your little army in small detachments, and the instant the Service is over they go on shipboard to return to their respective garrisons. The real service of a campaign here might be comprised in the operation of a fortnight in Europe.'[50] An even more fundamental problem was getting troops to the West Indies. After a force had been assembled, there still remained the usual problem of finding ships to transport them. In this instance, it was 15 December before all but one of the transports sailed from Portsmouth. They soon ran into strong westerlies which drove most of them back to Portsmouth, although two rode out the gales in Torbay and sailed as soon as the weather permitted. Then news that a French invasion fleet was heading for Ireland delayed the departure of the others. Only when Hoche's ships were known to have been dispersed by storms could the transports continue to the Caribbean.

Abercromby had originally intended to meet Rear Admiral Harvey in Barbados but when he reached the Caribbean he sailed straight for Martinique, where Harvey awaited him. Once again Abercromby immediately established a rapport with the Admiral, similar to that he had enjoyed with Christian. 'It was not the least of Abercromby's attributes as a general that he seems to have been almost unique in this period in being able repeatedly to establish good relations with the touchy senior service.'[51] When the army was dependent upon the navy to carry them to the theatres of war, this was a valuable characteristic. He also discovered, more disturbingly, that the troops in the Leeward and Windward Islands had been decimated by disease. And, of course, there was no news of the transports from England. Equally frustrating was the failure of his attempt to raise a black regiment. He did at least have time to study all the information that was available on Puerto Rico and Trinidad. And he received the good news that Victor Hugues was fast losing influence. As Abercromby told Dundas, 'he is not bold, he is grown rich and avaricious. He is sending his fortune to Santa Cruz and St Bartholomew.'[52]

The first troops, from the Irish Brigade, finally arrived on 30 January 1797 and proved fit only for garrison duty, which did at least release fit men for service in the field. More troops arrived on 6 February, and were soon joined by men Harvey collected from Barbados, St Vincent and Tobago. By 14 February Abercromby was able to muster 3,743 all ranks at Carriacou Island[53] and prepared to set sail, not for Puerto Rico but Trinidad. This was another change of plan. Abercromby had been ready to attack Puerto Rico before Trinidad since it was the tougher target and required fresher troops. Dundas, however, had given way to pressure from merchants and planters in the West Indies who wanted Trinidad in British hands. He had also instructed Abercromby to launch the attack as soon as he arrived in the Caribbean, without waiting for the troops from Britain but using men from the garrisons. If Harvey's information was to be believed, there were only 1,500 Spanish troops on the island, supported by four ships of the line and a frigate, but the weak state of the British garrisons prevented Abercromby from implementing Dundas' instruction.

On 15 February he was once more at sea with a naval contingent of the *Prince of Wales* 98, Harvey's flagship, the 74s *Bellona*, *Invincible* and *Vengeance*, *Scipio* 64, the armed transport *Ulysses*, the frigates and sloops *Arethusa*, *Alarm*, *Favourite*, *Thorn*, *Zebra* and *Victorieuse*, and the bomb vessel *Terror*. It was a formidable invasion force for an island where the garrison was known to be weak, and the detachment of so many ships from their normal duties left Harvey open to criticism, although he earned Abercromby's approval.[54]

The expedition was not sailing blind. Abercromby had with him Lieutenant Colonel Soter, in command of the black troops, who was familiar with the island. Similarly, Harvey's use of a black pilot who knew the Bocas del Dragón, the rocky islands that needed to be navigated in order to approach Puerto d'España, brought them safely into the Gulf of Paria, which they reached on 16 February. By mid-afternoon they were in Chaguaramas Bay, eight miles from Puerto d'España. Here they came upon the four Spanish ships of the line and the frigate lying at anchor, under cover of a fortified islet, Gaspar Grande, These five vessels, the 84-gun *San Vincente*, the 74-gun *Gallardo*, *Arrogante* and *San Damaso*, and the 34-gun

Santa Cecilia, combined with a strong battery on Gaspar Grande Island which covered an advance, threatened any attempt to land. Harvey anchored three of the British vessels, *Alarm*, *Favourite* and *Victorieuse*, almost within gunshot range of the Spanish ships, while the transports carried the troops towards Puerto d'España, escorted by *Arethusa*, *Thorn* and *Zebra*. The flotilla then took up a position about five miles from the town. Preparations were made for the landings with naval cover to take place at daybreak the next day.

At 2 a.m., however, before the plan could be implemented, the Spanish caused an unexpected distraction: '. . . it appeared that the Spanish had set fire to their ships and we were reduced to the necessity of remaining quiet spectators of the conflagration. This lasted till daylight with great fury.'[55] Four of the ships were burnt to the waterline. Only the *San Damaso* was salvaged. The garrison on Gaspar Grande had also abandoned their post. It later transpired that Admiral Sebastiàn Ruiz de Apodaca, in command of the ships, lacked the manpower to take them to sea. The whole island was now vulnerable. On land the governor, José Maria Chacón, although a Royalist, believed Trinidad had been abandoned by Spain. The people were disheartened. They had been suffering from the effects of a British blockade, and disease had been rife. There were also tensions among the inhabitants, Spanish against French, Royalists against Republicans.

With Abercromby and Captain Woolley supervising, the troops disembarked across a muddy shoreline under cover of a naval bombardment that targeted Puerto d'España. It was actually too far out to cause much damage but it succeeded in diverting the attention of the governor and his small force from the real point of attack. The invaders straggled towards the town unmolested. Towards evening Chacon became aware of what was happening and sent out his troops. These collided with Löwenstein's Chasseurs, who drove them back. Unfortunately, some of the British troops had found the stores of new rum and quickly drank themselves senseless while Hompesch's men engaged in an orgy of plundering in which some of the locals also joined. In the midst of this chaos Abercromby sent a sympathetic message to Chacon in which he showed understanding of the governor's difficulties. There was obviously no hope of Spanish relief, so he urged Chacon to surrender on honourable terms in order to avoid more bloodshed. Admiral Harvey was invited to join the negotiations. At the same time, Abercromby restored order to his troops.

The following day the governor signed a capitulation and duly surrendered the island. Trinidad had been taken with the loss of one officer and six men, while the spoils comprised the 600 men of the garrison and 1,600 sailors and marines as prisoners who were to be returned to Spain on parole until exchanges could be arranged. In addition, 100 guns, and one salvaged line-of-battle ship had been taken. Then there was the promise of prize money, which proved considerable. As for the inhabitants, they had the choice of swearing allegiance to the British king or leaving the island.

With Trinidad in British hands, Abercromby decided to leave 1,000 men under the command of Major Picton to hold the island while he moved on to Puerto Rico. He did not believe a longer stay was required and explained to Dundas, in a letter of 28 February:

> Every part of the conduct of the Spanish troops, both by sea and land, seems to indicate a decayed nation, and to point out the possibility of further conquests, if we were in a condition to keep what we might acquire, with a small additional force. It appears necessary to keep possession of Trinidad as an important post should the war continue, for which purpose I shall leave a garrison that will be sufficient for its defence. The inhabitants are a mixture of Spanish, English, and French. I shall endeavour as much as possible to gain them by a mild and equal government.[56]

In order to aid Picton in his new role, Abercromby instructed him to: 'Execute Spanish law according to your conscience. That is all that can be expected of you.' He also told the chief justice, John Nihell, to 'execute all things in due manner that shall belong to those different offices agreeable to the instructions and power which shall by my order be given you by lieutenant-colonel Picton'.[57] When Picton subsequently came under attack for his use of torture, it was claimed by his opponents that he had either hoodwinked Abercromby by disguising his true nature or had been given the governorship because he had powerful friends working on his behalf. It seems unlikely, however, that Picton could have hidden his true nature from Abercromby for over a year. Nor was Abercromby the man to be influenced by powerful interests, had such existed. The common ground shared by Picton and Abercromby was a belief that men were best motivated by firm discipline but also by fostering their sense of *esprit de corps*, and this was probably sufficient to recommend the former as the best candidate for governor.

Having experienced so little resistance in Trinidad, it is probable that Abercromby now contemplated the attack on Puerto Rico as a more viable expedition than he had thought previously. Nevertheless, he still had to return to Martinique to collect reinforcements and supplies coming from England. The first troops had already arrived. They were the 87th and some Germans, Löwenstein's Fusiliers, who had not impressed him when he inspected them on the Isle of Wight, and whom he now opined were little better than the condottieri on the sixteenth and seventeenth centuries

Under orders from Harvey, Captain Woolley had already departed to find pilots and guides. On 8 April Abercromby embarked with 4,100 troops.[58] His route was to take him to Puerto Rico by way of St Kitts, the appointed rendezvous with Woolley. On 17 April the fleet of sixty naval ships and transports was at Congrejos Point eight miles from the main town, San Juan, which was strongly defended. Situated at the head of a small island, it was protected by fortifications which prevented attack from either land or sea. Two redoubts guarded a narrow access channel and gunboats covered all other approaches.

The first obstacle, though, was a reef at Congrejos Point which had to be navigated before the troops could be landed at Congrejos Bay. The pilots Woolley had found proved their worth, however, and the troops prepared to disembark the following day. The Captain-General of Puerto Rico, Don Ramon de Castro, had sent a small force to oppose the invaders. As Abercromby led his troops ashore, he and they came under musket fire. The General threw his sword at the defenders, cheered and led the charge which put the defenders to flight, chased away by the British advance guard. This pursuit brought them to the broken San Antonio bridge. At this point Abercromby, who was with them, took stock of the task ahead. Although the town was already a daunting obstacle, the Captain-General had been busy during the previous twenty-four hours strengthening the defences. The entrance to the harbour was now blocked by pontoons and extra fortifications hampered access to the other bridges which led into the town.

Abercromby realized high cliffs made an attack from the seaward side impossible; the harbour was too strongly defended; and any advance from the east would have to overcome a series of daunting obstacles that would cause dangerous delay. In the face of these difficulties, he invited the Captain-General to surrender, an invitation that was immediately rejected. Not only was de Castro no Chacon, he also appreciated the strength of his own position. Nor was he hampered, as Chacon had been, by a population at war with itself.

It quickly became clear that a regular siege had no hope of success. When Harvey brought his ships inshore to reconnoitre he was immediately driven off by the guns of San Juan. The only tactic that might have worked was an assault on the San Antonio defences. Batteries were set up. In response the Spanish brought up more guns of their own. The British guns were brought into position on the 22nd, the working parties were attacked by a spirited sortie two days later, although the Spanish had not brought the means to spike the British guns. On the 24th the guns finally opened fire, which was immediately matched from the Spanish side. As the day wore on the defenders increasingly outperformed their opponents, although not without suffering losses themselves.

Another line of attack was needed, so on 25 April a detachment was sent to take possession of an abandoned powder mill on an island in the harbour. The plan was to set up a battery there that would target San Juan and the San Antonio defences from a different direction whilst also holding the Spanish gunboats in check. The Spanish made a sortie to disrupt the progress of the battery, but this was quickly driven off. When on the 28th the guns opened fire, however, they proved unable to reach San Juan. The Spanish guns positioned at San Christobal, with the advantage of higher ground, were soon inflicting casualties.

At this point Abercromby accepted that it would be impossible to take San Juan with his present forces. The garrison of San Juan was not only stronger than his own force; it was also receiving reinforcements from the local militia. As for his own troops, they were proving inadequate not just in numbers but also in quality. All the commander's attempts to encourage them had little effect and there was a steady trickle of deserters, mainly from the foreign regiments. Nor could the progress of the season be ignored. The weather would soon deteriorate into the rainfall which heralded the sick season. There was no choice but to raise the siege and depart.

The re-embarkation was conducted with some subterfuge. In order to suggest that another attack on San Juan was imminent and thus to concentrate de Castro's mind on defence, the scaling ladders were brought from the ships at the same time as the sick and wounded were embarked. Even the troops were not informed of the real intention in order to avoid a final spate of desertions. Late on the following day, the 30th, the troops were marched to the beach with unloaded muskets. On 1 May they re-embarked, taking with them eleven Spanish field guns, but at the cost of their own field train, which was abandoned after being made unusable.

His enemy's protracted silence raised de Castro's suspicions and he brought cavalry to the beach, but too late. The last man had safely left Puerto Rico and the Captain-General could only watch as the expedition sailed away. Not that he needed to reproach himself. Unlike Chacon in Trinidad he had shown determination from the start, aided by strong defences and a committed garrison. Abercromby's losses were 31 dead and 70 wounded, with 120 missing, many of them deserters.

In a later, private letter Abercromby explained why failure was inevitable:

> Perhaps the expedition has been undertaken too lightly. We had no sufficient information, and to say the truth, it is not easily obtained. Mariners, smugglers, and merchants, generally know little but their own affairs; it is only from military men, or men of great observation, that proper information can be got. Abbé Raynal passes for a writer of little credit, but in this instance he has been correct. At all events, after the reduction of Trinidad, the Admiral agreed with me, that something further was to be done, and as both he and I had received re-inforcements, and had been instructed to attempt Porto Rico, we determined to try our fortune, trusting a little to the weakness of the enemy. We found them well prepared, with a garrison more numerous than us, and with a powerful artillery. The troops, indeed, were of the worst composition, but behind walls, they could not fail to do their duty.[59]

There is evidence to suggest that Abercromby was never optimistic of success in Puerto Rico. While in Martinique awaiting the arrival of the troops he spent a day with Moore on St Lucia and confided that 'the object of the expedition was Porto Rico in consequence of orders from home; that he himself feared the consequences of taking so great a part of the force so far to leeward; that Porto Rico was a place of considerable strength; and that except General Hope he had not an officer on whom he could place dependence.'[60] Indeed, he had come to St Lucia to warn Moore that Hugues would probably launch an attack on the island once he realized the main force was occupied elsewhere, an attack which, however, never materialized.

Abercromby was not criticised for his failure to take Porto Rico, nor did he repine, but he was anxious to leave the Caribbean. He wrote to Dundas:

> With every wish to do my duty to the public, and to show my gratitude for the favours I have received, I hope that it will not be considered as a deviation from that principle, to ask permission to return to Europe after the campaign. I do not complain of want of health, but I find the complex nature of the civil and military duties of a commander too much for me, and I cannot discharge

both completely to my satisfaction. The control of the Army accounts, and the disagreeable task of keeping within due bounds the different departments, occupy much of my time, and give me much uneasiness. When I have a little leisure I hope to simplify this business, and make matters less a load on my successor.[61]

On 22 May he again confided in Moore, who had joined him on Martinique after a debilitating illness.

I told him that I was recovering daily, and made no doubt but in a fortnight or three weeks I should be perfectly able to serve, if he wished to employ me, anywhere but in St. Lucia. In that case I had no wish to go home; but if he had no employment for me, and the campaign was over, I should be glad to return to Europe . . . He told me that nothing more was to be done; the regiments were gone to their different quarters, and he thought the best thing I could do was go home; that he himself was against further conquests in the West Indies, and had written so to Ministers.[62]

Moore took his advice and returned to Europe. Before Abercromby followed him, he made a final attempt to raise more West Indian regiments. As Dundas had reported to the King in November of the previous year, 'Sir Ralph Abercrombie states in the strongest manner the great advantage which your Majesty's service has derived already from the few black corps which have been employed, and the great saving of British soldiers which may be made should a certain number of blacks be constantly kept in your Majesty's service . . .' The slave-owners, however, still valued profit above protection. They also resented the way the white officers treated the black soldiers, encouraging them to think of themselves as soldiers of the King and superior to other blacks. 'As it is found impossible to enlist them, and as the Islands do not seem disposed to give them, it is necessary that they should be bought.'[63] This would be a radical step but one that was implemented with government approval by Abercromby's successor, the American Loyalist General Cuyler, and men were bought directly (and secretly) from Africa. Dundas took this one stage further and ordered them to be freed. Thus the army took a small step towards realizing the wishes of Wilberforce and the other radicals who were campaigning for an end to slavery.

What had Abercromby achieved? The French had certainly been outfought, while the black rebels, Caribs and Maroons had all been overcome.

StVincent and Grenada had been pacified, St Lucia re-conquered, although still infested with brigands, and Trinidad taken from the Spanish. Although not directly due to Abercromby's presence, the Dutch possessions of Demerara, Berbice and Essequibo were surrendered to British control. The only failure had been at Puerto Rico, while the government had lost interest in St Domingue and Guadeloupe. Indeed, in May 1797 the Commons had proposed that St Domingue should be abandoned, despite Dundas's belief that the struggle should continue because success would so effectively weaken France. (A year later the last British soldiers finally left the island.)

Whether the gains made were worth the effort is open to question. Certainly, the cost in soldiers' lives has horrendous and the cost of the actual expeditions was higher than anticipated. Yet it has been argued that 'Britain's victory over France depended to a very large degree on the army's ability to hold on to British islands in the West Indies and to capture those of France and its allies. It is no exaggeration to state that the hallmark of British strategic policy in the eighteenth century was financial as opposed to manpower.'[64] War in the Caribbean was a potent economic weapon and provided Great Britain with the financial means to prolong the struggle where it mattered, in Europe.

There is evidence that Abercromby recognized the importance of an economic victory, tempered by his strong liberal sentiments. A later memorial he sent to the government makes clear that that he hoped for British intervention that would free the creoles and natives from what he saw as Spanish tyranny. Obviously the result of careful reflection, it is worth reproducing the part that concerns South America since it reveals so much of his thinking, both as a soldier and as a humane liberal.

> . . . of all objects which ought to claim our attention, the liberation of South America from the dominion of Spain seems to stand first. It can only be effected whilst we are at war with Spain, and if it should be happily accomplished, it would be beyond the reach of negotiation at a peace.
>
> It should be undertaken without any view to conquest, to exclusive commerce, or to plunder. Every port in South America, and the whole trade of that extensive continent should be declared free; every country would feel interested in it (Spain and Portugal excepted).
>
> Great Britain, however, from her enterprise, from her capital, and from her industry, would in reality possess nine parts in ten of

this great commerce. A market would be equally opened for British and for East India commodities. In a short time the Brazils (which would follow the fate of the Spanish settlements in South America), and the other countries now under the dominion of Spain, would produce more sugar, cotton, and indigo, than all of our West India islands, and at a cheaper rate. By degrees we should be enabled to drop our sugar islands, which we retain at a great expense, and which are frequently the source of wars.

Should Great Britain decline at this time to undertake this great enterprise, some other nation will attempt it on principles less liberal, and less advantageous to the happiness of South America, and to the world at large.

The present state of that country gives us reason to believe that it would not be difficult to accomplish this object.

The Creole Spaniards and Indians are oppressed beyond measure. No office can be held in that part of the world but by a native of old Spain, and the restrictions upon trade are severe in the extreme. Justice is venal, and extortion commonly practised by all in power. The clergy, who have great influence over an ignorant and superstitious people, are in general natives of New Spain, and consequently would favour a revolution. It seems only necessary that we should remove the Spanish forces; declare to the people what our intention are, and the Spanish government would fall to the ground.

Two expeditions should be fitted out, – one to proceed to the Cape of Good Hope, and from thence to the river Plate; the other should rendezvous at Barbadoes [*sic*], on the Gulf of Paris, and should act on the provinces of Cumans, the Caraccas, and Venezuela.

Monte Video is the principal port and rendezvous for shipping in the river Plate. It is situated on the left bank of that great river; Buenos Ayres, the capital of the country, is situated on the right. One or two line-of-battle ships, and as many frigates, are commonly stationed at Monte Video, and two battalions of Spanish infantry at Buenos Ayres, for the defence of that country. Of the force at Monte Video little is known.

The approach to Buenos Ayres by water, can only be made in vessels of a small draft, on account of the shoals. The climate is good, and the country abounds in provisions. Roads have been opened across the country to Chili [*sic*] and Peru, and European commodities are carried over land into those provinces, which are paid for in specie, and brought from Buenos Ayres to Europe.

The expedition against the Terra Firma should act in the rivers of Orinoco and Guarapichi, and against La Guayra and Porto Cabello; the above-mentioned rivers give an opening into the province of Cumana.

La Guayra is the port of St. Juan de Leon of the Caraccas, it covers the approach to that great capital, and is strongly fortified to the sea. A landing, however, may be effected to the right or left of La Guayra, particularly at the small river Tuy, and if the batteries to the sea can be turned (which they probably may) this fortress would soon fall, and consequently the capital of the province.

Porto Cabello is said to be a place of considerable strength, but probably like La Guayra it is not equally strong on the land side as on the water.

It may admit of a doubt whether in carrying on these operations, which should do more than blockade those fortresses, taking it for granted, that as soon as the revolution had taken effect they would surrender; but it is to be apprehended, that a people who possess so little energy as the Creole Spaniards would not venture to adopt so decided a measure as throwing off the Spanish yoke until they saw their enemies removed, and British garrisons in La Guayra and Porto Cabello.

If a revolution could be set fairly on foot in the principal settlements of the coast, it would spread with rapidity into the interior of the country. Emissaries would be sent to propagate the joyful event, and to assure them that the British troops should not quit the country till relieved from the Spanish yoke, and until a new government of their own should be established. All that would be required on the part of Great Britain in the first instance would be, to furnish them with arms and ammunition, and to assist them in framing a form of Government best suited to the genius and temper of the people.

Much information and many details will be necessary before these undertakings can be set on foot. Captain McDowell of the Ganges (who was an Admiral in the Portuguese service when Portugal endeavoured to establish a colony at St. Sacrement) certainly knows the navigation of the river Plate; and amongst the Spanish prisoners now in England, with a little address, some of them may be found who can give pretty accurate knowledge of the river Plate and of the coasts of Terra Firma, and General Miranda is still in London.

Lieutenant-Colonel Picton, the Commandant of Trinidad, was instructed, in 1797, to procure every possible information relative to the neighbouring provinces of Cumana, the Carracas, and Venezuela, and Colonel Maitland might be directed to go to Trinidad to arrange with Colonel Picton the plan of operations.

The province of Guyana is already nearly in our possession; there remains, however, in the possession of the French the small island of Cayenne, and some inconsiderable plantations on the mainland; it may be necessary to root out the French by removing the garrison, and the French settlers in this island, and by a total destruction of the fort, and adjacent town.

To insure the success of this great enterprise a very considerable force (probably not less than 12,000 men) would be required. Were it to fail, the unfortunate natives would be left to the merciless revenge of their cruel masters, and many of them would end their days on the scaffold, or in the mines.

The difficulty seems to be to find a sufficient disposable force; this, however, may be procured, provided the general principles in which this enterprise is founded shall be approved of.

Nothing has been said of Mexico. Unless the Americans were to co-operate we have not a sufficient force to favour a revolution in that part of the Spanish settlements; the probability however is, that the same spirit would prevail through that great continent.[65]

Chapter 3

Ireland – a Poisoned Chalice

A Most Wretched Country

Whan Abercromby returned to Britain in the summer of 1797, he may well have anticipated a welcome period of repose. In his absence he had been appointed Colonel of the 2nd Dragoons (Royal North British or Scots Greys); and was now governor of Forts St George and Augustus, as well as the Isle of Wight. In 1796, between his two stints in the West Indies, he had succumbed to his son's persuasion and stood once again for Clackmannanshire. He was duly elected, although it is doubtful that he would ever have been an active MP. There seems little doubt that a political life was not for him. Yet his next posting was to take him to the heart of political life, not in Westminster but in Dublin.

To describe Ireland as a wretched country is almost an understatement. There might be seething discontent in other parts of the British Isles but nowhere was it fed by such bitter and long-standing resentments as in Ireland. Catholics against Protestants; the military used as a weapon by the civil powers to repress dissent; political life dominated by a Protestant Ascendancy that represented about 15 per cent of the population; it was more like an occupied country than part of the realm of King George III. And complicating all these issues was the effect of two revolutions, in the American Colonies and France.

The successful outcome of the Colonists' war against the British crown persuaded many Presbyterians in Ulster to advocate republicanism. Then came the French Revolution and a new regime that seemed to provide an ideal model for reform of the British political system. On the other side of the religious divide, many Catholics warmly embraced the ideas of Thomas Paine which seemed to offer a corrective to their legal disabilities. In 1791, the year when *The Rights of Man* was published, Theobald Wolfe Tone, a lawyer based in Belfast, founded the United Irishmen. Presbyterians and freethinkers were attracted by the emphasis on parliamentary reform, but Wolfe Tone wanted to draw in Catholics as well and did so by focusing on Catholic rights. By these means he hoped to thwart what he perceived as the government's policy of divide and rule which kept Catholics and Protestants at odds. The movement grew rapidly and went beyond merely establishing a forum for the exchange of views, although this was subversive enough to cause disquiet. When units of National Guards, inspired by the French model, appeared in Belfast, Dublin and some other towns, the troops were called out to suppress the activities of the new movement.

In an attempt to conciliate, the government was prepared to offer some concessions to Irish Catholics. Ireland was part of Henry Dundas's portfolio at the Home Office. Early in 1792 he suggested extending the franchise (although not the right to sit in the Irish Parliament) and granting the right to carry arms to all Catholics who met the property qualification, and also repealing the laws that still restricted them in areas such as education, jury service and marriage. A Relief Bill was presented to the Irish House of Commons in February 1793. In March it went to the House of Lords, where John Fitzgibbon, Lord Clare, the Lord Chancellor, insisted that the property qualification should be raised from £200 to £300. The debate concluded on 15 March, and the bill received the royal assent on 17 April. These half measures, as so often happens, caused more discontent than satisfaction, but the voices that advocated the removal of all restrictions were overruled by the Protestant cabal that exercised power through the Lord Lieutenant. There already existed a Catholic underground movement, the Defenders. Formed in Armagh in the 1780s as an agrarian secret society, it became more radical in response to the extreme Protestant Peep o' Day Boys, also originally agrarian but now using the penal laws that prevented Catholics from carrying arms as an excuse to raid their homes. What were seen as the false promises of the Catholic Relief Act, as well as the implementation of the Militia Act (see below), encouraged more Catholics to look to the Defenders. To the better educated the movement offered the liberation which a French invasion would bring; to the rural poor it promised land reform and abolition of the tithes they were forced to pay to the Established Church.

The government was aware that both the Defenders and the United Irishmen were communicating with the French. The United Irishmen were officially suppressed in 1794 after the French showed some interest in their promise of support of an invasion. To ban a movement is not to eradicate it, but Wolfe Tone's departure to the United States certainly made it less of an immediate danger. As for the French themselves, seriously planning an invasion of Britain, they were well aware that Ireland was Britain's Achilles' heel.

The idea of an Irish Militia was first mooted in 1792, when war seemed imminent. A crucial point was whether Catholics should be allowed to serve in the proposed balloted force. The Lord Lieutenant, Lord Westmoreland, certainly favoured a Protestant-only Militia, but the Catholic Relief Act made such a view anomalous. If Catholics were required to serve, however, the burden would fall mainly on the poorest, causing hardship to their families. (The Relief Act had benefited wealthier Catholics.) Furthermore, it had not been made clear whether the Militia was for home service only. The Militia Act came into force on 8 April 1793, and riots broke out almost immediately. They soon drew in those with agrarian grievances and others who saw the disturbances in political terms. Violence quickly escalated, leading to about 230 deaths, including some soldiers. This compares with the fifty deaths in the various agrarian disturbances of the previous thirty years.

In the event, the solution proved straightforward: the ballot was dropped; generous provision was made for the families of those who volunteered; and there was a firm undertaking that there should be no overseas service. The consequences, however, were far-reaching. The presence of Catholics in a home-based armed force, combined with the Relief Act which gave some of them political power, was seen as a threat by Protestants, particularly in Ulster. Furthermore, during the worst of the riots the army had been acting on its own initiative rather than at the request of the magistrates, as the law required. This set a dangerous precedent. In the Militia itself, tension was inevitable when the officers and NCOs were predominantly Protestants and the men in the ranks were overwhelmingly Catholics whose motives for volunteering were open to question. It was suspected that many of them had been subverted to radical causes and the Militia would give them military training. This was worrying when the Irish garrison comprised two-thirds Militia troops (21,660 in 1795 out of total force of 32,000 at most).

To sum up, from this time onwards, outbreaks of violence acquired 'a character of savage ferocity, while organized outrage was encountered by a military repression which often exceeded the limits of law, led to horrible abuses, and . . . [demoralized] the forces that were employed in it'.[1] As Thomas Bartlett has argued this was the end of 'moral economy', which he defined as 'mutual obligation and shared responsibility'.[2] The Irish population was fatally at odds.

There was a brief change of mood when Lord Fitzwilliam was appointed Lord Lieutenant. Fitzwilliam, a leading member of the Portland Whigs, was known to be in favour of Catholic emancipation. His appointment was one of the conditions the Duke of Portland made when he agreed to serve with

Pitt in July 1794. Those who understood Ireland's problems hoped that by offering emancipation Fitzwilliam would be able to reconcile Irish Catholics to British rule, while weakening the Protestant Ascendancy. In order to strengthen his position, even before he set out for Ireland Fitzwilliam wrote to William Grattan and the Ponsonbys, vocal supporters of Catholic representation in the Irish Parliament. Their positive response seemed to strengthen his hand.

Fitzwilliam arrived in January 1795, to be confronted by continuing disturbances, exacerbated by the intervention of volunteer units, in existence since the 1780s but now more sectarian in their activities. The new Lord Lieutenant believed only the support of Catholics of rank would solve the problem. He planned a straightforward Emancipation Bill that would remove all restrictions and disqualifications. He had also been forewarned that the two most obdurate members of the Ascendancy were Lord Clare and John Claudius Beresford. He decided to deal with Beresford first, removing him from his office as First Commissioner of Revenue. This was a step too far, however. Beresford was a man of great wealth who exercised power through political patronage, so that many regarded him the de facto leader of the Ascendancy. Although Fitzwilliam had been warned by Pitt not to interfere with Irish administration, he had assumed that the protection of Portland, who as Home Secretary was responsible for Irish affairs, would grant him a free hand. He was mistaken. Pitt intended to allow emancipation only as a gradually process in order not to provoke the Ascendancy. Fitzwilliam was ordered to halt the progress of the bill, and was then recalled, having served only three months.

Lord Auckland, who was a regular correspondent with members of the Ascendancy, reported in a letter to Lord Henry Spencer:

> The conversation of the day much on the sudden break-up of Lord Fitzwilliam's government in Ireland. I have, in confidence, seen much of the whole course of that business. The short fact is, that Lord Fitzwilliam weakly and wildly committed himself to the direction of all the wrong heads in Ireland; and among them there were some who had a particular enmity to the whole system of Mr Pitt's government for the last ten years in Ireland, and to the persons who had faithfully supported that government. In addition to this, they were preparing to give, what they called, an emancipation to the Catholics, to an extent dangerous to the Protestant establishment in both kingdoms.[3]

Fitzwilliam's replacement was John Pratt, Lord Camden, who proceeded to display strong Protestant sympathies on the presumption that such was government policy. This earned him the support of Clare, Beresford and the Under Secretary of State, Edward Cooke. The consequent disappointment among Catholics, whose hopes had been raised by Fitzwilliam, inevitably strengthened the Defenders, particularly in the main towns of the north. At the same time there was a revival of the United Irishmen, now more overtly republican and, therefore, treasonous. Wolfe Tone had travelled from the United States to France, and it was not difficult to work out what he was doing there, particularly as he had established a good relationship with Carnot and the young and talented General Lazare Hoche.

The simmering disturbance was also aggravated by Fitzwilliam's departure. In County Armagh the rivalry between Protestants and Catholics, the former strengthened by the intervention of the volunteer companies, erupted into armed confrontation. Armagh was the centre of the linen trade, formerly Protestant dominated. Trouble was inevitable when Catholics encroached on what the Protestants regarded as their right to a monopoly. At Loughgall on 21 September 1795 Peep o' Day Boys and Defenders fought a pitched battle. It was noted at the time that the Protestants seemed to have been armed by local landowners and also carried volunteer weapons, which enabled them to kill about thirty of the Catholics and put the rest to flight. The Peep o' Day Boys now became subsumed into the Orange Order (known as the Orange Boys since 1793) and embarked on further outrages in Armagh. During the winter of 1795–6 they drove out 700 Catholic families, many of them into the arms of the Defenders.

The violence spread and the government reacted with harsh punishment. This included pressing offenders into the Navy without trial, a policy that backfired when the mutinies at Spithead and the Nore in April and May 1797 showed evidence of prominent Irish involvement. A more sensible policy decision was a plan to establish a properly constituted Yeomanry Force to preserve peace and enforce the law. In theory, this would release the regular army and the militia for their proper purpose, the defence of Ireland.

In 1796 the Insurrection Act was passed to deal with an upsurge of raiding parties by the resurgent United Irishmen as they searched for weapons. Their members were also receiving rudimentary military training and committing acts of murder. The act gave magistrates the power to proclaim a county as disturbed, whereupon they could impose a curfew, suspend trial by jury and exercise unprecedented powers of search and arrest. This was martial law in all but name, and inevitably exacerbated a dangerous situation. In defence of the government it can be argued that there was crime, even anarchy, in some areas. The probability of a French invasion meant that disarmament was vital; and the army was the only means to achieve it. Thus 'the Insurrection Act was an extreme remedy for a desperate disease, limited to a brief period and to the proclaimed districts'.[4]

On the other hand, the Irish legislature was controlled by members sitting for nominated boroughs, placemen who were the tools of the Protestant Ascendancy. That a small minority could possess such political power was at odds with the new world of the French Revolution and the *Rights of Man*. Instead of granting even moderate reform, which might have won over the United Irishmen, they opted for intransigence, particularly on the Catholic question. And by excluding from parliament the Catholic gentry, they had alienated the very men who might have exercised control of the Catholic majority.

The implementation of the Insurrection Act inevitably provoked discontent and further disorder. The magistrates' reliance on the support of the army undermined discipline in the ranks, while various Acts of Indemnity protected both magistrates and the military from the consequences of any unlawful activity. To make matters worse, it was suspected, with some justification, that the authorities were quick to punish the outrages committed by the Defenders but loath to pursue Orangemen. While the army was losing discipline, the Militia, the other military prop, was considered suspect. It was feared that the Defenders had infiltrated the ranks, while the officers were often neglectful of their duties. Indeed, John Moore later wrote in his journal: 'The officers of the Militia are in general Protestants, the men Roman Catholics. The hatred between these different persuasions is inveterate to a degree and the officers have so little sense or prudence as not to conceal their prejudices. The plots which have hitherto been discovered among the troops have been confined to the Roman Catholics.'[5]

Camden was initially opposed to the establishment of an Irish Yeomanry but popular disturbance, disaffection in the Militia and rumours of an imminent French invasion persuaded him to change his mind. Permission was reluctantly granted from London. On 19 September 1796 an announcement was issued from Dublin Castle and the first commissions were granted in October. This part-time volunteer unit could be made permanent in emergencies, and was open to both Catholics and Protestants. Certainly, some Catholics were to be found in the ranks but the majority, particularly the cavalry, were Protestant, including many Orangemen from the north.

A crisis came in December when a French fleet of seventeen ships of the line, thirteen frigates, six corvettes and seven transports, commanded by Vice Admiral Morard de Galles, sailed from Brest. Because Vice-Admiral John Colpoys, who was off the coast of Brest, believed that the fleet was heading for Portugal, he saw no danger and returned to Portsmouth for water. Thus the Brest fleet avoided the British blockade and sailed for Ireland. The plan was to land 15,000 men under General Lazare Hoche at Bantry Bay. With the United Irishmen and the Defenders united in a common cause and ready to welcome the French, such a landing, if successful, would have endangered the rest of Britain.

The Government was saved by the elements when storms dispersed the French fleet; yet the politicians chose not to register the well-reported fact that the poorer classes of the south and east had shown no sign of welcoming the enemy. The Lord Lieutenant did report to Portland that the peasants of Cork and Limerick anticipated the soldiers' wants by preparing potatoes for them on the road and clearing snow away but the inhabitants do not seem to have been given due credit for this in London.[6] Even when the Irish Parliament petitioned Westminster to reward the people's loyalty with further concessions, the motion was defeated in the Commons. Consequently, it is difficult to avoid the conclusion that the government was to a large degree responsible for what ensued. Indeed, after the events of 1798 it was strongly suspected that the government had been deliberately provoking unrest in order to justify an Act of Union.

The Commander of the Forces at this stage was General Lord Carhampton, appointed in 1796. A contemporary wrote of him that despite his limited military experience 'he was a man of the world, of courage, and decision, ardent, obstinate; – he determined, right or wrong, to annihilate the conspiracy. Without the consent of the Irish Government, he commanded the troops that, on all symptoms of insurrectionary movements, they should act without waiting for the presence of any civil law.'[7] He also continued the illegal policy of sending men to the fleet. In the autumn of 1797 he moved the garrison from Dublin without the consent of the Lord Lieutenant, posting them to the north and south of the city because he believed they had been infiltrated by rebels. His orders were promptly overruled and in November he was made Irish Master General of the Ordnance, in effect an enforced resignation.

General Lake now assumed temporary command of the forces. He had already been disarming the population in Ulster, specifically the Defenders and the United Irishmen. He resorted to terror tactics, flogging men and burning property, thus dragooning Ulster under the terms of the Insurrection Act. With the Lord Lieutenant's consent and the collusion of the civil powers he had effectively suspended both law and constitution. Further repressive measures were introduced, including a ban on all large assemblies, while members of the United Irishmen were hunted down and arrested. The brutality was explained by Sir Richard Musgrave in his *Memoirs*:

> To disarm the disaffected was impossible, because their arms were concealed; and to discover all the traitors was equally so, because they were bound by oaths of secrecy, and the strongest sanction of their religion, not to impeach their fellow-traitors.
>
> But suppose the fullest information could be obtained of the guilt of every individual, it would have been impracticable to arrest and commit the multitude. Some men of discernment and fortitude perceived that some new expedient must be adopted to prevent the subversion of government and the destruction of society, and whipping was resorted to. As to the violence of the forms of the law by this practice, it should be recollected that the law of nature, which suggested the necessity of it, supersedes all positive institutions, and as its ends will be baffled by the slowness of deliberation.[8]

Henry Grattan, born into the Protestant Ascendancy but keenly aware of the dangers of Catholic disaffection, published an *Address to his Fellow Citizens* in 1797. He included a list of all the abuses of power which had so demoralized him that he had resigned his seat in the Irish Parliament:

> . . . the convention bill – the gunpowder bill – the indemnity bill – the insurrection bill – the suspension of habeas corpus – General Lake's proclamation by order of Government – the approbation afforded to that proclamation – the subsequent proclamation of Government, more military and decisive – the order to the military to act without waiting for the civil power – the imprisonment of the middle orders without law – the detaining them in prison without bringing them to trial – the transporting them without law – burning their houses; burning their villages – murdering them; crimes, many of which are public, and many committed which are concealed by the suppression of a free press, by military force – the preventing the legal meetings of counties to petition his Majesty,

by orders acknowledged to be given to the military to disperse them; subverting the subjects' right to petition – and finally, the introduction of practices not only unknown to Law, but unknown to civilized and Christian countries . . .

His parting shot was a plea to those who held power: 'Combat Revolution by Reform – let blood be your last experiment.'[9] Unfortunately, the Ascendancy, with the tacit support of London, believed that repression was their most effective weapon.

The relief occasioned by the failure of the first French invasion was short-lived. By the spring of 1797 there more rumours, this time that both the Dutch and the French were preparing for invasion. In July Wolfe Tone was known to be at Texel, ready to sail with the Dutch fleet, a force of twenty-five ships of the line and frigates, supported by transports to carry over 14,000 soldiers to Ireland. The Dutch were to sail to Brest, where they would join the French for a joint invasion. (There was another fleet assembling at Toulon which was mistakenly presumed to have the same objective.) Again, circumstances saved the government when storms prevented the Dutch from leaving harbour. Admiral Duncan, most of whose ships had joined the Nore mutiny, then deceived the Dutch by keeping his two remaining ships off Texel and making signals to a non-existent fleet. The Dutch stayed in harbour, while Hoche's mortal illness threw French plans into disarray. The final blows came with the Dutch defeat at Camperdown on 11 September 1797 and Hoche's death eight days later.

Too Little, Too Late . . .

The government had been searching for another Commander of the Forces since Lord Carhampton's resignation. Lord Cornwallis, the first choice, refused because he was opposed to government policy in Ireland. Lord Moira, another possibility, was even more strongly opposed. It was fortuitous, therefore, that Abercromby had recently returned from the West Indies. Camden was eager for his appointment because here was a man whose reputation suggested that he could both exercise control over the army and defeat a French invasion. Furthermore, Abercromby, from his years in Ireland, recognized the difficulties he would face as commander of the forces which were compounded by the Lord Lieutenant's role as nominal head of the army. This meant that any decision taken by the commander, even the most trivial, had to be ratified by the Lord Lieutenant. It was an invitation to political intrigue; those with their own agenda, which was likely to be at odds with the commander's, could play one authority against the other.

Why did Abercromby accept such an invidious responsibility rather than remaining quietly in Scotland? It would seem that he was again motivated by the strong sense of duty that governed so much of his military life. It is unlikely that he was deceived by Camden's promise that he should have a free hand over everything except patronage. Although a man of liberal sympathies with no time for party, he appreciated the realities of political life and recognized that the situation in Ireland fostered self-serving machinations of power. That he believed he could work against such men might well be considered naïve. Leckie described Abercromby as 'a man of very independent and honourable character, and of liberal opinions, and he had the reputation of a commander who was not only skilful in the field, but also eminently successful in maintaining a high standard of discipline among his soldiers.' Like Lord Fitzwilliam before him, 'Such an officer was peculiarly wanted in Ireland, but such an officer was unlikely to find his task a smooth one.'[10] At the very least, he was likely to experience problems with one of his subordinates. Abercromby and Lake were reported to be on bad terms; and Lake's methods would certainly not receive Abercromby's approval.

From his own experience as a junior officer in Ireland, and later as colonel of the King's Irish Infantry, he knew that the gentry were the root cause of the country's problems. He believed them ignorant, neglectful of their duties and only interested in their own pleasures, while at the same time they oppressed their tenants unmercifully. 'Still more shocking to his Scottish soul, their chief interests were "the pursuit of pleasure or political intrigue". Now, when their country most needed magistrates of integrity and courage, they were deserting their posts, or crying to the army to rescue them from the peasantry they had goaded to rebellion.'[11] Since the Irish government represented the interests of the gentry, Abercromby anticipated conflict between his own principles and the government's actions. As for the people, they were what the government chose to make them. They were warm and generous when treated with kindness, intransigent when used harshly, and fully trustworthy soldiers when well commanded.

Abercromby had his own solution to the Irish problem, which he communicated to Pitt via Dundas even before he had accepted the position of commander. The Lord Lieutenant and the Commander of the Forces should be one and the same person, under whom he would willingly serve. He considered Lord Cornwallis the best man for the combined position.

He also warned Pitt that he would resign if the measures he advocated did not receive the support of the government. He recognized that his most pressing task, to restore discipline to the army, would prove contentious. The necessary measures would not receive the approbation of the gentry, or the support of the magistrates, who viewed the army as a vital prop to their authority. Yet he had to resolve the contradiction between the protection of Ireland, which required the concentration of troops, and the desire of gentry and magistrates to disperse them in order to maintain their authority.

Abercromby had requested that John Moore should accompany him to Ireland with the temporary rank of brigadier. Moore recorded that he

> attended Sir Ralph to the levee on the 15th November, and kissed hands. On the 24th we left London, arrived at Holyhead on the 28th, sailed the morning of the 1st December, and landed in Dublin the 2nd, after a most boisterous, disagreeable passage. An aide-de-camp from the Lord Lieutenant was ready to receive Sir Ralph, with a message that apartments were prepared for him and his suite at the Castle, where the Lord Lieutenant hoped he would remain till such time as the Commander-in-Chief's house was vacated by Lord Carhampton. Sir Ralph did not feel himself at liberty to refuse this offer. [Moore declined a similar offer.] The day after our arrival we dined with Mr Pelham, the secretary, and the day following with the Lord-Lieutenant at the Park, where I was introduced to him by Sir Ralph. The company was all military – the different Generals and staff.[12]

This was a warm-enough welcome to convince Abercromby that his appointment was welcomed, at least by Lord Camden, but not sufficient to ease his concerns. He soon realized that Lord Carhampton's laxness and the Lord Lieutenant's assumption of the commander's powers had created a situation inimitable to useful military activity. No Commander of the Forces could function effectively when the generals under his command addressed all communications to the Lord Lieutenant rather than to him. He requested Lord Camden to honour his undertaking that the new commander was free to make his own decisions. If he chose not stand by this promise, then Abercromby would feel at liberty to resign. Camden characteristically vacillated. He could not publically give Abercromby complete control, but he would nevertheless enjoy that control. Camden then confided to Pelham that he was finding the new commander-in-chief difficult to get on with because his manner was so peremptory.

Abercromby summed up the state of the army in a letter to a friend, written soon after his arrival. 'I found an army of upwards of 40,000 without any arrangement made for subsistence . . . No artillery was in a position to move. Even the guns attached to the regiments were not provided with horses. No magazines were found for the regiments. Little or no order or discipline.' He was equally damning of the cavalry, which was 'in general unfit for service'. As for the infantry officers, they were 'very little able to command their men'.[13] To Moore he further confided that 'every application, even of the most trifling kind' had to be made to and be directed by the Lord Lieutenant. 'In quiet times a Commander-in-Chief has been little attended to, and the army has been considered little more than an instrument of corruption in the hands of the lord-lieutenant and his secretary. So much has this been the custom that even now, when the country is undoubtedly in a very alarming state, both from internal disaffection and the fear of invasion, it requires, I believe, all Sir Ralph's temper and moderation to carry on the necessary business, and to obtain the weight that his situation and the times require.'[14]

Abercromby was particularly concerned by the dispersal of troops and sent an urgent order to General Lake to concentrate his forces in order to restore discipline.[15] They needed to be in garrison where they could be quickly mobilized against the French rather than distributed in small bodies to suit the requirements of the gentry. They could also be more easily sent to deal with unrest when in garrison, although this should happen only in support of the civil powers. Unfortunately, the civil powers' dependence upon the military had fostered the unbridled licentiousness which the army was prone to when not under strict control.

As Moore observed from the southern district: 'The mode which has been followed to quiet the disturbances in this country has been to proclaim the districts in which the people appeared to be most violent, and to let loose the military, who were encouraged in acts of great violence against all who were supposed to be disaffected. Individuals have been taken up upon suspicion, and without any trial sent out of the country.' These, of course, were the methods instituted by Carhampton and applied by Lake. Abercromby would definitely have agreed with Moore's further comments. 'By these means the disturbances have been quelled, an apparent calm produced, but the disaffection has been undoubtedly increased. The gentlemen in general, however, still call out aloud for violent measures as the most proper to be adopted, and a complete line seems to be drawn between the upper and lower orders.'[16]

Abercromby had already sent a circular, reminding his generals of the need for strict discipline, training, and the exercise of proper conduct. After a preamble which stressed that they should be prepared for all emergencies and ready to bring their troops into the field without notice, he continued:

> In this country it too frequently happens that the troops are called upon in aid of the civil magistrates, to support the peace of the country. Although on all occasions they ought to behave with firmness, yet they must not forget that they are only called upon to support the laws of the land, and not to step beyond the bounds of them. Any outrage or excess, therefore, on their part is highly culpable, and they are strictly enjoined to observe the greatest moderation and the strictest discipline when they are called upon to execute this part of their duty. Even in time of actual war, amongst all civilized nations, it is considered as disgraceful and subversive of all discipline if soldiers are allowed to be licentious.

He also encouraged the generals

> to have a confidential correspondence with the heads of the Yeomanry corps in their different districts, in whom the internal tranquillity of the country must in a great measure depend. The general officers will give these gentlemen such advice, instructions, and support as the local situation of the country may require, to enable them to preserve tranquillity, and to prevent insurrection, or the excesses of the banditti which may show themselves in any part of the country, and which must happen, unless they will exert with vigour and energy the means they have in their power to prevent it.[17]

Of equal concern were the reactionary attitudes of the landowning classes, as instanced by Musgrave. These people, strongly represented in the government of Ireland, expected the army to support their own interests. Their opposition to a Commander of the Forces who wished to use the army for its proper purposes would bedevil Abercromby throughout his tenure.

At this point, Abercromby's estimation of the situation was conveyed in a frank letter to Mr William Elliot, a military Under Secretary of State.

> . . . When I was to take command of the Army in Ireland, I then stated the objections which the nature of the government of this

country suggested to my mind, and I then felt the delicacy of my situation. I was then assured by those with whom I communicated, that I should labour under no difficulty or restraint in my command, and from the conversation I had with those well acquainted with the government of Ireland, I had reason to expect that in time of war the Army would be totally under my command, the patronage of it excepted; and I was taught to believe that my recommendation of deserving officers would be sufficient to entitle them to promotion. From the experience I have had since my arrival in this country, and from looking forward to future consequences, I find it indispensible for the good of the King's service, and to prevent any further embarrassment, that there should be a free and explicit explanation on this subject. A divided command in the direction of an Army is perfectly incompatible with those principles by which military affairs are guided. It is, therefore, necessary that the Lord-Lieutenant should take the sole command; or that he should delegate it to the Commander-in-Chief appointed by His Majesty. I can see no other alternative . . . With the highest respect for the situation and character of the Lord-Lieutenant, I request a clear decision on this point. I came here with no motive of emolument, and I may say of ambition, except that of being useful as far as my abilities went; and it is my earnest wish not to quit a station in which I have been placed. I trust to receive through you such an explanation as will settle this point.[18]

No explanation was forthcoming. Consequently, Abercromby never managed to square the circle of divided command, nor whether the army should be primarily concerned in defending the country against enemy attack or in supporting the interests of the ruling class by suppressing the disorder caused by their refusal to recognize the grievances and animosities that were at its root.

One man who fully supported Abercromby was the Commander-in-Chief. York now asked him for regular reports on the state of the army and his own actions. In the first of these, dated 28 December, he reported disturbances in the south, caused by the burden of tithes and oppressive rents, and the concomitant failure of the magistrates and gentry to do their duty. He stressed the variable quality of the regular and Militia troops, and the country's dangerous vulnerability to invasion. He also made frank reference to the difficulties of divided control. 'With an army composed of so various description of troops, and in a country so unprepared for war, it requires all the authority that the Lord Lieutenant can give me, to enable me to carry on the King's service. I have no reason to say that Lord Camden has refused me his support, but the difficulties and delays I experience will render my situation irksome and my labour unavailing.'[19]

After a month in Dublin Abercromby set out to tour the south, the most likely area for another attempted invasion, which made critical the state of the fortifications and posting of the troops. What he discovered was far from reassuring. The defences were in poor state of repair. He had identified Bantry Bay or possibly the Shannon estuary as the most likely landing point; he now reckoned that it would take a week to assemble a force to confront the invaders, and even then it would be only 15,000 or 16,000 men strong. On 23 January he wrote to Camden that the country was tranquil but 'it would now be desirable if the troops could, without alarming the gentlemen, be collected, and their discipline restored, which suffers exceedingly from their dispersed state. I am morally certain that many of the regiments could not, at present, take the field from their various wants, which cannot be known or supplied till more brought together. The yeomanry appear to advantage; they are well clothed and mounted, and expressed great willingness and zeal.' In case the implication that the Yeomanry could be trusted with maintaining peace was missed, he added, 'I am, however, nearly convinced that to bring them together, and to appoint officers to command them, must not be attempted. They must be left at home, and appointed for the defence of the interior.'[20]

Abercromby was more forthright in a letter to Pelham. As he later discovered, the Honourable Thomas Pelham was a man who shared many of his opinions on the situation in Ireland, a man described by a contemporary as although 'Without great talents, he had good sense, good manners, a frank address, with humane, honourable, and just intentions.'[21] To this potential ally he wrote: 'The dispersed state of the troops is really ruinous to the service. The best regiments in Europe could not stand such usage.' He needed to know how many regiments were needed to support the Yeomanry to deal with internal dissention. These he would willingly release, 'provided the remainder were to be kept together, and in a situation to move if a foreign enemy should appear'.[22]

To make the point even more specifically, he reported to York in a private letter of 17 February that

> The upper classes of men have fallen, in general, into a state of despondency, and seem to have given up the cause. To rouse them,

and to call forth their exertions, ought to be the great object of the government. On this principle, I have endeavoured as far as possible, to resist the interference of the troops in all matters where the civil magistrate ought alone to have interfered. I clearly saw that the discipline of the troops would be completely ruined, and that they would be led into a thousand irregularities contrary to the law, which would bring disgrace upon them, and in which they ought not to be supported by the government of the country. I flatter myself that the effect of this will be to force the gentlemen to exert themselves, and to trust to the yeomanry, on whom they must ultimately rely for the internal security in case the troops should be called to act against a foreign enemy. On no occasion, however, which has been really urgent, have I objected to the troops being employed, guarding them at the same time against any excess in the execution of their duty.[23]

He had certainly clarified the problem and stressed the need for well-disciplined troops, stationed in sufficient numbers to repel an invading enemy. He chose not to labour the suffering of the common people, as might have been expected, because he was dealing with men, particularly in Dublin, who were well aware of the licence permitted to the troops by commanders like Lake. After all, Camden had agreed to the imposition of military rule in all but name in the north. If Abercromby could bring about the concentration of the troops under officers who performed their duty, the irregularities, both military and legal, would ease, because magistrates would have to act within the law.

By this time it was clear to Abercromby that Camden was the main obstacle. Privately, he was an amiable man: in his public position he was at best weak-willed and at worse double-dealing. As Abercromby made his opinions clear he won the ready support of those who could appreciate the danger, internal and external, that Ireland faced. Too many men in public life favoured the status quo, however, and these were the men who had the ear of the Lord Lieutenant. This was not just a matter of saying to Camden what he wanted to hear. They also seem to have taken every opportunity to criticise and misrepresent the commander-in-chief's intentions. Abercromby might convince Camden of the justice of his views when they met face-to-face, but Camden would be swayed in the opposite direction when, as he put it, 'I must go to *my* friends and hear very different opinions.'

So that the senior officers knew what was expected of them, Abercromby was quick to commend the behaviour of a general who appreciated that the army should support, not replace, the civil powers. When General Johnstone behaved appropriately in the case of a double murder, Abercromby wrote appreciatively:

> Your exertions in assisting the civil magistrates in apprehending the perpetrators of a horrid murder are highly commendable, and promise to be the means of eventually bringing them to justice. I have always wished that the law should be supported by the troops when called on properly, but I have as strongly wished that they should not take any part that was not strictly legal, because when we once depart from that rule we subject ourselves to much inconvenience. I hope the magistrates have not put their intention of burning houses in force. I hope the soldiers have taken no part in it.[24]

This contrasted with a case in Kildare. In order to discover the murderers of a Fencible sergeant, the magistrates simply let the troops loose on the population. The result was the mayhem that Abercromby so much deplored. As he wrote to Pelham,

> It is much to be regretted that the civil magistrate has not hitherto discovered the murderer of the serjeant, and I still more lament that no evidence has been brought forward sufficient to convict the authors of the notorious acts of violence which have been, in some measure, the consequence of the murder. It is to be hoped, Sir, that the magistrates of the county of Kildare will be instructed to prosecute still farther the investigation of this business. Although they may not discover the murderer of the serjeant, they cannot fail to discover the soldiers who first set fire to the houses, and committed several acts of violence at noonday, and in face of all the inhabitants of Newbridge. The soldiers are all at Kildare, and every assistance shall be afforded in the further prosecution of the inquiry. The future discipline of the Army may depend on the conduct observed in this affair.[25]

For Abercromby, soldiers should never be above the law, nor should there be a supposition of guilt without inquiry and evidence. This attitude made him powerful enemies. For soldiers like Lake, house-burning was an acceptable instrument of repression. For Ascendancy politicians like Lord Clare and the Speaker, John Foster, the army had the right to inflict rigorous but righteous punishment. They may even have been eager for the rebellion such rigour might well provoke so that the dissidents could be crushed once and for all. On 26 February 1798 Abercromby published a general order that brought the situation to crisis point.

> The very disgraceful frequency of courts-martial, and the many complaints of irregularities in the conduct of the troops of this kingdom, having too unfortunately proved the Army to be in a state of licentiousness which must render it formidable to everyone but the enemy, the Commander-in-Chief thinks it necessary to demand from all Generals commanding districts and brigades, as well as commanding officers of regiments, that they exert for themselves, and compel from all officers under their command, the strictest and most unremitting attention to discipline, good order, and conduct of their men, such as may restore the high and distinguished reputation which the British troops have been accustomed to enjoy in every part of the world. It becomes necessary to recur, and most pointedly to attend to the standing orders of the Kingdom, which, at the same time that they direct military assistance to be given at the requisition of the civil magistrates, positively forbid the troops to act (but in case of attack) without his presence and authority, and the most clear and positive orders are to be given to the officers commanding the party for this purpose.[26]

Although this order might not seem controversial, since it merely drew attention to the standing orders, it contradicted a proclamation issued by Camden on 18 May 1797. This permitted the army to act without first receiving authorization from a magistrate, a decision which had caused concern in London. Furthermore, Abercromby's timing was unfortunate. Only six days previously Lord Moira, speaking in the Irish House of Lords, had accused the army of using illegal means of repression. Some suspected collusion between Moira and Abercromby over an issue that concerned both of them.

   Shortly before Abercromby issued the general order, Camden had written to Portland acknowledging Abercromby's careful consideration of the danger of external attack and the need for internal security. He agreed with

Abercromby that the troops should be concentrated, that the responsibility for internal security should rest with gentry, who should use their powers appropriately, and with the Yeomanry. So perfect was his agreement with the commander's views that he had already communicated with several gentlemen who shared those views. He continued: 'I propose very speedily to make some arrangements which will disengage the army from part of the duty that is now imposed on them in various parts of the kingdom.' As for Abercromby, he was a man in whom 'the greatest military experience is combined with remarkably good sense and knowledge of the world.'[27] Yet here was an order that directly challenged his authority. Camden initially decided that the best response was no response, in the hope that the matter would blow over. Pelham went as far as to defend Abercromby in the Irish House of Commons, arguing that the order was justified by the dangerous lack of discipline and the poor quality of officers in the Militia.

The Ascendancy saw the order as a direct provocation and took matters into their own hands. Clare and Foster arranged dinners for politicians who shared their views and were prepared to join them in getting rid of Abercromby by any means, even including impeachment. Clare revealed his feelings in a letter to Lord Auckland, written on 23 March.

> I feel the peevish indiscretion of Sir Ralph Abercromby's order as strongly as you feel it, and it is provoking that the critical situation in which we stand, made it ineligible to resent his intemperance as it merited. The order was issued without communication or notice of any kind to Lord Camden, on the day before he set out from hence on a tour to inspect the army in the Northern province. He disclaims all intentions of counteracting the proclamation issued last year under the authority of both Houses of Parliament, and professes his readiness to act under it. But he states in his defence that he found a general relaxation of discipline in the army, and that his only object was to restore it.
>
> If Lord Moira had not retracted his charges against the Irish army in the most explicit terms, both in public and private, this Scotch beast certainly would have given him strong ground to stand upon.[28]

Clare and Foster had already made sure the order was known in London and it was there, rather than in Dublin, that the first rumblings of the storm of protest were heard. Portland wrote urgently to Camden to discover whether the order could be a forgery, since it clearly played into the hands of the disaffected and also seemed to justify Moira's admonitions. He claimed that his Irish acquaintances felt they were being abandoned and would have no choice but to rebel.[29] The suspicion that Moira and Abercromby were conniving to undermine the Lord Lieutenant and, through him, the ministry in London, gained quickly credence. Yet if this were true, Abercromby must have undergone a complete change of character and abandoned his long-held principles, as those supported him (including York) clearly recognized. Abercromby rarely sought to defend himself in public, and this occasion was no exception. But later he wrote a long letter to his son which clarified his reasons for issuing the order.

> You know the reluctance I had in accepting the command of this country; it was in obedience to the King's pleasure; and having accepted it, neither inconvenience nor serious difficulties would have induced me to quit it at this time. Since my arrival I have been under the necessity of supporting myself by great exertions and strong representations, otherwise I should have been a mere cipher, or what is worse, a tool in the hands of a party who govern this country. Their dislike to me has of course been visible, and in my absence they took the opportunity of attempting to crush me.

He explained this as a deliberate plan to undermine him by bringing the matter before the Irish Parliament and writing letters to Portland and other men of importance in the government.

> This mode of proceeding was so precipitate and so hostile, that there can be no doubt of their intentions to ruin me. After this there can be no mutual confidence. In times so difficult, it is next to impossible to separate the civil and military business of the country, and with all the wisdom, all the vigour that can be shown, it is impossible for any General to answer for success. Should, therefore, any one thing go wrong, I could expect nothing but the fullest effects of their resentment . . .
>
> The abuses of all kinds I found here can scarcely be believed or enumerated. I tried various means with little success; it was necessary to speak out; the order is strong, but be assured it was necessary. The way in which the troops have been employed would ruin the best in Europe. Here are 35,000 Yeomanry, raised for the

express purpose of protecting the country. To them I have urged the necessity of applying for assistance, but in vain. I therefore restricted the troops to the standing orders of the kingdom, that their discipline might be pursued if possible, and that the gentlemen might be obliged to trust to the Yeomanry, on whom they must ultimately depend, in case the troops should be called away to oppose a foreign enemy.[30]

The order had brought the issue of who controlled the regular army and the militia into sharp focus. Was it the commander-in-chief or the Lord Lieutenant, who had been abrogating military powers for some time? Without resolution, no commander-in-chief would be able to function effectively in Ireland. Yet the question itself had an obvious answer. If a country was under threat of imminent foreign attack, then the primacy of the commander should have been recognized as not only desirable but inevitable.

When Abercromby returned from the north, where the situation he had encountered in the south was replicated even more disturbingly, he realized just how effectively his enemies were manoeuvring against him, particularly by associating him with the anti-government stance of Lord Moira. As he explained to Colonel Brownrigg, York's military secretary, 'Lord Moira is little known to me, and his politics have certainly never allured me, and the profession of a politician I have never followed. Independence has always been too powerful an attraction to allow me to engage with any set of men. I came here determined not to regard trifling inconveniences, and to struggle with more serious difficulties, but if I am to have a powerful host to contend with, I do not see how I am to keep my ground.'[31]

Abercromby was summoned to the castle. He came prepared, bringing a letter that he now read to Camden. 'Understanding from your Excellency's communication yesterday that the orders issued on the 26th February last had been construed as a political manoeuvre, permit me to lay before your Excellency, with candour and truth, what has passed in my mind and influenced my conduct since I took command of his Majesty's troops in this kingdom.' These can be summed up as the unbridgeable rift between people and government; the reluctance of the gentry to address the problem while they could use the army as a tool, and the resultant effect on the discipline of the army. He then outlined the efforts he had made to correct the situation, firstly by reconnaissance, and then by issuing orders to correct abuses and impose firmer discipline on the troops. Furthermore, the Yeomanry would have to be called out in consequence of widespread disorder if it coincided with an enemy attack, and he had distributed arms to the well-affected should such a crisis arise. He concluded the letter with a clear statement of intent and exculpation.

> The orders of the 26th February were issued expressly for this purpose, and the whole spirit and tenor of them tend to that end. I acknowledge that I did not consider the proclamation of the 18th May last as then in force; at the same time, I am clearly of opinion that the interpretation and execution of it could not have been left to officers of all descriptions without great inconvenience, and even danger.
>
> I beg leave to assure your Excellency that I never was a political man; and that I have no political connexion to the noble Lord who was lately in this kingdom, and but a very slight personal one. Previously to my coming to Ireland, I had no communication with any of his Majesty's Ministers on the state of the country. After my appointment, I communicated to Mr Pitt, through Mr Dundas, that if I did not meet the public mind, I should most willingly resign, or serve under a superior officer with whom I knew that I could act. I now renew to your Excellency what I then expressed, being perfectly convinced of the necessity of it, because, if I do not possess the confidence of those with whom your Excellency advises, I must impede the operation of your Government.[32]

Camden was torn between his own instincts, which favoured Abercromby's firm but humane approach, and the voices that chorused against the commander-in-chief. In London the initially antagonistic reaction to Abercromby's order had lost its fervour, particularly as the Whigs had made no attempt to exploit it. In Dublin, however, when the order was belatedly leaked to the Irish newspapers there was an extreme response from those officers and gentry who saw it as a deliberate attack on their interests. A cabal, led by Foster, sought to move an address to the Irish House of Lords that contradicted the order, while others agitated for impeachment.

Inevitably, Lake's was one of the loudest voices of protest. He maintained that, if observed, the order would lead to the loss of the north and was scathing in his opinion of Abercromby: 'Poor creature, I pity him . . . he is quite in his dotage.' There were voices raised in Abercromby's favour, however, not only Pelham and some of the English civil servants stationed in Dublin, but also soldiers like Moore and Robert Crauford. Moore wrote:

> The principal officers who had hitherto been used to be complimented, could not bear the language of truth. They had the folly to call out and make public what was meant for their private guidance and correction, and they have done so with all the effrontery of innocence and rectitude. Not, however, daring to deny the abuses, they have laid hold of that part which forbids acting without the presence of a civil magistrate. This is stated to be in direct contradiction to former orders, and to the Lord-Lieutenant's proclamation. In consequence of the disturbed state of the north the laws were extended and districts were proclaimed, but in the practice and execution the troops had infinitely exceeded what ever the laws thus extended authorized, and undoubtedly enormities had been committed extremely disgraceful to the military as well as prejudicial to their discipline. Sir Ralph was determined that this should no longer be the case, and his instructions, private and public, to the general officers tended strongly to forbid such practices. But as the above conduct in the north had terrified the people into submission, the cry of the gentlemen throughout is that nothing but *strong measures*, as they are called, will do; and upon every murmur of the people they call upon the military and urge them to every act of violence. A cabal has by these means been raised against Sir Ralph for his moderation, and it is surprising to what length it has been carried.

Moore informed Abercromby that he would join him in resigning, should it prove necessary. He received a typical response. Abercromby,

> in terms friendly and flattering, entreats me to take no hasty resolution with respect to myself. His resolution not to retract his order nor to submit has afforded me much pleasure and I have taken the liberty of writing so to him. In fact, his conduct since his arrival in Ireland has been so exemplary, the motives upon which he has acted have been so honourable and upright, that he stands upon grounds which reflect great credit upon him, and happen what may, he must have pleasure in the reflection through life . . . He has already done much good; the country allows it, and

should the perverseness or weakness of Government by yielding to unjust clamour force Sir Ralph to resign, Ireland will repent it I am confident, but unfortunately when it will be too late.[33]

However strongly Moore, Crauford, Pelham and others who understood the need for the order expressed their support, their voices were lost in the storm of condemnation. Pelham even drafted a letter to Portland (although it was never sent) which went as far as to accuse the ministers in London of listening to a coterie of self-interested men. He claimed that by failing to support Abercromby, they had also undermined the authority of Lord Camden and himself; furthermore, they had trusted the veracity of unauthorized reports produced by a self-interested cabal. These men, he asserted, had taken advantage of his recent illness to attack Abercromby.[34]

It was probably inevitable that Camden would eventually come down on the side of the cabal. These were the men whose advice he habitually adopted, men who may have believed that provoking a rebellion was the only way to ensure the paramount position of the Protestant Ascendancy. At first Camden procrastinated, assuring Abercromby that he realized the order was not a political manoeuvre and that he had no wish for his resignation. But neither did he offer unconditional support. He conceded that

A responsibility is thrown upon the Army, which is unpleasant to him who commands it, and upon the officer who may be called upon to exert himself individually; and although I may lament the necessity, that necessity exists, and since it does exist, it appears to me that the proclamation must be acted upon. I therefore look with confidence to some explanation of that part of your orders which you issued under the impression that the proclamation was not in force, to determine whether it will be most agreeable to you to make such alteration yourself, or whether you would be desirous to receive an intimation to that effect from me.[35]

Abercromby responded by informing the general officers of his intention to resign, urging them to recognize that Camden's proclamation still required them to act within the law and advocating leniency whenever possible. He also counselled Camden to request disciplined troops from England, since these would be better able to oppose a French invasion. Nor did he abandon his responsibilities as commander-in-chief, as he made clear in a letter to Dundas which was surprisingly generous to Camden.

If the virtuous character of any man could interest me, as I am now situated, it is that of Lord Camden; and I hope you will think so when I tell you, that to ease his government I have consented that I should contradict my own order, and I should go into the south to compose the disturbances that now prevail in certain districts in the provinces of Leinster and Munster. Before I yielded these points, I informed my brother officers that I expected soon to be relieved. This I considered as an attention due to myself, and I hope my letter is conceived in such terms as to preclude any misconstruction, or even the most distant idea of my endeavouring to create in the minds of others any improper sentiment or sensation. It must however be considered as a pledge that I shall not on any account remain in the chief command in this country. Although I have consented to the revocation of my own order, I cannot consent to my remaining a degraded man. As to the propriety of the order, I trust that I shall hereafter be found to stand on the firmest ground.[36]

Clare, always ready with his pen, again wrote to Auckland.

I should suppose that Sir Ralph Abercromby must have lost his senses. Lord Camden kept his resignation perfectly secret, nor would it have been made known by him until he was apprised that the King had accepted it. However, on Saturday Sir Ralph thought fit to write to General Craig, who commands the garrison of Dublin, to inform him that he was about to give up his command and his resignation is now public. It looks as if the last act of peevish folly was dictated by his resentment at being forced to countermand his absurd order, which has led to a degree of confusion unexampled here since the rebellion of 1688.

Clare then described outbreaks of anarchy in Munster and Leinster, making the point that under Abercromby's order the soldiers had to stand by helplessly. This is disingenuous because according to the order the local magistrates could still call upon the army. Instead, the army was still taking the initiative against the United Irishmen's efforts to encourage murder and robbery. This, he told Auckland, 'we know by private information'.[37]

Even before he had received official permission to resign Abercromby had written to Camden that there is one point on which no man who is fit for public employment can be indifferent. No man can be indifferent to his own character. He cannot trust it in the hands of those who have endeavoured to deprive him of it. Were I to remain under your Excellency's orders, I should feel diffidence and distrust from the experience which I have had of the past conduct of those with whom your Excellency advises, which would render me very unfit for the command in such a time as the present. I, therefore, entreat you will be pleased to move his Majesty graciously to permit me to resign my situation, in which I cannot be continued with advantage to his service.[38]

Camden made a last attempt to retain Abercromby, offering to mediate between him and those who had worked against him, but Abercromby pointed out that his would be an invidious position if he were supported only by the personal authority of the Lord Lieutenant. Dundas urged him to compromise so that he could retain his command, assuring him that he had the support of Portland. Both men urged him to do his duty, which meant remaining in Ireland. If there was any criticism, it was of his outspoken comments on army indiscipline which could be misinterpreted as providing ammunition for the government's enemies. Indeed, the government needed Abercromby to remain because no-one else wanted the position, as Cornwallis, David Dundas and Sir William Howe all made clear. Lake was a possibility, but Camden believed him to lack judgement.

Abercromby remained adamant in his determination to resign. He wrote to Dundas on 24 March that 'the principal members of Lord Camden's cabinet have lost their confidence, if they ever had any, in me, that they did, during my absence, attempt my ruin by their machinations here and in England, is a matter beyond all doubt. It is perfectly impossible for me to act with them in future, but with the greatest distrust, which, in these difficult times, must cramp every endeavour of mine to render any essential service, if I were to remain here.' Having reiterated the justice of his own policy, he concluded: 'I have nothing to charge my conscience with, and whatever is the consequence, I cannot abate one single fact or sentiment I have now the honour of expressing to you.'[39]

When there were further outbreaks of violence Abercromby was held responsible. His order had encouraged the bloodshed, it was claimed. Camden found himself under such pressure from the cabal that on 30 March he signed a proclamation declaring Ireland to be in a state of rebellion, which meant that the Insurrection Act now applied to the whole country. This gave the cabal just they had wanted: the imposition of martial law.

Several weeks later Abercromby wrote another letter to his son which was designed to reassure his 94-year-old father.

> Be so good as to tell him in a few words, that the struggle has been, in the first place, whether I was to have the command of the Army really or nominally, and then whether the character and discipline of it were to be degraded and ruined in the mode of using it, either from the facility of one man, or from the violence and oppression of a set of men, who have for more than twelve months employed it in measures which they durst not avow or sanction. Lord Camden, in weakly yielding these points, has betrayed the situation of the Commander-in-Chief; has thrown the army into the hands of a faction; has made it a tool under their direction; and has, I think, overset himself; for, although the British government has prejudged me, they cannot but see the weakness and folly of all that has been done here. Within these twelve months, every crime, every cruelty that could be committed by Cossacks or Calmucks, has been transacted here . . .
>
> Such a degree of insubordination has been allowed, that the general officers write directly to the Castle, overlooking every decency and order. Almost all of those who were here before me have a plot or a conspiracy which they cherish, and which is the subject of their correspondence and consequence; and instead of attending to their duty, and to the discipline of their troops, they are either acting as politicians, or as justices of the peace, a situation which most of them have solicited. In short, I feel the greatest satisfaction in quitting a country where I have been betrayed. Of this I am certain, that there must be some change, otherwise the country will be lost. The late ridiculous farce acted by Lord Camden and his cabinet must strike everyone. They have declared the kingdom in rebellion, when the orders of his Excellency might be carried over the whole kingdom by an orderly dragoon, or a writ executed without any difficulty, a few places in the mountains excepted . . .[40]

To dispel any idea that Abercromby's suspicions were indicative of paranoia, it is important to note that while he was dealing with the disorder in three troubled counties those he identified as his enemies convened a secret

meeting to plot their next move. They decided to proceed with impeachment
and were only thwarted when a gentleman who had once served in the same
regiment as Abercromby informed Pelham of the plot. Pelham immediately
intervened to prevent its implementation.

In another letter home Abercromby revealed just how clearly he
understood the strength of the cabal.

> In a letter to my brother, I informed him that I desired to be recalled
> from my present command. This step is no doubt unfortunate
> at this moment, but it is much better for the King's service and
> for Lord Camden's Government that a successor should be sent
> over, than that there should exist an open war between my Lord-
> Lieutenant's cabinet and myself. The breach is too wide to be
> closed, and they and I must be always at variance. They will never
> forgive me, but have used every means in their power to ruin me,
> and it is impossible that I can ever have any confidence in men
> who have endeavoured to deprive me of my good name. I shall not
> enter at present into any detail on my own conduct since I came to
> Ireland. I trust that it is irreproachable, and that I have reason on
> my side. It is some satisfaction to have the opinion of the reasonable
> men, both civil and military, with me, and that the man, not the last
> in this kingdom [Lord Camden], is among the number.
>
> The hue and cry has been raised in London by letters from
> hence, and has been carried on, as I hear, principally by that
> immaculate character, Lord Auckland. I shall keep my temper, and
> patiently wait for the moment when I can be heard . . . This is a most
> wretched country. The upper orders have fallen into a lethargy,
> and are only occupied in eating and drinking, or in uttering their
> unmanly fears. They know that they have been the oppressors of
> the poor, and that the moment of vengeance is at hand when they
> can glut their revenge, and hope for a more equal share of the good
> things in this life.[41]

At the beginning of April Camden in Council ordered Abercromby to
deal with what he described as the rebellion. In obedience to such a direct
command, Abercromby reluctantly instructed the troops to comply with the
Order in Council, which meant acting without the authority of a magistrate.
He then travelled to Munster, where he used the generals in command to
disseminate the message that those who surrendered the arms they had

seized would be pardoned. He also warned them against trusting the French and reminded them that they would be severely punished if they joined the King's enemies. The officers in command were instructed to identify the instigators of any trouble, while offering support to the well-affected and encouraging the magistrates and the gentry to do their duty. As for his own interpretation of the situation, he believed the disturbances were the work of agitators and were exacerbated by the price of grain, the harsh measures adopted by rent collectors, the absence of the gentry, and the violence of religious feelings. These factors helped to explain why an area which twelve months previously had shown loyalty in the face of a threatened French invasion was now on the point of insurrection.

Abercromby applied his own guidance. The troops were ordered to act with moderation. Every operation had to be overseen by an officer. Thousands of proclamations were printed and dispersed to inform the population that after ten days' grace, if all weapons had not been surrendered, there would be general punishment. In Queen's County, one of the areas most strongly suspected of subversive activity, he chose not to target individuals, as Lake had done in the north, but to apply a more collective punishment in order to bring about the surrender of arms. His chosen method was to send troops into free quarters in the most disturbed areas in order to persuade the population to surrender their concealed arms. This proved unexpectedly successful. As one of the Wellesleys reported, 'To my utter astonishment in two days we got in nearly all the fire-arms that had been taken . . . About 250 muskets, blunderbusses and pistols – and above 300 pike heads which had been buried in peasants' gardens.'[42] This effectively disarmed the peasantry, who later confessed (possibly under instruction) that they had been misled by troublemakers, and also reassured the gentry. Yet there was a snag. It was a system that would only work with a highly-disciplined army. When Abercromby or some other commander who ascribed to his views on discipline was in command there would be no problem. But Abercromby was on the point of departure, and there were too many commanding officers who abused free quartering, preferring the exercise of power to the exercise of discipline.

From Dublin Abercromby sent another letter home. 'I returned last night from the South. I had reason, from the proclamation and instructions I received, to believe that an insurrection had taken place in the province of Munster. I have been through all the disaffected districts. And found nothing but tranquillity, the people employed in cultivating their lands and following their usual avocations. They were civil and submissive, and although I never took any escort or anything more than one servant, I was under no apprehension, even the most distant, of any danger . . . ' He was not blind to the realities of the underlying situation, though, and forecast that 'if an enemy land, the Roman Catholics will rise and cut the throats of the Protestants'. Nevertheless, 'I really think that Lord Camden is ill-advised to declare the Kingdom in rebellion, and to establish something more than martial law over the whole kingdom. It was perhaps right to do something in that way in some particular districts where the greatest outrages had been committed . . .'[43] In other words, there was a case for applying the terms of the proclamation judiciously, instead of as a default punishment to the whole country.

While in the south, Abercromby confided to Moore his own reading of the situation.

> He explained to me confidentially all that had passed; he spoke of Lord Camden as one of the best men in the world but one of the weakest, and completely guided by a set of violent, hot-headed men. Sir Ralph told me that the proclamation and order in consequence of it, formerly issued in Lord Carhampton's time, had never been acted upon; but a special order and Act of indemnity and pardon having since passed, they were considered as thereby annulled. At one instance only since his arrival at a place in the north had an officer acted without a magistrate, and he was immediately stopt. In the south, where colonel Manser St George was murdered General Johnstone wrote that he was going to burn houses etc. His letter was sent to Mr. Pelham, and from him to the Lord-Lieutenant, and orders were instantly sent down to stop General Johnstone. When Sir Ralph issued his order desiring officers never to act without a civil magistrate he conceived he did nothing beyond what Lord Camden approved of. In the different councils he had always disapproved of the violent measures proposed and of dispersing the troops. His opinion was that the civil magistrates should be encouraged to act. He had already succeeded in getting them to attempt it in some parts where he had been.
>
> The Chancellor and his party would never explain exactly what they wished; but it was evident that they wished the Commander-in-chief with the army to take upon themselves to act with a violence which they did not choose to define, and for which they would give no public authority. Their approbation would therefore

depend upon the success. Sir Ralph said he never chose to understand them. It was during his tour to the north that the cabal was formed against him, and it was not until his return to Dublin that he found his orders to the army had been the subject of discussion, and his character and conduct traduced and misrepresented both in this country and in England. He had done all he could with Lord Camden to show him the danger of the measures pursued. His Lordship agreed with him, but could not resist the other party. Upon the proclamation Sir Ralph issued the order he was desired to do [the resurrection of Carhampton's order], because he did not wish to be said to have disobeyed, but he immediately wrote to be recalled. The Lord-Lieutenant than asked him to come to the south where the disturbances were, to carry into execution the orders which he disapproved. He told the Lord-Lieutenant that since it was his desire he should comply, but it was a sacrifice which he did not expect would have been demanded of him; he hoped it would be the last, and that upon his return to Dublin he should be permitted to quit the kingdom . . .

There was also further discussion of Moore's desire to resign his command because he realized that:

The measures likely to be adopted will be most odious, and whoever attempts to execute them with leniency or moderation risks giving displeasure and being ruined. Should an invasion be attempted there will be no head to direct, and no previous arrangement made; the scene will be disgraceful, and I wish to retire from it . . . He begged I would be cautious, both for my own sake and his; he should be sorry that anything we did should bear the appearance of party. Sir Ralph said, 'I shall be blamed for what I have done in this country, but I never felt more satisfied with myself, or my conscience more clear. I meant to act well, and feeling this, the calumny of the world does not affect me.' I told him I was sure that in time all prejudice would subside and his conduct would obtain the approbation it deserved. I was convinced the part he had acted would always be a source of pleasant recollection to himself.[44]

Needless to say, Camden's advisors strongly disapproved of Abercromby's conduct in the south and persuaded Camden to countermand free quartering in favour of more drastic punishment. The blindness of such men, who could not appreciate how successful Abercromby's policy proved when the gentry and the magistrates did their duty and used the Yeomanry for their designated purpose, was inexorably leading the country towards violence. This was made even more certain when Lake was appointed commander-in-chief in April, and immediately set about encouraging the very military excesses that Abercromby had battled against. To make the point, on 7 May General Sir James Stueart published an order in Cork making clear that leniency was no longer an acceptable policy. Instead, to counteract the willingness of the people to enter into general subscriptions which raised money to feed the troops, thus spreading the burden through the whole population rather than confining it to the guilty, officers were to increase the number of billeted soldiers severalfold, and send out foraging parties. The troops were to be moved from station to station until all arms had been surrendered and the area was at peace, and until all landowners reported that rents, taxes and tithes had been paid in full. The rebellion broke out three weeks later, almost as if Abercromby's resignation was the trigger for the horrendous violence that followed. Henry Grattan was right that 'the policy of Sir Ralph was sound and wise, but that he came a little too late', but it is also worth noting that the policy he advocated was never given a chance to prove itself. And the alternative, as practised by men like Lake and Stueart, consistently proved disastrous.

Abercromby returned to England at the end of April. Upon his arrival he was appointed Commander of the Forces in Scotland. As he wrote on 14 May,

> It seems determined that I must accept of the command in Scotland; it is by no means with my good-will, as it will expose me to more company and expense than I could wish and can add neither to my fortune nor my fame. Were I to choose, I should have said, allow me to be quiet until there is occasion for me. But the King is determined to give me the highest mark in his power, on account of the injury done to the service, not in removing me, but in removing his Commander-in-Chief by a political blast.[45]

As if to publically demonstrate this final point, at a royal levee the King told him that he had been very ill-used in Ireland, and would enjoy more respect in Scotland. The King later confided to a member of the government that he had waited until he was within hearing of some Irish politicians before he made the comment.

Failure in Ireland continued to haunt Abercromby. In January 1799 he told an Irish friend that he was

> not afraid of being charged with prejudice. If I have any, they are in favour of a country in which I have lived long, in which I formed many valuable friendships, some of which are still fresh in my mind . . . Long observation has convinced me, that all your misfortunes, that all the evils with which you are threatened, proceed from the illiberal, the unjust, and the unwise conduct of England. Your legislature and your Executive Government partake of course, of the vices flowing from the wretched system of English domination. The vices of the government infect the manners of the people. If I find a peasantry cunning, deceitful, lazy, and vindictive, I cannot attribute it, without impiety, to the hand of God. It must come from the iron hand of man. Although the French Revolution and Jacobin principles may be the immediate cause of the events which have lately taken place in Ireland, yet the remote and ultimate cause must be derived from its true origin, the oppression of centuries. Do not imagine that I am weak enough to believe that a few effusions of lenity or benevolence are to soften or subdue the minds of a people hardened by oppression. It will require the wisest system you can devise, and length of time, to effect it. In the meantime, you must trust to the due execution of the Law, and to a powerful and well disciplined Army for your protection. The Irish people are not a thinking people, they have strong prejudices. However, people will think for them. Till a new system has begun to take effect, they will remain the tools of a foreign enemy, or of domestic agitators and demagogues. God grant that the measures on the affairs of Ireland, which, they say, are now under consideration, may be well weighed, and that the spirit of party may give way to true wisdom.[46]

To those who had opposed Abercromby's policy from the beginning, his resignation was a reason for congratulation. Yet it remains difficult to understand why those with military experience could not grasp the vital importance of a well-disciplined army that was used, not as a supernumerary police force, but for its proper function, the defence of the country. There were magistrates and the yeomanry to enforce law and order. An army allowed, or even encouraged, to rampage was a pernicious factor in a situation that was simmering towards rebellion. That even the vacillating Lord Camden recognized this simple fact demonstrates the wisdom of Abercromby's policy. But an enlightened liberal like Abercromby would always be suspect to those who believed in a status quo which so effectively supported their interests.

When the Whig grandee, Lord Holland, wrote his *Memoirs of the Whig Party during my Time* he offered a damning assessment of the ruling powers: 'The measures which led to that event [the Rebellion], suggested by Lord Clare, and by the remorseless faction of Orangemen who called themselves the Protestant Ascendancy, roused the indignation of every men who had a sense of justice, or the feelings of humanity.' He added later:

> The premature and ill-concerted insurrections which followed in the Catholic districts, were quelled, rather in consequence of want of concert and skill in the insurgents, than of any good conduct or discipline of the King's troops, whom Sir Ralph Abercrombie described very honestly, as formidable to no-one but their friends. That experienced and upright commander had been removed from his command, even after those just and spirited orders, in which the remarkable judgement just quoted was conveyed. His recall was hailed as a triumph by the Orange faction . . . Indeed, surrounded as they were with burning cottages, tortured backs, and frequent executions, they were yet full of their sneers at what they whimsically termed 'the clemency; of the government and the weak character of their Viceroy Lord Camden.[47]

Perhaps the most crucial question is not what Abercromby could or should have done, but why did the government send to Ireland a man whose principles would always be in conflict with the Protestant Ascendancy. They should have learnt from Lord Fitzwilliam's experience that there was no place for liberals in late eighteenth-century Ireland. As Grattan remarked, Abercromby's efforts were too little, too late.

Abercromby's good friend and aide-de-camp in Flanders, John Hely-Hutchinson, who had been involved in the suppression of the rebellion, wrote to him from Dundalk in the June the following year:

> In my opinion, the Rebellion in this country is entirely put down. The rebels seem to be sick of their own machinations, by which they have been themselves the chief sufferers. I suppose you know that I support the Union. After all my patriotism, I have

been obliged to vote for the annihilation of the Irish Legislature, but such are the hopes of man, and such the termination of his most proud designs . . . If ever there was a country unfit to govern itself, it is Ireland: a corrupt aristocracy, a ferocious commonalty, a distracted government, a divided people. I solemnly believe that the great mass of every religious persuasion in this country have no wish so near their hearts, as to enjoy the power of persecuting each other. The Catholic would murder the Protestant in the name of God; the Protestant would murder the Catholic in the name of law. Both sects seem to consider their common country only as an extended field of battle, where each are at full liberty to display their sanguinary dexterity . . .[48]

It is possible to argue that Abercromby had played a part in bringing about the rebellion, and the Act of Union that followed. His general orders were undoubtedly provocative to the political classes and potentially damaging to army morale. Furthermore, such public criticism of a force intended for the defence of Ireland could be said to have given encouragement to the French. On the other hand, the authorities were undoubtedly using the threat of rebellion in order to justify the repressive methods that, ironically, would bring it about. Pushing the argument further, the authorities were using repression in order 'to accelerate the explosion of the insurrection in order to confound the plans of its leaders. For this reason it was necessary to drive the people mad with terror; and the subordinate agents of this policy were allowed to take their own ways of accomplishing the minister's [Castlereagh's] designs.'[49] If such were the case, then there was little that Abercromby or any other man of liberal sentiments could have done to prevent the cataclysm that struck Ireland in May 1798. And yet there is an ironic twist. Having been hooted out of Ireland by his enemies, after his death he became an Irish national hero, and his health was frequently drunk on formal occasions.[50]

Chapter 4

The War of the Second Coalition

A New Coalition

Abercromby's next command is best understood in the context of a complicated exercise in strategy and diplomacy undertaken to establish a new coalition. After the defection of Prussia in April 1795 (Peace of Basel), Spain in July and Hesse-Kassel in August, the First Coalition had limped on with Britain and Austria as its only active members, although no longer co-operating with each other. Even this loose agreement finally collapsed in 1797, with the Franco-Austrian Treaty of Campo Formio. Before this, Pitt had made overtures of peace to the French, using Lord Malmesbury as an intermediary. He was prepared to surrender Martinique and St Lucia to the French and to return the Cape of Good Hope, taken from the Dutch in 1795 to prevent it falling into French hands. (This had been followed by the seizure of another Dutch possession, Ceylon, in February 1796, to prevent it being used as a French base for operations in support of Tippoo Sahib, the Sultan of Mysore, who was challenging the British in India.) Pitt was also ready to acknowledge the Rhine as France's eastern frontier, although not as a northern frontier that would deprive Austria of Belgium. It was all in vain, however. The French were still thinking in terms of bringing Britain to its knees, initially through an attack on Ireland. (Wolfe Tone and Lord Edward Fitzgerald had travelled to Basel to discuss plans for a French invasion with a French government representative.) Some pretence of negotiation was sustained for several months before Malmesbury was abruptly ordered to leave France.

Campo Formio followed a victorious campaign in northern Italy which forced Piedmont out of the coalition and secured French possession of Nice and Savoy, while Napoleon Bonaparte demonstrated at Lodi, Castiglioni, Bassano and Arcola that he was the leading French general of the day. He also enjoyed the favour of the Directory, the five-man committee which eventually replaced the Committee of Public Safety after the fall of Robespierre, coming to power in November 1795 after months of constitutional discussion. In May 1795, while these discussions were under way, the Jacobins had tried to seize power. There had also been a Royalist rising in Brittany in June and July which, despite some British support, was harshly suppressed by General Hoche. These disturbances concentrated people's minds and the new constitution was finally agreed at the end of August. Although Paul Barras had formed a provisional committee, the Directors had still not been officially named when reports surfaced of a planned *coup d'état* by Royalists and constitutional monarchists (who were normally at odds). Barras gave complete command to Bonaparte, with the result that the planned mob-march on the Tuileries, where the Convention was sitting, was defeated by the famous 'whiff of grapeshot', as Carlyle termed it. The rising general not only won the kudos of saving the constitution; he also gained the interest of Barras' mistress, Josephine de Beauharnais.

Bonaparte's successful Italian campaign was matched in part by the Archduke Charles' activities in 1796 against Moreau and Jourdan, who had been sent to drive the Archduke from the Rhine to the Danube. In this they were initially successful, at which point Württemberg and Baden defected from the coalition. The Archduke struck back at Jourdan, defeating him at Amburg in August and Würzburg in September; but Moreau was successful at Schliengen in October, which left the situation in a stalemate. Then in January 1797 Bonaparte defeated the Austrian General Alvinczi at Rivoli. With the Austrians in total disarray, he turned his attention to Rome and quickly brought the Pope to heel. As soon as the snows had melted he prepared to threaten Vienna itself. By 30 March he was at Klagenfurt and making peace overtures to the Archduke Charles. When he received no reply, he advanced to Judenburg. The Emperor realized that he was in a hopeless situation and on 17 April agreed to an armistice, the Peace of Loeben. This was despite Thugut's opposition. 'In the midst of these accumulated calamities M. de Thugut retains his firmness, and [is] determined not to be the instrument of concluding a disgraceful peace.'[1] By the autumn the peace party in Vienna had triumphed over Thugut; the Treaty of Campo Formio was signed on 17 October; and Thugut resigned as Foreign Secretary, to be replaced by Baron Cobenzl. He was still in control, however, and was already anticipating the next campaign against France.

By the terms of Campo Formio Austria acknowledged the legitimacy of the French Republic, conceded French possession of Belgium and territory on the left bank of the Rhine, and recognized the Batavian and Cisalpine Republics, the latter now a French satellite state which included Milan, Modena, the western part of Venetian Republic and the Ionian Islands. In return the Austrians received Venice itself, Istria and Dalmatia.

With the Austrian Netherlands no longer an issue, Pitt was ready for further peace negotiations. Malmesbury travelled to France once more only to discover that Paris was in the grip of a power struggle. This made serious discussion impossible. In September the *coup d'état* of 18 *Fructidor* (4 September) led to the ejection of suspected Royalists from the Legislative Council and the imprisonment of the two most moderate Directors, Carnot and Barthélemy. Their fault had been to advocate *les anciennes limites*. Now the policy of *les grandes limites,* advocated by Barras, Reubell and La Revellière, could be pursued with the support of Jacobin deputies in the Legislative Assembly, and the army. (Hoche and General Pierre Augereau had played a vital part in the coup at Bonaparte's instigation.)[2] In other words, France would no longer limit her aspirations to the traditional boundaries she had long claimed such as the lower Rhine but now intended to dominate whatever territory her armies could conquer. Campo Formio pointed the way forward: French hegemony in Europe seemed within reach. The next step was the Congress of Rastatt. Campo Formio was a treaty made specifically between France and Austria. Rastatt would establish peace with the Holy Roman Empire, on French terms.

Britain was now isolated, a dangerous position because, as Lord Auckland pointed out to the House of Lords, 'The security of Europe is essential to the security of the British Empire.'[3] And Grenville believed the Directory planned to overthrow all other governments. Jervis' victory at Cape St Vincent on 14 February 1797 had restored faith in the power of the navy (although the mutinies at Spithead and the Nore two months later demonstrated the danger of overconfidence) but the navy alone could not win the war. The establishment of a strong combination of powers against the French was vital to Britain's safety. Grenville's thinking was opposed by both Pitt, who hoped to use the navy to fight an economic war, and Dundas, who had developed a deep suspicion of foreign alliances which seemed to cost much and achieve little.

Grenville understood that any alliance would only succeed if all parties were agreed on their political aims. Failure in this respect had brought about the collapse of the First Coalition. He planned a quadruple alliance which would enable the coalition powers to drive the French back to their pre-Revolutionary boundaries. This presupposed that Prussia could be persuaded to abandon neutrality and Austria would reject Campo Formio. The latter was the more probable of the two events, although there was some hope that the new King of Prussia, Frederick William III, who succeeded in November 1797, might be persuaded to adopt a more bellicose policy. Russia was the fourth ally. Bonaparte's success in Italy in 1796 had finally convinced Catherine the Great that the French threat could no longer be ignored. She responded to an Austrian appeal for help by offering 64,000 men. This seeming generosity was hedged around with conditions that were unlikely to be met, however. There was little chance that Prussia would provide an equal number of men or that Britain would agree to further subsidies. Catherine's death in November 1796 and the accession of her son, Paul I, created even greater uncertainty. It was difficult to gauge the new Tsar's likely actions. On the one hand he fulminated against the Revolutionaries: on the other, he protested that Russia was exhausted by her wars against the Ottomans. His order to General Alexander Suvorov to stand down the troops he had been assembling on Catherine's order sent an ominous message. When the Directory took possession of the Ionian Islands in September 1798, however, and seemed intent upon turning the Mediterranean into a French lake the Tsar rescinded his order to Suvorov.

Some form of international action was becoming increasingly urgent because, despite Campo Formio, it was obvious France still had expansionist ambitions. The treaty had yet to be ratified by the German states, and during the ensuing discussions at Rastatt the French emissaries continually made demands that would extend French power. Then on 8 December Bonaparte and Reubell held discussions with a prominent Swiss patriot, Peter Ochs, who welcomed French intervention in order to overthrow the moribund Swiss Convention. Invasion swiftly followed, leading to the establishment of the Helvetic Republic. The French also took possession of Geneva and Mulhouse. More significantly, they now had control of the Alpine passes. Unfortunately, they could not resist their usual tactics of pillaging, raising taxes and passing laws that interfered with local traditions, with the result that the new republic lasted only five years. This lay in the future. In the present, another French satellite state clearly indicated the Directory's insatiable appetite for territory.

Nor was Switzerland the only gain. The Directory used the murder of a French general in a street brawl as an excuse to seize Rome, ejecting the Pope and establishing the Roman Republic. La Revellière's claim that France would establish a united territory from the Netherlands to northern and central Italy seemed about to be realized. And there was good reason why France needed all this extra territory, other than for *la gloire*. As already noted, one of Carnot's army reforms had been the policy of living off the land. By doing away with depots and a supply train he created greater mobility, but there was an obvious disadvantage if the Revolutionary forces were confined to French territory. Better that subject peoples should feed them.

The Directory was equally determined to exercise influence over the Holy Roman Empire. On 1 December, during a visit to Rastatt to chivvy the Imperial delegates into accepting French demands, Bonaparte was able to persuade Austria to evacuate the crucial Rhenish city of Mainz in return for the French evacuating Venice. French power was encroaching on Imperial territory.[4] Early in 1798 the Emperor confided in the Archduke Charles that the current state of peace was worse than war. He recognized that it was only a matter of time before Austria and France were at war, and warned his brother accordingly.

Thugut had always seen Campo Formio merely as breathing space. He also shared Grenville's views. 'Like his Austrian counterpart, Grenville viewed revolutionary France as the scourge of the times, a threat not only to the existence of his own country but to the entire social and political fabric of Europe. And like Thugut, Grenville believed that the only way to resist the daemonic force was to enlist all the monarchies in a just and honourable struggle for their mutual salvation.'[5] Despite this compatibility, however, there remained a seemingly insurmountable problem. Austria had not only proved an unreliable ally but there was also an ongoing financial conflict between the two states. Before the collapse of the alliance, Britain had given Austria an advance of £1,600,000, to be followed by a loan of £4,000,000. The preliminary peace talks started before the latter amount had been paid in full. Grenville then demanded the repayment of the advance with interest on the grounds that it was the first instalment of a loan. Thugut agreed to repay the advance, but without interest, which had been set at a very high rate. The resultant stalemate made it impossible for the Foreign Secretary to contemplate an alliance with Austria.

As for Prussia, Frederick William continued to temporise. Indeed, he probably enjoyed a certain degree of *schadenfreude* at the humiliation of his German rival. In Russia the Tsar was proving himself volatile and possibly unbalanced. As the British ambassador at St Petersburg, Lord Whitworth, reported to Grenville: 'How much under the influence of passion and sometimes of caprice is the first moment in which he decides.'[6] Furthermore, Grenville was well aware of the rivalries that obsessed the three central European powers, yet because he believed that Campo Formio would prove short-lived, he continued to plan, even if his plans could not yet be realized. But Grenville was a patient man.

The Congress of Rastatt continued its deliberation without the Imperial delegates coming any closer to a formal peace with France. Then in May 1798 Bonaparte set sail from Toulon, not for Ireland as the British had feared but for Egypt. On the way he stopped at Malta and without any declaration of war forced the surrender of the Order of St John. He then took possession of the island, leaving a garrison of 3,000 men before sailing on to Egypt and yet more victories. Malta was a miscalculation. As a boy the Tsar had conceived of the Order of St John as the epitome of Christian chivalry. Its surrender to the godless French inspired him to appoint himself protector of the Order and also to offer 16,000 troops to the Austrians. Nor were the British prepared to accept this latest French conquest. Then on 1 August came the Battle of the Nile and the destruction of the French Mediterranean fleet. This trapped Napoleon and his army in Egypt, changed the balance of naval power in the Mediterranean, and persuaded both Russia and the Ottomans to declare war on France. Old enmities temporarily forgotten, Turkey granted the Russian fleet access to the eastern Mediterranean. The Tsar was also ready to send men to the Rhine in return for British money, in addition to the men sent to aid the Austrians. At the same time unrest in Switzerland and the Papal States promised well for the proto-alliance that was forming. A Cabinet minute dated 20 January 1799 acknowledged the beginning of a second coalition.

It was at this point that the idea of attacking French interests in the Netherlands first seems to have been mooted. The British government, fed information by the Hereditary Prince, chose to believe in the existence of an underground pro-Orangist movement. This required them to forget the unpopularity of the Stadtholder, and make no allowance for Dutch reaction to the British seizure of their colonial possessions. Even if this justified an attack on French interests, such an attack would need careful planning. In the event, 'there was such a degree of ineptitude and want of preparation as virtually ensured in advance the ignominious failure that resulted in the end'.[7] The government seemed unable to learn from their own misjudgements. In May 1798 they had succumbed to the persuasion of Captain Home Riggs Popham and landed a small expeditionary force near Ostend. The objective was the destruction of gates and sluices on the newly-completed Bruges canal in order to disrupt French plans for yet another invasion of Britain. In this respect the troops were successful but the whole force was lost when high winds prevented its evacuation to the waiting naval ships.

As far as Thugut was concerned, by the beginning of 1799 Campo Formio was dead and buried. Like Grenville, he recognized the need for joint planning from the start so that the French could not pick off their opponents one by one. Yet no formal alliance was possible until the question of the loan had been settled. At the same time Grenville had been concentrating on

Russia and had won the Tsar's agreement to co-operative action in return for a subsidy. Naples, Portugal and some minor German states had also committed themselves to the new coalition.

So conducive was the atmosphere in Europe to an attack on the French that the Neapolitans overstepped the mark and invaded the Roman Republic in November 1798. They were soon put to flight, and pursued back to Sicily. Their defeat led to the establishment of yet another satellite republic, the Parthenopean Republic. This, in effect, made the French the rulers of all Italy except for those territories ceded to Austria by Campo Formio; but what should have been a mere distraction led to valuable troops being transferred to the south from a defensive position on the Po. With the seasoned soldiers of Bonaparte's Army of Italy far away in Egypt, this dispersal was the factor most strongly in the allies' favour.

The Swiss were already chafing at the French bit. The first outbreak of violence, led by Alois von Reding, came close to success. The second resulted in violent reprisals. Grenville saw the possibilities of exploiting Swiss disaffection. If Switzerland could be brought under Allied control, using Austrian and Russian troops for the purpose, it could then become the launch point for an invasion of eastern France. Grenville also anticipated that Austria would campaign to regain its lost Italian territory. Thugut, however, wanted to concentrate on the Tyrol and the Rhine, although a combined Austro-Russian attack in north Italy was also part of his wider plan. In this he had the agreement of the emperor, whose primary concern was the protection of the Hapsburg crown lands. Suvorov's Russian force could be used to regain Piedmont and Lombardy, while the archduke focused on the Rhine.

Even Prussia seemed on the verge of joining the coalition. Count Haugwitz had previously proposed a Prusso-Russian invasion of Holland, financed by Britain. A popular rising in Belgium against conscription in October 1798 seemed to suggest that the overall situation was more volatile than it had previously appeared. Grenville judged the time right to challenge French hegemony with the Austro-Russian invasion from Switzerland that he had already envisaged, and a Prussian attack across the Rhine into Belgium. In a two-pronged attack the major operation would focus on Switzerland, while a smaller Anglo-Russian expedition would first attack the French in Holland, before moving into Belgium to support the Prussians.

These strategic designs continued to ignore Dundas's instinctive suspicion of Continental allies and failed to win the wholehearted commitment of Pitt, who had no wish to embroil the country in yet another

Continental war. And it was one thing to plan, quite another to effect, for much might be lost in the detail. Even after Grenville eventually won over the other two members of the triumvirate to his way of thinking, the three of them then prepared to assemble a force 'without any concrete plan for using it. They were indeed determined that a force should sail from Britain, land somewhere and do something in Holland; but where and to what purpose were questions to which they had no answer.'[8]

Neither Austria nor Russia had yet committed themselves to Grenville's plan for Switzerland but they were enjoying success elsewhere. As soon as winter conditions permitted, General Jourdan had crossed the Rhine near Kehl with the Army of the Danube, in violation of Campo Formio. The Archduke Charles marched against him and defeated him at Ostrach and Stockach in March 1799. Charles then invaded Switzerland and defeated General André Masséna at the first Battle of Zurich early in June, forcing him to withdraw. Suvorov took command in northern Italy on 14 April. In a bludgeoning campaign he then defeated General Moreau twice, General Macdonald at Trebbia River, took Mantua, and finally defeated General Joubert at Novi on 15 August, thus undoing all Bonaparte's success. Yet just as Grenville saw his plans coming to fruition, Prussia defected. On 22 July Haugwitz formally announced that Prussia had decided to remain neutral.

However, after the Archduke's victory at Zurich early in June Austro-Russian relations turned sour. Just when Grenville could congratulate himself on the success of his diplomatic manoeuvring the Austrians created difficulties. The Archduke had expected to remain in Switzerland and link up with the Russians, including both Suvorov's force and 30,000 men under General Alexander Korsakov, who were still on the march, but the Austrians had become suspicious of Prussian designs on Belgium. In May 1799 the Archduke was ordered to move to Swabia, an imperial decision that he knew was a mistake but was obliged to obey. As a result, when Korsakov finally reached Switzerland he found himself isolated. There were no Austrians, and Suvorov, who should have crossed the Alps to reinforce him, had been delayed by the difficult terrain. As a result, Masséna overwhelmed Korsakov at the second Battle of Zurich on 25 and 26 September. Korsakov withdrew to Schaffhausen, leaving Suvorov at the mercy of the French. As the winter snows set in Suvorov retired in the most difficult conditions with the French snapping at his heels. The Russian general, 70 years old and as tough as old boot leather, refused to call this retrograde march a retreat, but it still meant that the Allied campaign in Switzerland was over, and there would be no further co-operation between the Austrians and the Russians.

The Do-Something Campaign

The unravelling of Grenville's strategy lay in the future as he set in motion his plans for a northern diversion. Should the Prussians fail, the million-pound subsidy intended for them could be used to finance an Anglo-Russian expedition to Holland. But money was not enough. No campaign could be fought without an army. By the second half of the 1790s the shortage of recruits had become critical. An attempt was made to resolve the situation in January 1798 when an Act of Parliament permitted a proportion of men in the Militia to enlist in the regular army. Since there was neither financial inducement nor exemption from service in the West Indies, the take-up was limited, only Norfolk producing an appreciable number of men from the supplementary militia. By 1799 the situation in Ireland had stabilized sufficiently to allow the detachment of some regulars to the expeditionary force; but too many regiments were still critically short of men.

On 5 June Dundas wrote privately to Abercromby, who was still in Scotland:

> Although there is never dependence to be placed on the disposition of Prussia, governed as she is by a corrupt and weak administration, still she must be ready, if actuated either by her fears or interest she shall be induced to come forward. By our most recent intelligence it is not impossible that at any hour she may call upon France to evacuate Holland, with a menace of marching a Prussian army into it, if she does not. If she takes this step, she will at the same time call upon us to co-operate with our fleet, and to seize on the island of Walcheren. We must be ready if such an event takes place, and I have this morning arranged with the Duke of York to carry the accompanying disposition of troops into execution. I have not time to enter into further details, but if you wish to command the expedition, you must come away as soon as you can after the receipt of this letter.[9]

Although there was already an agreement between Britain and Russia, on 22 June a further treaty stipulated that Britain would supply 13,000 men and Russia 17,000, for which she would receive £88,000 as a subsidy and £40,000 a month to cover their expenses. The objective, as Dundas informed Abercromby, was Holland; the purpose, to draw off French troops from the Rhine and Switzerland, destroy Dutch naval resources and eventually attack

France from the north. By mid-July Home Popham was on his way to the Baltic to organize the transport of the Russian troops. Although entitled in government papers 'The Secret Expedition', the plan was reported in the newspapers. Nor could the Directory remain unaware of British intentions when preparations were in evidence in every dockyard.

Abercromby travelled to London in response to Dundas's letter and on 2 July he was summoned to a meeting with Grenville and Dundas to discuss plans for the expedition. It is significant that, despite the extended nature of Grenville's negotiations, this was the first time that a military opinion was sought. Abercromby made the soldier's predictable observation: whether the landings took place at Walcheren or somewhere else, they could only be effected with sufficient landing craft. This obvious point seems not to have occurred to the political planners who had entered into binding commitments with foreign allies but had not considered such basic practicalities. Shortage of landing craft was to prove one of the many issues that would leave the expedition ill-equipped, even though the shortage was eased somewhat when Captain Popham persuaded the Tsar to adapt Russian craft instead of relying on British boats. One decision was taken, however. The Duke of York was appointed to overall command because the Russians would only serve under a general of royal blood, and Abercromby would command the advance force.

An even greater challenge was to find 30,000 men fit for service, when only 10,000 men at most were immediately available. In July, therefore, a Militia Reduction Act reduced the strength by up to a quarter, and the supernumerary men were encouraged to enlist into fourteen nominated regiments.[10] This time it was made quite clear that they would be limited to European service, they could also choose which regiment to join, and they would receive a £10 bounty, which were sufficient inducements to persuade more than enough men to volunteer for the regulars. The ministers obviously expected these men to be integrated into their new regiments and ready for service by late summer, which proved that, 'after all the bitter experience of the past six years, [they] had not yet learned the difference between an army and an assembly in red coats'.[11] The result was that

> Many thousands of stout fellows were obtained by this measure; but for the time they ceased to be well-drilled, orderly soldiers of our Militia regiments, without becoming men on whom their new officers could rely for regular service. So numerous were the volunteers that many regiments, which in August could hardly

muster one or two hundred wasted old soldiers, found itself 2000 strong; healthy, athletic young men, and well drilled as far as mere drilling could go. But these men were hardly sobered from the riotous jollity of their volunteering; their minds were unsettled; to them their new officers and sergeants were utter strangers; everything was new and bewildering.[12]

The arrival of so many volunteers posed practical problems. Major Alexander Jackson, only recently appointed to the 40th Foot, recorded in his journal how his new regiment had been a skeleton unit when it returned from the West Indies. Now it had to accommodate 1,400 volunteers. 'Recruits were pouring in from all quarters, in the various uniforms of their late Regiments, and the parade displayed a motley group of all the colours of the Rainbow. It required unremitting attention to methodise and arrange them, and then there was not an officer who could call one minute his own.'[13]

The first troops assembled near Southampton. Then, as the summer progressed, the handful of fit-for-service regiments and 10,000 volunteers so far assembled, were encamped on Barham Downs and this Kentish location suggested an expedition across the North Sea. Although most of the volunteers were from the Militia, as noted, there were also some regulars who had transferred from other regiments. These men received a bounty of a guinea and a half as an inducement. Abercromby received a letter from Colonel Brownrigg, the Duke of York's military secretary, which offered him the chance to nominate the general officers and staff who would accompany him. He was also instructed to join Pitt and Dundas, who were at Walmer, so that plans could be formalized.

The idea at this point was for the conquest of the Batavian Republic as far south as the Waal and the restoration of the Stadtholder with the support of those Dutch who were loyal to the House of Orange, plus those who resented the French. Thus a Dutch rising remained a crucial factor in the subsequent planning, nor was the expectation totally unjustified.

The departure of the Stadtholder in 1795 had raised expectations that a new era was dawning, with the proposed National Assembly as its epitome. It took over a year to bring such an assembly into being and it soon became clear that 'instead of a disinterested forum of the Public Good the National Assembly had degenerated into a battlefield of faction'.[14] At the heart of the conflict lay the struggle between radical unitarists who wanted the Dutch nation to be one and indivisible and the more conservative federalists who wished to retain the old United Provinces. There were outbreaks of violence, most notably in Amsterdam, Holland being the dominant unitarist province. When the National Assembly finally produced its proposals for the new constitution they were at best a series of compromises. For example, although the Dutch would no longer be 'a confederated state' but would function as 'one single sovereign state', the provinces were still granted a range of devolved powers. Compromises have the unfortunate result of pleasing no-one and both sides expressed their dissatisfaction. The French had been watching what was happening with growing impatience. The Batavian Republic was in a state of virtual interregnum, which did not suit the Directory's purpose. François Noel, the resident French agent, decided to intervene by recommending that the constitution should be put to the vote. Unfortunately, the Dutch increasingly resented their obligation to support 25,000 French troops, and on 8 August 1797 the voters rejected the constitution almost four to one, as much in response to French interference as in dislike of the actual constitution.

In 1795 the victorious French had been reasonably moderate in their approach. They demanded a war indemnity, annexed some territory and forced the Dutch to declare war on Britain, a war which eventually cost the Dutch both colonies and trade. Britain and the Dutch Republic had long been economic rivals, and the Dutch had a strong suspicion that the British would never return the Cape, Ceylon and Demerara. For the French the northern Netherlands were essentially a 'defensive buffer: protecting the North Sea coast and the Scheldt estuary against a British naval offensive, and shielding the Belgian *departéments réunis* against any sign of Austrian revival'.[15] Under the aggressive prompting of Jean-François Reubell, a different role for the Dutch emerged. Reubell advocated the establishment of dependent states, including the Dutch Republic, as France went in pursuit of Austria. After the collapse of the First Coalition there remained one intransigent foe. The Dutch were now required to lend their naval strength to the French as they went on the attack against the British. Unfortunately, this resulted in Admiral Duncan's victory at the Battle of Camperdown on 11 October 1797.

The outcome of the popular vote and defeat at Camperdown gave the Directory the excuse to replace the moderate Noel with the Jacobin Charles-François Delacroix. Furthermore, those Patriots who had remained in Paris had been feeding the Directors with stories that suggested the Netherlands was on the verge of anarchy. Although these were baseless exaggerations, there certainly was festering discontent, caused not only by the cost of maintaining French troops but also by the imposition of the paper *assignats* currency. After Camperdown the French expected the Dutch to rebuild their fleet, which could only be done with a rise in taxes but when an 8 per cent tax was finally proposed, all the provinces except Holland rejected it.

Delacroix's instructions, which he brought with him to The Hague in December 1797, required him to 'put the Batavian Republic in a condition of being able to act *effectively* in the alliance which she had contracted with [France]'.[16] In other words, the Dutch were to be allowed considerable licence when devising their political system, as long as the resultant government was prepared to work for French interests. The most extreme radicals in Paris, however, had their own view of what that system should be and were able to flatter Delacroix into supporting them. Soon the new French agent was identifying himself as the saviour of the Dutch.

The coup took place against a heightened sense of excitement as all parties realized a crisis point had been reached. On the evening of 21 January 1798 Dutch troops under the arch Patriot, General Daendels, took up position in The Hague so that no-one could enter or leave. French troops under General Barthelémy Joubert their new commander, were strategically placed to intervene if necessary. Warrants were signed ready for the arrest of those deputies identified as enemies. By the next afternoon the radicals were in power and Delacroix was able to write to Talleyrand in Paris: 'At last the Batavian regeneration has been consummated this very day! An 18 *Fructidor* as wisely conceived and as happily executed as that which saved France has taken place this morning. The people are perfectly calm. At two o'clock this afternoon the soldiers were able to return to their barracks and the National Assembly to pursue its business in peace.'[17]

In imitation of 18 *Fructidor*, a five-member Interim Executive Directory was established which, under the influence of Delacroix, introduced yet another constitution. In March this was as enthusiastically accepted as the old one had been rejected. If the radicals had stopped at this point, their Batavian Republic might have lasted longer. Instead, they embarked on the mass disenfranchisement of men identified as counter-revolutionaries, which lost them the support of Daendels and Joubert. Daendels travelled to Paris where he was able to convince the Directors that the new regime in the Netherlands was very much against French interests. On 12 June Daendels, pistol in hand, held Delacroix in his own ambassadorial residence while the radical Dutch Directors were arrested. Although the new constitution was still implemented, all those who had been arrested in January were released and the disenfranchised had the vote restored to them. Later even those arrested in this second coup were released, but the danger of a Jacobin dictatorship had been avoided.

It is possible that Anglo-Russian intervention during this period of political turmoil might have been successful, but the opportunity was lost once Daendels' second intervention had resolved the situation. Yet there was still anti-French feeling. The Dutch were paying more than 10 million guelders a year to support 25,000 French soldiers when little over 10,000 were actually in the Batavian Republic, and they were certainly not satisfied with the specious argument of the Directory that 'the defence of Zurich or the capture of Naples contributed, by crushing the Coalition, as much to the defence of the Netherlands as if the armies were kept on its own territory'.[18] On the other hand, all but the most conservative Dutch saw little to choose between the status quo and a return to British domination of the trade routes. Nonetheless, optimists like Tom Grenville, who had been employed on some of the diplomatic missions so vital to his brother the Foreign Secretary's strategy, believed the Dutch would rise and overwhelm the French. Perhaps influenced by his brother's optimism, perhaps feeling something was needed to counteract the Austrian withdrawal from Switzerland, Grenville now decided that once Holland had been taken the Anglo-Russian army should advance into Belgium, even though it was already late in the campaigning season.

There still remained the question of where the troops should land. The Meuse estuary was an obvious choice. The area was known and an advance inland, along the course of the Maas, would enable an attack from the rear on enemy lines at Ijssel and Vecht. But the estuary was guarded by the fortresses of Brikke and Helvoetsluys. This problem could be overcome by simultaneous attacks on Voorne and the mainland, but failure at any point would leave the other units vulnerable to enemy counter-attack, particularly those trying to take the forts. Other ideas were floated, including a two-pronged attack. Pitt favoured landings at Voorne, and at Groningen in the far north, the area reported to be most loyal to the House of Orange. He even proposed a timetable. Abercromby, however, insisted that it would be more effective to launch one concentrated attack.

Abercromby, innately cautious, had serious doubts about the viability of the campaign. In a memo he pointed out that if there were to be an invasion of Holland, then it should wait upon the arrival of the Russian first division. Far from heeding these doubts, the planners looked for other options. If the Meuse estuary posed too many difficulties, the idea of Walcheren could be resurrected, particularly if the Prussians, even at this late stage, could be persuaded to co-operate in Belgium. When it became clear that King Friedrich Wilhelm, deterred by French threats, would not join forces,

Abercromby pointed out that without Prussian support a large garrison would be needed to hold this notoriously unhealthy area.

So the discussions continued. Possession of Walcheren, Goree and Ameland would usefully support the anticipated Dutch rising. Alternatively, landing 15,000 men at the Ems would establish a position in Groningen. Yet an advance into Holland from Groningen would only be possibly if Koevorder fortress on the Vecht was taken. This might well extend the campaign into the winter, and Abercromby knew only too well what a Dutch winter was like. Scheveningen was also suggested, even though the exposed beach was notoriously dangerous and easy to defend.

Abercromby, when pressed, inclined towards an attack on the Meuse islands. Disembarkation at Voorne would be risky because the water was too shallow for the larger ships to get in close. Yet if the expedition was to go ahead, possession of Voorne was vital. On balance, though, he believed all the options were too risky. This was not what Pitt wanted to hear. Abercromby's caution provoked him to remark that 'There are some persons who have a pleasure in opposing whatever is proposed.'[19] His irritation missed the simple point that Abercromby was looking at the situation from a practical, military perspective. After his experience in Flanders and the West Indies, the soldier, who was not without political acumen, could not fail to notice that previous mistakes were about to be repeated, the worst being that an inadequate force was being sent in anticipation of a local uprising that might never materialise. Of all the peoples of Europe, the pragmatic Dutch were possibly the least likely to risk their security on such uneasy terms.

The minister most inclined to take Abercromby's doubts seriously was Dundas, who countered Grenville's optimism with the warning that 'Unless the Dutch co-operate with us cordially and actively, I do not think it possible to do as much by mere force of arms in this campaign as we flatter ourselves. I cannot forget the American War and the disappointment of our hopes.' It was a sign of his friendship with Abercromby that he repeated Grenville's view to him, explaining that it would justify him if 'he should be led to dash more than military rules and tactics would warrant'.[20]

Even though it had still not been decided where the expedition should land, on 25 July the four brigades intended for the advance force mustered on Barham Downs. As for the quality of the troops, Moore, who was to serve as a brigadier at Abercromby's request, wrote in his journal: 'The Guards are certainly a fine body of men. The regiments of the Line are in general but poor, and few of them are formed or disciplined. The 92nd (Highlanders) are an exception. They are excellent; my next best are the Royals and 25th;

the 79th are weak, but not bad. The 49th have not been a sufficient time embodied; the 64th are not fit to be sent upon service.'[21]

If further evidence were needed that Abercromby would be commanding too many raw troops, William Surtees, newly enlisted in the Militia at the time, remembered how 'none of us finished our drill; for, in July of the same year, an order was issued, permitting such men as chose to extend their services, to volunteer into the line, in order to recruit the army then destined for Holland'. Surtees volunteered into the 56th. At Canterbury 'we joined the skeleton of our regiment, just then returned from the West Indies, where twice, during the war, it had been nearly exterminated by disease . . . The regiment had not at this time either arms, appointments, or clothing; but, being in a few days sent off to Barham Downs, where the army for Holland was assembled and encamped, we soon after were supplied with the necessary equipment, and commenced without delay to drill and get the men ready for embarkation.'[22] Since the 56th were to sail with the Duke of York, it is easy to imagine just how ad hoc were the arrangements for the troops in the advance force.

In addition to the doubtful quality of the troops, there were insufficient horses to pull the guns and wagons, despite the creation of the Royal Wagon Train, which was embodied on 15 August. Nor were there enough naval ships to carry the flat boats that would be needed for disembarkation, while the search for sufficient boats was still ongoing. Abercromby sent another memo in which he pointed out that 'The British troops want the means of conveyance for artillery, sick, baggage and provisions, and you know we have not a foot on the continent until we acquire it. I hope it is not a crime to state such facts.' Two days later he wrote: 'The Emperor of Russia may make a general into a private man by his fiat, but he cannot make his army march without their baggage . . . and rest assured, that an army cannot move without horses and wagons.'[23] Abercromby also contacted the Duke of York, as commander-in-chief of the army, and York persuaded Pitt to requisition monies from the Treasury for anything that was lacking. This presupposed that wagons, horses and supplies were available in the numbers required, which proved not to be the case.

In one area, though, was there a reasonable chance that earlier mistakes would not be repeated. Dr Young, recently returned from the West Indies, was again appointed as Inspector General of Hospitals. Here was a man with whom Abercromby had already established a warm relationship; a man known for his indefatigable efforts on behalf of the sick. There was also a generous complement of medical staff, two physicians, four surgeons,

1. Sir Ralph Abercromby
(1734–1801), after Hoppner.
(*Author's collection*)

2. Sir John Moore
(1761–1809), Abercromby's
most trusted lieutenant,
from *The Royal Military
Chronicle*. (*Author's
collection*)

3. William Pitt the Younger (1759–1806), Prime Minister at the outbreak of the French Revolutionary Wars, by John Hoppner. (*National Portrait Gallery*)

4. Henry Dundas, later 1st Viscount Melville (1742–1811), Secretary of State for War 1794–1801, by Sir Thomas Lawrence. (*National Portrait Gallery*)

5. William Wyndham Grenville, 1st Lord Grenville (1759–1834), Secretary of State for Foreign Affairs 1791–1801, by Gainsborough Dupont. (*National Portrait Gallery*)

6. The Duke of York at the Siege of Valenciennes, 1793. (*Anne S.K. Brown Collection*)

7. The Battle of Tourcoing, 1794. (*Alamy*)

8. The Winter Retreat, 1795. (*Alamy*)

9. The 27th (Inniskillings) take Morne Fortuné, 24 May 1796. (*The Inniskillings Museum*)

10. The Capture of Trinidad, 18 February 1797, by Nicholas Pocock. (*Public domain*)

11. John Jeffreys
Pratt, 1st Marquis
Camden (1759–1840),
Lord Lieutenant
of Ireland 1795–8,
by William Salter.
(*Public domain*)

12. British troops under General Abercromby landing in North Holland,
27 August 1799. (*Courtesy of Michael Crumplin*)

13. The Battle of Egmont, 2 October 1799, after Jan Langendyk. (*Public domain*)

14. The Departure of the Anglo–Russian Expedition from North Holland, November 1799 (*Author's collection*)

15. Aboukir Bay, March 1801. (*Author collection*)

16. British Troops landing at Aboukir, 8 March 1801, by Philip James de Loutherbourg. (*Anne S.K. Brown collection*)

17. The Death of General Sir Ralph Abercromby K.B., after Thomas Stotha (*Anne S.K. Brown Collection*)

three apothecaries, a purveyor and three deputies. Although Abercromby had reservations about general hospitals, based on the problems of 1793–5, he accepted their necessity and had the consolation of knowing that they would be well supplied with medical stores, although on a basis of the normal allowance for a 10 per cent casualty rate they might yet prove insufficient. Young, however, suggested a solution. A hospital ship should be fitted out so that the most seriously sick and wounded could be transferred to hospitals at Deal, Harwich and Yarmouth. It was a typical feature of military planning, however, that while Deal possessed a dedicated military hospital, the casualties would have to be transferred to shore in open boats. Fortunately, Dr Jerome Fitzgerald, who was now Inspector General of Health and Transport, intervened and decided that the wounded would all be landed at Harwich.[24]

Abercromby received his first orders on 3 August. These established the main objective of the campaign, which was to liberate the Dutch, and then outlined the organization of the army. He was instructed to take command of the first division, comprising 10,000 men, who would sail ahead of the rest of the army and secure territory for further operations. He was specifically required to take Goree and Overflakke, to the south of Voorne, Rozenburg to the north, and then Voorne itself, followed by an attack on the mainland north of the Waal, at which stage he would receive an extra 4,000 troops. Suggested mainland targets were Maasland, Hellvoetsluis, Schiedam, Rotterdam and Dordrecht. If Abercromby had reservations about advancing further than the islands, the 4,000 troops would be held back until the arrival of the Russians. There was also a suggested of diversionary naval activity at Texel to threaten what remained of the Dutch fleet.

General Don had already been sent to warn the Orangists east of the Zuiderzee that they must resist the temptation to take any action before the first British landings. They would be sent arms once an attack had been made on Ameland. To further assist the Orangist cause, Abercromby was instructed to issue a proclamation from the Hereditary Prince. This would make British intentions clear, establishing that it was

> not as Enemies, but as Friends and Deliverers that the British troops enter into the Territory of the United Provinces. It is to rescue the Inhabitants of this once free and happy Country from the oppression under which they groan; to protect their Religion from the intolerant and persecuting spirit of Infidelity and Atheism; to deliver their Civil Government from the Despotism of a rapacious Anarchy, and to re-establish their ancient Liberty and

> Independence by restoring to them the Benefits of that Constitution
> for which, under the Auspices of the Illustrious House of Orange,
> their Ancestors fought and conquered, and in the enjoyment of
> which they so long flourished in Friendship and Alliance with
> Great Britain . . .[25]

The only positive element in these first orders was an assurance from
Dundas that if upon reaching the Meuse Abercromby discovered that the
risks of proceeding were too great, he could withdraw. This proviso was
welcome when the expedition was sailing blind, and dangerously dependent
on information from unreliable sources. Although Dutch refugees had given
assurances that Goree and Overflakke were viable landing places, they could
provide no definite information. Nor had a freebooter called Johnstone,
who was reported to be familiar with the Dutch coast, proved any more
helpful, and the only apparently reliable information came from a Dutch
prisoner-of-war.

   Grenville's plan for the expedition was straightforward, if unrealistic.
Once the landings had been accomplished, Holland must be overrun as
quickly as possible, easy enough if the government remembered the need for
wagons and horses and the Dutch rose: difficult to achieve without popular
support. Grenville, however, expected Abercromby to advance rapidly into
Belgium. His information suggested that there were only 6,000 French
troops in the Batavian Republic, and the troops in Belgium would be drawn
south by the projected invasion of the Allies from Switzerland, which at
this point was still viable. With these comfortable assumptions influencing
his judgement, Grenville wrote: 'Sir Ralph Abercromby would neither do
justice to himself, nor to us, if he were to apply the same mode of military
calculation to his military operations, as he has to his demands, and were
to act in Holland as if he were in a country armed against him.'[26] A more
delusional opinion it would be difficult to conceive of.

   Abercromby's doubts about the whole enterprise were, if anything,
increasing as he considered the realities of the preparations. Nor was he alone
in his misgivings. Even after the expedition had set sail, Moore confided to
his journal similar reservations.

> The original destination of the expedition was the island of
> Walcheren; this has since been altered; Goeree and Vorne are
> now the objects. The information with respect to the force upon
> these islands, their state of defence, etc, is extremely imperfect.

The expedition has undoubtedly been hurried beyond reason, but
the country having been put to the expense of assembling it, it is
necessary that we should be sent to attempt something. We are now
upon a voyage of adventure.[27]

Pitt was anxious that the expedition should be launched as soon as possible
as evidence that the government was indeed attempting something but
Abercromby refused to sail while preparations were still incomplete. He
needed time for the Militia volunteers to settle into their new units and,
more importantly, for sufficient shipping to transport not only men but also
horses and landing craft. Indeed, there was no need for haste because the
landings would need a spring tide, and the next springs were not due until
the middle of the August.

On 6 August Dundas, Abercromby and Admiral Andrew Mitchell,
who was to command the supporting fleet, met to consider their options.
Also present were Captain Flynn RN, a Yarmouth man and thus familiar
with the relevant area of the North Sea, and a foreign officer who was also
supposed to be familiar with the Meuse estuary. This meeting failed to
satisfy Abercromby's reservations. He had proved in the West Indies that he
could co-operate with the navy but on this occasion he found the Admiral
over-optimistic to the point where all difficulties were brushed aside. Flynn
was reluctant to offer any opinion beyond stating that the seaward approach
to Voorne was unsuitable for the landings because access was impossible
for large ships. The only certain point to emerge from the discussions
was that Voorne must be taken, but this would first require silencing the
Goree battery and taking possession of Rozenburg with all its navigational
difficulties.

Dundas now suggested to Abercromby that instead of Voorne he
should land at Scheveringen, then march south, through territory held
by the enemy, to take Goree. Alternatively, if Mitchell agreed, he could
sail north to Texel and Den Helder in order to take the Dutch fleet. If that
proved too dangerous, there was always the Ems. If he landed near Delfzyl
he could take the provinces of Groningen, Friesland and Drenthe. Of the
three options, Goree seemed the least practicable, but the government had
promised loyalists in the area that British troops would be sent there in
support of a rising. Essentially, though, this new order passed the initiative
to the commanders. Grenville declined to be involved in this re-thinking,
even after Dundas had shared his concerns with him. As far as the Foreign
Secretary was concerned, heavily-defended Walcheren was to be the place

for the landings since it was convenient for the next stage of his strategy, the invasion of Belgium.

Abercromby now sent his aide-de-camp, Major James Kempt, to Dundas with a paper drawn up by Sir John Hope, his Deputy Adjutant General, under his direction. This made the case for an attack on den Helder and received Pitt's warm approval.[28] It also explains the decision Abercromby made when he finally set sail with 10,000 men on 13 August. If he landed at den Helder, the aim would be to seize the Dutch fleet, and such an objective would justify risking British troops in an ill-conceived expedition. The troops themselves had started to embark as soon as Kempt returned from Walmer. Abercromby also summoned General Coote from headquarters and gave him instructions for a demonstration on the Dutch coast, away from den Helder. Then he joined his troops on board ship.[29]

At this point General Don returned from the United Provinces with less than encouraging information. The enemy was strengthening his defences, which were generally in good repair, while the Dutch people, although resentful of the French presence, were unlikely to rise against them. He also recommended either Scheveningen or den Helder as the best places for the landings. In fact, Abercromby and Mitchell had already abandoned any idea of taking the islands in the Meuse estuary. Abercromby saw his task as fighting a military campaign that had some hope of success, instead of one that would end in stalemate at best and failure at worst. He had realized the futility of an expedition to the Meuse and the Maas once it was clear that there would be no Prussian support. He also recognized that political strategy was taking precedence over sound military considerations. He knew that no member of the triumvirate was 'a suitable supervisor of the war machine. Dundas specifically disowned the title of war minister. Grenville was indifferent to military problems; and the information on which his political considerations were based seems to have lain concealed in his own office . . . War was not Pitt's *metier*; and he allowed the political and military elements in British strategy to drift in parallel courses.'[30] Abercromby, and later York, were to be the unfortunate instruments of their wrongheadedness.

The Greatest Stroke

On 13 August 1799 Pitt started his day early in order to witness the departure of the fleet, 180 transports with their naval escort sailing up the Channel in calm conditions. According to Edward Walsh, he was witnessing the departure of 'the flower of the British Army . . .' while 'the commander-in-chief was an officer who had devoted a long life to the service of his country, during which, on many trying occasions, he was distinguished for his courage and ability, and the most unblemished reputation'.[31] Pitt probably thought they were sailing off to South Holland but Abercromby, with Mitchell's ready agreement, had already chosen den Helder as the objective. This surprised even Moore.

> A signal was made pretty early to the Generals and Captains of the fleet. When I went on board the *Isis* I found the original plan was changed. The difficulties attending the landing at Goeree and Voorne induced both the Admiral and Sir Ralph to give it up, and they determined to attack the Texel. The army lands, it is hoped, to-morrow. We are now standing for the shore, and shall anchor this night or to-morrow at daylight.[32]

Abercromby also sent Dundas notice of this decision.[33] Since Dundas had also doubted the viability of the Meuse plan, he sent his agreement as soon as Abercromby's letter reached him, instructing him to attack Texel, and then the mainland as far south as Haarlem and Amsterdam.

The wind that carried the fleet across the North Sea was fair at first but then the weather turned foul, as was so often Abercromby's experience. By 20 August, though, the fleet was off Texel, Mitchell having succeeded in keeping transports and warships in close contact. Here Admiral Duncan, with the North Sea fleet, had set up a blockade of the island and the Dutch fleet. Abercromby and Mitchell met with Duncan on his flagship, the *Kent*, to discuss the particulars of the landings. It was decided that Duncan would continue the blockade while Abercromby landed just south of the batteries of den Helder. He would then establish a defensive position on a spit of sand hills and open communications with England. A landing was planned for the following day and the landing craft were anchored two miles from Texel in preparation but a boisterous wind whipped up the sea and drove the ships further out. The landing craft had to raise anchor and the landings were abandoned. This delay, however, enabled Colonel Maitland and a naval officer to go inshore and summon the garrison of den Helder. More importantly, they were able to take a good look at the shore. They identified the most favourable part of the coast for landings if the wind was blowing from the south-west, as had been the case so far.

By 25 August, although the surf was still high, it was possible to anchor under the shore of den Helder. The following day the transports were brought inshore, ready for a landing between Kycksduin and Callantsoog, just south of den Helder, which was believed to be heavily fortified. By this time, conditions on board were increasingly uncomfortable, and 'all the fresh provisions and vegetables in the fleet were consumed; the wine, vinegar, and even water began to be scarce'.[34] Had the weather not held, the fleet would have been obliged to continue north to the Ems where they could re-supply. Also, the longer the delay lasted, the more time the enemy would have to plan his counter-offensive. Both the French and the Dutch had been aware of the preparations for the expedition but had no idea where it would land, a fortuitous result of the ministers' indecision. Thanks to the weather, though, they now had a good idea where they should concentrate their first line of defence.

In overall command of the Franco-Dutch forces was General Guillaume Marie-Anne Brune, who had joined the Revolutionary army as a volunteer in 1791. A protégé of Danton, he had risen rapidly through the ranks, being appointed general in 1793, and he would finish his career as a marshal before being murdered during the White Terror of 1815. Having commanded the expedition that successfully occupied Switzerland (where he acquired a reputation for plunder), he had assumed command of forces in the Batavian Republic in June 1799, and would prove himself a determined opponent of the Anglo-Russian army. Despite the notional 25,000, the French forces in the Batavian Republic actually amounted to no more than 15,000 at most, of variable quality. The Dutch could field about the same number but half of them were conscripts of uncertain loyalty. A further problem for Brune was that despite enjoying overall command, he soon discovered how obstructive the Dutch would be when he wanted to inspect their military resources.

When Brune learnt that the British were off Texel, he immediately called up reinforcements, even sending urgent messages to Belgium demanding troops. He then used the delay between the arrival of the British fleet and the landings to concentrate his forces in North Holland. The first division, under the command of General Louis-Jean-Baptiste Gouvion, was sent to Haarlem while Daendels, in local command, opposed the landings with about 13,000 men. Daendels had disposed his troops so that one brigade was defending the coast from den Helder to Groete Keeten while the other occupied Callantsoog, Petten, Kamp and Groet, and held a line from Schagen to Bergen. In addition, a small reserve had been left at Alkmaar. Brune also made sure he could feed his troops without having to call upon the local population because he knew the easiest way to alienate the Dutch was to demand supplies from them.

The position taken by the British fleet on 26 August suggested that Groete Keeten was the landing place, and Daendels adapted his position accordingly. He recognized that the configuration of the coast would make his troops vulnerable to the heavy naval guns, so he decided to attack the enemy on the flank as soon as they were in the dunes. He posted one of his brigades between Petten and Callantsoog, with two battalions in the centre of the dunes, another battalion in reserve, and two further battalions with their right on Groete Keeten and their left by the sea. Another three battalions, two squadrons and four guns were positioned in front of Huysduinen, obliquely to the sea, while several companies were told off to protect den Helder.

Abercromby faced a more immediate problem than the intervention of the enemy. Such had been the determination to press ahead with the campaign that the ministers had failed to collect the vital flat-bottomed boats needed for the landing. Instead, naval boats had to be used but they could land only 3,000 men at a time. At 3 a.m. on 27 August the naval guns opened fire on the beaches and at dawn the first troops were rowed ashore. These were men of Coote's 1st Brigade comprising the 2nd, 27th, 69th and 85th, with some of Macdonald's reserve, commanded by Abercromby's second-in-command, Sir James Pulteney (Sir James Murray of the Flanders campaign who had subsequently changed his name to his wife's to secure an inheritance). They were to establish themselves at the southern end of the chosen beach as Coote had already been informed. The rest of the army, under Abercromby's direct command, would land further north, with the Guards on the right and Moore's brigade on the left, closest to den Helder.

There were losses when some of the boats were swamped by the heavy surf. The troops that did reach the shore found themselves in a willy-nilly state because the naval officers directing the landings had failed to appreciate the importance of keeping companies and battalions together. The result was chaos rather than brief disorganization. Moore wrote that they landed 'with great confusion and irregularity. I was put on shore with not more than 300 men of my brigade, and those a mixture of every different regiment; the ground was such as to render the fire from the shipping to no avail. Had we been opposed we must have been beaten with little resistance; but the enemy had made no disposition to oppose the immediate landing.'[35] Furthermore, the full extent of the beach was not used as had been planned, possibly because a strong south-west wind had sent Pulteney further north than intended, close to where Moore was landing. The resultant crowding of the troops prolonged the confusion Daendels had anticipated. Nor had any kind of order been established when Pulteney somewhat prematurely gave the command to advance in the direction of Groete Keeten.

Daendels had hitherto kept his distance but Pulteney's advance was his opportunity.

> . . . the first Division had scarcely begun to move forward, before they got into Action, which continued from five in the Morning until three o'Clock in the afternoon. The enemy had assembled a very considerable Body of Infantry, Cavalry and Artillery, and made repeated attacks on our Right with fresh Troops.
>
> Our position was on a Ridge of Sand hills, stretching along the Coast from North, to South. Our Right Flank was unavoidably exposed to the whole Force of the Enemy. We had nowhere sufficient Ground on our right to form more than a Battalion in line. Yet on the whole, the position though singular, was not in our Situation disadvantageous, having neither Cavalry nor Artillery.
>
> By the Courage and Perseverance of the Troops, the Enemy was fairly worn out and obliged to retire in the Evening, to a Position two Leagues in his Rear.
>
> The Contest was arduous, and the Loss has been considerable. We have to regret many valuable Officers lost to the Service who have either fallen or been disabled by their Wounds . . .[36]

To add more detail to this bald account, when some sailors who had strayed towards the dunes came under fire, Pulteney's leading troops climbed a ridge of sand hills and charged the leading Dutch battalions, driving them back on their own reserve, southwards to Groete Keeten. At this point Pulteney should have focused on taking up a defensive position to protect the men who were still being landed. Instead, his troops advanced in increasing disorder. The pursuit brought them to an extensive hollow where a concealed enemy detachment had guns loaded with grape. Daendels immediately send forward two further concealed battalions, and also called up troops from Callantsoog, to put pressure on Pulteney's right flank. Pulteney tried to reform but the limited area of flat ground made this difficult and the British were forced back. This lured the enemy from the shelter of the dunes and they now became targets of naval gunfire.

Abercromby had landed by this time, along with Brigadier General Francis d'Oyley's Guards brigade, while on the left Moore was being reinforced as more of his brigade came ashore. This enabled him to take up a position opposite den Helder and thus hold off an enemy attack on Pulteney's left flank, while Abercromby brought up infantry reinforcements who effectively disrupted the progress of an advancing Dutch column. Daendels tried to seize control of the inner line of sand hills, but Coote's brigade and the reserve were now settling into entrenched positions, while Abercromby and the 1st Guards brigade advanced to attack the enemy. The struggle became general along the length of the sand hills until, at about 5 p.m., Daendels withdrew four miles. Abercromby was unable to pursue him because he lacked cavalry, while transport and supplies were still to be landed. Instead, he gave his attention to den Helder.

There was a price to pay for what must be considered successful, if disorganized landings. Abercromby's dispatch continued: 'During the course of the Action I had the Misfortune to lose the Service of L[t] General Sir James Pulteney from a Wound he received in his Arm, but not before he had done himself the greatest Honor, and that I was fully sensible of his Loss. Major General Coote supplied his Place with Ability. Colonel Macdonald, who commanded the Reserve, and who was very much engaged during the Course of the Day, though wounded, did not quit the Field . . .'[37]

As was his wont, Abercromby had commanded from the front. Two of his staff officers were wounded, one of them being his deputy adjutant general and trusted subordinate, John Hope. He also lost his chief engineer, a loss that Abercromby felt personally. He wrote to Dundas on 28 August, 'Lieutenant Colonel Hay, whom I highly valued, was killed by my side. He has left a widow and six daughters without a shilling. I trust that you will recommend Colonel Hay's family to the King's goodness. If I have endeavoured to render any service to the public on this occasion, the only reward I ask is, that this poor family may not be left destitute.'[38] He had made a promise to the dying Hay, whose thigh had been shattered, that he would ensure his family was provided for.

Abercromby had achieved a victory out of the confusion on the beach and against Daendels' sustained attack. There was no cause for celebration as yet, however, because 'Our situation at this moment was unpromising. An enemy was on both our flanks and we were in a position which, however favourably it had been represented by maps, proved to be extremely bad. Sir Ralph determined that at night I should attack the Helder. A part of the Guards were to assist. It was evident that if we failed, immediate measures must be taken for re-embarking.'[39]

Despite Moore's pessimism, there was no failure. As Jomini later wrote, the Dutch had always depended upon their naval force to protect them from seaborne attack but on this occasion there had been no sign of the Dutch ships. Yet there were the first signs of another enemy, impossible to overcome and with the power to weaken the British forces. 'The weather was rainy, cold, and tempestuous; and presage of the autumn season in the humid and trying atmosphere of North Holland. Its fatal effects would necessarily soon become visible in an army exposed, and without camp equipage of any sort . . . It is the parent of those unhappy fevers which undermine, unnerve, and wither all the faculties of the hardiest frames.'[40]

Fears about the strength of the defences at den Helder proved groundless; there were 'heavy batteries towards the sea, commanding the channel of the Texel and the deep water within it' but 'on the land side the works were imperfect and neglected' held by 'a motley garrison'.[41] Abercromby subsequently wrote:

> As the Enemy still held the Helder with a Garrison of near two thousand Men it was determined to attack it before day break on the Morning of the 28th, and the Brigade under M General Moore support'd by M Gen. Burrard were destined for this Service, but about Eight O'Clock yesterday Evening, the Dutch Fleet in the Maes Diep got under Weigh, and the Garrison was withdrawn, taking the Route through the Marshes towards Midenblick, having previously spiked the Guns on the Batteries, and destroyed some of the Carriages. About nine at Night M Gen. Moore, with the 2nd Batt. Of the Royals, and the 92nd Regt, under the command of Lord Huntley, took possession of this important Post, in which he found a numerous Artillery of the best kind, both of heavy and field Train.

There were further gains when 'that part of the Dutch Fleet in the Nieuwe Diep, together with their Naval Magazine at Nieuwe Werk, fell into our hands this Morning . . .'.[42]

Daendels knew he lacked the resources to offer further resistance and gave the somewhat controversial order to abandon den Helder. He then withdrew to a position that placed his left at Petten by the sea and his right at Oudesluis on the Zuiderzee. He had earlier advised closing the entry to the Texel but this had not been done. There was also a suggestion that the Dutch crews had been worked on by emissaries from the Hereditary Prince because seven Dutch ships surrendered after den Helder had been abandoned, while others sailed eastward. Mitchell was now able to buoy the channel, allowing safe access to his own ships. He raised the Orange flag and offered negotiations to the Dutch commander, Admiral Samuel Story. These were refused, and Story prepared to take on the much stronger British fleet, whereupon mutiny broke out on some of his ships.

Many of the British troops were in position to witness what happened next.

> We described [*sic*] Admiral Mitchell cautiously advancing through the mouth of the Texel . . . and we saw immediately before us the Dutch fleet drawn up in line of battle. The whole line turned out anxiously awaiting a conflict which, tho' we in no way doubted the result, yet every mind filled with anxiety. In a little while we saw the Boats passing backwards and forwards, and some time after the Dutch flags flying in the Batavian fleet. The result was soon communicated to us and is well known, but the acquisition alone was a most essential advantage obtained by the expedition, and filled our hearts with exultation.[43]

Having been summoned to surrender, Story offered as an excuse for his capitulation that his men had refused to fight. As a result, the navy had acquired a further eight ships of the line, three frigates and a sloop of war, as well as ninety-five guns and the stores held at Nieuwe Diep.

Abercromby had much on which to congratulate himself, and would have been gratified by Moore's opinion:

> Thus the greatest stroke that has perhaps been struck in this war has been accomplished in a few hours, and with a trifling loss. The expedition, though it has terminated so successfully, began with every appearance against it. We were a fortnight at sea, and the enemy perfectly apprised of our design. It showed great enterprise in Sir Ralph to persevere in the attempt, and he has met with the success he deserved. The chances of war are infinite. The number which were against the success of this expedition were incalculable.[44]

Dundas' response to Abercromby's dispatch was equally enthusiastic, yet along with the fulsome congratulations there was an implicit sense of relief. Dundas at least had glimpsed something of the military difficulties of the campaign. Now he wrote:

The cool judgement, military ardor, and superior abilities you have
displayed on the occasion, have justly drawn from His Majesty the
warmest commendation. It is to these great qualities, directing
the enterprizing Courage of the Troops and the able assistance of
Lieutenant General Sir James Pulteney, and the other Generals and
Staff Officers engaged on the occasion, that His Majesty ascribes,
under Providence, the brilliant opening of the Campaign, and the
important events by which it has been so rapidly improved.[45]

Grenville had anticipated a rapid advance into Belgium once the position
in Holland was secured. He now became impatient with Abercromby.
He could see no reason for him to await the arrival of the Duke of York
with the remainder of the British troops and the Russians. The reality of
the situation, however, made such an advance difficult, if not impossible.
Abercromby confided to his family, 'This expedition has hung heavy on my
mind ever since it was thought of. The risk was far too great, and now all
is not daylight.'[46] The disembarkation on 30 August of Major General Don
with the 17th and 40th and Major General Lord Cavan with the 1/20th,
2/20th and 63rd, plus the 11th Light Dragoons, added a useful 5,000 men
of all ranks. There was still a lack of horses and wagons, though, and an
advance towards Alkmaar could not be accomplished without transport.
Only General Coote and part of his brigade formed an entrenched front
towards Alkmaar. The rest of the troops bivouacked in the sand hills for four
days without camp equipment and all the while the unseasonal wind and
rain was unremitting. The means to support an advance with the necessary
provisions and stores did not arrive until 1 September, although the heavy
baggage was still at Deal and the shortage of transport meant that tents had
to be left at den Helder. The problems York had faced in Flanders were once
again in evidence.

Both the strength and the disposition of the enemy were as yet
unknown. According to Grenville, the enemy lacked the men to challenge
Abercromby's advance on Amsterdam, and what force there was would be
more than counterbalanced by the Dutch, who would now rise in support of
the House of Orange. For a soldier such an optimistically unsupported view
was delusional; and for a cautious man, the first requirement was reliable
information so that the odds could be assessed. Abercromby, therefore,
brought his first line into a strong defensive position, from Oudesluis on
the Zuiderzee on his left, twelve miles south-west to Krabbendam, and
then following a line sharply north-west along a canal to Petten. This was

a country of meadows and cultivated land, intersected by canals and dykes which usefully protected the position Abercromby had taken up. There were two potentially vulnerable points where the Amsterdam–Alkmaar–den Helder canal and the road running up from Amsterdam and Alkmaar crossed the lines, the former at Zijpe Sluis and the latter at Krabbendam. The two battalions of the 20th were designated to hold these posts, while the Guards were given responsibility for the crossing point on the canal to Petten. A further crossing point at St Maartens was held by the 40th. The line was well-defended because 'An immense Dyke or Mound of earth which stretched from the North Sea to the Zuyder Sea was about ¾ mile in our front' and within 'a day or two very excellent Batteries were very advantageously erected upon this Mound [and] several others were afterwards established.'[47] The remainder of Don's brigade, along with Moore's, were either watching den Helder or, in the case of Coote's and Macdonald's, functioning as a reserve which could be brought forward to support any part of the line that was under threat. In this position Abercromby waited for York's arrival.

In the meantime the disposition of the enemy became clearer, and Abercromby responded by altering the position of his own forces. According to Moore,

> The enemy have about 5,000 French, 8,000 Dutch. The French are posted in Alkmaar, and have posts to the sea at Camp. The Dutch are upon the right, their headquarters at Schermeer Shoorn. Our position with respect to theirs is oblique, the right advanced. Our right opposite to the French, is more immediately threatened. Sir Ralph wished to reinforce it. I received an order in the evening of the 5th to march with the Royals and the 92nd Regiments, and take post upon the left of the Guards in first line, my right on Zype Sluys, my left on St Marteens and Brug. General Don's brigade was ordered to close their cantonment to the left to make room for me. The 20th Regiment of two battalions was put under my command in lieu of the other regiments of my brigade, which I left at Ouder Sluys. A high dyke in front of the canal and generally within cannon shot of it, is now our line of defence instead of the canal, though our cantonments are chiefly on the other side of the canal. Four bridges cross it, four more are being made with boats, and communications are being opened from the canal to the dyke. Our picquets are upon the dyke, and command an extensive view, besides which we occupy as outposts the villages in front of the

dyke . . . The enemy occupy Camp Groet, Shorldam, and Oude Karspel. Our sentries and videttes are pretty near each other . . .[48]

Abercromby has been criticised for choosing to take up a defensive position, and not only by contemporaries like Grenville. Jomini, writing in the 1830s, was strongly of the opinion that he could have advanced further south and put the Franco–Dutch forces under pressure.

> This easy conquest, by fulfilling the naval aim of the expedition, secured for the English free navigation of the Zuiderzee, and should have enabled Abercrombie to profit from his superior numbers and advance into the interior, stretch his resources and provoke the inhabitants to insurrection. But although the reinforcements that he had received raised his force to more than 16,000 men, he contented himself with chasing Daendels from his position on the Zijpe. This one, a long way from thinking on the defensive, fearing to be turned on his left, behind which the English could easily throw troops, decided to move closer to Alkmaar, and on the same day as the surrender of the fleet, he decamped and took position before Scheermer, between Avenhorn and Alkmaar. From there he could quickly take himself to the line from Purmerend to Monikendam, if the enemy pushed [forward] or made attempts against Amsterdam.[49]

Abercromby's decision to take a defensive stance could be ascribed to his shortage of so many campaigning essentials or to his generally negative feelings about the whole expedition. As far as his troops were concerned, he judged only the Guards and the 92nd truly fit for active service. At the other extreme, Don and Cavan had brought over many of the battalions filled with untrained volunteers. In contrast, the force under Daendels had proved itself unexpectedly effective. Furthermore, although Abercromby now had some wagons and horses, the total number of bread wagons available was only thirty-five, and there was only one forge cart. Nor were the local farmers showing any inclination to release their own horses and wagons, let alone to rise in rebellion. In a country intersected with dykes and canals water transport might have seemed the obvious alternative to wagons but the enemy had destroyed the small craft that plied the canals. Furthermore, although waterways were excellent barriers for a defensive operation, they made offensive manoeuvres difficult. In fact, the whole countryside was, as Jomini described it, a chessboard of canals and high dykes.

Despite having some awareness of the practical problems Abercromby faced, even Dundas had expected him to press on towards Amsterdam, particularly once Don's and Cavan's brigades had arrived. He made this clear in his initial response to the success of the landings when he surmised that, having secured den Helder, Abercromby would soon be in possession of North Holland as far south as Beverwyk and Haarlem in readiness for the march on Amsterdam. Abercromby himself had initially thought in terms of an advance towards Alkmaar, but influenced by the practical shortcomings of his situation and also, possibly, by the risk of strong Dutch resistance, he changed his mind and decided to hold ground on the lines of Zijpe.

At the same time he was prepared for pressure from the ministers, telling Dundas that although his 'determination to remain on the defensive until reinforced may not meet with the approbation of His Majesty's Ministers or professional men, yet I am certain that I have acted right.'[50] Ironically, although this decision may not have satisfied His Majesty's ministers, it would certainly have been approved by His Majesty. The King, a lone voice against the enthusiasm for further action, was concerned that matters were being rushed. Abercromby was not alone in feeling the need for caution. 'I doubt whether the over ardour of Mr Dundas may not incline him to press the remaining troops forward before they are in order, which may render success less certain than if a little more time be given.'[51] Like Abercromby, he believed it would have been wiser to wait for the arrival of the Russians.

Abercromby also realized that any forward movement would be strongly opposed by the enemy, whom he reckoned to be at least 15,000 strong, against the 14,000 he could bring into action. If he remained behind his defensive line until York arrived, then the Franco-Dutch would have no choice but to withdraw from their own positions under the threat of attack. He was also aware that he had the best British troops with him, which was all the more reason not to gamble with them in an uncertain action. Significantly, Moore, having described the British disposition, concluded: 'We must remain in our position till reinforced; upon the arrival of the Russians we shall instantly move forward.'[52] Admittedly, Moore shared Abercromby's cautious approach, but he was also a better judge than Grenville or Dundas.

While he waited for York and the Russians, Abercromby sought to open communications with the Dutch. He wrote a letter to the Batavian Directory which General Don carried to Daendels' headquarters. Here he hoped to acquire a passport to The Hague, but General Brune, who was now on the scene, refused the request. This seems to have been provoked by Don's absent-mindedness. When he pulled the papers he was carrying out of his pocket he also inadvertently revealed a length of orange ribbon which was intended for any adherents to the Stadtholder that he encountered. A further search revealed that he was also carrying proclamations to the Dutch. Brune's refusal of the passport, however, convinced Abercromby that an attack was imminent so he concentrated on strengthening his defensive line with guns, fortifications and forward piquets. Petten and Oudesluis at the ends of his line received particular attention. He also strongly occupied the villages between Schagen and Krabbendam, which served as advance posts.

Brune was aware that the enemy would soon be reinforced from Britain, and had been collecting his forces, as well as calling out the National Guard. He left sufficient troops in Zealand to protect it from attack, directed the rest of his French troops to Haarlem and summoned General Dumonceau from the east. He expected Mitchell to move into the Zuiderzee, so he also concentrated upon defending Amsterdam by posting a fleet of gunboats on the fortified Pampus Island and covering the tongue of land of Brink Sloot with batteries. When the last reinforcements arrived on 8 September, they brought Brune's force up to 21,000 men, one-third French and two-thirds Dutch.

In the meantime Daendels had evacuated Avenhorn and had concentrated his division between Rustenburg and Koedyk. To his left, Vandamme commanded a force of 7,000 men to defend the area from the sea to Alkmaar, with outposts at Oudescarpel, Schoorldam and Schoorl. When Dumonceau arrived with the last 6,000 men they were posted at Koedyk. Brune believed he now had the resources necessary to drive the British from their lines before the arrival of York and the Russians. He reasoned that, even if the British successfully repulsed the attack and continued to hold their position, nothing would have been lost.

At the same time, British patrols had located the enemy three miles to their front. This certainly indicated the imminence of an attack but 'As the whole Army was in the constant habit of being under arms at their Post an hour before day light, no confusion could possibly follow . . .'[53] Such proved the case.

Brune planned to attack at daybreak on 10 September and turn the British right flank, a task given to the 7,000 reliable French troops under General Vandamme. Having debouched by Schoorl, they would take Groet and Kamp and penetrate as far as Petten. As Vandamme's troops were leaving Schoorl, the 6,000 Dutch to the right of them under General Dumonceau would move by way of Schoorldam to Krabbendam, where they were to take the bridge and force the entrenchments at the vulnerable angle of the British lines. Further right Daendels with a further 6,000 men was to advance northwards from St Pankras, also five miles north of Alkmaar, and traverse the Langdyk towards Eenigenburg.

Abercromby was still struggling to get supplies forward, and was also frustrated by the inaction of Admiral Mitchell, who was out of contact dealing with the Dutch ships rather than sending gunboats and the local flat-bottomed boats into the shallow Zuiderzee to threaten the Franco-Dutch force. The only naval presence was a small flotilla of gunboats under Home Popham on the Alkmaar Canal. (These would, however, render significant support.) Convinced that Brune was about to make a forward movement, Abercromby expected the strongest attack to fall on his right flank at Krabbendam and back towards Petten. This section was held by the Guards, with the two-battalion 20th at Krabbendam itself. As already noted, he had ordered Moore, whom he regarded as his most competent brigadier, to take command of the line between Sint Maarten and Krabbendam with two of his best battalions.

What followed, like the following engagements, was 'of the most peculiar kind. Restricted to dikes and causeys, intersecting in different directions a low and swampy ground, it consisted of detached conflicts at insulated points rather than any general movements; and . . . was to be determined chiefly by the intrepidity of the heads of columns.'[54]

Brune had hoped to take the British by surprise, but his opponents were forewarned by the noise of gun carriages and drums which suggested units getting into position. The period of quiet that followed confirmed this suspicion. Abercromby instructed Moore to be ready to respond at first light, while Moore himself received a warning from Lieutenant Colonel Smith of the 20th that a sizeable force was advancing on Krabbendam. This was Vandamme's right column. According to orders, Vandamme's division advanced in three columns, preceded by a swarm of skirmishers and headed by grenadiers with bayonets fixed. While the right column marched towards Krabbendam in order to support Dumonceau's attack, the centre advanced towards Slaperdyk, and the left made for the coastal dyke and Petten. It was this column that broke first, coming under heavy British fire supported by a frigate and some gunboats. Having taken heavy losses, the French had no choice but to retire. The centre managed to reach Slaperdyk where they were confronted by Burrard's 2nd Guards brigade, lined up to oppose them. Under steady British fire the French attack eventually disintegrated. After two hours they were in full retreat.

Further right there was some delay at the outset when one of Dumonceau's brigades was late moving. The other was misdirected and marched in the direction of Eenigenburg. This brought them onto the road where Daendel's force was advancing, also towards Eenigenburg. Afraid of losing the momentum of the attack, Dumonceau let the brigade which had gone astray continue on the wrong road and marched rapidly with the rest of his division to Krabbendam. Here he divided his force into two columns, both of which attacked with great determination. The smaller of the two, which came under enfilading fire from the British, took refuge in the first houses they came to. The larger column headed towards the entrenchments at the dyke. Abercromby immediately responded to Dumonceau's attack by sending the 2/20th towards Eenigenburg, leaving the five companies of the first battalion to face the French onslaught. At first the impetus was with the Dutch, who were able to advance into the village and engage in a hand-to-hand struggle. 'The enemy had driven our people from Krabbendam and from a redoubt on the right of it, but were not able to penetrate further. Colonel Smith and six officers of the 20th Regiment had been wounded, and the corps composed of drafts from the Militia, behaved, Sir Ralph Abercromby told me, with great gallantry.'[55] Abercromby, as was typical of him, had dismounted and put himself at the head of the British defenders, who rallied and held the position until re-joined by the second battalion. Together the two battalions put Dumonceau's troops to flight.

Meanwhile, once he had sorted out his disordered troops, Daendels moved north to Sint Maarten where he was able to take the outer British defences. He then went to Eenigenburg, where Dumonceau's stray column had initially taken the village but had failed at the entrenchments. According to Daendel's own account, he had hoped to rally the troops. Instead, he found them in retreat. After this failure he returned to Sint Maarten, to continue the attack there. He then became aware that there was no fighting on his left. When the 40th of Don's brigade threatened his flank as they advanced from Schagen, he retired to Sint Pankras.

Brune's army had been driven back at all points, having suffered some 2,000 casualties. Acknowledging that any further attack would waste his resources unnecessarily, he decided not to oppose the landings of York's troops and the Russians. Instead, recognizing that an Anglo-Russian advance was now inevitable, he concentrated upon fortifying his original position. Roads were broken up and redoubts constructed at salient points on the dykes in order to make the terrain even more difficult for an advancing force.

The British took little more than a tenth of Brune's losses, and Abercromby had the further satisfaction of witnessing the fighting spirit even of battalions with large drafts from the Militia. The action had 'confirmed the confidence of the British troops in themselves and in their commanders; and it proved how easily the position on the Zuype might be held by 12,000 or 14,000 men.' At the same time, 'The Dutch troops had fought against us with great bravery; nor, though they had been beaten, was the desertion from their ranks considerable.' Similarly, the civilian population evinced no support for the House of Orange.

> The farmers and others within our lines lounged about with their pipes in their mouths; as silent and sullen spectators of an unpleasant disturbance . . . it was sufficiently clear that, however odious the French domination might be in the provinces on the other side of the Zuyder Zee, there was little goodwill towards us in North Holland. If the Allies were to make their direct way to Amsterdam it must be done by sheer fighting; and the enemy was every day receiving reinforcements and fortifying his successive lines of defence.[56]

Thus Abercromby cannot have been disappointed by York's arrival that same evening with the long-awaited main British force and the first of the Russians.

On the Attack

Abercromby received general praise for the success of the landings, including the freedom of the city and a sword valued at a hundred guineas from the Corporation of London. Dundas wrote a remarkably frank letter to Abercromby's eldest son in which he admitted ministerial culpability.

> Gratified as the country is by the complete success, neither the Minister who planned, nor the General who executed, the enterprise, would have escaped censure if it had failed. In so far as I could, I took the responsibility on my shoulders. From what Sir Ralph stated to me, I was aware that risks were to be run, not justifiable by the rules of military prudence, and therefore, when I gave my last instructions, I expressly took responsibility on myself. Thanks to Heaven and to Sir Ralph, we stand on a pinnacle of glory and fame . . .[57]

It is doubtful whether Abercromby shared this sentiment. Despite the victory of 10 September, which was not known in England when Dundas wrote his letter, the practical problems of supply and transport, combined with an enemy growing stronger by the day, still remained. These were now York's problems, however. He had arrived off Den Helder on the day Brune was repulsed, and landed three days later. He brought with him three brigades of infantry, Chatham's, Manners' and Prince William of Gloucester's, as well as the 7th Light Dragoons and a detachment from the 18th Light Dragoons, and artillery. All but one of these infantry battalions had taken in Militia volunteers. These British troops were accompanied by 12,000 Russians of unknown quality. As for their commander, General Johann Hermann von Fersen, 'it can only be said that, with a great deal of boasting and pretension, he was no better than his men'.[58] To put it more kindly, although 'probably a bad general . . . he was a brave, zealous, and straightforward fellow'.[59] Hermann's ability was crucial because, although York was commander-in-chief of the Allied force, the Russian general was in direct command of his own troops as stipulated by the Anglo-Russian treaty. Unfortunately, York quickly conceived a dislike of the Russians and did not refrain from expressing his contempt.

York's qualities as a commander in the field were also open to question, however, even if he had the social rank that was crucial to persuade the Russians to accept his authority. In the judgement of one of his aides-de-camp,

> much as I loved the Duke personally, much as I felt many good and amiable qualities in his character, much as I owe to him of gratitude for long kindness to myself, I cannot but acknowledge but that he was not qualified to be even the ostensible head of a great army on arduous service. At home he administered the business of our military establishment sedulously, zealously, clearly, and impartially; but he possessed none of the higher qualities which influence the fate of a campaign, or turn the fortune of a battle. He was of a cool courage; he would have stood all day to be shot at; but he had no active bravery. With a very fair understanding, he had little quickness of apprehension, still less of sagacity in penetrating designs or forming large views; painstaking, yet devoid of resources, and easily disheartened by difficulties. Even his good nature and kind temper were injurious; for it too often happened that he could not say No when he ought to have said No. To these defects must be added habits of indulgence and a looseness of talking, after

dinner, about individuals, which made him enemies or inflamed the rancour of Russian generals.[60]

Abercromby recognized the necessity for a royal commander, and was happy to serve under him. Indeed, he would have been ungrateful in the extreme to resent being superseded by the man who had offered him so much support during his period of command in Ireland. The ministers' doubts were made clear, though, when they insisted that York should act upon the advice of a council of war. This was composed of Abercromby, David Dundas and Pulteney, the three lieutenant generals with the British force, along with Hermann for the Russians. Pitt's elder brother, Major General the Earl of Chatham, was also designated to join the discussions, although there is no evidence that he did so. Abercromby's opinion of this arrangement is not recorded, although as a thinking soldier he may well have shared the view of later historians, that it was the least effective way to conduct a campaign. There is no evidence, however, that York consulted the council with any frequency.

York was specifically required to occupy Holland as far south as Utrecht and the Waal, and then use his discretion. Grenville needed troops for a planned attack on Brest, and believed that, once taken, Holland could then be held by a smaller force throughout the winter. In the spring there would be an attack on Belgium, on the presumption that the Belgians would rise against the French. The Foreign Secretary, however, was continuing to make these assumptions against a wider situation which, in Switzerland, threatened to become catastrophic for the Allies (see above).

York had 48,000 troops under his overall command, three-quarters of them British but in the haste to dispatch reinforcements much vital materiel had been left behind. Two brigades had not even been supplied with greatcoats. This was ominous when 1,700 of Abercromby's original force were in hospital, most of them suffering from the effects of incessant wind and rain. Nor had the problem of transport been solved. The number of bread and forage carts, hospital wagons and forge carts remained seriously inadequate for the size of the army. In addition, the ammunition wagons were of a design which York himself had condemned as inadequate in 1793. On 10 September, the chances of success had been put at risk by the difficulty of bringing up ammunition. The ministers had assumed there would be plenty of water transport but, as already noted, the enemy had pre-empted this belief by removing or destroying most of it during the days when the British fleet hovered off the coast. There were no sutlers with the army, which would have meant no supply of spirits, had not the King allowed 'a gratuitous dole' of rum, which Walsh considered good for the soldier's health.[61] Indeed, anyone from the Fens would have been able to testify to the efficacy of spirits as an antidote to cold and damp. Coal was still to arrive from England and there was a critical lack of bread, as well as nowhere convenient to store it. On 9 September, with only six days' supply remaining, the chief commissary responded to Abercromby's concern with the simple statement that the troops would have to starve. If there was any source of comfort in this depressing situation, it was the efficiency of Dr Young and the efficacy of the hospital ship, plus the adapted transports that had to be pressed into service as the casualty rate rose. (It would finally reach 24 per cent in this malarial area.)

Nor was the North Holland terrain ideal for manoeuvring an army. It was impossible to advance over a wide front because of the constricting nature of Jomini's 'chessboard'. Much of the land was waterlogged marsh, and the enemy controlled the means of flooding large areas, as Brune had already demonstrated. He had also ordered bridges to be broken, while roads were already in a poor state of repair. Any advance would have to imitate Brune's columnar tactics at Krabbendam.

In effect, 'The Ministers were so busy planning campaigns, of which they understood nothing, that they could spare no time for the humble details whereby an army is kept in the field.'[62] Even though it could be argued in the ministers' defence that they had not intended the landings to take place at Den Helder, this proviso only applied to the terrain. All the other shortcomings would still have been apparent if any of the other proposed plans had been adopted. As a further burden, York was required to organize the Dutch loyalists, even though so few of these had made an appearance. The Hereditary Prince had been on the border with Westphalia, where he had been able to raise a small force of about a thousand men. Some Royalist officers had also offered their services. The plan was to create a diversion but the Prince's advance early in September was opposed by the local population, forcing him to withdraw to Emden, where he embarked to join the British army (and was safely confined to the island of Texel). Similarly, when Mitchell had finally sent a flotilla into the Zuiderzee to take Medemblik and Enkhuizen there was no positive response.

The Hereditary Prince had already plagued Abercromby with a series of impracticable plans. 'I listen,' Abercromby informed Dundas, 'but follow what appears to me to be our interest . . . I believe the Prince has been deceived into thinking that he has more friends than enemies in this country.

If we can advance, every one will be on our side, but there are few who will risk anything.'[63] This was a cynical view of the Dutch, but not unjustified as an assessment of the clear-headed inhabitants of Holland. The Prince continued to pester, however, including making frequent demands for money to pay for levies that had not yet appeared.

Despite all these difficulties, York recognized that the campaigning season was drawing to a close; immediate action was required to break the enemy. He had been assessing the situation since his arrival, and his plan was to push forward by way of Bergen and Alkmaar, or by taking Hoorn and advancing on Amsterdam from that direction as well as from Alkmaar. All the troops had been landed by 15 September, so he needed to reorganize the position that Abercromby had taken up in order to accommodate the greatly enlarged force. The Russians took the place of Moore's brigade on the right at Eenigenburg and Petten, while Moore himself moved further left, towards Hoorn. From here he sent patrols to assess the situation in Hoorn and towards Rustenburg.

Brune had taken up a strong position that extended six miles from strongly-entrenched Bergen on his left to Oudkarspel on his right. Beyond the village almost into Bergen, the country was wooded, with thick undergrowth, while beyond Bergen lay the dunes. Oudkarspel, on the causeway that ran north from Alkmaar, was also strongly defended. Between the two ends of the line Schoorldam and Warmenhuizen had been heavily fortified, as had Schoorl, Groet and Kamp, which served as outposts. The enemy needed to be dislodged from this formidable position before reinforcements and further fortification rendered it impregnable. For his part, Brune was under orders from the French Directory to contest every inch of territory, and to act on his own authority even against the wishes of the Batavian Directory. Since he was already holding the Dutch troops responsible for his earlier failure, he felt no reluctance to obey his masters in Paris.

York had the advantage of greater numbers but it was known that Brune was expecting another 9,000 troops from Belgium, so speed was essential. The plan York devised, seemingly without reference to his lieutenant generals, required four separate columns, each with its own objective. The overall aim was to prevent the enemy withdrawing from one strong defensive position to another. To stiffen the new troops, too many of them Militia volunteers, each column was reinforced with one of Abercromby's original brigades. The objective was to turn the Franco-Dutch flanks and drive the whole force back to Alkmaar. The right-hand column comprised twelve Russian battalions, more than 7,000 men under General Hermann, with Major General Robert Manners' British brigade and the 7th Light Dragoons under their colonel, Lord Paget, in reserve. They were to debouch by Slaperdyk, take the outposts at Kamp and Groet, then follow the roads by way of Schoorl until they came to Bergen and Brune's left.

Next to them a second column under David Dundas, 7,000 strong and formed of D'Oyley and Burrard's brigades, with two squadrons of the 11th Light Dragoons, was to march on Schoorldam and Warmenhuizen, thus supporting Hermann's advance. A separate corps, 2,000 Russians under General Sedmoratsky, was posted at Krabbendam in order to establish and maintain co-ordination between the two columns. Prince William of Gloucester's brigade, at Sint Marteen and Eenigenbrug, formed a reserve.

Pulteney, in command of Coote and Don's brigades, was to advance on Langedijk and Oudekarspel, which were strongly entrenched. Only 5,000 strong, this third column was to demonstrate in order to draw troops from Brune's left. If the chance arose, however, Pulteney could threaten Schoorldam and attack the positions on his left in order to establish communication with the fourth column. (This would later prove significant.) On Pulteney's right was the great canal that would enable the three gunboats under the command of Home Popham to keep pace with the advance.

The fourth column, under Abercromby, was numerically the strongest with 10,000 men. Comprising Moore's, Cavan's and Chatham's brigades, Macdonald's reserve, two composite battalions of grenadiers and light infantry, and two squadrons of the 18th Light Dragoons, its first objective was Hoorn, which lay twelve miles south-east of Oudkarspel. A further advance, south to Purmerend, followed by a march in a north-westerly direction would allow Abercromby to attack the Franco–Dutch from the rear. Obviously, this would only be possible if the other columns were successful, and if Abercromby was kept informed of progress on his right, hence the significance of Pulteney establishing communications with him. The advance to Hoorn required a much longer march than those undertaken by the other three columns, so Abercromby was to depart on the evening of 18 September and reach Hoorn in the early hours of the following morning.

Should the plan succeed, Brune's left would be overwhelmed, which would open the road to Haarlem, while Pulteney and Abercromby on his right would prevent him from re-aligning his troops. Brune was well aware that the most vulnerable section of his line lay between Alkmaar and the sea, and placed his elite French troops under Vandamme in that section of his line to cover Bergen, while the Dutch under Daendels and Dumonceau held positions between Schoorldam and Oudkarspel.

The time for the first Allied advances was fixed for dawn on 19 September. Abercromby started his march at about 8 p.m. the previous evening and soon discovered the challenge of marching twenty miles with raw Militia troops across broken roads that did not run straight and were deep in mud in places. Nineteen-year-old William Surtees was typical of the troops which had to undertake this march.

> We moved off as soon as it became dark, but such was the state of the roads that it became the most trying and distressing march that I believe ever troops undertook; the roads were literally knee deep in mud in most places, while every now and then they were rendered nearly impassable, both by the enemy having broken down the bridges over the innumerable canals and dikes which intersect this country, and those canals in many places having overflowed their banks. None but those who have experienced this or something similar, can form an idea of the fatigue attending a night march in such a country, where the column is large. Conceive, then, your arriving at an obstacle which the darkness of the night multiplies a hundred-fold. Not more than one man will attempt to pass this obstacle at the same time, and he has to grope his way; consequently all the other fifteen men must stand still, or nearly so, till he is over, before they each move on in turn. Not surprisingly, this problem not only slowed the march but, because of the continual stop-start, rendered it the most tiresome and trying situation that I know of.

It was 2 a.m. before the head of the column reached Hoorn, in a state of exhaustion.

> . . . just before daylight, I became so excessively weary that I could not continue in the ranks any longer; indeed men had been dropping out for some hours, so that, I suppose, when the head of the column reached Hoorne, one half of the number had fallen out; for it was beyond the powers of human nature to sustain such excessive fatigue. I, with two or three others, got behind a house that stood by the roadside, and laid ourselves down on a paved footpath which led from the back-door . . . I laid myself down and slept as soundly as ever I did in my life for about an hour, which quite refreshed me. We then set off with all despatch to over take the column which we came up with and joined just as they halted after reaching the city.[64]

Fortunately, bearing in mind the state of the troops, the Dutch defenders were asleep. Even the gatekeeper failed to respond to the summons to open the gates until threatened that they would be blown open. (This had the unexpected effect of sending some of the 27th and 55th into precipitous flight.) Once the gates had been opened the town was quickly taken, with a haul of 160 prisoners. At this point Abercromby decided to rest his men, who were certainly in no condition to continue the advance, but he was motivated equally by the realization that if the other Allied attacks failed he would be dangerously exposed at Purmerend. Whether this was sound common sense or over-caution merits further discussion. For Surtees and his fellows it was a welcome respite. 'All now lay down to rest, and such as had houses near them, occupied them; but those who had not, chose the driest parts of the canal bank or road, and all were soon buried in profound sleep, excepting those who were placed on guard.'[65]

At about the time Abercromby reached Hoorn, that it is to say well before dawn, some Russian light infantry and grenadiers under General Schutorff were setting off far too early on a march along the beach to Kamp. Hermann, although informed, did nothing to bring them back. Instead, hearing shots at about 3.30 a.m., he sent his first line of troops forward to support Schutorff. He also ordered the 7th Light Dragoons to bring up the horse artillery, and Manners to advance closer to Petten. Dundas, who was supposed to be co-ordinating his advance with that of the Russians, remained unaware of what was happening on his right.

At first, the wild impetus of the Russians drove the French from Kamp, although in this undisciplined attack many of the attackers fell to friendly fire. They then took Groet, and with their second line now in support advanced in two columns towards Schoorl and the dunes, driving the French before them. Manners, in reserve, had no choice but to follow the Russians who by this point were out of control. At Schoorl they met the first resistance. The French Adjutant-General, Rostolland, managed to restore order to the retreating forces and posted them in front of Schoorl, supported by light artillery, whereupon the Russians came under concentrated French fire. Despite this, General Ivan Essen, second-in-command, managed to sustain the wild momentum. Turning by the dunes, the Russians fought their way into Bergen, which was held by General Gouvion with five battalions. A two-pronged attack finally forced Gouvion out and he took up a position further back to await reinforcements. Manners, meanwhile, pressed in on Schoorldam but then moved towards Bergen when he recognized the risk of being cut off.

Brune was soon aware of what was happening on his left and hurried his reserve from Alkmaar. He also detached some of Dumonceau's troops from further on the right. These reinforcements were directed to Bergen and the dunes, thus taking pressure off General Vandamme's division, which was holding the left flank. Vandamme now ordered Gouvion to turn Bergen by the right, while Rostolland was ordered to take two battalions into the nearby woods. Despite initial Russian resistance, this counter-attack turned into a rout when Vandamme launched four further battalions who attacked with the bayonet. Hermann was forced to surrender while Essen extracted as many troops as possible and called up Manners, who had been engaged in a tough fight of his own, to cover the Russian retreat as they fled to Schoorl or the dunes. If British accounts are to be believed, the Russians were not withdrawing empty-handed.

Elsewhere, matters were under better control. At 5 a.m., as soon as there was sufficient light, Dundas, accompanied by York, advanced towards Warmenhuizen. He was followed by Sedmoratsky's three Russians battalions, who were to behave with as much elan but more discipline than their compatriots. Warmenhuizen was strongly defended but fell when attacked by Sedmoratsky from the left and the 1st Foot Guards from the right. Dundas had already detached the Guards grenadiers to cover Hermann's left. He now took a further two battalions to establish contact with Pulteney. The rest of his force moved along broken roads towards Schoorldam, to support Hermann's Russians. The village was finally reached at 9 a.m. and, despite strong fortifications, was quickly taken. It then became necessary to repair the bridge over the canal, and by the time the troops were able to cross the full extent of the Russian catastrophe had become clear.

Although York ordered Manners to Schoorl in an attempt to stabilize the Russians, it was too late. Not only were the Russians beyond help but the enemy were back in the battle and Manners found himself struggling to contain a French counter-attack at Schoorl. When Schoorl was lost, and despite Dundas's troops still holding Schoorldam, he had no choice but to follow the Russian withdrawal to Krabbendam, which he accomplished in good order.

While the Allied right was suffering defeat, Pulteney had finally reached Oudkarspel after a difficult advance. Don's brigade launched a frontal attack while Coote's brigade debouched at Nieudorp-Werlaet to attack Dutch entrenchments from the rear. The first attacks were beaten off with heavy casualties. Don's brigade then began to make progress and were able to set up their own guns to answer the Dutch guns. Coote's brigade, however, continued to struggle until Dundas arrived with his detached battalions. As a result, a Dutch counter-attack was beaten off and the Dutch resistance disintegrated into a disordered retreat towards Koedijk and Sint Pankras, with the loss of 700 prisoners and most of their guns. According to his own report, Daendels was lucky to escape the rout when his horse was shot and he was saved only when a trumpeter gave him a horse. Pulteney went no further and seems to have expected that the battle would continue the next day. Instead, he (like Dundas) received an order from York to retreat to the lines. According to Major Jackson of the 40th, this retreat was 'highly distressing to a man of any feeling'.[66] He was probably not alone in habouring this sentiment.

As the struggle developed on his right, Abercromby had remained at Hoorn. Although he could hear the guns, it was not until noon, about the time he judged his men fit to march, that he received a message from York. This reported Dundas's success at Warmenhuizen, but said there was no news from Pulteney. Since Pulteney's movements were crucial to his, Abercromby decided to remain where he was rather than advance and find himself cut off. Four hours later he finally heard that Pulteney had taken Oudkarspel but also learnt of the Russian debacle. He then received an instruction to return to the lines. He left the 55th to hold Hoorn, in acknowledgement of the kindness shown by the townsfolk, for which they might suffer repercussions, and delegated Moore to bring the troops back on another difficult march in torrential rain that turned the muddy roads to quagmires, and caused many to straggle. Abercromby himself rode to join York, as requested.

One of the problems of assessing Abercromby's conduct is a common misunderstanding of his order. Burne, among others, claimed that from Hoorn he should have marched on Alkmaar, a distance of thirteen miles, rather than to Purmerend and then on to Alkmaar, which is twenty-two miles. Yet York's order specified that Abercromby should 'push forwards with all possible expedition for Purmerend',[67] thus bringing his force to the rear of the enemy. Despite its merits, such a plan would only have worked effectively in a different terrain, with campaign-hardened troops and with more time for its implementation. Furthermore, his task was not to support Pulteney but to function as a detached force; in other words, he was not required to intervene in the main action but to capitalise strategically on a victory. Furthermore, if he had intervened as Burne, for instance, thinks he should, by moving towards Pulteney at Oudkarspel, he would have had to cross two 40-foot canals where the bridges had already been destroyed.

Bunbury, who was with Abercromby, gave a full account of the situation, making the point that the fourth column had been expected to reach Hoorn at midnight, which would have allowed the troops to enjoy three or four hours' rest and still be ready for action when the other three columns were co-ordinating their own movements.

> But see what took place. Sir Ralph's 10,000 men, with their cannon, had to march in a pitch dark night, and under torrents of rain, along one narrow paved causeway, flanked in both sides by low stripes of deep mud, which was confined only by broad ditches filled to the brim. We did not arrive at the gates of Hoorn till between three and four o'clock in the morning, and then there was some delay in entering. Our men had been under arms twelve hours: they were dead tired; nor could they have been fit to resume their march much before midday. But before midday the main body of the Allies was beaten out of the field. Sir Ralph Abercromby dispatched me at an early hour to apprise the duke of York of the state of affairs on the side of Hoorn; but though I was well mounted, and took short cuts across the marshes, I did not join his Royal Highness till the Russians were in full retreat and Dundas was beginning to fall back. Another aide-de-camp was dispatched immediately to recall Abercromby personally, as his advice was required without delay; and to order that his column should retread their steps, and resume their quarters within the lines of the Zuype.[68]

Bunbury added a footnote which suggests that, instead of being recalled, Abercromby's column should have been ordered to co-operate with Pulteney, once that general's success was assured, in a joint attack on Alkmaar. Moore was critical of the whole operation, but came to the same conclusion as Bunbury.

> The whole attack was hurried, before the Generals perfectly understood their parts, and before those who were to lead the different columns had communicated together. The detaching of Sir Ralph with so large a body of men so late as the evening before the general attack was ill imagined. Such a body, taking advantage of the first successes of the Russians, might have decided the day. It should have been detached, if at all, at least ten days earlier. Had that been done and the bridges and roads upon the flank of the enemy

been repaired, the detachment might have given him jealousy, but even as it was, this body might still have profited by the advantages gained by Sir James Pulteney, and at least to have made it possible to retain Oude Karspel.[69]

Jackson also recognized the potential value of an advance from Hoorn, but he added a vital caveat.

Had we secured the Posts we had taken, what incalculable advantage would have arisen from the movements of Sir Ralph Abercrombie who on the night of the 18th marched to Hoorn . . . 18 miles in our advance with 14,000 of the best British troops and was to have fallen on their rear and right flank of the Enemy . . . But as I have described, our best hopes were blasted when upon the eve of being accomplished.

This was a reference to the Russian indiscipline that enabled the French to re-form and inflict 'a most horrid and disgraceful carnage'.[70]

Even Jomini remarked, somewhat ironically, that 'it was fortunate for [Abercromby] that the bad state of the roads and the weariness of the troops prevented him from going on to Purmerend, in agreement with his orders; because nothing prevented Brune from crushing him before the Duke of York could support him'.[71]

Against this we have Burne, picking up the action at the point where Pulteney had finally put the Dutch to flight, and commenting somewhat disingenuously, 'The moment was ripe for the intervention of the Abercromby columns [*sic*]. But there was no sign of it. Where was it and what was it doing – nothing. A few hours later it moved – back to the British lines!'[72] Burne, of course, was thinking of a march towards Alkmaar rather than to Purmerend. Nor does he recognize that Pulteney had not yet had the opportunity to establish any communication with Abercromby's column. Having driven off the Dutch, he was not thinking of an advance on Alkmaar because he expected to hold his ground until the morning.

Looking at the action as a whole, it is easy to criticise York after the event. He could not have anticipated the Russian debacle, even though their lack of discipline, which had already attracted attention, might have given some intimation of it. He has been criticised, however, for detaching so many troops on his left while still having as the main objective the attack on the enemy's left flank, the French division under Vandamme which was the strongest part of Brune's army. As Moore commented, secure in his position at Hoorn, and with time to repair roads and bridges, Abercromby could indeed have advanced on Alkmaar and threatened the enemy from the rear, a move that would have made it difficult for Brune to use his reserves against the Russians. Mackesy suggested further that if the general advance had been held back until after Abercromby launched an attack, Vandamme would probably have been overwhelmed by the Russians and Dundas's troops.[73] Perhaps the most serious criticism to be made of York is that he launched the whole attack prematurely. None of this suited Burne, however, who blamed York only for entrusting Abercromby with so much responsibility, as if Abercromby's column were the lynchpin of the battle plan.

Captain Hussey Vivian, now in the 7th Light Dragoons, probably summed up the majority British opinion when he wrote to his father: 'I can only say that the Russians, after advancing like a brave mob, retreated like a cowardly one. The slaughter was dreadful and they made it worse by their savage acts of cruelty on the wounded French. Our left succeeded completely, and but for "Russeman" the day would have been a brilliant one.'[74] Overall, British casualties on this frustrating day were 6 officers and 127 men killed, 44 officers and 397 men wounded and 490 men missing, many of them Abercromby's stragglers. The heaviest losses, about 500, were taken in Manners' brigade when it became caught up in the Russian disaster. The Russians lost 3,067 men, including over a thousand taken prisoner. On a more positive note, sixteen enemy guns and 3,000 prisoners had been taken. Among the Russian prisoners were Generals Hermann and Jerepsoff. The latter died of wounds the following day. Whatever his failings, Hermann was straightforward and co-operative. His successor, Essen, 'without possessing more military abilities, was false, intriguing, and ill disposed towards the British'.[75] He was also the butt of York's careless talk and in command would become a recalcitrant ally.

The Franco-Dutch losses were similar to their opponents' in this stalemate affair: 3,427, over two thirds of them from the Dutch divisions, including more than a thousand prisoners. Yet, according to Jomini they took seven flags and twenty-six pieces of ordnance. Furthermore, their morale was undoubtedly raised by their success in holding their position while the Anglo-Russians had ultimately gained no ground except Hoorn, and had ended the day where they started. In addition, while the French might still have had some reservations about the Dutch, who had collapsed at Oudkarspel, the British now knew beyond doubt that their Russian allies could not be depended upon even to act within the parameters of a pre-arranged plan, while the Russians' taste for pillaging might have been designed to alienate a neutral population. At the same time, the Russians blamed the British for lack of support.

Brune was quick to capitalize on his success in holding back the Allied attack. He abandoned Warmenhuizen but continued to strengthen his right by flooding the area from around Oudkarspel to the Zuiderzee, thus making an attack from the rear impossible. Koedijk and Schoorl were still more strongly entrenched, and the roads to Purmerend and Monniken were placed under permanent guard, thus protecting Amsterdam. A sixty-gunboat flotilla was brought up from Dunkirk via the canal network to provide further protection for the city. The arrival of more reinforcements meant that Brune was now 25,000 strong, which enabled him to establish a second French division.

The Allies also received further reinforcements, between 3,000 and 4,000 Russians, including 200 Cossacks, three troops of the 15th Light Dragoons and some riflemen of the newly formed 6/60th. York, meanwhile, had been weighing up the possibilities for a further attack, which he presented to Abercromby and Dundas on 24 September. There were three options. The first was to send a strong detachment eastwards and then launch an attack on the enemy's right flank while the navy threatened Amsterdam. Abercromby pointed out that even without the problem of the flooded countryside, the necessary size of the detachment would dangerously weaken the Allies' overall position. The second option was to shift the action further north by sending 7,000 men to Friesland and Groningen. Although this would exploit the strongest area of support for the House of Orange, it had to be accepted that 7,000 men would achieve very little, while Brune would be free to strengthen his position. A third option, which required a general attack on the enemy's left, was finally adopted.

York now set about planning another four-column attack, set for 29 September. Once again Abercromby had the strongest column and the best troops, Moore and Cavan's brigades, Macdonald's reserve and d'Oyley's Guards brigade in place of Chatham's. Attached to the 8,000 infantry were a troop of the horse artillery and nine squadrons from the 7th, 11th and 15th Light Dragoons, 750 men under Henry Paget's command. He was given the place of honour on the right (the van), and was to advance from Petten, along the shore and over the dunes towards Egmond-op-Zee [modern Egmond-aan-Zee], thus threatening the enemy's left flank. According to Jackson, 'the principal hope was placed and justly upon Sir Ralph Abercrombie'.[76]

To Abercromby's left 8,000 Russian infantry and 200 Cossacks under Essen would follow the road that lay to the east of the dunes, advancing via Groet and Schoorl to Bergen. Detachments to the left were to maintain contact with the third column, commanded by Dundas and comprising Chatham's, Coote's and Burrard's brigades, 4,500 infantry, with a squadron, 100 strong, from the 11th Light Dragoons. Coote was to follow Abercromby's advance guard as far as Kamp before turning east to attack the enemy's defences which barred the Russian advance. He would then cover the Russian right. Chatham's task was to support the Russian attack on Bergen, while Burrard advanced on the right of the Alkmaar Canal in order to link up with Sedmoratsky's Russian detachment, supported by seven gunboats, which would be advancing on Schoorldam. Thus Dundas would essentially be protecting the Russians, apparently at Essen's insistence. Pulteney on the extreme left was in command of Prince William's, Don's and Manners' brigades, two Russian battalions and two squadrons of the 18th Light Dragoons. This gave him 4,800 infantry and 150 cavalry to advance towards the Zuiderzee, thus covering the Allied left and threatening the enemy right.

York's decision to use the same columnar formation that had failed at Bergen might be open to question but the terrain made any other form of attack impossible. Yet it meant a smaller army had every chance of holding off a larger one that was obliged to traverse a land intersected by dykes and canals. Nevertheless, York seems to have anticipated that the attacks, delivered in some kind of echelon formation from the right, would drive the enemy back towards Haarlem in such disorder that they would not be able to take up any intermediate positions.

Once again everything depended upon co-ordination. Several difficulties suggested themselves. There was the challenge of traversing waterways, while Abercromby's column would struggle to maintain cohesion as they advanced across dunes that rose and fell steeply and extended as much as four miles wide in places. Marching through loose sand was never going to be easy, while those further inland would have to contend with sodden, muddy ground as the rain continued to fall. As at Bergen, maintaining communication would be vital. Unfortunately, the terrain suggested that it would prove a problem even within Abercromby's column. The state of the tide was crucial because the horse artillery and the two 6-pounder guns could only accompany the column by keeping to the beach. The dunes were ideal for the concealment of sharpshooters, which posed another challenge. Then, because of the exhausting effect of marching through sand, the column would be particularly vulnerable as it emerged from the dunes to face the fire of the enemy, who were already occupying ground ideal for the deployment of troops and guns.

On the evening of 28 September Abercromby's troops were in position on the beach near Petten. Each man carried three days' rations, ammunition and a greatcoat or a blanket. Then, once again, the weather frustrated Allied intentions. A storm blew up from the south-west; the surf was soon running too high for the guns and cavalry to use the beach; and a sandstorm in the dunes made an advance by the infantry impossible. York had no choice but to send staff officers to halt the march, and postpone the attack until 1 October.

Abercromby now wrote in a private letter:

> Our situation does not improve; the weather is bad, the enemy gain strength from inundations, and they fortify every other point. The Russians, *entre nous,* seem to be a strange kind of people. There may be bravery, but there is no discipline. The general may cane an officer, but he does not prevent plunder and robbery. Our people have behaved uncommonly well in that respect. We must expect sickness from the climate and the weather, and I wish the nation may prepare itself for a disappointment. If the expedition had ended with the surrender of the Dutch fleet, everybody would have been satisfied. In short, my reason does not tell me that we are to have any success. Perhaps those who are better informed have a right to see things in a different point of view.[77]

The final sentence is interesting. He cannot have been talking about the military, since they would have been aware of the very conditions he described in the letter. If he meant the politicians who had organized (or failed to organize) the campaign, then a note of irony may be detected. For Abercromby's fiercest critic, this letter is just another example of his moral cowardice. A more generous view might call it the observations of a realist.[78]

On 1 October torrential rain led to another delay. Even when the attack finally took place the following day conditions were still so windy that the gunboats had difficulty operating on the Zuiderzee in support of Pulteney's column. Abercromby's column began their advance at 6 a.m,. when the tide was at its lowest ebb. Ahead of the troops lay a five or six-hour march across difficult terrain. In the lead were a squadron of the 7th Light Dragoons, two horse artillery guns and an advance guard from Moore's brigade. The first warning the enemy received was when a piquet fired a signal gun and withdrew from Kamperduin.

When the column reached the dunes, they deployed as planned. By this time the cavalry was actually in the water. On their left Moore marched into the dunes, keeping his right flank close to the sand hills nearest the beach. Macdonald's reserve, on the right of the column, and the two composite grenadier and light infantry battalions, plus 300 Russian light infantry acted as a covering force. Further right, Coote, from Dundas's column, moved sharply east towards Schoorldam, where he would be in contact with the Russians and might be able to prevent a repetition of the lack of discipline at Bergen.

The first breakdown in cohesion occurred when Macdonald's men came under fire from French light infantry concealed in the dunes.

> Abercromby had reckoned on his protégé, Colonel Macdonald, for the security of his left flank during the march along the beach. The latter was to have hung on the seaward side of the sand hills, clearing the flank, and at hand to receive support if necessary. But Macdonald was a very wild warrior. On first entering the hills he met with small parties, afterwards with larger, of the enemy; he got excited, followed them up, met with more, entangled himself in the waves of these great sand-dunes (which are from two to four miles wide), had a battle to himself, and so completely lost sight of Sir Ralph's column, which he did not rejoin till dark.[79]

Abercromby was obliged to weaken his column by throwing out the 25th and 79th of Moore's brigade to act as a covering flank guard and at this moment of confusion, the French launched their first attack. They were driven off with the bayonet, but Moore, the most trusted of Abercromby's brigadiers, was among the wounded, although he stayed on the field. The French remained a hovering threat, and the Royals, the 49th and Guards grenadiers were drawn in to resist another attack. There was also a considerable gap between the 25th and the rest of Moore's brigade as the column continued its advance.

Further east things had initially been going better. Coote and Burrard's brigades and the two Russian battalions had forced the enemy to abandon Groet and Schoorl. They encountered more determined resistance at Schoorldam but Burrard and the Russians finally drove out a Franco–Dutch force under General Simon. Then disaster struck. Essen halted the main Russian column and refused to move forward until the arrival of Abercromby. This hampered Burrard's advance to Koedyck, where Dumonceau had taken up position, and left only Coote and Chatham to attack Bergen. As Coote advanced slowly through the dunes, Dundas sent Chatham to his right, where he was surprised to find Macdonald. The reserve now joined in the attack, and the British troops not only forced Gouvion to withdraw, they also severed enemy communication between Bergen and the beach.

The loss of Schoorl and Schoorldam, combined with Abercromby's advance, forced Brune to change his arrangements on the left. He sent Gouvion with two battalions and artillery support into a redoubt on the right of Bergen, and provided him with a five-battalion covering force under Simon and Barbou. A further three battalions were posted on the crest of the dunes, four battalions held the ground between Bergen and the sea, and two battalions hitherto in reserve at Alkmaar were sent to Egmont.

After five hours of hard marching, Abercromby's column were now approaching Egmond. As the first troops emerged from the dunes they came under heavy fire from Boudet's and Fuzier's brigades, who were supported by cavalry and guns. The 25th in the lead and three following companies of the 92nd took heavy casualties. Moore was again wounded, this time stunned and rendered *hors de combat*. The rest of the column now came into action, the 92nd and the 1st Guards on the right of the 25th and the Royals, 49th and Guards grenadiers on their left, and the French were finally forced to withdraw after an hour's hard fighting. This cleared the road to Egmont. When the French withdrew, however, they left behind an exhausted British commander, who had remained at the head of his troops throughout, and equally exhausted troops. Moore's brigade had suffered greatly, losing its commander, 44 officers and nearly 700 men. This meant Abercromby was reliant on the two Guards battalions, their grenadier battalion and three Militia battalions against an enemy once more securely entrenched, stronger in guns and bringing up reinforcements.

This was the time for moral courage. Despite having received no information from his left, although he did learn that Macdonald was at Groet, three miles out of position, Abercromby seems not to have considered a withdrawal. With the light fading, and aware that both he and his troops had pushed themselves to the limit, he took up a position for the night that would allow him to continue the fight the following day. Burne was quick to criticise this decision. 'Bergen had not been captured when Abercromby's battle was over. He thus found himself in a somewhat similar position to that at Hoorn, being to the flank and in the rear of the French position. The smoke from the Bergen battle, three miles away, could be seen from the dunes (though Abercromby himself was too blind to see it), and an opportunity presented itself to strike a decisive blow, but Sir Ralph decided that his troops were too tired, and as at the Helder he put them to bivouac on the battlefield.' Then comes a surprising concession. 'It is hard to blame the general for this decision, for his troops were really tired and his ammunition supply had run low.' Yet this seems to be contrasted with Brune, who 'was only too glad, as soon as darkness fell, to abandon his whole position and retreat south'.[80] This seems somewhat disingenuous; an uncontested withdrawal is rather different from forcing exhausted men to continue the fight. It may usefully be contrasted with the view of the medical officer, Walsh, who was on the spot and wrote: 'But it was to the inspiring example, and cool orders of the veteran general, Sir Ralph Abercrombie, that his brave column owed its success. He exposed his person every where amidst showers of bullets, with the vigour and vivacity of five and twenty; and though two horses were shot under him, he seemed wholly insensible to danger.'[81]

There was a final burst of activity on the Allied right before night set in. In Bunbury's version of events, after Abercromby had halted for the night he sent a troop of horse artillery forward with an escort of light dragoons to counteract some French artillery fire. The dragoons took up a position behind a sand hill, where the men dismounted. Because the cavalry were concealed from view, the gunners looked like a tempting target. Vandamme, now in command at Egmond, had brought up reinforcements from Alkmaar, including a squadron of hussars. These he sent forward to seize the guns. When they reached the battery, however, they were charged by Paget and a dozen officers and sergeants who had remained in the saddle. This allowed the rest of the escort time to mount, with the result that all the hussars were either killed or taken.[82]

Walsh also witnessed this attack.

> They even cut down several men of the corps and carried off in triumph two guns. Their success was short-lived; for some squadrons of the 7th and 11th Light Dragoons, with Lord Paget at their head, suddenly issuing out from a recess between two sand hills, charged them at full gallop. The French cavalry, wholly incapable of sustaining the shock, were either cut to pieces, or rushed into the sea, to avoid the British sabres. A small proportion, favoured by the approaching darkness, effected an escape – without making any attempt to carry off their prize cannon.[83]

Macdonald had now re-joined Abercromby, while Dundas had taken up a positions on ground gained from the enemy and also prepared to bivouac for the night. Pulteney on the left had effectively threatened Oudkarspel, which was occupied by Daendels, although there had been no opportunity to advance further. For Abercromby's troops the situation was particularly uncomfortable. They were without their packs, which had been left behind as not needed. Furthermore, marching through the dunes had been thirsty work and they had soon run out of water. For dry-mouthed men, their rations were too salty to swallow, so when the inevitable rain arrived it was welcomed as a blessing.[84] As for Abercromby himself, not only had he lost two horses shot under him, but he also felt as if he had lost his right hand. Yet whatever his own physical discomfort, he was more concerned about his 15-year-old son's. 'The evening was cold and the troops were to sleep on their arms. Sir Ralph's son was there, a mere youth and the father took off his cloak. "Here", says he, "Sandy you must have my cloak to keep yourself warm, my Boy."'[85]

Egmond-op-Zee might best be described as a Pyrrhic victory. Fortescue considered it 'the kind of victory which ruins an army'.[86] Allied losses were heavy: 11 officers and 226 men killed, 74 officers and 1033 wounded, 5 officers and 218 men missing, while 125 horses were also lost. Not surprisingly, the heaviest casualties were taken by Abercromby's column, particularly Moore's brigade. The experience of this brigade in the dunes as they led the advance clearly established what Abercromby and Moore had both already grasped, that the lack of light infantry was a serious disadvantage because it meant the troops had to face French sharpshooters with the bayonet. Somewhat surprisingly, given their recalcitrance, the Russians suffered 600 casualties. The Franco-Dutch force must have taken similar, if not heavier, casualties, particularly the French who anchored Brune's line on the left and who had been overrun. As well as dead and wounded, several hundred men were taken prisoner. The enemy also lost seven guns. Furthermore, Brune had lost communication between Bergen and Egmont, while Dundas threatened any retreat from Bergen. The French general recognized that his troops were both exhausted and demoralized, so he decided upon an early morning retreat to Beverwyck, five miles from Bergen. At 3 a.m. the first troops moved away from Bergen under the cover of fog. Gouvion and Bonhomme's brigades, covered by Simon's cavalry, marched towards Alkmaar. Boudet's brigade remained at Egmond to protect the retrograde movement of the centre before retiring to Wyk-op-Zee during the evening. Daendels had already moved back to St Pankras and now withdrew further to Purmerend. Thus Brune was able to extricate his troops without attracting allied attention.

In his dispatch York was unstinting in his praise of Abercromby, writing that although

> Sir Ralph Abercromby's column had proceeded without meeting much resistance in the early part of the day, it was nevertheless much inconvenienced, and his troops harassed by the necessity of detaching continually into the sand hills to his left to cover the flank against the troops whom the enemy had placed on them. The admirable disposition, however that he made of his troops, and their determined spirit and gallantry, enabled him to arrive within a mile of Egmont [English spelling]. Here he was seriously opposed by a considerable corps of French infantry which occupied Egmont-op-Zee, and the high sand hills in its front, and who had formed a very strong corps of cavalry and artillery on the beach. The engagement was maintained during several hours with the greatest obstinacy, and in no instance were the abilities of a commander, or the heroic perseverance of troops more conspicuous. Animated by the example of Sir Ralph Abercromby, and the general and other officers under him, the troops sustained every effort made upon them by the enemy their superior in number and much favoured by the strength of their position.[87]

The next few days were used to take stock of the situation. Although Brune had been driven back, he had merely withdrawn from one strong position to another. He had also received six more battalions from Belgium, and these reinforcements enabled him to deploy in three lines, stretching from South Bakkum to Akersloot and Lange Moor, from Heemskerk to Uitgeest, and from Wyk-aan-Zee to Beverwyck. Daendels was holding ground at Knollendam and Purmerend in a position protected by flooded terrain. He also had a reserve at Monnikendam. York had to decide whether it was now possible to dislodge the Franco-Dutch, who had received further reinforcements from Belgium. The terrain hindered military activity and made it difficult to bring supplies forward. The area was unhealthy enough without the wet weather, and the numbers of sick were daily increasing. Nor could York deceive himself that the Dutch would eventually offer support. He decided, however, to advance on Haarlem as a preliminary move on Amsterdam.

Abercromby remained at Egmond-op-Zee, somewhat isolated from the rest of the Allied force. The Russians established themselves at Egmond

Binnen; Dundas's division was posted at Alkmaar and Herloo, on the road to Haarlem; Pulteney held a position between Alkmaar and Schoorldam; and Prince William of Gloucester's brigade was at Hoorn. Undeterred by his ignorance of Brune's exact deployment, on 6 October York ordered his front line to take and fortify the villages ahead of them. Abercromby was then to move through the dunes to the coast while Essen advanced to Bakkum, and Coote and Burrard, to Limmen and Akersloot. A successful general advance forced the French back to Kastrikum, with Essen in pursuit. When Brune became aware of what was happening, he ordered Boudet to unite his division at Noordorp and check the Russians while Gouvion manoeuvred in the dunes to prevent the British from rescuing him.

General Pacthod was at Kastrikum with three battalions and folded before the Russian attack. (Jomini does suggest that he merely made a pretence of retiring.) He was saved by the arrival of Brune with most of Boudet's brigade and there followed three hours of indecisive fighting. Burrard, who had been watching Bonhomme's brigade, intervened on the Russian left flank but was checked by three French battalions. Then the full force of the counter-attack fell on the Russians, who retreated in disorder, overwhelmed by a bayonet charge. Essen was able to rally them at Kastrikum, placing his guns at the entrances to the village. He now called for support from Abercromby, who was on his flank and who came in person with his reserve, but too late to save the Russians. Pacthod, supported by Boudet, advanced towards Kastrikum and after a dogged struggle took the Russian guns. The Russians were then driven back towards Bakkum and Limmen, followed by French cavalry in what seems to have been a wild pursuit. At this point British cavalry, probably the 7th Light Dragoons under the enterprising Paget, intervened and sent the French horsemen back onto their infantry, who panicked and retreated.

Pacthod was then brought to a halt by a broken bridge, beyond which some of the Russians were re-forming. They were now joined by two battalions from Dundas's division. As soon as the Russian had repaired the bridge, an Allied force, including men from Abercomby's division, went on the attack. In Jomini's account, the Franco-Dutch forces were described as exhausted and short of ammunition. Not surprisingly, therefore, they gave ground when attacked by what Jomini calls fresh troops. Brune immediately brought up Dutch cavalry against the British cavalry, who were leading the Allied attack and overwhelming the enemy right flank. The Dutch cavalry pushed them back on their own infantry, and Vandamme then led a vigorous attack with some of Boudet's battalions which forced the Allies back towards Bakkum and Limmen.

The rest of Abercromby's division had been engaged with Gouvion's battalions in a lively back-and-forth combat in the dunes. After Abercromby had brought a brigade to Essen's assistance, the engagement settled into a stalemate situation. When the missing British brigade returned, Abercromby made tentative movements against Gouvion, but before anything could come of this the French general received orders from Brune to retire to his former position. All this while, Pulteney on the left had remained inactive against Daendels, ostensibly because of the inundations that separated them. He sent General Don to parley, but this only led to Don's arrest on the pretext that he was trying to disseminate an incendiary proclamation. On Brune's order he was sent to Lille.

As the battle became general,

> the Duke of York in Alkmaar was wondering what had fallen out and what had become of his army. Though the rain poured down in torrents, the musketry was incessant, aide-de-camp after aide-de-camp was sent forth to make out what were the causes and objects of this off-hand engagement, and I was carried up and perched on top of the tall steeple of Alkmaar, with a spying-glass, to try to ascertain for the Duke what was the direction and where were the main points of the fight. But all was confusion, and in fact the troops were intermingled: they had been brought irregularly into action, without any definite plan on either side: engaging wherever they happened to meet with an enemy, and advancing or retreating in various directions as the one or the other party proved the stronger.[88]

The choice that had faced York after Egmond lay between either a quick strike or retreat without dishonour. Buoyed by what he perceived as the victory of 2 October, he had opted for a quick strike. It can be argued that his plan, which seems to have been to overwhelm the enemy outposts on 6 October and advance in force the following day, was frustrated by Russian impetuosity (or disobedience) when Essen advanced on Kastrikum. This caused a premature general action which York was unable to control. He had allowed more and more battalions to be drawn into an unplanned battle that ultimately achieved nothing, since his troops finished up in their original positions. As Bunbury makes clear, there was no way York could have understood what was happening, and it might be suggested that sending aides-de-camp in all directions was a substitute for taking firm control

When he received a message from Abercromby, carried by Major Kempt, warning him that the Russians were embroiled in a serious fight, he gave it only cursory attention before inviting Kempt to dine with him and his staff. Only when the firing could no longer be ignored did he give the order for withdrawal. This was conducted in disorderly fashion, and was only saved from complete chaos by the steadiness of the more experienced troops. Furthermore, the cost was once again heavy, 800 British killed or wounded and 600 taken prisoner, while the Russians, who had borne the brunt of the action, suffered 1,100 losses. Jomini put Franco–Dutch losses as 2,000, including 500 prisoners.

Brune was proving impossible to dislodge and retreat was now the only sensible option. On the night of this last action Abercromby, Dundas, Pulteney and Hulse, having presumably already discussed the matter, strongly represented to York the need to retire to Zijpe. They also individually wrote to Henry Dundas to explain why retreat was necessary. Their reasons were cogent: five actions had caused losses of between 9,000 and 10,000 men; the Russians were difficult and unpredictable allies; the country was either marshy and waterlogged or sand dunes that offered little cover, fuel or means of sustenance; the inhabitants were indifferent; the enemy had destroyed roads and bridges, making any movement difficult. Worst of all, it was perilously late in the campaigning season. Abercromby was even more specific in a private letter he wrote on 8 October. 'Were we to suffer a severe check, I much doubt if the discipline of the troops would be sufficient to prevent a total dissolution of the army. This is melancholy, and is the natural consequence of young soldiers and inexperienced officers – all-powerful if attacked, but without resource if beaten.'[89]

York heeded the arguments and a disorderly retreat began on 7 October. 'The intense darkness was still accompanied by deluges of rain. There was no sure footing; all was quagmire; but the firmest bottom, and, on the whole, the safest way, lay through pools of water, though it was impossible to guess whether the next step would be up to the knees or the neck.'[90]

Bunbury vividly described how 'our jaded, drenched, and dispirited army was withdrawn in silence and unmolested within its former lines. The weather had continued, with few and brief intervals, to be dreadfully bad; torrents of rain, attended by storms of wind. The roads were becoming impassable; but as the enemy had not discerned, or at least had not molested our retreat, this circumstance became favourable to the Allies when they set themselves down as the defenders of a position.' Not surprisingly, 'Everybody was out of humour and out of heart.' Expectations of success had been high but 'Here were the troops in their old lines, minus nearly 10,000 of the bravest men and officers, fatally convinced that they could not make their way forwards, though still numerous; pent up in a narrow corner of a dismal country, which afforded very insufficient quarters for the troops, and the great number of sick and wounded men; and of which the cattle were already eaten up.'[91]

The following day the Allied force was behind the lines at Zijpe, although the wounded had been left behind because of the lack of transport. (Fortunately, they were dealing with humane opponents.) The enemy offered some harassment as the Allies retreated, picking up about 500 stragglers, but nothing that suggested a serious threat. (Three hundred women who had been taken were sent back three days later, along with their children, who had been given new clothes.[92]) Daendels made a more concerted attack on Prince William's brigade at Hoorn but was beaten off. Even at Zijpe, though, problems remained. There were provisions for only nine days, and ships that had been sent to Hamburg and Bremen for flour in early September had yet to return. All York could do was strengthen his defensive position by flooding the country, await further orders from the government, and hope they would arrive before the food ran out. He could certainly do nothing about the demoralized state of the troops, who had expended so much effort for so little reward.

The mind that had conceived this ill-judged and ill-prepared campaign was only too ready to blame Abercromby. According to Lord Grenville, 'With common exertion they could now be in Amsterdam.' More realistically, George Canning, Under Secretary of State for Foreign Affairs, pointed out that it was 'Better to have an army without Holland than Holland without an army'.[93]

On 10 October Abercromby wrote frankly to Huskisson that the war department needed to consider what they were to do with 'an army of 24,000 men, cooped up in an inhospitable country. I am unwilling to write to Mr Dundas on the subject; my mind always went in opposition to the undertaking, and I spoke my sentiments on it so fully before I left England, that it is decent to be silent in my correspondence with him, or the consequences likely to result from it.' He dwelt on the inadequacy of the Russians, the increasing sickness, and the unlikely chances of success should the action be transferred to Friesland and Groningen. He also stressed his continuing support for York, and there was a final word on 'the abilities and heroism of General Moore. I have seen so much of his conduct, that I can speak confidently. To him you may safely look as a most promising officer. He goes to England covered with honourable scars and were I King of England I should administer a salve.'[94]

The army was certainly in a difficult situation. The troops needed to be evacuated from Holland as soon as possible, but that would mean the loss of horses and guns, since neither Zijpe nor den Helder could be held against a committed enemy attack for any length of time. Engineers who had been sent to inspect the defences at den Helder conceded that if the defensive works currently being undertaken continued for another fortnight, 3,500 men would be able to hold the place for just two or three days. In other words, although a rearguard at Zijpe might hold back the French in the first instance, enabling some of the troops to embark, all too soon there would not be enough men remaining to contain the enemy, nor could den Helder hold out against a strong artillery attack.

When news of Masséna's victory at Second Zurich reached York, he realized that the campaign had lost its relevance to Grenville's collapsing strategy. Capitulation was the only option. He sent General Knox to the Franco-Dutch headquarters, whereupon Brune unexpectedly offered his opponents the option of opening negotiations for an armistice. Discussions began on 14 October and were completed four days later by the inevitable Allied capitulation. Initially Brune insisted on the return of the Dutch fleet and all prisoners, but moderated his demands to embrace only the prisoners, either because York threatened to let his troops loose on the Dutch, or Brune imagined the catastrophe for the whole area if the enemy troops were allowed to rampage through the countryside. On 20 October Abercromby wrote to his family, 'We have entered into an agreement to withdraw the Allied Army from Holland on or before the 30th November, and to restore to France and Holland 8000 prisoners. An armistice has taken place. What do you think of this? I have given my consent, but I do not consider that this convention gives us any security.'

Eleven days later he wrote again.

What could tempt the French to agree to it I cannot conceive. One-half of this army must have fallen into their hands, with all our artillery, stores, etc. It would have overset the Ministry, so great would have been the indignation of the nation, however ill directed. I am sure they ought to thank the Duke of York for listening to the advice which he got on this occasion. Whether our conduct is approved or not, is to me a matter of indifference, being conscious that we were in the right. The first hint came from the

French Army, which was taken up by the Duke's Etat-Major, then proposed by them to me, I desired them put it down in writing. I heartily concurred with them, and desired them to carry it to Lord Chatham, which was done. As to the number of prisoners to be returned, whether 5000 or 8000, it appeared to be of no great importance. The chief objects were not to commit, by any act of ours, the ministry, and not a word to be said about the [Dutch] Fleet. All inferior articles were left to be adjusted by General Brune and General Knox. The agreement has been ratified, hostages have mutually been given, and more than two-thirds of the Anglo-Russian Army are embarked. It would not now be worth while to break from the Armistice for so small an object.

A great change has taken place in the manners of the French since 1794. They are now perfectly civilized, they have not exactly the tone of the old system, but more frankness and apparent candour. Nothing can exceed the humanity that has been practised between the rival nations.[95]

Another letter to Dundas, written on 26 October, sums up Abercromby's view of the whole campaign, including some positive thoughts for the future of the army.

It has apparently suited the convenience of the French Directory to sanction the Armistice. We shall get off with some difficulty, and not without risk, from the badness of the port of the Helder, and the inclemency of the weather. With a superior army in our rear, it is difficult to see how the Army would have got off, especially as the works ordered at the Helder, on my arrival, had been long neglected, and in a very imperfect state. Whatever may be the opinion of others, I shall boldly set my face to the Convention signed by the Duke, and when the welfare of an army is at stake, one cannot allow feelings and such unmeaning words to have any weight. If an army were so situated as to be able to open a way with their swords, any agreement might have been a disgrace, but that was not the case. The army you sent to Holland will return with the real loss of three or four thousand British. Many of the wounded and sick will rejoin their regiments. In the spring you will have a fine army if the brigades are put under major-generals who are capable of instructing young officers and training soldiers. They must remain stationary and not be allowed to dance all over Great Britain. I have been cautious in blaming the Russians. I must, however, acknowledge that I have seen nothing to admire. I am sensible of the great exertion made to send a considerable force to Holland. So much is wanting to enable an army to act, that unless we could have kept our ground during the winter, we could not have hoped to be in an active state until spring. From apathy this country seems contented under its present governors. I have not seen anything like opposition, and there have been no acts of cruelty as far as I have heard. The Hereditary Prince of Orange is the most ungracious, weak prince in Europe. Except one man from Hoorn, no person has come near him. He knows so little of the country as if he had been born in Sweden. He is not a man whom you can support from any motive of personal character. My further services are not worth offering. I am not, however, discouraged; and I have but one wish in this world, – the honour and welfare of the country.[96]

There were also letters from Huskisson and Dundas. The former, in response to Abercromby's of 10 October, praised him for 'having, without accident, borne so principal and distinguished a share in the gallant but bloody conflicts our Army has so honourably sustained in Holland'. At the same time, the writer admitted that 'considering the season, the importance of not totally ruining our Army, the apathy of the Dutch, and the efforts of the French, I have wished since the attack of the 19th, that the campaign had ended with the brilliant *coup-de-main* that gave us the fleet. That battle opened my eyes on several points, and I believe others saw things as I did, but they were naturally over sanguine . . .'[97]

Dundas similarly conceded that some decisions had been misguided. 'If I had foreseen, that in the month of August you were to have had a hurricane, and in the months of September and October a deluge, I probably should not have ordered the armament to sail at the time I did.' Unlike Huskisson, however, Dundas still believed that

If the thing was to do again, and I was certain, that with all the loss we have suffered, the result was to be the capture of the Dutch Fleet, I would order the armament to sail. I say so, taking into calculation all the hurricanes and all the deluges that have obstructed us . . . I therefore desire that none of you will return with heads hanging down in despair, or as if you were returning as condemned criminals. I hold you up in a very different tone, and I have the satisfaction to feel the country does the same.

A final sentiment would prove significant. 'Bring me back as many good troops as you can, and before next spring I will show you an Army the country never saw before. How to dispose of them must depend upon circumstances at the moment.'[98]

Despite storms and sickness, all the troops had embarked by the appointed day. Bad luck still dogged them, however. Three ships were wrecked on the Dutch coast, two with all hands, and a transport carrying the 23rd was also lost, with only twenty survivors. The rest landed in various East Coast ports, from whence the Russians were carried to the Channel Islands.

Abercromby sailed separately from the rest of the army. He was blown by a gale to South Shields and then travelled on to Scotland, where he resumed his duties as commander-in-chief. His failure to report to the ministers in London was interpreted by the Foxite Whigs as an indication of his condemnation of the whole campaign, and they found it a useful stick with which to beat the government. As Lord Holland wrote in his memoirs, 'This failure was occasioned by many causes: the delay of General Abercromby after taking the Helder, the consequence, it was alleged, of positive instructions from home, the rawness of the militia drafts, the original badness of the whole plan, and the incapacity of the royal commander. Strong suspicions were entertained that the operations had been suspended after the first landing that the triumph of entering Amsterdam might be reserved for the Duke of York; he was to receive 40,000L. as a reward for his success.'[99] Did the ministers instruct Abercromby to hold his ground after the landings? There is no evidence of such an order, while Grenville's impatience tends to suggest the contrary. That such a belief existed, however, indicates how failure at den Helder undermined the government.[100]

In order to defend themselves the ministers made much of the bad weather. And if that was not enough to deflect criticism, they maintained there had not been enough shipping available in the whole of Britain to transport an adequate number of wagons to Holland. As for the rawness of the troops, they claimed the political situation had made it impossible to take men from the Militia before July, another dubious assertion. Their lowest device, however, was to quote some words of Abercromby intended to encourage York but which, when taken out of context, seemed to imply that he had anticipated a successful campaign. When he protested at this cavalier misuse of his words, they tried to pacify him with a peerage.

Bunbury had his own explanation of why the expedition failed so miserably. He agreed that den Helder was probably the best place for the landings as far as topography went but it failed in all other respects.

> There was undoubtedly in the Seven Provinces a party favourable to the restoration of the House of Orange, and a much larger proportion of the inhabitants desirous to get rid of the French and to see the independence of their country re-established. It was particularly in that peninsula which we chose for our campaign that the dislike of the Stadtholder was the strongest and the animosity to the French had been least excited. In North Holland, the people were of the old republican character; and in 1799 they preferred the French as being republicans and as enemies of the House of Orange, to the English who hoisted the yellow flag and circulated proclamations on behalf of the Stadtholder. We found scarcely a friend in the country: a very few Dutch gentlemen came into our army, but they made their way to us from distant quarters. It was fancied that the Batavian troops (as they were called) would not fight; but we found to our cost that their battalions under Daendels fought as hard as the French under Brune and Vandamme.[101]

Since den Helder was Bunbury's only experience of serving in one of Abercromby's campaigns, his later assessment must have been formed by the events of 1799.

> Of the lieutenant-generals who were associated to the control of our military operation, Sir Ralph Abercromby stood foremost . . . [he] was a noble chieftain. Mild in manner, resolute in mind, frank, unassuming, just, inflexible in what he deemed to be right, valiant as the Cid, liberal and loyal as the prowest [sic] of black Edward's knights. An honest, fearless, straightforward man; and withal sagacious and well skilled in his business as a soldier. As he looked out from under his thick, shaggy eyebrows, he gave one the idea of a very good-natured lion, and he was respected and loved by all who served under his command.[102]

Whatever Grenville's opinion of Abercromby's conduct in the first days of the campaign, there was a strong feeling in the government that he deserved some reward. On 10 October Dundas wrote to York:

At the time the news arrived of the success of the Army on the Helder, and the subsequent capture of the Dutch fleet, Mr Pitt observed to me, that no such brilliant service had been performed during the war, or perhaps any war, without receiving a distinguished mark of His Majesty's approbation, and he mentioned his wish of carrying to His Majesty his opinion that a peerage should be conferred on Sir Ralph Abercromby, which he considered to be the more necessary as so many distinctions of that nature had been conferred on naval services, but none in the course of the war upon services of His Majesty's forces.[103]

York had been thinking along similar lines to Dundas because he wrote to the minister after Egmond:

What I have much at heart is, that the opportunity should be taken of showing some mark of His Majesty's approbation to Sir Ralph Abercromby. I know his delicacy about accepting a peerage. It is for you to consider how far his own feelings ought to be consulted, when certainly it would be a compliment to the Army. The action was fought between Bergen and Egmont; that, therefore, would certainly be the title most complimentary to himself. Should, however, any difficulties arise on account of the Egmont family,[104] may I say, that I should consider it as a favour done to me if he was to receive the title of Bergen.[105]

When Dundas sent the correspondence to the King, he had added some interesting comments that harked back to Ireland.

Independently of his feeling of duty as an officer and a good subject, Mr Dundas has personally reason to know that no reward he could ever receive, no distinction that could ever be conferred on him, would give Sir Ralph Abercromby half the satisfaction he derives from every opportunity afforded to him of proving the high sense of gratitude he feels from the generous support your Majesty and the Duke of York administered to him on his last return from Ireland, a time when every support was necessary to protect him from the unprincipled faction that was then combined against him. Mr Pitt has never said so to Mr Dundas, but he cannot help thinking that part of Mr Pitt's anxiety to mark Sir Ralph on this occasion, may arise from his recollection of some circumstances that occurred at that time.[106]

The King, perhaps more sensitive to Abercromby's feelings than York or Dundas, suggested that instead of a peerage he should be rewarded with Caribbean lands. He also made the pertinent observation that he was 'not surprised Mr Pitt feels that Sir Ralph was not justly treated in Ireland. I know he has a heart, when he has had time for reflection, that ever inclines him to judge equitably.'[107]

Dundas had already broached the matter of a peerage with Abercromby and had received an unequivocal response. 'I deprecate a title either for myself or any of my family. Allow us to go on in the paths of industry in our different pursuits.' When Abercromby realized that the government intended to put the King's suggestion into effect he wrote to Dundas,

> It has been hinted to me that in consideration of the services I may have done in the way of my profession I am to receive a grant of Caribbean lands, or a sum of money arising from them. If it is thought that I am deserving of any mark of public favour, it is from the public alone that I can receive it. I am not a beggar or a covetous person to ask private honours or private grants. Good God, sir, what opinion should I have of myself were I to profit from the crimes and forfeitures of such a set of miscreants as the Caribs! I hope I shall trouble you no more on my services or their rewards. As long as my body and mind remain entire, I am bound to the service of my country.[108]

It is possible that if Abercromby had been offered a peerage in the first days of the campaign, he might have accepted. What cannot be denied is that he considered the expedition to Holland to have been misconceived from the beginning. He did his best to convince the ministers of military realities, and when he failed, fell prey to increasing pessimism which, according to Burne, coloured his actions and his advice to York. Yet a different view suggests that while political objectives dominated British foreign policy and sent the army on difficult operations, 'Abercromby's qualities may have been the ones that were most needed. He had the moral courage to say no, yet in the last resort he did not flinch from risk . . . If his halt on the Zijpe disappointed his political directors, this was because he faced a conflict between military realities and political hopes.'[109]

Pessimism, born of realism, is no fault in a general who knows he is in command of a half-trained army, hastily assembled, inadequately supplied, and sent late in the season to a country where the chance of a popular uprising existed only in the minds of the ministers. This applied particularly to the Foreign Secretary, who was so besotted with his political objectives that he was incapable of giving due regard to military considerations. Yet 'one may wonder whether the cold mind of Lord Grenville ever dwelt on the men who had stayed behind, never again to fear the winter's rage as they lay in their scattered graves in dune and polder'.[110]

As a final word, a contemporary letter, written by Henry Dundas's wife, Jane, to Lord Mornington, Governor-General of India, conveys how the expedition might be interpreted if one were inclined to take an optimistic view:

> The first twelve days or rather fortnight after the sailing of the expedition were such as, living on the stormy Deal coast I can never forget – what in this generous and well planned expedition was to have been done, and must have been accomplished as a <u>coup de main</u> in less than week, by the delay in landing the troops and all the other incalculable bad effects of the storms, has ended in being the hardest fought campaign that was ever known and one of the most honourable – and after being victorious in five severe engagements, having struggled against difficulties and disadvantages of various sorts, we are now withdrawing our troops from a country that I do not believe is worthy of our exertions in their favour, and which we now leave much in the same state we found it, except the loss of their whole navy. I ought to add that I speak of our own British army, not including our allies, and their proceedings when I say that we were always successful. <u>We</u> have not taken Amsterdam and <u>your</u> army <u>has</u> taken Seringapatam, but we feel an inexpressible pleasure in reflecting that one spirit has animated both these armies, and that the credit of the British arms never was greater or more conspicuous than this year.[111]

One may take issue with some of these comments. Yet Abercromby, sent to *do something*, had effected a successful landing on a difficult coastline and brought about the surrender of the Dutch fleet, the one tangible achievement of the campaign. Less discernible at the time, although it is a point that Jane Dundas makes with some force, he had also bloodied an army that would soon prove itself able to take the war to the French – and win.

Chapter 5

The Last Campaign

Grenville's Strategy

Although the conduct of the British troops in Holland held promise for the future, Grenville's grand strategy had ended in failure: the ignominious departure of the Anglo-Russian force from Holland; Korsakov's defeat at Zurich which left Switzerland in French hands; Austria seemingly more interested in acquiring territory in north Italy than aiding its allies; and Prussia on the sidelines. Nor was the situation at home any better. A poor harvest had inevitably caused social unrest, forcing the government to purchase grain to replace the failed wheat, oats and barley crops. Such expenditure necessarily borrowed from resources needed for the war against France.

The government now had to decide whether there should be further intervention on the Continent. Grenville still believed in exploiting popular resentment of France, and using subsidies to attach allies. Dundas firmly advocated a war of economic attrition. He believed any direct attack on France should be limited and clearly focused. In addition, he instanced the acquisition of Trinidad as a means to strengthen trade with the Spanish colonies in South America, undermine Spanish influence, and liberalize those same colonies, a view he shared with Abercromby. He was also alarmed by Napoleon's expedition to Egypt, recognizing the threat it posed to India.

Dundas was castigated by Fortescue for the failure in Holland, and was indeed held responsible by his contemporaries, even though the plan was Grenville's. Yet, with nothing but failure on the Continent, his attitude might be interpreted as more rational than Grenville's. A more balanced view than Fortescue's recognized that 'Strong-minded and decisive, sanguine yet canny, he was the ideal political friend for Pitt, complementing his strengths and compensating his weaknesses.'[1] Pitt was given to rash enthusiasm, or, as Dundas expressed it, he was 'either in a garret or a cellar'. A loyal and level-headed friend (and drinking partner) like Dundas was invaluable to such a temperament.

It would be impossible to describe Grenville, a classical scholar of distinction who lacked normal human sympathies and Dundas's *joie de vivre*, in the same terms as Pitt. Yet, without demonstrating any of Pitt's unbounded enthusiasm, he was still in a sense as unrealistic as his cousin: unrealistic in his belief that the practical Dutch would risk all in a popular revolt; in his confidence that to plan a strategy was to make it happen; and in his notion that armies could be created out of thin air. Different in character, different in their view of how France could be beaten, it was inevitable that Grenville, the Foreign Secretary, with his political priorities and broad concept of international diplomacy, and Dundas, the Secretary for War, concerned with the reality of finding men and means and using them to best advantage, should be at loggerheads.

Grenville continued to make the Russians central to his plans, even after Zurich. Then he received a letter from William Wickham, the agent whom he most trusted, which changed his mind. Having described the disorderly conduct and pillaging of Korsakov's army, Wickham continued: 'I am most truly sorry to have to add that the conduct of the Italian army is still worse, and the pillage carried on with infinitely more audacity. The Cossacks not only steal whatever they can lay their hands on, but they stop passengers on the road, and enter the peasants' houses and force them to give them both provisions and money.'[2] Grenville now decided that Austria should attach at least 25,000 of her own troops to the Russian force and then organize and staff the joint army. He ignored Dundas's more level-headed suggestion that such arrangements should be left to the Austrians and the Russians, and failed to recognize that he was writing the script for the other members of the coalition. He was still thinking in terms of an attack on eastern France from Switzerland, with a second attack from the west. Dundas conceded that it would be possible to put 80,000 men into the field, 20,000 less than Grenville believed necessary, but he was less convinced that even a limited British attack on the French and Spanish fleets at Brest, which Grenville favoured, was worth the risk when it depended upon a successful Allied attack from the east. Yet the news of an uprising in the Vendée, which arrived on 30 October, seemed to justify Grenville's thinking, if only the Russians and Austrians could be persuaded to co-operate, and the Anglo-Russian army could be speedily extricated from Holland.[3]

In one respect the time was ripe for an attack on France. The Directory was in its death throes. In Paris Abbé Sieyès, a director since May, was trying to frame a constitution which would negate the power of the failing Directory and regenerate a socially and financially exhausted country. When Bonaparte landed at Fréjus on 9 October, having abandoned his army in Egypt, he found France in turmoil. Sièyes welcomed him as the means to achieve his own objectives. The coup of 18 *Brumaire* (9 November) swept away the Directory. Bonaparte was appointed one of three Provisional Consuls and immediately took over day-to-day business. Sièyes' constitution was finally promulgated on 15 December 1799. This officially marked the end of the Revolution. Bonaparte emerged as First Consul, his feet firmly on the path to despotic power. Thus the moment for Allied intervention was lost.

Grenville had been convinced that just one more campaign would bring France to peace negotiations on Allied terms, but on 19 November news arrived that the Tsar no longer intended to co-operate with the Austrians. The Foreign Secretary was sanguine enough to believe he could persuade the two coalition partners at least to undertake complementary campaigns. Separate attacks could be launched across the Channel, from the Mediterranean, and from the Alps. This was merely a skeleton idea and even Grenville recognized that everything depended upon General Bonaparte's intentions. And these were difficult to read.

Dundas remained a dissenting voice. There was still the problem of the French army in Egypt. Nor did he believe the war-weary British people would tolerate another Continental disaster, particularly when problems at home were so serious, not just food shortages but also the ongoing radical dissent which had been countered with harsh reactionary measures, including a second suspension of habeas corpus in April 1798. And it seemed that another severe winter was on the way which would increase the suffering of the poor and the discontent of the politically powerless.[4]

On 25 November Bonaparte made the first move towards peace in a letter to George III, whom he addressed as an equal. From the start his motives were questioned, and have remained a matter of debate. It might have been a move to court popularity in France but his reputation was already high. On the other hand, protracted peace negotiations would buy him time to deal with the Vendean rebels (he had used a similar technique at Rastatt) and the other internal problems France faced. Ultimately, though, 'France had *not ceased to be revolutionary*; but its energies were now, under a skilful and enterprising chief, turned to military objects. He was still, however, borne forward upon the movement, and the moment he attempted to stop he would have been crushed by its wheels.'[5] As Bourrienne commented, 'His fixed opinion from the commencement was, that if stationary he would fall;

that he was sustained only by continually advancing, and that it was not sufficient to advance, but that he must advance rapidly and irresistibly.'[6]

Furthermore, his letter to the Emperor insisted that Austria should accept the terms of Campo Formio as the basis for negotiations. When the situation in north Italy had changed so drastically in the past year it could be argued that he knew his initiative would be rejected, and was playing to a French audience. Whatever his motives, the offer was rejected by both Britain and Austria. Grenville, no doubt annoyed on the King's behalf by Bonaparte's assumption of equality, adopted a tone so peremptory in his reply that it was certain to provoke rather than conciliate. In the Commons, Fox described it as 'a lofty, imperious declamatory, insulting answer to a proposition professing peace and conciliation'. Yet, as Pitt replied, 'Buonaparte would acquire immense popularity by being the means of bringing about an accommodation with this country; if we wish to establish his power, and permanently enlist the energy of the Revolution under the banners of a military chieftain, we have only to fall into the snare which he has so artfully prepared.' The government carried the division with a majority of 201.[7]

Bonaparte next offered an armistice. This too was rejected, whereupon he adopted a third option; if there were not to be peace, he would make war instead. Brune, recently returned from Holland, was despatched to Brittany in the middle of January. Within a month the Vendean uprising had been defeated. Then Bonaparte focused on the campaign that would culminate at Marengo the following June. At the beginning of 1800, however, it still seemed possible that Grenville's plan for an allied attack on France might come to fruition. But British troops would need to be put into the field.

Dundas had written to Abercromby, 'Bring me as many good troops as you can, and before next spring I shall show you an army the country never saw before.'[8] Whether he anticipated that only 24,000 troops would return from Holland is doubtful. And the quality of those 24,000 was variable. In addition, 15,000 cavalry and 10,000 infantry were already stationed in Britain, including the Guards battalions, while 6,000 Fencibles had volunteered for service in Europe. These last could be deployed in the Gibraltar and Minorca garrisons, thus releasing the regulars serving there. In total, though, all these troops still fell short of the 80,000 Dundas needed to assemble for Grenville's purposes. If a further 25,000 volunteers came in from the Militia, the number might be reached, although the newcomers would need further training before they could be sent into action. Yet, as Abercromby had pointed out, with the right training men from the Militia were potentially excellent soldiers.

Abercromby had resumed his position as commander-in-chief in Scotland and was not involved in raising or training the necessary troops. He had a clear idea of how they should be trained, however, which he shared with Colonel Alexander Hope, who had been on his staff in Flanders and was an old friend.

> I am most anxious that the troops should be attended to during the winter with prudence and good sense. The Militia men are rather a better species of man, they understand the use of arms, and can move tolerable well, but they have not been accustomed to due subordination, to this they must be led by degrees, they must not be treated with too much harshness and severity. It is well worth while to bestow some time on such men, and rest assured if they are used with judgement and discretion you will have a fine army.[9]

While Dundas was searching for men and ships, the nature of an attack on western France remained undecided. Targeting enemy shipping in Brest made sense if conceived as an independent campaign rather than part of joint Allied action. Nevertheless, Dundas doubted whether the necessary transports could be found. Belle Ile, off Quiberon, was another possibility, although it would not match the effect of destroying the enemy fleets. At the same time the Royalists were urging their own agenda. Pitt was initially enthusiastic but when investigated by General Grey the Royalist plans were found to be unworkable. Then Napoleon sent Brune to Brittany and all plans for an attack from the Channel became academic.

One of the consequences of the hard winter was a disruption of communications across Europe. Ironically, when a thaw finally set in early in February, it coincided with the defeat of the rebels. Other news was mixed. The Russians were no longer players in central Europe; while the availability of Russian troops further west depended upon the whim of the Tsar. There was better news from Austria. Not only was Wickham enthusing over the excellence of the Austrian army, in sharp contrast to the Russians, but Thugut had also become more accommodating. As a result, the contentious loan agreement was finally settled and the first advance was quickly ratified by Parliament, despite strong opposition from the Whig rump. In their opinion the only justification for the war had been the destruction of the Jacobin elements. Bonaparte's rise to power meant there was no longer a Jacobin threat. For Pitt, though, Bonaparte was the heir of Jacobinism.

As ever, Thugut kept his exact intentions concealed, but he did seem to imply a major attack on eastern France. There were dissidents in France ready to act with any invasion force, and Wickham now busied himself with the task of co-ordinating them. This apparent undertaking by Austria meant that Britain could focus on an attack from the Mediterranean or land at Belle Ile with Russian support. General Charles Stuart was to have 20,000 British troops that, once assembled, could be shipped to Minorca. In the meantime, he was to meet Wickham in Germany so that plans could be co-ordinated.

Stuart was an able soldier but a difficult personality, quick-tempered and over-protective of his honour. He also suffered from uncertain health. His talent had been displayed at the taking of Corsica and Minorca: his defects became apparent in his quarrel with Sir Gilbert Elliot in Corsica. He was determined to conduct this new campaign on his own terms. As a result, the Ordnance protested that his demands were excessive. He also insisted upon the right to appoint his own staff, including John Moore, whom he knew well from Corsica. When it came to the medical staff for the expedition, he pointedly ignored the list prepared by the Army Medical Board at York's command and selected men of his own choosing, many of them very junior. When checked, he toyed with the idea of resigning his command.

While Stuart was causing practical difficulties, Dundas continued to nurse his own reservations. York had produced a list of the battalions he intended for the expedition, and it made depressing reading.[10] The harsh weather had caused training difficulties for units that were trying to absorb large numbers of Militia volunteers, and York had inadvertently compounded the problem by allowing officers to take extended periods of leave. Dundas nominated twenty battalions for service in the Mediterranean. York considered none of them ready. This led Dundas to confide to Lord Spencer at the Admiralty that he believed the army unfit for service anywhere. He was also at odds with Grenville over the existential question of for what purpose was the war being fought.

Although there was considerable disagreement within the Cabinet, Dundas was probably alone in his conviction that Britain's only successes had been achieved when fought explicitly for British interests. Such a view might be anathema to an internationalist like Grenville but Dundas believed Britain would best contribute to the international effort by small demonstrations designed to distract, and relevant to her own concerns. He subsequently produced a memorandum that he circulated to the Cabinet. This focused on trade, and suggested the establishment of fortified trading posts, particularly in Spain's South American colonies. But such a policy would have spread British troops across the globe, and deprived Britain of an army that could be sent to the Continent, thus undermining Grenville's strategy.

The February thaw had been followed by yet another freeze and communication was not re-established until well into March. Thugut was now demanding clarification of British intentions. In the west these were nebulous; take Belle Ile with Russian help, certainly, but beyond that nothing had been decided. The Mediterranean plan was offered to prevent Austria making a separate peace with France. Yet just as the first preparations were put into execution, Grenville received word from Wickham that Thugut was opposed to it. Wickham also doubted whether Thugut would sanction supplying the British with Italian resources. Nor did it seem likely that Austria intended to attack eastern France. To Grenville this was Thugut being his usual duplicitous self, but there was actually good reason for the change of focus. Bonaparte had been gathering a large reserve force in Dijon for an attack on either Germany or Italy. Thugut's priority was to protect the German lands. Thus Britain should forget the Mediterranean and make Brittany or Holland the targets.

Dundas was now able to persuade Pitt to hold back two-thirds of Stuart's 15,000 men until Stuart's meeting with Wickham produced some clarification. This would save the army from another unfocused, 'do-something' campaign. In the meantime, the 10,000-strong force could take Belle Ile, and then await transportation to wherever British interests dictated.

Grenville remained optimistic, insisting that the Austrians would recognize that by co-operating with Stuart, and with a dissident force forming in Provence, they would distract Bonaparte from whatever he was planning. Grenville also recognized that by the time preparations were completed it would be high summer. Any delay and the season would be lost, just as had happened in Holland. Before all else, he was determined that something should be done. As he urged Dundas,

> Do this or anything else you prefer but for God's sake, for your own honour, and for the cause in which we are engaged, do not let us, after having by immense exertions collected a fine army, leave it unemployed, gaping after messengers from Genoa, Augsburg and Vienna till the moment for acting is irrevocably past. For this can lead to nothing but disgrace.

He later wrote:

> . . . whatever decision you adopt respecting the bulk of your
> force, all the late events make it more important than ever that the
> Belleisle Expedition should go on. If you send 12,000 men to the
> Mediterranean, you can have no other equally good employment
> for the remainder of your force as that of Belleisle, nor is it possible
> that anything can so much distract Bonaparte's plans and operations
> in Germany and Italy as the necessity of giving his attention to
> Belleisle and the Vendée.[11]

The difference of opinion between the two ministers now became
acrimonious.

Dundas regarded Grenville as a theorist who had no understanding of
practicalities, while Grenville felt only contempt for Dundas and (along with
Pitt) found amusement in mocking his idiosyncratic grammar. Yet despite
coming at the situation from different directions, both ministers were in
agreement that half of Stuart's force should be held back for whatever kind
of attack Austria wanted. Grenville continued to believe, however, that the
Mediterranean expedition was now a lost opportunity and that it would
have succeeded with better execution. The more cynical Dundas suspected
that if Bonaparte gave the Austrians what they wanted in Italy, they would
soon be out of the war.

The Mediterranean expedition might be dead but there remained
5,000 men destined for Minorca. A month after their intended date
of departure, though, they were still awaiting sailing orders; their
commander, who was to consult with Wickham, was still in England;
and it was not clear what they were to do once they reached Minorca.
In the eastern Mediterranean a force under Colonel Thomas Graham
had successfully penned up the garrison Bonaparte left at Malta. Stuart
was now instructed to accept the French surrender there and then allow
a Russian force to occupy the island. This was an attempt by Grenville
to humour the Tsar in his self-appointed role of Grand Master of the
Knights of St John, and thus retain him as an active ally. Dundas saw
the situation somewhat differently. The Russians had already claimed
ownership of the Ionian Islands. Possession of Malta would enable them
to attack the Ottomans at will while posing a threat to British naval
superiority in the Mediterranean. Grenville refused to be persuaded by
these arguments, however.

When Stuart was given the order to surrender Malta to the Russians, for that is what it amounted to, he refused to obey and resigned his command. His volcanic temper, possible linked to declining health, had betrayed him once too often and his resignation was accepted. As the Duke of York commented, 'jealousy of temper and impatience of control from any superior authority' made him unemployable.[12] As a result 5,000 troops set sail on 24 April without a commander, while General Fox, in command in Minorca, received as his only instruction that they should be kept in a state of readiness.

From his post in Scotland Abercromby had been aware of what was happening elsewhere, thanks to his close friendship with Dundas. They had spent time together during Dundas' Christmas visit to Scotland and had exchanged views on both the situation and the principal players. On 21 January 1800 Dundas had summoned him to London. The Portuguese believed they were under threat from Spain, in furtherance of French interests, and needed British support. Specifically, they wanted Abercromby to take command of their army. Abercromby informed Dundas that he would not serve under a foreign ruler, although he would take command of a joint army if the situation warranted it. In the short term he agreed to travel to Portugal to inspect the defences and the state of the army. Before he could set off, however, Stuart's resignation led Dundas to rethink where Abercromby might best be employed, with the result that he was offered command of the Mediterranean force. This was a generally popular appointment, although Grenville could not resist suggesting 'that the Dutch business does not sit very easy upon him, and that he would not be sorry to do something brilliant.' There was undoubtedly some truth in this assessment, but the Foreign Secretary added waspishly, 'I doubt whether his character is naturally enterprising enough to give fair chance to Royalist plans.'[13] Abercromby's delay on the Zijpe still rankled.

Abercromby was famed for his equable temper and this led General O'Hara in Gibraltar to point out to Admiral George Keith, in command of the Mediterranean fleet, that the new appointment was fortuitous. While Stuart could not 'bear any difference of opinion from his own, and [is] certainly the least accommodating of any man on earth, Sir Ralph, on the contrary, I hold to be a reasonable, considerate good soldier, and listens with temper and patience to every proposal made to him.'[14] His capacity to work with the navy had already been proved in the West Indies and Holland, and once in London he demonstrated his understanding of combined operations by requiring that the transports which had taken the troops to Minorca should be retained for his further use. As far as could be determined, the Austrians intended that Abercromby's force should create a distraction from the Austrian General Melas's operations in North Italy by landing at various points on the Italian coast.

The Marengo Campaign

While Abercromby was considering the implications of his new command, Wickham was sending what sounded like excellent news from the Continent. He was able to report that Bonaparte lacked the resources for a successful attack on either Germany or Italy; and even if he were to launch an attack General Kray in Germany and General Melas in Italy were confident of being able to deal with him. Dundas might still have reservations about the durability of the coalition but he could no longer persist in his view that Continental adventures should be avoided At best, he could only ensure that there would still be a British army when the coalition finally collapsed. From Minorca Abercromby was instructed to send 2,500 or 3,000 men to Malta to force the French garrison into submission. He would then receive a further 6,000 men, whom he should use to support or even co-operate with the Austrians. If no opportunity occurred, however, he might undertake the conquest of Tenerife, a vital stopping point for voyages to Central and South America. This, of course, was an element in Dundas's plan to extend British trading interests into the Spanish Americas.

Once the planned reinforcements for Abercromby had been deducted, Dundas still reckoned on a further 25,000 men who could be used for limited attacks on Belle Ile and Walcheren which even Grenville conceded would be no more than demonstrations. Neither the state of the troops nor the attitude of the Russians made possible any greater commitment. Dundas was prepared to send an initial 4,000 men to Belle Ile, later augmented to 25,000, while the émigré Dutch brigade would be sent to Walcheren. From Belle Ile it would be possible to seize whatever opportunities presented themselves. He was definitely thinking of the far side of the Atlantic.

An advance force, three battalions strong and under the command of Colonel Miles Nightingall, sailed from Ireland to occupy the unguarded islands of Houat and Hédic, close to Belle Ile. Once the main body under Colonel Maitland had arrived, there would be a concerted attack on Belle Ile itself, planned for the beginning of June. This date was soon overtaken by events. The Austrians began their new campaign in mid-April when Melas manoeuvred to trap Masséna and the right wing of the Army of Italy in Genoa, while also forcing General Suchet with the left wing into a retrograde movement. Fresh news from Wickham, however, suggested that the force holding western France had received orders to join the Army of the Rhine. They needed to be stopped, so Maitland was urged to attack Belle Ile as soon as possible. But Maitland was unlikely to reach Quiberon Bay before the middle of June.

At this point it is necessary to focus on Bonaparte. When he left Paris in the early hours of 6 May to join the Army of Reserve, the British Government optimistically believed that it was a response to the threat of British landings in Brittany and Holland. This delusion was compounded by another mistaken assumption, that the Army of Reserve was composed of inferior troops. There had indeed been some making-up of numbers, but there was also a core of well-trained demi-brigades, amounting to 35,000 infantry. Nor was it deficient in cavalry and artillery. Far from intending to go on the defensive, Bonaparte was planning an aggressive campaign that would put Austria out of the war and consolidate his own position as First Consul and de facto ruler of France.

Even before he joined the Army of Reserve, Bonaparte was already planning an attack on Kray. Kray himself had received instructions from Vienna that required him to cross the Rhine and then remain on the defensive until Melas joined him from Italy. Bonaparte expected to work in concert with General Moreau and the Army of the Rhine. When Moreau proved less than accommodating, Bonaparte simply changed his objective. Orders issued on 25 March instructed Moreau to put Kray under sufficient pressure to force him back into northern Bavaria and then to send a quarter of his force, 25,000 men, to join the Army of Reserve. Bonaparte planned to move into Switzerland, cross the Alps into Italy and attack Melas.

His intentions did not become clear to the British ministers until mid-May. By this time, Moreau had been putting Kray under pressure for several weeks, although in a rather stop-start fashion. Kray had been waiting for news of Masséna's surrender of Genoa, which was his signal to bring his troops across the Rhine. He then became a victim of false news, that Masséna had been killed and Genoa had fallen. Having moved into position with all the necessary paraphernalia for a river crossing, he found himself confronted by Moreau. He had no choice but to make a stand. As a result, he was worsted at Stockach and Engen on 3 May, before being driven back towards Ulm.

Having completely misread Napoleon's intentions, Wickham now urged Grenville to send every available man to the Mediterranean to support the Austrians in Italy but even Grenville agreed with Dundas that it was too late in practical terms to resurrect the Mediterranean plan. The only possible concession was to send Abercromby the two extra battalions he had been asking for. Abercromby himself was still in England. Although he had boarded the frigate *Seahorse*, on 13 May, his first attempt to sail to Minorca had been frustrated by adverse winds. This led Grenville to remark that 'Abercromby and his convoy are as usual blown back. If I were a seaman, with half the superstition that belongs to them, I should certainly throw him overboard as a second Jonah.'[15] More seriously, he deplored the delay because from Minorca Abercromby could easily have aided the Austrians. Whether Melas would have accepted this support is problematic because he had already refused the assistance of a well-commanded dissident force from Provence.

As already noted, Melas was confident that he could hold his position at Alessandria. There was some suggestion that General Berthier was advancing on Savoy, but his force was estimated at no more than 15,000 men, thus posing no real threat. This was old news, though; Grenville could have warned Melas differently because he suspected, rightly, that a part of Moreau's victorious force would now be detached to support the Army of Reserve.

The Belle Ile plan remained viable, but with troops still assembling on Houat and a shortage of landing craft, there was no chance of an immediate attack. Then reports were received from 'Chouan Georges' (Georges Cadoudal) that the garrison was stronger than previously believed. Undeterred, Maitland planned for landings on 19 June, only to be frustrated by a violent storm. The next day Maitland was assured that the garrison was 7,000 strong, with some additional Militia support. This proved to be a wild exaggeration but with a force of only 4,200 men Maitland decided to delay the attack until reinforcements arrived. Then he received an order to send all his troops to the Mediterranean.

By this time, though, any British intervention in Italy would have proved futile. Moreau had indeed been detaching troops to support the main French attack in Italy, although fewer than half the number Bonaparte had demanded. Dundas might well send 4,000 troops to Abercromby, and direct Maitland to the Mediterranean, but it was too late. News that Masséna had surrendered in Genoa was followed almost immediately by further news that Bonaparte had reached the Po. Maitland received another message instructing him to resume the attack on Belle Ile, but he had already sent his troops, under Lord Dalhousie, to join Abercromby on Minorca. It is also difficult to see how a diversion at this late stage would have halted Bonaparte.

The day after the French capitulated at Genoa, Melas wrote to Admiral Keith urging him to hold the place with the troops from Minorca. Keith then wrote to General Fox with the same message, arguing in addition that possession of Genoa could save the Austrian position. The French were known to be moving towards Genoa, where General Peter Ott, who had been in command, had left a garrison of 5,000 on his own initiative. These troops, reinforced with the British troops on Minorca, could hold Genoa against any French attack. Fox was now faced with a dilemma. He had orders to retain the 4,000 men that had been sent to Minorca until General Abercromby arrived, and he had only one transport ready to sail. Then he received another peremptory message from Keith. The French were advancing in strength; there was little chance Genoa could be held without extra troops. In response, Fox began to make arrangements for the troops to sail to Genoa.

Among the battalions on Minorca were the 40th Foot. About this time a French admiral was brought into Port Mahon as prisoner of war. He later reported that the British troops, who were drawn up on the hills around the harbour in celebration of the King's birthday, were 'well cloathed but badly disciplined, disaffected to their officers and so fat as to be incapable of exertion'. Major Jackson, who later read this report, commented, 'I could not have believed this if I had not seen it in the French papers.'[16] It was, however, useful disinformation about troops that were soon to show that they could outfight the French.

Mediterranean Command

Abercromby finally reached Minorca on 22 June, to be greeted by a critical situation, with messages from both Keith and Melas importuning him to come to Genoa. His arrival was also a surprise to the troops, who had been expecting Stuart. '[It] gave new life and spirit to the whole army, and that anxiety with respect to our future destination, which had so often evaporated in idle conjectures, was now likely to be satisfied.'[17] In Jackson's opinion, Abercromby had been speedy in his acceptance of the command and 'With the same dispatch his movements were guided on his arrival at Minorca, where he had not been more than two or three days before orders were issued for the Regiments to be divided into two Divisions. The 1st Division, Major General Hutchinson with B. Genl Doyle under him, consisted of the 2 Battns of 40th, 48th and 90th Regiments. The other Division under M. General Moore consisted of the 18th Regiments [*sic*], which were on board in the harbour from Malta, the 28, 42 and De Rolle's Regimt.'[18] The

40th were under arms at 5 a.m. the following morning, and embarkation was complete six hours later. This was replicated throughout the army thanks to Fox, who had kept the troops in a state of readiness as ordered.

A few days later, Abercromby learnt that Genoa had fallen and Keith had sailed to Leghorn (Livorno). Abercromby redirected the transports to join him while he decided on his next move, only to receive the worst of all news from the Admiral. On 14 June Bonaparte had comprehensively defeated Melas at Marengo, whereupon the Austrian general had immediately signed an armistice and withdrawn to the east of the Mincio. Bonaparte was now in possession of Lombardy, Liguria and Piedmont. The First Consul, with characteristic speed and determination, had put himself into an unassailable position, both militarily and politically, and not a single British hand had been raised against him.

The crucial question was whether the Austrians were now beyond British help. Although a message was received from Lord William Bentinck, who was with the Austrians, that Melas believed himself capable of continuing the fight, Abercromby had sufficient doubt to send two of his staff, Colonel John Hope and Colonel Ludwig Lindenthal, who was Austrian, to discover the true situation and establish whether any reasonable action by the British could aid Melas. These officers duly reported that no British action could redeem the Austrian disaster.

Before Abercromby could send the troops back to Minorca, he was accosted by Maria Carolina, the Queen of Naples and Sicily. Fearing an attack on her own kingdom, she had travelled to Leghorn, along with Nelson and the Hamiltons, in the expectation that her imperial nephew would give her assistance. Now that the fortunes of Austria were in such a dire state, she begged Abercromby to come to her help by landing his troops and marching them to Naples. Knowing that his own force was not strong enough for such an enterprise, and harbouring doubts about the quality of the Neapolitan troops, he refused. Although Admiral Keith supported his decision, she persisted, only accepting his refusal when he pointed out that he could undertake no action without the consent of the British Government.

Abercromby sent some of the troops back to Minorca, which led Anderson to comment:

> Thus did we appear, at least, to traverse the Mediterranean, without any fixed or determined object. Our advantage, however, was derived from this erratic campaign; that our army kept the enemy in continual dread and apprehension along every part

of their coast, and consequently obliged them to detach large bodies of their troops to the frontiers to watch our motions, as well as to be prepared for them; and we have greatly to regret that this circumstance did not prove more fortunate to our allies.[19]

This may be to exaggerate the influence of Abercromby's force, but its presence in the Mediterranean was certainly a cause of concern to the French while its purpose was still unclear.

Abercromby now sailed for Malta, whence he had already dispatched the 28th, 2/35th and part of the 48th, under General Pigot, to reinforce the blockade that Colonel Graham was conducting with the 30th and 82nd. He had also written a tactful letter to Graham.

> I send in compliance with my instructions, Major-General Pigot, with a reinforcement of 1,500 men for the blockade of Malta, which you have hitherto carried on, with a much inferior force, with great perseverance and credit to yourself. I am convinced that you will not feel your zeal in any degree abated, and that you will continue to act with the same degree of spirit as hitherto, and, that you will afford General Pigot all the assistance which you have it so much in your power to give.[20]

Abercromby, who arrived in Malta on 17 July, was accompanied by General Hutchinson and together they inspected the island, particularly the defences of Valletta. Abercromby made a point of praising the Malta Regiment, which Graham had raised, and the disposition of the troops. He also found waiting for him a letter from General Melas, written on 5 July, urging him to land at Livorno and defend central and southern Italy. There was only one answer he could send. He had too few troops for such an enterprise, and the situation had changed since Melas wrote. The French were now threatening Modena and Bologna.

When Abercromby returned to Minorca he was surprised to discover Dalhousie and the 2nd, 20th, 36th, 82nd and 92nd from Maitland's Belle Isle force on board their transports in the harbour of Mahon. This required another reorganization of the troops. He also spent his time, as he waited for further orders, 'in paying the vigilant attention to the state, discipline, and comfort of the troops under his command, which formed such a prominent feature in his illustrious character. He accordingly directed that sheds might be fitted up for the accommodation of the troops that were still on board the ships in the harbour, in order that they might be landed for a short time to refresh themselves after such a long and painful confinement.'[21]

He also ordered a general review, which was to take place on 9 August. The interim was 'in a great measure, employed by the different Generals and Officers commanding brigades, in preparing them for the review of the Commander in Chief, who was himself occupied in examining the troops in the most remote parts of the island, in order to ascertain the service for which they were best qualified, previous to his final arrangement of the army. The troops were daily practised in the most useful manoeuvres for actual service . . .'[22]

This attention to detail, coupled with concern for the welfare of the troops, is evident in many of the general orders that Abercromby issued between 3 and 24 of August. For example, he required all the battalions to check whether their men had the sixty rounds and three flints which was normal issue. Those with a superfluity were to surrender the excess to Colonel Aliston RA so that those with a shortage could be fully supplied. Commanding officers were ordered to hold regular field days at a time that they judged convenient and 'On these occasions [the troops] should be practised in performing with exactness and precision a few simple manoeuvres; and in order to accustom the soldiers in the free use of their arms, when encumbered with their necessaries, they ought, when ordered to fire with blank cartridge, sometimes to parade in full marching order.' The men were commanded to show respect to their officers at all times. The sick were to take a change of clean clothes when admitted to hospital, and regimental surgeons were to send in monthly returns of the first day of each month. Another order stipulated exactly what each man should carry in his knapsack, with the further proviso that knapsacks should be packed neatly. Taken together they clearly convey Abercromby's view of effective soldiering.

He had always shown concern for the treatment of recruits, and that was demonstrated in a further general order.

The Commander in Chief, having finished the inspection of the troops near Mahon, has, in many particulars, sufficient reason to be satisfied with their appearance. Several of the regiments, however, ought still to be considered as newly raised. The greatest care and attention, therefore, are necessary; and he has the fullest reliance on every officer, from the General to the Ensign, in the forming of troops so worthy of their care, whom they may command in action, and of whose conduct their own honour and the welfare of the public depends.'[23]

Although Abercromby had to wait for most of August to discover where he was to take his army, there can be no doubt that thanks to how he used those few weeks he had under his command the best-prepared troops of the war so far.

He had received a set of instructions from Dundas, written on 16 June, two days after Marengo but before the news of Napoleon's triumph had reached London. These ordered him to use all his troops to defend the Riviera coast, and thus assist Melas. A few months earlier these instructions might have had the desired effect but they had been overtaken by events. Instead, Abercromby sent Hope to Melas to assure him that the British troops were being held ready for action and would co-operate in any way that helped the Allied cause. This led to a further plan from Melas. Abercromby should return to Leghorn, and exploit an increasingly favourable situation. The Neapolitans were in Rome and Austrian officers were nurturing an uprising by Tuscan peasants. There was an Austrian force at Ancona, which would support the uprising, while Melas himself was ready to re-cross the Mincio. Furthermore, Bonaparte, the mastermind, had returned to Paris, and command in Italy had devolved first on Masséna and then on Brune. Abercromby judged the plan unviable: he had too few troops, even for the more limited role Melas had assigned to him; he had reservations about the dependability of the Austrians; and he knew the Cabinet to be is a state of disarray.

Bonaparte had not been wasting his time in Paris. His objective was to break up the coalition, and to this purpose he offered the Austrians a general armistice, to be followed by peace talks. In his grandiloquent letter to the Emperor he was careful to present Britain as 'perfidious Albion'. On 15 July the Armistice of Alessandria, signed by Melas after Marengo, was extended to the German theatre. At the same time Napoleon was courting Tsar Paul and Godoy, Charles IV of Spain's principal minister. He offered the former what he so desperately wanted, the Grand Mastership of the Order of St John, even though he was in no position to fulfil the promise. He also undertook to equip 7,000 prisoners of war so that they could constitute the garrison of Valletta. As for Spain, she was (as suspected) being manoeuvred into an attack on Portugal, the bait being the promise of Portuguese territory for Godoy.

On 4 July, as the government was still digesting the implications of Marengo, the long-anticipated Austrian ratification of the treaty of alliance had finally arrived from Vienna. By one of those ironies with which history abounds, Thugut had signed it on 23 June, the day before he heard the first news of Marengo. For Britain the ratification had financial implications in the form of the promised £2 million loan, while the Austrians undertook not to make peace with France before 1 February 1801. This persuaded Grenville that he could still preserve the coalition, even as the Cabinet openly discussed the possibility of peace negotiations. There were voices enough urging Pitt to take this step: the Foxite Whigs, experienced military and naval men like Cornwallis and St Vincent, even George Canning, still a junior minister but an ardent advocate of war. Questions were raised whether the country would be prepared to stomach further fighting, particularly as there had been so few victories. As a result, the diplomat Lord Minto (Gilbert Elliot) was instructed to inform the Austrians to this effect.

Dundas had long predicted the collapse of the coalition but he now took his time before offering a strategy that would take note of the changed circumstances. Thus Grenville was able to assure the Austrians that 25,000 British troops remained available for diversionary operations on the French coast. When Dundas finally presented his views they were similar to his earlier memorandum, but also recognized that Britain would be continuing the struggle alone. His premise was that Bonaparte would use the naval resources of France, and of its Spanish and Dutch allies, to challenge British naval supremacy. In response, Britain must increase her colonial power, both for economic security and to obtain a stronger hand at any peace negotiations. In the short term, Britain should attack the naval resources of Spain, the most vulnerable of the three Allied sea powers, and secure Malta as a strong naval base. There should also be a concentration of British troops in Gibraltar, whence they could be sent in any direction.

Dundas had a strong ally in Lord Spencer, who was proving an efficient First Lord of the Admiralty, familiar with naval procedure and, in the opinion of Lord St Vincent, a better naval officer than the triumvirate that ran the Navy Board. Spencer, like Dundas, saw Spain, and particularly the naval base at Ferrol, as a fair target. Furthermore, General Pulteney believed an attack on Ferrol was possible, with every chance of success, a view he was strongly advocating to anyone who would listen.

As Dundas refined his strategy, Grenville continued to focus on preserving the coalition. Although he accepted that Britain might continue the war without Austria, he recognized that only with Austria's involvement could there be a victory decisive enough to ensure peace. He had known for some time, through Wickham, that Austria would have to agree to the armistice, and the subsequent peace talks. According to Wickham's latest report, Kray's forces in Germany were totally demoralized, while in Vienna there was every expectation that the peace party would oust Thugut, whom they regarded as an enemy to Austria's interests.

On 24 July Dundas presented his regenerated strategy to the Cabinet. Its naval premise was approved, and there was general acquiescence that Pulteney should be allowed to attack Ferrol. Then Abercromby, reinforced by Pulteney's troops, could target Cadiz, another Spanish naval base. The concentration of 20,000 troops in Gibraltar was also accepted as reasonable. There was some cavilling at Dundas's insistence there should still be a policy of colonial expansion, even if Britain joined Austria in peace talks, and this final piece in Dundas's strategy was not conceded. Nevertheless, Dundas might have been satisfied that the Cabinet had gone as far as they did to agree with his plans, had not the King created problems. When George received the minutes of the Cabinet discussion he was infuriated, as head of the army, to discover that his ministers were planning military action without reference to him. He reacted by refusing his consent to the Ferrol expedition until he had been fully informed of the reasons for its authorization.

Dundas was on the point of visiting the Duke of York to finalize arrangements for the expedition when the King's letter of protest reached him. He could not proceed without the King's agreement. He contacted Pitt, who was out of town, and Pitt advised him to temporise by writing to, or even visiting, the King and offering a moderate explanation of why the Belle Ile expedition had been abandoned and why a speedy attack on Ferrol was so necessary. If he stressed that the idea for the attack had come from Pulteney, who enjoyed a sound military reputation, he would win the King's agreement.[24] Pitt's advice had the desired effect, up to a point. The King conceded that any military activity that delayed making peace with France was to his liking. He had only opposed the idea because he deplored the waste of life that had been a feature of previous expeditions like those to Holland and the West Indies. There needed to be proper evaluation and preparation before any expedition to Ferrol took place.[25]

The King's insistence on yet more delay compounded Dundas's frustration, and only Pitt's intervention prevented him from offering his resignation.[26] Instead, he pointed out to the King that if the attack on Ferrol were to have any chance of success, it would need to be prosecuted expeditiously, before the enemy became aware of Britain's intentions. On 31 July Dundas sent orders to Pulteney and Abercromby to prepare immediately for the destruction of Spain's naval resources. The next day Abercromby was instructed to persuade the Russians, as tactfully as possible, not to land in Malta. Speed was now of the essence. Dundas felt he was alone in appreciating that Britain faced an existential crisis which could only be avoided by a rapid strike against French interests. To Abercromby he confided that something was needed to counterbalance the sequence of failure and defeat. A brilliant intervention now might change everything. Yet even as preparations for the Ferrol and Cadiz attacks were underway, there were other problems that needed to be dealt with. Despite the armistice, Austria still expected Britain to undertake diversionary activities. Again they requested that Abercromby should take his troops to attack Leghorn. The planned raid on Cadiz made this impossible but Grenville repeated his promise that if the Austrians resumed the fight British troops would be available to support them.

In Russia the Tsar was becoming ever more erratic, and seemed to be moving towards a rapprochement with France. He had resurrected the anti-British Armed Neutrality of 1780, which threatened Britain's access to the vital resources of the Baltic. In late July a Danish convoy was stopped so that the ships could be searched for contraband. This led to an exchange of fire and the convoy being forcibly escorted into Deal. Worried that the Danes would turn to Russia for support, and Russia would close the Baltic to British shipping, Britain tried negotiation. Sir Charles Whitworth, whom the Tsar had recently expelled from Russia, was sent to Copenhagen, but with an armed naval escort. When Whitworth realized that the Danes were prevaricating while they waiting for a response from Russia, he withdrew from the negotiations. Two British bomb vessels were brought up close to the city and their presence persuaded the Danes to capitulate. On 29 August they agreed not to send merchant ships in convoy. This was not the end of Britain's difficulties with Russia and the Armed Neutrality, but it bought time to concentrate on Spain.[27]

Meanwhile, peace negotiations between Austria and France were still in their early stages. Austria sent an emissary to Paris in response to Napoleon's initial offer. Once there he was manipulated into signing the preliminaries for an eventual peace. Thugut managed to evade ratification by insisting upon joint negotiations with Britain. Bonaparte immediately agreed to extend the armistice to Britain, although the offer was delivered in the form of an ultimatum. The First Consul's motives were obvious enough. An armistice that kept his two most determined opponents inactive would enable him to build up his own army and supply his forces in Malta and Egypt, particularly as he expected the armistice to include naval activity. In order to render Britain impotent, the First Consul chose to ignore the obvious fact that an armistice on land did not presuppose an armistice at sea.

Inevitably there were differences of opinion within the Cabinet. The most telling argument for Pitt was public opinion, which was becoming increasingly volatile and dangerous to the stability of the country. He decided, therefore, that they would have to accept the conditions of the armistice and the subsequent tri-partite peace negotiations. Dundas was taking the waters at Cheltenham when this crucial Cabinet meeting took place. He had then intended to travel on to Scotland. Instead, he responded to an urgent letter from Huskisson, who had been primed by his friend, Evan Nepean, the Secretary to the Admiralty, and hurried back to London to avert what he regarded as a potential disaster. He obliged the Cabinet to focus on the strategic dilemma: whether to sanction the attacks on Ferrol and Cadiz which, if successful, would strengthen Britain's hand but, if ending in failure, would give even more power to the French negotiators. Lurking as a complicating factor was the ongoing French invasion threat, an option never completely abandoned, while Portugal similarly feared a Spanish invasion, possibly aided by French troops. Grenville, in particular, felt an obligation to support Britain's long-standing ally. Attacks on Ferrol and Cadiz would certainly distract the Spanish from any planned invasion of their Iberian neighbour.

Dundas, still thinking in commercial terms, argued for an attack on Spanish interests in the Americas, and on 24 August he won qualified Cabinet support for an expedition to Cuba. He began an immediate search for the necessary number of transports and also informed Abercromby that he would be in command. Should an invasion of Cuba prove too challenging, then he could direct the attack elsewhere. The Canaries, the River Plate, Caraccas and even Puerto Rico again were among places mentioned.

At the same time, however, Dundas continued to have concerns about Egypt. Bonaparte's departure in August 1799 might have been interpreted as a signal that French possession of Egypt was finite. Certainly, the reaction of General Kléber, left in command, crudely expressed his anger. 'That bugger has deserted us with his breeches full of shit,' he is supposed to have exclaimed. 'When we get back to Europe we'll rub his face in it.'[28] Furthermore, the orders Bonaparte left for Kléber suggested a temporary stay. If not relieved by May 1800, and if losses to the plague were running at more than 1,500 a year, Kléber should make peace with the Porte. As so often with Bonaparte, there was a subtext that delivered a different message. Kléber could make peace but he was then to play for time rather than leave Egypt. By this means, Egypt would remain in French hands when peace was finally made in Europe and no-one would have the power to deprive France of her new colony.[29]

In January 1800 Kléber came to an agreement with the Turks. The Convention of El Arish, negotiated by Sir Sidney Smith, who had both naval command, under Nelson, and diplomatic authority, and who recognized that the Turks would never defeat the French. The convention allowed the repatriation of the French army with arms and baggage. Nelson, who was in Sicily, and Lord St Vincent believed it wiser to keep the French army out of the European theatre. There was a similar division of opinion in London when it became known that negotiations were taking place. Dundas, who still saw the French presence in Egypt as a springboard to India, welcomed the agreement, but Grenville shared the naval view, particularly as the Austrians opposed the repatriation of these battle-tried French warriors. The Mediterranean fleet was ordered to stop the French transports reaching Egypt, an order rescinded when it became known that the convention had been signed. Too late, because Kléber considered the agreement nullified. The Turks had assembled a strong multi-national army, led by the Grand Vizier, who now advanced on Cairo. When he refused to negotiate with the French emissaries who visited his camp, Kléber brought up his own forces and on 20 March routed the Turks at Heliopolis, even though outnumbered four to one. Three months later Kléber was assassinated by a Syrian fanatic and command passed to General Menou, an efficient administrator but a far less impressive commander and a man who was disparaged by many of the senior officers.

Ferrol and Cadiz

While Dundas continued to press the economic case, Grenville had won the Cabinet's agreement to the attacks on Spain. Pulteney took his troops, including three companies of the newly-formed 95th Rifles, to Ferrol as planned. They disembarked on the evening of 25 August and by early the following morning were in position to drive the enemy from the high ground that overlooked the town and harbour. When the Spanish attacked, they were quickly driven off. An inspection of the defences of Ferrol, however, convinced Pulteney that the place was too strong to be taken by escalade with the troops he had, while he lacked the resources for a blockade, particularly as the supporting naval ships were subject to the vagaries of the weather. That evening he gave the order to re-embark, to the disgust of the navy but to the approval of many of the more experienced military officers, who shared their commander's assessment. He then sailed on to Vigo, but finding nothing there to justify an attack he went to Gibraltar to join Abercromby, arriving on 19 September. Abercromby had arrived eight days earlier with 10,000 men.

Unfortunately for Pulteney, Britain was becoming uncomfortably familiar with failure. The protests of the naval officers were echoed by some of the military, and were soon taken up in Parliament. In February of the following year he was obliged to defend himself before the Lower House. He pointed out, with justification, that the task was impossible considering the resources he had been given, that no naval officer had seen the defences from the land side, and that as commander it was his responsibility to decide whether to proceed or withdraw.

To return to the summer of 1800, orders for the proposed attack on Cadiz had reached Gibraltar on 24 August, coincidentally the same day that the French garrison on Malta finally surrendered. The expedition was to land at Cadiz and Caraccas and destroy as many naval resources as possible. There was a proviso, though, that Abercromby should only undertake a landing if it were safe to do so; and safety would depend upon Admiral Keith's covering fleet finding secure anchorage. Without it, re-embarkation would be impossible, as would land-sea communications. For this reason, Rota, six leagues north of Cadiz, was identified as the most convenient landing point. From there the troops, once landed, could take Santa Catalina fortress, which defended Cadiz to the north, while the fleet lay at anchor in the bay. Abercromby, however. was about to discover that his naval equivalent, George Elphinstone, Admiral Lord Keith, was 'A selfish careerist who held the record for accumulating prize money' and 'would never share responsibility for a decision if he could dodge it',[30] Furthermore, in the opinion of Captain Alexander Cochrane, he was also incompetent and untruthful, while his language was known to be intemperate.

With Pulteney's forces as well as his own, Abercromby now had 20,000 infantry, 200 cavalry and 772 gunners, formed into two wings, the left under Pulteney and the right under Hutchinson. Because of a shortage of water in Gibraltar, most of the ships had sailed on to Tetuan, where the commanders now joined them. The fleet then set sail, passing the Straits of Gibraltar on 2 September and reaching Cadiz the following day. Two days later two engineers and a naval officer reconnoitred the beach at Rota. They discovered that the town was well fortified, while several batteries, strategically placed between Rota and Santa Catalina, would be difficult for the navy to silence. North of Rota however, there was another beach and this was considered more suitable for the landings.

Orders were given for disembarkation at 10 a.m. on 6 September, and once again Abercromby was precise in his requirements. Everything from the men's rations to the position of the surgeons in relation to their battalions was included in his general orders. Most significantly, though, the troop ships and transports were to be arranged as far as possible by brigade. There was to be no repetition of the confusion in Holland.

Moore provided the clearest account of what followed when he wrote in his journal the following day:

> I went on board the *Ajax* (Captain Cochrane). Captain Cochrane had the direction of the landing, and had said that he would take me on shore in his barge. The second signal was soon made for the troops to get into the flat boats. I found the different captains, who under Captain Cochrane were to superintend the landings, all on board the *Ajax* asking for directions. Captain Cochrane was extremely busy but confessed he was as ignorant as themselves. The fleet was all this time under way, seven or eight miles from the shore. Many flat boats were assembled alongside and astern of the *Ajax,* full of troops, but not near the number that were expected. I begged of Captain Cochrane to go to the *Foudroyant* and mention to Lord Keith the great deficiency of boats; and the necessity of their rendezvousing round some ship anchored inshore, etc. etc. Captain Cochrane returned soon afterwards, but apparently not better informed than when he went. The signal was made to know if we were ready to land. We answered from the *Ajax* No. I told Captain Cochrane that my orders were to land with my whole brigade (the reserve) and the Guards: in all about 5,000 men. As boats had come sufficient to hold 2,500 or 3,000 only, I could not take it upon me to land without particular orders from Sir Ralph; the more so as the fleet was still under way so far from the shore, and there was no probability of the boats, after landing the 1st Division, being able to return and land a second division before night. Sir Ralph had left the *Foudroyant* soon after the first signal was made to prepare to land, and had gone inshore to the *Phaeton* frigate. I went to the *Foudroyant* to explain to Lord Keith the situation we were in. I found him all confusion, blaming everybody and everything, but attempting to remedy nothing. He made the signal for the flat boats to row to the *Phaeton,* where they would receive their orders from Sir Ralph. He said that he could not help the want of boats, and that his orders had not been obeyed. I left him, determined to go with all speed to Sir Ralph and let him know how matters stood. As I was

leaving the ship I met one of Sir Ralph's aides-de-camp, who told me he had come from the general with a message to Lord Keith. I went with him into the cabin and heard him deliver his message: 'That Sir Ralph understood from a Captain of the Navy that only 3000 men were in boats. It was now one o'clock, and before they could land and return for more it would be dark. He therefore desired that the troops might be re-embarked, the ships brought to an anchor nearer to the shore, and a proper arrangement made for landing them at daylight next morning.' The Admiral said that it was impossible to anchor nearer the shore, so as to make a better arrangement, that the same confusion must occur tomorrow as did this day. He went on repeating much more incoherent nonsense. It was with difficulty I persuaded him to make the signal to the troops to re-embark. He would not issue it until I had said to him more than once, with some firmness, that Sir Ralph, who was inshore, must be a better judge than his Lordship of the propriety of risking 3.000 men on shore without the possibility of support for six or eight hours, perhaps till next morning; and that it was the first time any person had attempted to land an army from a fleet under sail.[31]

When Moore reported to Abercromby on board *Phaeton*, he stressed not only Lord Keith's state of confusion but also the opinions he had received from other naval officers that the anchorage was dangerous and communication with the shore would be lost if the wind blew from the south-west. Despite this, the order was given for a daylight landing the following day, which provoked Moore to write: 'we expected that nearly as much confusion would attend the attempt in the morning as had attended that of the day before.' During the night the wind veered to the south-west and at daylight the signal was given to cancel the landings. '. . . everything indicates that the expedition is given up. Whether this is in consequence of the weather, or of any previous determination, we know not. At any rate, the surf on shore makes it impossible to land, and the officers of this ship say that if I had landed with the reserve yesterday it would have been impossible, from the weather in the night and this morning, to have afforded us any support.'[32]

Why the expedition was aborted remains somewhat contentious. According to Bunbury, even before the departure from Gibraltar,

Sir Ralph had learnt that the yellow fever, in its most fatal form, was raging in and about Cadiz, the place which he had secret orders to attack. The General was disposed, in consequence, to suspend his operations against that unhappy town; to repair with his great army to the Tagus, and to wait there until fresh instructions could be received from England. Lord Keith put a different interpretation on the orders which had been received from our Government. He considered them to be peremptory, particularly as to an attack on the Caraccas, and the capture or destruction of the Spanish ships. Under these circumstances, Sir Ralph acquiesced, though reluctantly, in the prosecution of the enterprise.[33]

Whether Abercromby knew in advance that Cadiz was in the grip of an epidemic, a letter the Governor addressed to the admiral and cited by Moore certainly claimed such was the case:

That at a time when the town and neighbourhood of Cadiz was suffering under so severe a calamity as the plague, he saw with surprise the force under his Lordship's command upon the coast, with the view no doubt to take advantage of their present state to destroy the town and arsenal; that a conduct so inhuman was unbecoming to a nation like Great Britain; that he still hoped his Lordship would desist; that if he did not, he was not to expect an easy conquest; that the force collected was sufficient to baffle him; and that the garrison and inhabitants, however reduced by sickness, would prefer an honourable death in defence of their country, to that which was at any rate awaiting them from disease.[34]

Moore also mentioned that local fishermen and the crew of a recently-captured American ship maintained that large numbers were dying daily in Cadiz.

Yet this alone does not seem to be the reason for the abandonment of the expedition because in response to the governor's letter, and with Abercromby's agreement, Lord Keith wrote that unless the Spanish ships were surrendered, the troops would be landed and the expedition would fulfil its purpose.

An alternative explanation is the attitude of Lord Keith. Both Moore in his journal and Bunbury in his later account make much of the admiral's vacillation. Even after the engineers had identified a safe landing place, Keith was still cavilling. At dinner, when Moore was also present, Abercromby tried to pin the admiral down to a decision on whether it was safe to attempt the landings. He needed to be sure that communication could be maintained with the fleet, and the troops could be safely re-embarked, and only Keith could give him such assurance.

> Lord Keith said he could not be answerable for the winds; that if the weather was fine he could be answerable; but if a South-West wind blew, he must put to sea. Sir Ralph had heard, Lord Keith said, the sentiments of the naval officers, as well as his own. They were more averse to the undertaking than he was, but he had no objection to try it if Sir Ralph chose. Sir Ralph said, 'It is true that I heard the opinions of Sir Richard Bickerton and of the naval officers, but I do not feel myself competent to judge them. My orders are to land if I can be assured of embarking the troops. It is for your Lordship to form your opinion from your own knowledge and that of the naval officers under you, and to give a pointed answer. I do not wish to take to myself, or to throw upon others more than their share of responsibility. I shall take the whole responsibility of the land operations on myself; I am willing to share with your Lordship half the naval. If you will say that it is an undertaking to be risked, I am willing to undertake it, and to share with your Lordship the merit or blame which may attach to the issue. If you say it is not, let us withdraw, and I am also willing to share equally the merit or blame of that; but I must have a determined answer one way or the other.'[35]

It seems that while Lord Keith was in Gibraltar he had been confident that after taking Santa Catalina he would be able to anchor the fleet in safety, but once he was in Cadiz waters he was warned by Admiral Sir Richard Bickerton and other officers who knew the coast of the dangers of a south-westerly wind. At that point he appears to have lost his nerve, which would explain his confusion at the time of the aborted landings. Bunbury also considered him ungenerous to Abercromby, since he would neither give an opinion whether communications could be maintained once the troops were ashore nor commit himself to a decision to abandon the expedition. Bunbury was caustic in his criticism: of the ministers who 'brought together a mass of twenty or twenty-five thousand soldiers for a great undertaking, without having informed themselves whether their landing could be safely made'; and of Lord Keith, who 'might have informed himself as well (if he did not) with respect to the safety of the anchorage off the bay of Cadiz while he was lying at Gibraltar, as when he brought the fleet of transports to that insecure station'.[36]

The troops had been keyed up for action. The countermanding order 'occasioned much speculation, as we certainly had lost one very favourable opportunity for landing. At the same time I cannot pass by, without observation, the high spirits and enthusiastic ardour of the troops, which promised an additional example of British valour and victory, had they been permitted to display the one and to have obtained the other.'[37]

The reaction in Britain to yet another failure veered between anger and contempt. The country, it seemed, had an army not fit for purpose while the ministers played games with undertrained troops and inexperienced officers. Inevitably, Dundas was the target of much of the criticism. The Secretary for War, in response, deplored what others were holding him responsible for, the squandering of military resources to keep the Austrians happy or to support the wilder proposals of the Royalists. This was a dig at Grenville's Continental focus and obsession with coalition, and the Secretary at War William Windham's refusal to accept any future for France except the restoration of the Bourbons.

Abercromby now brought his force back to the Straits of Gibraltar. There was an urgent need for water, which meant sending boats into Tetuan on the North African coast. Grenville had called Abercromby a Jonah, with some justification. Once again, his presence at sea seemed to invite trouble when a violent storm hit the fleet. The boat parties had to be abandoned as cables were cut and the ships headed out to the Atlantic. The troops were sick, not only from the sea but also from the effect of rotting and maggot-infested food. The transports were unseaworthy. The whole force was in danger of destruction before it had achieved anything.

Collapse of the Coalition

The talks to set the conditions for an armistice dragged on, until it was finally recognized that Bonaparte was playing for time by continually introducing new conditions, just as his emissaries had done at Rastatt. When Dundas examined the latest version that Count Louis Guillaume Otto, the French resident agent in London, had brought from Paris he realized that Bonaparte's emphasis on a naval armistice was designed to allow him to augment the Army of Egypt. When this was confirmed by a similar report from Madrid, Dundas decided that Abercromby's troops should be sent to Egypt. On 18 September he put the proposal to the Cabinet. The Austrians wanted Abercromby's force to sail to Venice and some of the ministers saw this as the most effective use of the troops. As for Egypt, Sir Sidney Smith insisted that 20,000 men would be needed to drive out the French. Abercromby had only 15,000, the remainder having accompanied Pulteney to the Tagus in response to reliable information that Spain did indeed intend to invade Portugal with French support. Spencer also undermined Dundas by pointing out that it was too late in the season for naval activity in the eastern Mediterranean. Undeterred, Dundas presented a paper to the Cabinet in which he argued that it was time to abandon Continental expeditions and concentrate on British interests, which meant Egypt. Any delay and the Sultan might make peace with France. He urged Pitt to force the Cabinet into agreement. On 23 September, however, the Cabinet sanctioned aid to Portugal, which would now be Abercromby's destination, while a small force from India could deal with the French in Egypt.[38]

Dundas did not give up, particularly as Bonaparte was now demanding that the Malta garrison should receive a daily allowance of 10,000 rations, and six ships should be allowed to land their cargo in Egypt without inspection. To counteract Spencer, Dundas explored a wealth of naval data, and questioned men who had experience of the eastern Mediterranean. He also discovered through Nepean that the officer who informed Spencer of the conditions in the eastern Mediterranean, Admiral William Young, had never sailed there. Spencer was stubborn, however, maintaining there was not enough shipping available to transport the troops. In his view, Egypt should be postponed until Portugal was safe.

Paradoxically, Dundas's best ally proved to be Bonaparte's emissary, Count Otto. Although there might be some compromise on Malta, Otto made clear that Bonaparte intended to keep a French army in Egypt. Furthermore, that army needed extra troops and arms to retain possession of Egypt, which was a principal element of Talleyrand's negotiating stance. Britain must accept they had no choice but to agree to a naval armistice. Should they refuse, the First Consul would attack Austria, take Naples and Sicily, and then operate freely in the eastern Mediterranean. This concentrated the ministers' minds on whether an armistice was acceptable in any form.

At the same time, Bonaparte was playing the two allies against each other. On 19 September Moreau informed the Emperor that Britain was refusing the offer of an armistice. Bonaparte, therefore, would have no choice but to attack Austrian forces in Germany. Francis could avoid more bloodshed, though, by surrendering the three fortresses that Moreau was blockading, Ulm, Ingolstadt and Philipsburg. At the same time, the First Consul maintained to the British that the situation with regard to the fortresses was still under discussion. The Emperor agreed to surrender the fortresses when his own brother pointed out that the regeneration of the army was dependent upon a period of peace. Thugut promptly resigned in disgust. He was replaced by Count Johann von Cobenzl, who had led the negotiations that resulted in the Treaty of Campo Formio three years before. Cobenzl was dispatched to Paris with instructions to stall for as long as possible so that nothing would be signed before February 1801 but also making clear that Austria was ready to negotiate.

The Emperor had also decided that Kray should be replaced. He wanted his brother to take command but Charles, who believed that even a bad peace was preferable to yet more military failure, pleaded sickness. Francis then turned to another of his siblings, 18-year-old Archduke John, who was given a military theorist, General Franz von Lauer, as his second-in-command. Needless to say, Lauer's thinking had not adapted to the realities of Revolutionary warfare. At the same time, Bonaparte was making his own arrangements for renewed action that would force Austria to capitulate. General Augereau was sent with a Franco-Dutch force to threaten the Rhenish princes while Brune brought 10,000 men into Switzerland. Thus Moreau's flanks were secured ready for the inevitable campaign against Austria.

Britain might be at war with France, but the government could not ignore internal affairs. At the end of September, six months after both the British and the Irish parliaments had passed legislation for the union of the two kingdoms, the Cabinet was summoned to discuss the question of Catholic emancipation. Dundas, however, took the opportunity to hijack the meeting and introduce the topic of Egypt. He maintained that the threat to Portugal had been exaggerated and argued that an extra 3,000 troops in Lisbon would be sufficient to protect that country. This would release 12,000 men who could join Abercromby in Minorca, whereupon a choice could be made between Egypt and the Adriatic. The argument was won when Pitt agreed that Egypt should be the first concern. This change of mind set him against Grenville, who still believed that supporting Austria by fighting within Europe was the priority, and the King, who deplored the inevitable loss of life, while the Royalist-obsessed Windham twitted Dundas that having lost one army in a contest with yellow fever, he was now about to lose another to the plague. Pitt, however, realized that Egypt would be a potent bargaining chip in what he now regarded as an inevitable move towards some kind of negotiated peace. Indeed, his capitulation is not surprising considering the poor state of his health, the burden of heavy debts, the emancipation question and the increasing social unrest, which made the conflict between his two principal ministers one problem too many.

On 3 October the Cabinet agreed that 15,000 men should be sent to Minorca, while a further 1,500 should be taken from the Mediterranean garrisons to augment Abercromby's force. The plan for the campaign was now taking form. Abercromby's force would attack from the Mediterranean, while a force from India would advance from the Red Sea. Instructions were sent to Lord Wellesley to raise a force of 1,000 Europeans and 2,000 Sepoys, to be joined by a battalion from the Cape of Good Hope. At the same time Lord Elgin, Ambassador Extraordinary at Constantinople, and British Officers with the Turkish forces were forewarned of the government's intentions, while the Portuguese were told that Pulteney's force was all the help that Britain could supply.

Admiral Home Popham advised a point of assembly in the eastern Mediterranean, not only to secure fresh provisions and purchase horses but also to obtain intelligence. Based on this advice, Dundas intended that Abercromby should be off the coast of Egypt by December. He would then conduct a rapid (and successful) campaign, after which he could return to help Portugal. This was wildly optimistic, but seems to have been based on the presumed state of the Army of Egypt, only 15,000 strong, demoralized, and short of supplies, information gained from papers thrown into the sea during an attack on a French polacca. At the time Kléber was in negotiations with the Turks and may have sent the message back to France to justify his actions, or even to discredit Bonaparte, whose ambitions he suspected, and feared as a staunch Republican. Sir Sidney Smith estimated the French force at 20,000, however, and when the Army of Egypt was finally evacuated it numbered 24,000 military personnel.

The ships scattered by the storms off Tetuan finally reassembled without loss. Repairs were effected on those that needed them; the others sailed fairly aimlessly, waiting for news of a destination. Eventually, because they recognized that there was no safe anchorage in their present position, the two commanders decided they should make for Lisbon where there was both safety and provisions. On 24 October, however, the brig *Lavinia* arrived with dispatches, and Abercromby finally discovered that the government intended to send an expedition to Egypt. This was good news because such a campaign, which would secure the overland route to India, was genuinely in Britain's interest. He too recognized that possession of Egypt would give Britain a definite advantage in any peace negotiations. In his view the Revolution had run its course; it was now necessary to come to some kind of agreement with the France that had emerged from the decade-long upheaval. As Abercromby wrote to Huskisson, 'I ardently wish that public affairs may go well, and they cannot go better than in obtaining what I have always longed for, a reasonable peace . . .'[39]

Dundas wrote to Abercromby:

> . . . Other persons may have different sentiments, but the necessary course of events, seems to counteract *their views,* as much as they accord with mine upon this momentous subject, which are, that a negotiation without a naval armistice, is the best line we can follow for bringing the War to a safe and not disgraceful conclusion, and Providence seems to interfere to prevent our adopting any other. Entertaining this opinion, I have no uneasiness with respect to the footing on which we shall meet the enemy, except what arises from his being in possession of Egypt. From the moment of the unfortunate rupture of the Convention of El Arisch, I have watched with unceasing concern the unavailing efforts made by the Turks to drive him from the province, and coupling the weakness of that ally, with the disasters of our other Allies on the Continent, and the direction of British politics during this campaign, I own I have seen with great alarm the necessary moment of negotiation draw near, without perceiving any certainty that either by any military effort, pending that negotiation, or by any compensation it might afford us an opportunity of offering to the enemy, it might be in our power to compel or entice the French to withdraw from Egypt . . .[40]

Events would justify Dundas and completely undermine Grenville's coalition strategy. By early November Napoleon knew that his peace demands would not be met. He ordered Moreau to drive the Austrians back behind the Inn. Augereau and Macdonald, who had replaced Brune, were to co-operate on the flanks of Moreau's advance, while Brune, now in Italy, was to create a diversion. On 11 November the Archduke John was forewarned of the resumption of hostilities in accordance with the terms of the armistice. Moreau intended to march to the road hub at Hohenlinden fifteen days later. The Archduke moved first and actually worsted the French at Ampfing on 2 December. The following day, however, Moreau routed the Austrians out of the war at Hohenlinden. By 24 December Austria was suing for peace. The Truce of Treviso was signed on 16 January 1801, followed by the Treaty of Lunéville on 9 February which forced Austria to fulfil the conditions of

Campo Formio. As if this was not enough to scupper Grenville's hopes of pan-European action against the French, there were further setbacks when the Tsar, taking umbrage over Malta, persuaded the Scandinavians to close all ports to British ships. By March the Neapolitans were also out of the war. With Britain and the Ottomans now left alone to continue the struggle, it was obvious that there was no sensible alternative to Egypt.

An Eastern Mediterranean Front

Abercromby was aware that his only real successes had been in the West Indies and the taking of the Dutch fleet at den Helder. Flanders in 1793 and Cadiz were failures (although he had acquitted himself well in the former), and Ireland had been a personal disaster. He was now anxious to be associated with a campaign that would raise the reputation of the army, strengthen British interests and bring peace to Europe. It may be for this reason that he wrote to Lord Spencer with a request that command of the fleet in Egypt should be transferred from Lord Keith to some other officer. By this time he had experience in the ways of naval officers, and recognized that Keith might cause as many problems in Egypt as he had at Cadiz. Spencer refused the request, but in the short term he sent Keith to watch Sicily.

Abercromby was instructed to set up a rendezvous with the Turks (Rhodes, Cyprus, Candia and Syria were suggested locations) so that, even if he was prevented from landing by the season and the weather, the British government could dispute French possession of Egypt in any negotiations. Once the campaign started, he was to proceed against Alexandria. Dundas believed the fall of Alexandria, combined with a Turkish attack from Syria, would force the French to evacuate Egypt. Even if they decided to stay put, control of the northern coast, and of the Red Sea ports by the force from India, 5,000 men under General Baird, would effectively trap them. Dundas estimated the French strength as 13,000. Only 3,000 were thought to be in Alexandria, which was said to have weak defences. Furthermore, some intercepted officers' letters suggested that the French were desperate to leave Egypt, so Abercromby was permitted to offer them transport back to France. If the French commander-in-chief refused the offer, it was to be publicized to the rank and file.

Some of the Cabinet, as well as the King, initially opposed Dundas' plans. He won over the former by pointing out how victory could contribute to peace with the French. The King was concerned that the climate of Egypt might prove even more injurious to the army than yellow fever in the West

Indies. Later, though, when news of the first successes arrived, he praised the perseverance of the ministers who had steadfastly remained in favour of the expedition. Dundas was, however, prepared to listen to Abercromby if the information he received from naval and local sources convinced him that the project was unsound. He knew that Abercromby would not be motivated by any 'false point of honour or feeling', nor put off by any 'difficulties to which characters of less energy or less standing than your own may allow themselves to yield'.[41] In fact, Abercromby and Dundas were of one mind in their understanding of what could be achieved by expelling the French from Egypt. As an objective it was preferable to any other military option.

Abercromby had already grasped that the forthcoming campaign would be crucial to the British war effort and he now characteristically devoted all his energy and zeal to the necessary preparations, even though he was aware that Dundas had failed to give due weight to the practicalities of the expedition. He was instructed to divide his forces by sending 8,000 men (later reduced to 5,000) to Lisbon, where they would join Pulteney. His complement of senior officers comprised Lieutenant Generals Hutchinson, Coote, Craddock, Ludlow, Moore, and Lord Cavan, and Brigadier Generals Stuart, Hope, Doyle and Oakes, with Hope as his Adjutant General, and Colonel Robert Anstruther as his Quartermaster General. His force amounted to 16,488 infantry, 200 cavalry, 614 artillery under Brigadier General Lawson, and a small number of artificers under Major McKerris and Captain Fletcher RE.

Abercromby had been granted the choice of senior officers, and he had opted for men he considered competent. All but three of the infantry battalions, which had been completed from the Irish Militia, were soldiers with some experience, and generally under effective command. Significantly, even before the arrival of the *Lavinia* with new orders, Abercromby had already consulted with Keith about shipping requirements and had sent Hope to Lisbon to obtain supplies. He had also identified those battalions comprised of men who had volunteered for Europe-only service, his intention being to exchange them for unlimited-service men from the garrisons at Gibraltar, Minorca and Malta. It was, in fact, the best British army that had been assembled since the outbreak of war. Captain Thomas Walsh of the 93rd, and aide-de-camp to Major General Sir Eyre Coote, felt there was a feeling of 'sanguine expectation. To meet the justly celebrated army of the East, was now the favourite hope, and little doubt was entertained of the event. Few English armies were ever better composed; few, if any, expeditions more judiciously arranged; and never did general officers more fully enjoy the confidence of those under their command.'[42]

As for the medical services, Dr James Franck, Head of Medical Services in the Mediterranean, was originally appointed as Inspector General for Egypt. Upon further consideration the Medical Board realized that Franck lacked experience and Thomas Young was then appointed to the position. This obviously suited Abercromby, and Young did not disappoint him. He showed his usual energy from the beginning. When confronted by a sick rate of 12 per cent at Marmoris, he demanded and received help from the depots at Gibraltar and Malta. Franck remained with the expedition, and was later responsible for establishing a plague hospital in Aboukir.[43]

As soon as Abercromby discovered that the objective was Egypt, he had sent a message to Lord Elgin, instructing him to buy horses, while Anstruther and Lieutenant Colonel George Murray sailed for Rhodes to arrange for supplies and set up communication with the Turks in Syria. The original plan was for the whole fleet now to make a stop at Minorca and on 27 October about twenty ships set sail for Port Mahon. In the event, only the ships that were in the most need of repair stopped at Minorca and the rest sailed directly for Malta. Many of the troops, as a result, found themselves crammed into transports with leaky decks, and a shortage of stores and anchors. They left behind in Gibraltar between 400 and 500 sick men, while the 2/27th, suffering a serious outbreak of fever, were sent back to Lisbon in some of the ships intended for the expedition. By 11 November the ships were underway for Tetuan to take on water before heading for Malta, whereupon the weather turned boisterous. As the British ships reached Malta, though, they were given a warm welcome. Maule described how 'In entering this noble haven, between the forts of St Elmo and St Angelo, a boat, with musicians, according to their usual custom, met us, and preceded the vessel. The music was simple, but, like all compositions of that latitude, extremely pleasing.'[44]

Abercromby arrived on 19 November aboard the *Diadem* and immediately organized quarters either in barracks in Valetta or in nearby villages for the men who had fallen sick. The remainder of the troops had to stay on board, although they were landed in rotation for exercise, and so that the ships could be cleaned. They were also provided with fresh beef and vegetables. Abercromby took the opportunity to inspect the defences of Malta and informed Dundas that it was a more valuable possession than Minorca. Maule later wrote, 'Malta, situated between Europe and Africa, is a stupendous fortress, and presents the most formidable aspect, both from its singular situation, and the numerous bastions, forts, and ramparts, by which it is surrounded and defended . . . Nature has combined with art, and rendered the military strength of this important fortress truly noble and magnificent.'[45] It was certainly a prize worth keeping.

As the only information that Abercromby had so far received from the government was a sketchy report produced by Admiral Thomas Troubridge, a poor map of Egypt and copies of 'Intercepted Correspondence' which painted such a dispirited image of the Army of the Orient, he used his time in Malta to find out more about the geography of Egypt, the state and strength of the French, and the newly constructed defences of Alexandria. He learnt about the weather conditions on the coast, and also the possibility of Aboukir Bay as a landing point. Overall, though, his knowledge was unsatisfactory. Consequently, he wrote to Dundas: 'During my stay here I have procured a little information respecting Egypt, and have been able to form some notion on the operations of the campaign, with which I shall not trouble you at present, but I think it necessary to apprise you that the service on which we are going will not probably be so soon performed as you may expect.'[46]

He now acquired two further battalions to strengthen his force, the 30th and the 89th who had been engaged in the blockade of Valletta and were now replaced in garrison by the 40th and 63rd, both full of limited-service men. Abercromby, however, was made aware 'that a great part of the 40th regiment were eager to accompany him on the expedition, under the command of Colonel Spencer'. He chose the flank companies of the two battalions.

> They were accordingly removed to Riscoli, where they were seen on the following day, by Sir Ralph Abercromby, who said, that he did not come to inspect them, having had that pleasure so lately when he had every reason to be satisfied with them; but to return them his sincere acknowledgements for their gallant offers of service, which, while it manifested a zeal for their King and country, so honourable to themselves, enabled him to avail himself of the assistance of their gallant commander Colonel Spencer, an officer equally distinguished for his zeal and military talents.[47]

If Major Jackson was typical, it was not only the men in the ranks who were anxious to volunteer. 'I offered my services to Col. Spencer who received my offer and named me to Sir Ralph Abercrombie, who very handsomely acceded to my wishes.' Jackson was to be disappointed, however. Owing to some shenanigans involving Colonels Paget and Hill of the 28th and 90th, he learnt the day before the departure that he would not be going to Egypt.

The next morning I got up to witness the sailing of the fleet. It however overpowered me and I retired to the Library. Whilst reading there, General Moore came from an inner room, tapped me on the shoulder and said I shd. be too late for the ships. I apprised him of the mistake, I shall never forget the handsome and feeling manner he expressed himself which if possible made my regret the greater for the 40th flank companies were attached to the reserve which he commanded. They sailed with the good wishes of all, and the envy of two thirds who were left behind.[48]

Abercromby had already sent Moore an intercepted report from General Kléber's Chief Engineer. Although the information was twelve months old, it still gave some indication of the defences of Alexandria. On 28 November Moore received another paper which was an outline of Abercromby's plan of campaign. Since it takes us into his mind, it is worth reproducing in full:

Although it is allowed by all who are well acquainted with the navigation of the Levant, that the weather during the months from November to April is unfavourable for any naval and military operations on the coast of Egypt or Syria; yet, from the report of Captain Hallowell and Mr Smith of the *Theseus*, it appears that many days at that season are clear and moderate, and nowise adverse to the landing of troops on the coast of Egypt. Even when it blows, ships well found may ride at anchor off the coast without any danger, and the gales in general are not very violent or of long duration. If on further inquiry and fuller information it shall be found that a landing can be effected at this season without too great risk, it certainly will be advisable to attempt it for the following reasons. First, Alexandria is the only port on the coast of Egypt where ships can remain in safety. Second, when once we are in possession of that port all communication between France and Egypt will be effectually cut off. Third, the fatigue of a long blockade by sea will be avoided. Fourth, after a sufficient garrison has been placed in Alexandria, we shall be enabled to detach largely for the purpose of reducing Rosetta and Damietta, or to assist the Turks in expelling the French from Cairo and Upper Egypt.

If, however, we shall be disappointed in our expectation of getting possession of Alexandria, we have it always in our power to land at Damietta, where ships of war and transports can ride in great safety, although at a greater distance from the shore than near Alexandria. It will in that event change the plan of campaign. We shall either singly or in conjunction with the Turks ascend the Damietta branch of the Nile, and, after reducing Cairo, descend to Rosetta, cut off all communication with Alexandria, and prevent the annual supply of water from the overflowing of the Nile reaching Alexandria, which must from that circumstance, as well as other causes be under the necessity of surrendering without the labour of a siege. In acting in conjunction with the Turks we shall profit by the services of their cavalry. We shall be supplied with gunboats and other craft fit for the navigation of the Nile, and with horses and camels, and we shall experience the effects of terror and of fanaticism on the minds of the inhabitants and of the Bedouins. Although the disembarkation at Damietta must be made at three leagues' distance from the shore, yet it will be in smooth water, and as small craft is ordered to be provided for that purpose there will be no difficulty. Greek boats, which will carry 100 men, and not drawing more than 3½ feet water, will fully answer for this service. If the Turkish army shall have advanced from Jaffa towards Damietta we shall meet with no opposition in landing. At any rate, the French are not in sufficient force to oppose us with any effect without abandoning Cairo or Alexandria. Should the fleet meet with no disaster there is a reasonable prospect that the expedition will be successful. Most of the regiments are amongst the best in the service; the general officers men of high honour, with the advantage of vigorous health joined to experience. Independent of the *éclat* that will attend the defeating the most splendid project of modern times set on foot by a man of a great and comprehensive mind, we shall have the more solid satisfaction of rendering secure our possessions in the East, and of removing perhaps the only bar to general peace.[49]

Abercromby instanced HMS *Swiftsure*, which had cruised off the shore or lain at anchor in Aboukir Bay during the winter months, as evidence that the fleet would be able to cope with the conditions at sea, while the temperate conditions on shore would enable the army to function effectively. He also shared with Moore some initial ideas about the landings.

Troops must disembark at four or five miles' distance from the shore near Alexandria. The boats of the fleet will carry 4,000 men, and if sufficient small craft are obtained, of which there is little doubt, 3,000 more may come very near the coast. Eight artillerymen and twenty sailors must land with each piece of ordnance. Seven thousand men may be landed nearly at the same time. It will require two trips more to land the remainder of the army. With diligence and arrangement 7,000 men may be on shore in three hours after the boats and small craft take their departure from the rendezvous, and in seven hours more the whole army may be landed, provided the weather is favourable during the space of ten hours. All this, however, is subject to a degree of uncertainty.

There were further thoughts on the need to protect an army without cavalry, such as the one he commanded, when on the march. The solution was to place the steadiest troops on the flanks. These troops would need to be able to move quickly into square or, if there were no time for such a manoeuvre, to close into a mass and face outwards. Most interesting is the final sentence. 'The General Officer commanding the reserve, to whom the advanced and rear guards, and the most important service of the army may be entrusted, is requested to turn his mind to the different situations in which he may be engaged.' That officer was John Moore.[50]

While the final arrangements were being made Abercromby occupied himself in ways which demonstrate his attitude to command. On 27 November he inspected the 30th, 35th and 48th, praising all three and distinguishing the 30th

with peculiar expressions of approbation. The troops, on this occasion, were dressed in complete marching order, and his Excellency was pleased to pay particular attention to the manner in which the men carried their knapsacks; when he ordered them to be worn higher, the pack raised up on the shoulders, that the weight might fall as light as possible on the chests, while, at the same time, the men might enjoy a more free use of their arms . . .

During the remainder of the time he passed here, the whole of his mornings were employed by the General in reviewing the troops, and regulating the state of the army; and from twelve to three he gave audience to his officers, and such persons as had any business to transact with him: though, at the calls of justice or humanity, he was ready at all hours, and to persons of every denomination, to administer the relief in his power . . .[51]

Time Wasted: Experience Gained

The government intended the expedition to sail directly to Egypt. Indeed, Dundas had expected the campaign to open by December. However, Abercromby realized that they needed another rendezvous to acquire water, small craft, the horses that Lord Elgin was purchasing, supplies and somewhere to leave the sick, another indication of how seriously out of touch even Dundas was with the reality of campaigning. The plan was to leave Malta on 13 December but adverse winds delayed the departure until the 20th, when the 1st Division finally set sail. At this point Abercromby had 16,000 NCOs and other ranks fit for duty, and a further 1,270 sick. Inevitably, sickness was destined to become an increasing problem.

By 27 December Abercromby and the 1st Division were off Rhodes but could not anchor because of the south-easterly gales. They did, however, make contact with the *Petrel*, which Sir Sidney Smith had sent to liaise with the fleet, and Captain Inglis brought them to a safe anchorage in Marmoris Bay, to the relief of seasick soldiers in the overcrowded transports. A week later the second division joined them, having come via Crete. On realizing at one point that they were near the site of the Battle of Lepanto, Maule mused: 'These very Mohametans were now in alliance with the English nation, in order to drive away and destroy Christians of almost similar persuasion in religion, arts, and customs.'[52] The war was indeed throwing up some strange bedfellows. One of the strangest pairings was that between Tsar Paul and Napoleon, which was warming towards an alliance.

> The entrance into the Straights, which conducts to the spacious Bay of Marmorice, is marked by the appearance of several large mountains. We arrive at a narrow pass: as we wind along these delightful banks formed by mountains, towards the mouth of the Bay, we catch a glimpse of several villages romantically situated. These mountains majestically arising above each other in the figure of pyramids, whose summits are crowned with myrtle, orange, and citrus trees, present a charming and interesting scene ... The Bay of Marmorice, our destined anchorage for some weeks, completes a circumference of three leagues, and is encompassed by hills, covered with lofty trees, beyond which are extended on every side considerable forests and woods.[53]

Storms were frequent, and created such an impression that they are often referenced in the memoirs of the campaign. The most dramatic 'came on from the south-east, with showers of hail or lumps of ice, the largest seen by any of us. The tents on shore were beaten down and riddled as if by musket balls. Trees were broken down and rooted up. When night came on it was dismal to hear the wild beasts howling in the woods . . .'[54]

The 2nd Division had arrived in the wake of such a storm.

> The morning was gloomy, and the appearance of the horizon did not promise a speedy termination of the gale . . . About one o'clock our anxiety was a little relieved by the prospect of land, which we rightly concluded to be the western point of the gulf of Macri. At two we entered the bay of Marmorice, following the headmost ships, which were our only guidance into it. The sight of so many vessels sailing between the two narrow ridges of elevated mountains, which form the intricate entrance into this bay, joined to the dismal and lowering aspect of the atmosphere, rendered more awful by long and repeated flashes of lightning, made the scene impressively grand and solemn.[55]

Abercromby now needed to ensure that they had Turkish support. Anstruther was already in Rhodes, and Murray, the Assistant Quartermaster General, went on to the camp of the Grand Vizier at Jaffa. Anstruther initially reported positively, but the promises made to him were not fulfilled. As a result, Abercromby found himself without the small boats he needed for the landings, without crews for the gunboats that were still at Rhodes, and without provisions and horses. To make matters worse, Murray reported that the state of the Vizier's army precluded any useful assistance. However, Abercromby still announced his arrival at Marmoris Bay to the Vizier and explained the possibility of joint operations, urging the Vizier to get his army fit for action. Moore was the intermediary for this. His main task was to familiarise himself with the real state of the Turkish army. He was also to make clear that the British forces were ready to adapt their plans to those of the Turks, although this did not prevent Abercromby instructing Moore to give the Turks a route for their advance towards Alexandria. The two armies would then be able to act together while remaining two distinct forces, a lesson learnt from Holland. Moore was also to request a sufficient number of horses to mount the British cavalry, and some small craft for the disembarkation of the army. Finally, he was to assure the Vizier that Britain had but one objective, to drive the French from Egypt.

Moore was well received by the Vizier and won his general agreement to Abercromby's plan. He soon came to the same conclusion as Murray about the condition of the Turkish army, though. 'From a view of his troops and from everything I could learn and observe of their composition and discipline, I could not think they were otherwise than a wild ungovernable mob, incapable of being directed to any useful purpose; and as they were destitute of everything that is required in an army, while their chief, the Vizier, was a weak-minded old man, without talent, or any military knowledge, it was in vain to expect any co-operation from them.'[56] 'For what could be effected by a disorganized army, composed of an assemblage from all countries and nations, without any dependence on its officers, without discipline, with little or no authority in its chief, without any magazine, and afflicted with the exterminating plague?'[57]

Abercromby suspected that the Turks were being deliberately obstructive; he agreed with Moore that they would receive no Turkish assistance and must rely on their own resources. He took the pragmatic view that support would only be forthcoming if he gained a foothold in Egypt. His instructions required him to land as close as possible to Alexandria, but to use his discretion and choose any other place if it seemed advisable. Damietta had seemed preferable when there was the option of linking with the Turks. Now he made a definite decision to land near Alexandria. He knew there was a good anchorage in Aboukir Bay, and that communication could be maintained between ships and shore. He had no knowledge of French strength at Aboukir, however. He also realized that if the French were expecting a landing at Aboukir they would have made preparations to defend the position. This might make it impossible to disembark; and even if the British established a foothold, a determined French attack might drive them back to the ships. Such a 'defeat' would weaken the British negotiating position, but the risk had be taken. He also recognized that he would need to take Alexandria to establish a safe haven for the fleet and a secure base for the army before moving against the main French army, whose position he did not know. Yet, despite these uncertainties, he was not in the mood to give up when victory would prove so valuable to the interests of Great Britain.

George Baldwin, who had been the British consul in Cairo for thirty years and had joined the expedition at Malta, volunteered practical assistance. He warned that there was no fresh water between Aboukir and Alexandra and that the coast between Aboukir and Alexandria was too rocky and the surf too high for boats to approach the shore, except at one small creek four miles from Alexandria, which could be used only if the weather was good. In order to supply water, wood and all the stores and provisions required the fleet would have to remain in Aboukir Bay and land what was needed either at Aboukir, ten miles from Alexandria, or in the creek when weather permitted. Abercromby suspected this might be asking too much of Lord Keith.

It might now have been decided where the landings should take place but nothing could be done until the arrival of the small landing craft from Smyrna, and the ships carrying the 200 horses purchased by Lord Elgin, which were required for the recently-arrived 12th and 26th Light Dragoons. As Walsh commented, until the horses arrived the dragoons would be of no use because, having come from Lisbon without their own horses, 'The officers were the only mounted men in the regiments. This circumstance was the more distressing, as the four or five hundred horses we had received from the interiour of the country were so miserably weak and bad, as to be totally unfit to mount our cavalry.'[58] Smyrna was only a two-day sail away, but there had been a two-month delay. Although 500 mules had been bought at Smyrna, the *Greyhound* frigate, acting as escort, reported that the mule transports had been scattered by gales, while there was no news at all of the small landing craft.

There were other practical problems. Sir Sidney Smith had been blockading Alexandria in response to information that a French relief fleet had put to sea. He now arrived at Marmoris and informed Abercromby that the French strength was 30,000. (As already noted, this was more than the number of men that would eventually be evacuated from Egypt.) Abercromby was confident this was an exaggeration, his own guess being that the French had only 10,000 men at most to oppose the landings. This was still a formidable opposition because even when the small boats arrived there would only be enough of them to accommodate 6,000 men in the first wave. Furthermore, even after the beach had been secured, transport would remain a problem. Without wagons or draft animals, the soldiers and sailors would have to drag everything from the landing point to the camp. Men were already at work constructing wooden sledge-like structures that could be towed rather than carried.

On 16 February Abercromby wrote to Colonel Robert Brownrigg, York's military secretary:

> It is impossible for me to say how much we have been disappointed
> in our expectations of assistance from the Turkish Government.

I firmly believe, that both the Quartermaster, Colonel Anstruther, and Lord Elgin did use, before our arrival here, every exertion to procure us those articles of which we most stand in need, and I know, from my own experience, the impossibility of rousing the Turks to any effectual aid or co-operation. We are now on the point of sailing for the coast of Egypt, with very slender means for executing the orders we have received. I never went on any service entertaining greater doubts of success, at the same time with more determination to encounter difficulties. Our own character, and the honour of the profession to which we belong, urge us all to use every effort in the discharge of our duty . . .[59]

On the same day he wrote to Huskisson in a similar vein:

The Turkish government has been lavish of promises, but in no one circumstance have they been fulfilled, and we now go to fight their battles without their assistance or co-operation in any one article. I am not willing to state difficulties, but I should deceive you if I did not speak truth. You may rest assured that everything shall be done that it is possible to accomplish, but I cannot, and I will not, promise success.[60]

Not surprisingly, perhaps, Moore echoed Abercromby's sentiments in his journal: 'I cannot but think the enterprise in which we are about to engage extremely hazardous and doubtful in the event. We cannot, however, hesitate; we must attempt it.'[61]

At this point, the soldiers' pay was three months in arrears and a hundred cavalry horses bought at Marmorice had to be paid for out of the staff officers' own pockets. Abercromby might be in command of potentially the best British army assembled so far during this war, but he was also suffering from the incompetence of ministers who still had not grasped the simple truth that expeditions needed to be properly equipped, not left short of wagons and the horses to pull them and the right number of gun crews for the artillery. He did now have between ten and thirteen gunboats, however, Turkish from Rhodes and British naval, along with enough brigs and cutters to cover the landings. The engineers had prepared fascines and gabions, and every attempt had been made to supply the army from local resources for an arduous campaign.

On 21 January a council of war had been held on board *Foudroyant*. Representing the army were Abercromby, Hutchinson, second-in-command,

Moore, Anstruther and Hope. Keith, his second-in-command, Rear-Admiral Sir Richard Bickerton, and Captains Benjamin Hallowell and Sir Sidney Smith were present for the navy. Moore reported in his journal that after Abercromby had explained his reasons for preferring Alexandria as the first objective, he

> wished for a naval opinion how far the anchorage in the Bay of Aboukir could be depended upon for the fleet, and how far the navy would be able to land the ordnance, ammunition, provisions, and water which would be necessary for a fortnight or three weeks that the army might be employed in besieging Alexandria. Captain Hollowell and Sir Sydney Smith, but particularly the former, did not doubt from the experience he had of the coast that the fleet, when anchored in Aboukir Bay, would be able to land a sufficient quantity of water and provisions for the army for a fortnight immediately after the troops had landed.[62]

This was encouraging information, particularly as Hallowell pointed out that during the advance to Alexandria the army would never be more than a mile from the sea so that small boats would be able to replenish supplies. He also maintained, in welcome contradiction to Baldwin's information, that despite some rocky areas, there were still places where the boats could land.

According to Dundas's timetable the expedition should already have been in Egypt but Abercromby was detained in Marmoris Bay for over four weeks while he waited for boats and horses. The time was not wasted, though. As he had in the West Indies, he framed a code of conduct for the campaign. He was particularly concerned about the health of his troops. Several regiments were suffering from confinement on board ship, so he ordered that all the sick men be sent on shore and there encamped. The result was a rapid improvement in their health. Change of diet also contributed much to this desirable end. Both Abercromby and Keith realized that maintaining supplies was crucial. Ships were sent to Macri, Rhodes and neighbouring places to obtain cattle and vegetables. Even fresh bread was occasionally issued.

> It is a custom in the navy, to victual the soldiers at only three quarters allowance; this quantity being deemed sufficient for men who work little, and are only for a short time at sea. But in a case like the present, where soldiers, on board troop ships

weakly manned, are obliged to do as much work as the sailors, and detained on board for months together, the pittance is too small, and it is but fair, that they should receive the same allowance as the sailors. Sir Ralph Abercromby, fully aware of this circumstance, represented the business to Admiral Lord Keith, who immediately placed the soldier on the same footing as the sailor in this particular.[63]

Once again, and despite the debacle at Cadiz, Abercromby had established a good working relationship with a senior naval officer

As well as the construction of carriers with shafts that could be pulled either by two horses or a group of men, ammunition boxes were adapted to be fitted to camels. As was normal for a campaign where siege work was anticipated, soldiers were set to work on fashioning gabions and fascines. There was also a need for tent pegs and mallets, another task for the troops, which served the secondary purpose of keeping them occupied. Nor were the sailors idle. They aided the soldiers in their tasks, while naval coopers and carpenters produced casks and barrels for supplies, and more sledges for transporting them.

Nor did Abercromby neglect the general efficiency of his force and its good behaviour. As on Malta, and before that, Minorca, there were daily reviews of the troops in which Moore and Hope played their part. These two men, in some sense his protégés, shared his idea of what constituted a good soldier: sound health, equipment in good order, general cleanliness and a disciplined response at all times. There was regular drill. Abercromby was committed to neither the German nor the American system but appreciated the value of both in their proper place. With an Italian destination, he would probably have employed the American approach, which had formed part of the drill on Minorca because it would have been appropriate to the terrain. Egypt was open country and the French had cavalry, so the German system was more appropriate and formed the basis of drill at Marmoris. Like most competent officers, he realized that the eighteen manoeuvres, as required by Dundas's principles, were ineffectual in battlefield conditions, so he simplified them. He concentrated on tactics against cavalry, which required practice of forming square, and a variety of different squares, as well as instituting drill for marching in square. In this respect, rotating the troops on land not only improved their health by allowing the ships to be fumigated, it also meant that regular drill and inspections increased their efficiency.

It was also important to maintain good relations with the local population both in Marmoris and in Egypt. Officers and men alike were reminded of the need to show respect to the customs, manners and religion of the local population, since the ultimate success of the expedition could well depend upon their goodwill. Failure to do so would occasion 'the disagreeable consequences of punishment, which he assures them must inevitably follow every offence of this nature'.[64]

It could be argued that at the end of his military career Abercromby was establishing a pattern for the command and organization of an effective campaign. He also seemed to be enjoying a command where he was too distant to be plagued by the vagaries of politicians and where he had time to make all the necessary preparations. As Moore noticed, he seemed a decade younger than his sixty-six years. Nor did he ever sacrifice humanity in order to preserve the status of commander. He might be a strict disciplinarian but he also made the men's comfort a high priority. Lieutenant Macdonald remembered him tucking a blanket more securely around a sick soldier and requesting a pin to hold it in place.[65]

Moore summed up what had been achieved by Abercromby's attention to his troops.

> The Commander inspected the regiments and brigades separately. He gave praise where it was due, and was severe in his animadversions wherever he observed carelessness or inattention. He became thus acquainted with the state of every corps and the character of its commander. Discipline was improved and emulation excited. Corps were landed daily for exercise. The men were warned of the importance of preserving invariably their order in open country exposed to the attack of cavalry; and the attention of general officers was called to adopt the simplest and most speedy modes of forming from the column of march to the columns to resist the shocks of cavalry.[66]

Now that Aboukir was the designated landing point, the problems peculiar to that bay could be addressed. The water was shallow, so the ships would have to remain out at sea. It could be assumed that the French would strongly defend the bay with battle-hardened soldiers, very different from the Dutch who had opposed the Helder landings, although they had certainly fought with spirit and determination. Consequently, there should be no repetition of the chaos at Callantsoog; and the first wave of British troops would have to be reinforced as quickly as possible. Normally, the first wave would be brought inshore and boats would then row back to the fleet and pick up the second wave. If the ships were as much as seven miles out at sea, the first wave would suffer cruelly while they waited to be reinforced. In addition, the oarsmen would be exhausted. Abercromby decided, therefore, that the second wave should be held closer inshore while the first wave would embark from the naval ships and be rowed past their reinforcements. Anstruther and Cochrane were to oversee the landings, and the former was instructed, as an additional safeguard, to make sure that the latter understood the importance of landing the troops in order of battle.

The expedition to Egypt was a genuinely *conjunct* operation. Even after the landings, sailors would still have a vital role in the expedition. They would help bring ashore everything needed for the campaign, and their muscle power would assist in the transportation of guns, ammunition and supplies. Without abandoning his habit of temporising rather than giving answers to questions, Keith did agree that nearly half the naval strength and a battalion of marines could be spared to go ashore with the army. With men of the calibre of Alexander Cochrane and Richard Bickerton, however, Abercromby could confidently expect willing naval support of the kind he had enjoyed with Christian.

Taken overall, the stay in Marmoris Bay had proved a mixed blessing. Abercromby probably shared Moore's assessment that:

> By coming here we have got about 400 cavalry mounted, horses for the field-artillery, mules, which will be of use in the transport of stores, besides fascines, palisades and other materials necessary for a siege; but we have lost two months and the advantage of a surprise. Had we sailed straight from Malta to Alexandria, or after staying here a few days to water, we should certainly have taken the French unawares. They have now had time to prepare and digest their mode of defence . . .[67]

Nor was Moore alone in his misgivings. General Hutchinson, who had served as a volunteer aide-de-camp to Abercromby in Flanders and Holland, and was a trusted friend as well as second-in-command, strongly expressed his belief that the whole expedition was a mistake, although when challenged he explained that it had been his duty to state his doubts and he nevertheless promised his full support. Abercromby himself, although preserving in public that serenity of demeanour that he was so noted for, wrote to David

Dundas, another trusted confident, that he was concerned about the state of the Turkish army and anticipated that the forthcoming campaign would prove arduous, its outcome uncertain.[68]

These reservations were justified when a captured French corvette was brought in. It had sailed from Toulon with two frigates, which had reached Alexandria with 800 soldiers and military supplies on 10 February, having been able to avoid the British covering ships, *Minotaur* and *Northumberland*. Letters taken from the corvette revealed that other frigates were presently waiting to sail from Toulon; Bonaparte was obviously determined to retain Egypt as Europe moved towards peace negotiations. After the double blow of Marengo and Hohenlinden, the Austrians were effectively out of the war, while the Russians were on the verge of entering into an alliance with France. For Bonaparte, Egypt would be the main prize, and reinforcements were on the way to keep it firmly in French hands. Unknown to Abercromby at Marmoris, seven ships under Admiral Gauteaume had been able to slip out of Brest on 23 January when gales dispersed the British blockade.

Nevertheless, even if the delay enabled the Army of the Orient to tighten its grip on Egypt, the time had not been wasted. As Private Nichol of the 92nd reported:

> The army was exercised by brigades in landing in flat bottomed boats, with regiments keeping in line and advancing or retreating on signals from the naval officers stationed in the boats. The men-of-war launches had field pieces fastened on the prow, with slides for the wheels; when the lashings were cut, the guns were run on to the beach ready to act with the troops; this was an excellent plan which we had felt the want of in Holland.[69]

The first rehearsal took place on 21 January. Cochrane's ship, the *Ajax*, served as the assembly point for the landing craft which then proceeded to their appointed ships to load up with the troops of the two brigades which had been nominated for this initial practice. All went perfectly to plan, and the men were ranked in their battalions within minutes of landing. The process was repeated, not always successfully. On 2 February a practice by the 2nd, 3rd and 4th Brigades was notably disordered. Admittedly, by this stage the idea of an assembly point had been abandoned and the landing craft went straight to their allotted ships, which required more precise control, particularly as these manoeuvres would take place in the poor light of early morning. With repeated practice, however, the point was reached where every officer, military and naval, knew exactly what he and his men should do, while both soldiers and sailors had become experts in the planned manoeuvres. The constant repetition 'accustoms the men to get into the boats, teaches them how they are to place themselves in them, and instructs them in what manner they are to form as soon as they reach the shore. It also ascertained the number of men which the boats of the fleet were capable of containing. The wisdom of this measure is obvious; and it will, doubtless, prove very beneficial.'[70]

The horse transports, the last hold-up, finally arrived on 16 February and the horses were immediately embarked. The following day Abercromby summoned his generals to the *Kent* for a final issue of orders and those troops still on shore were sent to their transports. The total strength of the infantry was 14,444, although 750 were considered incapable of landing. The cavalry comprised 1,063 men and 454 horses, the artillery, 630 men and 173 horses. The battalion of marines seconded to the army was 500 strong. In total this amounted to 16,237 men and 627 horses.[71]

Egypt

The long-desired embarkation finally took place on 18 February 1801. The weather immediately turned foul and it was not until 7 a.m. four days later that the fleet finally set sail. Fortuitously, during the delay the small craft from Smyrna had arrived. By dusk all the vessels were clear of the harbour. It seems to have been a majestic departure. Colonel John Abercromby, the General's son serving with the adjutant general's department, wrote in his journal:

> It was impossible not to contemplate with an awful but interesting sensation the noble sight of this grand fleet issuing from under the stupendous mountains of Asia Minor. Never was there an expedition attended with more important and extraordinary circumstances. Never was the honour of the British army more at stake, or its animated exertions more required: and never was the interest of the country more deeply involved than in its ultimate success. Our difficulties, as far as we are able to view them, are great indeed; but I can venture to assert that an equal number of Britons were never assembled who were more determined to uphold their own and their country's honour.[72]

Elsewhere in the fleet Maule observed:

> Scarcely had the favourable breeze filled our sails, when our neighbours, the Regiment De Rolle, accompanied us with their noble music.
>
> Their vicinity, indeed, was always coveted by me, and on subsequent occasions, I have been still more gratified in an acquaintance with that regiment. At all times, when on duty with them, I have observed with delight their correct discipline and military department.[73]

Daniel Nichol of the 92nd was also impressed by the departure of the fleet:

> As the fleet consisted of about 200 ships, many of which were large and elegant vessels, it had a grand and interesting appearance . . . to see the last golden beams of the sun glancing on the wide spreading white sails with the wind beginning to blow fresh, brought to my mind what has happened on this very coast, of people being driven from their country going to found a new settlement under some adventurous chief.[74]

The voyage was not a pleasant one, however. 'On the 25th, being nearly half way across, the wind suddenly changed, and became completely foul. The gale continued to increase til the 27th, when it blew tremendously. The sea ran mountains high, and the heaviness of the swell made the ships labour exceedingly.'[75] The next morning the wind eased but it took the entire day to reassemble the fleet. The small Greek horse transports and the Turkish gunboats had run for cover in Cyprus and took even longer to re-join.

Land was sighted on 1 March and the fleet was ordered to 'bring to'. '. . . We stood in so near to Alexandria as to distinguish the vessels in the harbour and the colour of the signals. We lay for some hours in this situation, and at dusk made sail to the North-East. The weather was extremely unsettled and did not promise to be such as to admit of disembarkation. I thought we should have stood off until it became more favourable, and I was at a loss to conceive why Lord Keith had shown himself before Alexandria.'[76] Moore was not the only one to be puzzled by Keith's decision, but the Admiral chose to anchor close in because he wanted to observe the signals in the harbour. He also learnt that the water in the bay was at most only six to nine fathoms deep to seven miles out, becoming even shallower closer inshore, so that even the transports would be able to anchor only two miles closer than the warships. On 2 March the order was given to prepare provisions for three days and the fleet ventured further into the bay, which suggested that the landings were imminent, until 'boisterous and uncertain weather'[77] drove them further out. According to Maule, although the French showed their usual 'Alacrity, great military talents and unbounded assiduity, the attributes invariable in a French army', General Menou, in command, was guilty of a serious military fault, 'namely, that he despised, or rather that he did not hold in sufficient respect, the force and the nature of the enemy opposed to him'.[78] In fact, Menou was still in Cairo at this point, but the comments may be considered fair in the light of his later conduct.

So who was Menou, appointed to command of the Army of the Orient after the assassination of the talented Kléber? As already noted, he was certainly not an imposing military figure. Fifty years old, he was running to fat. He was one of several senior officers who had converted to Islam, taking the name Abdullah and a Muslim wife. He was happy to be in Egypt, while other French officers, like Reynier, Friant and Lanusse were anxious to return to the European theatre. These three men despised Menou and he, in return, did not trust them. Menou also shared with Bonaparte the conviction that Egypt should be possessed and colonized by the French. He acknowledged that the British navy was certainly a formidable opponent, but he only needed to look at the record of the army to believe it would pose little problem to his forces. Surprisingly, though, while he felt such contempt for the British army, he had considerable respect for the Turks, whom he considered difficult opponents.

Nevertheless, he still needed to take some decisions against the British threat. He suspected there were two British forces: the one at Marmoris, he might delude himself, was preparing for a land-grab from the Ottomans; the other, from India, was an unknown quantity whose purpose was unclear. Needing to defend himself against all possibilities, he decided to retain half his forces in Cairo, where he had established himself. As for the state of his army, it suited the British government to believe it was thoroughly demoralized. There is little doubt that the vast majority of the French troops, like their officers, were anxious to return to Europe. Stranded in Egypt, they had missed the latest French triumphs. In appearance they were not an impressive sight, the infantry in particular clad in make-do-and-mend uniforms. Yet they were crack troops, veterans of Bonaparte's first Italian campaign and men whose pride preserved them against the indiscipline of a truly demoralized force. It remained to be seen to what extent the promise of action would rouse their fighting spirit.

As the British fleet came to anchor off Aboukir, Captain Louis of the *Minotaur* boarded the *Kent* to report that the *Régenerée* had brought 200 infantry and 600 artillerymen into Alexandria; and the French were also expecting the arrival of Admiral Gantheaume with a further 6,000 men. Louis also informed Abercromby that Major McKerris and Captain Fletcher, who had been sent from Marmoris to reconnoitre the coast, had been surprised in a small boat and taken prisoner. This was a double blow: engineers were always a scarce commodity. Now the expedition had lost both its chief engineer and one of his most talented subordinates; and there was still no definite information about the shoreline.

Having learnt of the fate of the two engineers, Abercromby immediately took a cutter and, accompanied by Moore, went close inshore to reconnoitre and identify the most practicable landing places. These proved to be on the eastern front of the peninsula in a bay two to three miles wide. The castle of Aboukir was situated at the northern point, and was well armed with guns, the biggest of which could enfilade the beach, while a French ship anchored under the castle was in position to rake the beach. (Admiral Keith claimed that he could not spare a ship to deal with it.) A sand hill that rose over sixty feet dominated the middle of the bay, while further south the ground was a confusion of smaller sand hills and scrub. Nearer Lake Maadieh the area was wooded. There was also a blockhouse at the southern point with at least one heavy gun. Moore was of the opinion that the French had not bothered to entrench this position because of its innate strength. Picquets were visible, however. Bearing in mind the range of the castle guns, it became clear that the landings would have to focus on the area south of the dominant sand hill, which extended to a width of no more than a mile. The hill itself would be the objective of the British right.

By 2 p.m. Abercromby was back on board the *Foudroyant* and orders were given for the landings to take place the following morning, 3 March, but by 6 p.m. the weather had once again turned frustratingly rough, too rough for the landing craft to row to the shore. This day, however, an emissary under a flag of truce came from Alexandria to report that Major McKerris was dead. The engineer had decided against instructions that he and Fletcher should land in order to acquire a better understanding of the terrain, whereupon they had been spotted by the French. They were able to return to their boat and head for the sloop that had brought them to Aboukir Bay. When they ignored an order to surrender, the French gunboat which had been sent to intercept them opened fire. Mckerris had been killed and Fletcher taken prisoner. This news only intensified the sense of loss: 'Endowed with a great share of professional talent, active, enterprising, and ever indefatigable in the prosecution of the public service [Mckerris'] death was no less a misfortune to his army, that a calamity to his friends.'[79]

There was no improvement in the weather for the next two days, during which the *Romulus* arrived with the news that Ganteaume had safely avoided the British fleet at Brest and was now in the Mediterranean. On 5 March Abercromby again sent Moore to reconnoitre, accompanied by Colonel Lindental. They were able to use one of the bomb vessels, which was moored less than two miles from the shore, as a viewing platform. A close inspection confirmed what had been surmised from the previous reconnaissance, that 'the ground is favourable to the enemy, as he can be concealed close to the shore. The enemy have the means of concealing their force. They show none, but they have had time to collect one, and it is but reasonable to suppose that they have availed themselves of it. I could see their picquets extended along the line above-mentioned, and there seemed a constant movement of individuals and small parties along it. The captain of the bomb concludes that fresh troops have joined from a greater bustle appearing this day than before.'[80] The crucial question, how strong was the defending force, remained unanswered.

The next day Sir Sidney Smith was sent to destroy a French gunboat at the entrance to Lake Maadieh and to cut the rope of a pontoon bridge that allowed communication between Alexandria and Rosetta. A prisoner taken at the scene reported that Friant planned to oppose the landings with 3,000 men, itself an exaggeration, but very much better than the 10,000 Abercromby had anticipated. Nevertheless, the advantage would initially be with the land-based force and heavy casualties were inevitable. Despite this, Abercromby was anxious that the landings should take place as soon as possible, and once more gave orders for the following morning. But 7 March dawned to freshening winds, although these died down as the day progressed, causing a postponement of only one day.

Meanwhile, in Cairo, Menou knew of the British arrival by 3 March. This would have been the moment to send reinforcements to oppose the landings, had he not suspected that the force off Aboukir was diversionary and their true objective was Damietta, where they could link up with the Turks and attack Cairo. As a result, he sent only 600 men from Ramanieh to Alexandria. General Friant, who had last met the British in Flanders and was now in command at Alexandria, had about 2,000 effective troops and much the same number of invalids and sailors. He sent a small detachment to Rosetta, and another further south-west. Then he took up position at Aboukir with 1,600 infantry, 200 cavalry and 15 guns, confident that he could repulse any British landings. It had been proved time and again how easily troops could be brought into a state of confusion as they tried to establish a foothold.

Reynier, who may have been justified in his belief he would have been a more competent commander of the Army of the Orient, was able to convince Menou that it was crucial to focus on preventing the British from gaining a foothold. Under pressure, Menou now sent Lanusse's division to Alexandria, to be followed by a cavalry regiment (in addition to the one that was on its way to Friant) and one of Reynier's demi-brigades. Lanusse departed on 5 March. Then Menou learnt that the Turks were not expected to mobilize for several weeks, which seemed to confirm his suspicion that Aboukir was a diversion. Even if not, he shared Friant's confidence that it would be an easy matter to defeat the inferior British troops under their inferior commanders. He recalled some of Lanusse's troops and instructed the others to halt at Ramanieh, which left only a demi-brigade to join Friant. He also assured Friant that most of the British troops were still on Rhodes, a deliberate piece of misinformation brought to Aboukir by a Greek ship.

During the evening of 7 March preparations for the landings were resumed. Because of the practice at Marmoris, these proved straightforward. The boats of each ship knew which transport to approach when the signal was given for the first division to prepare to land. There were two field pieces and artillerymen on board each warship, and launches had been fitted to take guns so that they could fire immediately on landing. The flotilla was to advance in three lines: the first of flat boats 50 feet apart; the second, cutters in support of the boats; and the third, cutters towing launches for the conveyance of the artillery. The flat boats containing the grenadier companies of the various battalions were to hoist their camp flags as markers upon landing while the boats with the remaining companies would fall in to the left while maintaining the correct sequence to be able to take up their allocated positions once on shore. The Reserve under Moore was on the right, the Brigade of Guards under Ludlow in the centre, and the 1st (Royals) and the 54th under Lord Cavan on the left. It was important that the fifty-foot gaps were preserved so that the cutters in the second and third lines could land between the flat boats. These manoeuvres had already been practised many times, of course, yet from Abercromby to the Helder veterans in the ranks there must have been doubt whether even all the hours of practice would prevent the confusion of the Dutch landings.

At 2 a.m. on 8 March a rocket was fired from Keith's ship and the landing craft were rowed from their ships to the transports, where the troops waited. By 3 a.m., when a second rocket was fired, the troops of the first line were already in the fifty-eight flat boats, about fifty men per boat. They had with them their muskets, unloaded, sixty rounds of ammunition, supplies for three days and anything else, like spare shirts and stockings, that they had been able to cram into pouches and pockets. 'The moment was awful; and the most solemn silence prevailed, as the boats pulled to the rendezvous, a distance of about five miles. Nothing was heard but the hollow and dismal sound of the oars, as they dipped into the water.'[82] They had left the transports under a dark, starlit sky. As they came nearer to the shore dawn broke, showing them what lay ahead. At Marmoris there had been no concealed enemy to hinder the landings. Here it would be very different.

Cochrane was on a brig that marked one flank of the line. By 8 a.m. all the boats, including the ones that had been rowed the furthest, had reached the small vessels stationed to cover the landings, which also served as assembly points and from which naval officers directed the landing craft into position. In the first of three lines were the troops. Behind them men were taking up their positions in cutters which would fill the gaps between the flat boats and act as rescue boats. The third line comprised the launches carrying fourteen guns and their crews, and about 500 sailors, under the command of Sir Sidney Smith. The flanks of the flotilla were protected by the two bomb vessels, *Tartarus* and *Fury*, while three ships with the lightest draught came as close inshore as possible to afford further protection by bombarding the castle and the blockhouse. The soldiers in the landing craft were close enough now to see the enemy getting into position. They could also seem the muzzles of the field guns that crowned the dunes, and, even more threatening, the heavy battery at the foot of the highest sand hill.

Had the waiting troops but known it, for General Friant the sight as he looked out to sea was a daunting one. Like General Menou, he had doubted whether there would be any landings. Now he was confronted by the reality. He knew his own resources were not strong enough to withstand the force that was on the verge of attacking him. His only hope was to disrupt the landings, which was easy enough for determined soldiers at that moment of confusion which was surely inevitable when men were scrambling out of boats and trying to sort themselves into proper order under enemy fire. At that moment his troops would be able to drive the British back into the sea.

As his forces got into position, Abercromby was aboard the *Tartarus*, along with Admiral Keith. Knowing their commander's tendency to lead from the front at the risk of his own life, Hope and the General's son, John, had made sure he would not be able to succumb to the temptation to join the initial assault. They had instructed Lieutenant Richardson, in command of Abercromby's landing boat, to delay pushing off until the landing was secure. They intended that he should stand, watch and hope that all the planning and practice was about to pay off. There was good reason for him to be anxious; and perhaps to convince himself that he had done everything that could be done he sent Hope to Moore, who was on Cochrane's launch with his staff,

> to say that if the fire from the enemy was so great that the men could not bear it he would make the signal to retire, and therefore desired Captain Cochrane and me to look occasionally to the ship he was in. General Hope then said that Sir Ralph wished to know if I was still of the same opinion with respect to the point of landing on the right or if I did not think it would be better to extend a little more that way towards the bottom of the hill, as the latter appeared to be very steep in front. I said that I did not think a change was necessary; that the steepness was not such as to prevent our ascending and was therefore rather favourable.[82]

When this reply was reported to Abercromby, he commented with a smile, 'This is really taking the bull by the horns.'[83]

At 9 a.m., Cochrane gave the order for *Tartarus* to hoist the signal to row to shore. As the landing craft moved forward, the gunboats and bomb ships immediately opened fire. In reply, the French guns launched their own cannonade. Two boats were sunk, although most of the men were plucked from the water by the rescue cutters. Then

> a flat, conveying part of the Coldstream guards, was struck in the middle by a shell, which, bursting at the same instant, killed and dreadfully wounded numbers; the rest went to the bottom . . . Nothing, however, could dismay troops so brave. Surrounded by death in its most frightful shapes, their courage was not to be damped. Through a fire rendered doubly tremendous by the impossibility of resistance, we continued steadily to advance, cheering and huzzaing as if victory had already been in our grasp, though yet without the power of returning a single shot.[84]

From his position in the second line Nichol observed how

> The scene now became dreadful, the vessels pouring whole broad-
> sides, the bomb ketches throwing shells and the gunboats and
> cutters exerting themselves to the utmost. All eyes were directed
> towards the boats and every flash of the enemy's guns was noticed
> to see whether the shot struck the water or the boats, and when
> there was any confusion among them we wondered how many
> might be killed or wounded.[85]

Something of Abercromby's concern as the boats moved towards the beach
is conveyed in the letter he wrote to Lord Elgin on 16 March: '. . . .the
weather did not permit any disembarkation before the 8th; on that day it was
happily effected under the most trying circumstances. The boats had nearly
a mile to row, and were for some of the time under the fire of 15 pieces of
artillery, and the musquetry of 2,500 men; still the intrepidity of the troops
overcome every difficulty.'[86]

As the assault force drew ever closer, the French gunners changed from
the shell and shot designed to sink boats to grape which was intended to
maim and kill. Despite this, the sailors with the reserve and the Guards
rowed straight towards the shore. Coote's battalions were carried to the left,
however, possibly because the merchant seaman rowing them had not been
subjected to the rigorous discipline of their naval rivals. Despite this, Friant
realized that he was witnessing something very different from the haphazard
approach he had anticipated, something highly organized, something which
would not be disrupted by firepower alone. In response, he sent his cavalry
through the dunes with infantry support to fall on the assault force as it
landed.

Moore and Cochrane had been the first to strike bottom under both
artillery and musket fire. With others quickly following,

> the officers and men sprang out, formed on the beach, and landed.
> I then ascended the sand hill with the Grenadiers and Light infantry
> of the 40th, 23rd and 28th Regiments in line. They never offered
> to fire until they had gained the summit, where they charged the
> French, drove them, and took four pieces if cannon, with part of
> their horses. We followed them, they firing as they retired to the
> border of a plain, where I halted in favourable ground until I could
> perceive what was being done upon the left, where a heavy fire of

musketry was still kept up. Brigadier-General Oakes with the 42nd, 58th Regiments, and the Corsican Rangers, which composed the left of the reserve, landed to the left of the sand hill. They found the enemy ready to receive them. They formed expeditiously, were attacked by both infantry and cavalry, both of which they repulsed, and they also followed them into the plain, taking three pieces of artillery.[87]

Maule, who like Nichol was in the second line, described the attack by the reserve as

a moment of anxious doubt. On its success depended the character of the British army. The attempts, as may easily be imagined, were bravely and skilfully resisted by the French troops, who upon this, and upon every other occasion, during the campaign, maintained their high military character.

A corps of the enemy's cavalry, hitherto unperceived, debouched from the rear of the Sand Hills, and wheeling rapidly, attacked the left of the troops before they had sufficiently formed. The shock of this charge was serious, and was repulsed only after some considerable time by the succession of reinforcements arriving from the boats.[88]

This seems to refer to an attack on the Guards as they were still scrambling out of their boats, at which point the 58th, on the flank of the Reserve, turned and fired on the horsemen, some of whom had ridden into the sea, the better to get at the enemy. With the cavalry driven off, the Guards quickly formed up.

The last to land were Coote's battalions. They were greeted by a single French volley, after which these troops joined their compatriots in a precipitous withdrawal. With the British now in possession of the first line of dunes, the French retired initially to the dunes that lay further back and there was some exchange of musketry fire. Then Friant pulled his whole force back to the plain referenced by Moore, having his right flank by Lake Aboukir. He also sent a detachment to reinforce the garrison of the castle.

Despite the efforts of his quartermaster and adjutant general, Abercromby called for his boat and went ashore with his son and Colonel Kempt, his military secretary, while the struggle was still ongoing. He personally directed the troops and took pleasure in their conduct. In particular he noticed the good conduct of the 23rd, whom he had previously castigated for inefficiency, even going as far as to put them under the direct control of General Oakes, in whose brigade they served. Now, having witnessed their good conduct on the beach, he shook the hand of Lieutenant-Colonel Hall, who had only recently resumed command of them, and said, 'My friend Hall, I am glad to see you; I shall never abuse you again.'[89]

For an inexperienced soldier, the scene on the beach was harrowing.

> During the time we were actively engaged with the enemy, I had no time to observe particularly what was going on, or to think of my own situation. I felt all eager to reach the shore along with the rest of my comrades; but after reaching it, and when the affray was over, feelings arose in my breast such as never penetrated it before . . . The groans of the dying and the wounded, with the ghastly visages of the dead, that lay upon the field, were fearful to hear and witness. My very heart shuddered at the sound and at the sight, and I felt thankful and greatly relieved when we were called from the sad scene . . .[90]

In making his preparations for the landings there was one other vital requirement that Abercromby had not overlooked. As the fighting drew to a close, surgeons were already on the beach treating the wounded. He had witnessed the suffering caused in Flanders by the inadequacies of the medical provisions, the suffering that so moved a new recruit like David Robertson of the 92nd. Some of the wounded were already being taken back to the ships aboard the *Petrel*, one of the smaller naval vessels that had been able to come close inshore. The landing craft were also returning to those transports flying an ensign at the stern, the signal to indicate there were troops waiting to be brought ashore, while launches collected artillery, ammunition and the engineers' paraphernalia. All this was in accordance with the original planning.

The men of the first wave had halted several hours before the last reinforcements joined them. Now the whole British force advanced a couple of miles in column, led by the Reserve and the Guards, followed by Coote's, Craddock's and Cavan's brigades. They then halted for the night on a strip of land forty miles long between Aboukir to the east and the Arab Tower (Mandora Tower) to the west, the right flank against the sea and the left against Lake Aboukir. They were now eleven miles from Alexandria. After the warmth of the day, the night was cold, as were the following nights, and the men shivered without their tents. (A lucky few were able to occupy huts built by the French.) When George Baldwin came ashore on 9 March, dripping wet after his boat was swamped, Abercromby offered him little comfort. 'Baldwin, you will live with us a soldier's life; but we shall all fare alike.'[91] Interestingly, the soldiers felt differently, and built a small hut from date-palm branches for their commander. A strict disciplinarian he might be, but his troops recognized that his first concern was always their welfare, and they responded in kind.

The French losses were not excessive: one general, Martinet, killed, and anything between 200 and 400 men killed, wounded or taken prisoner. The enemy fought bravely, as their opponents acknowledged. British losses were heavier: 31 officers and 621 men killed, wounded, missing or taken prisoner from the army and 7 officers and 90 men killed or wounded from the naval contingent. Despite these losses, Abercromby had achieved what few ever managed, a meticulously-planned landing which had been readily effected by troops who knew exactly what was expected of them and by naval personnel who had with equal skill enabled them to achieve it. Not surprisingly, there was satisfaction and relief that all the planning and practice had been so well rewarded. Abercromby wrote in his general order: 'The gallant behaviour of the troops in the action of yesterday claims, from the Commander in Chief, the warmest praise that he can bestow; and it is with particular satisfaction that he observed their conduct marked equally for ardent bravery and by coolness, regularity, and order.' As well as commendations for the officers who had commanded the landings, there were thanks to Admiral Keith and the navy.

General Coote wrote to Prince William of Gloucester, 'The undaunted courage and coolness of the troops was such that they never loaded until disembarked from the boats and while loading were charged on the shore by the cavalry and infantry. Nothing can exceed this disembarkation, certainly the first and most glorious act of valour that is imaginable.'[92] These sentiments were echoed in many other accounts, while even the French prisoners of war informed their captors that it had been generally believed that a successful British landing was impossible. Of course, once the assault force had established itself on the beach, it was probably inevitable that 5,000 men would overwhelm 2,000. What Abercromby could relish, though, was the efficiency of the landings and the excellent behaviour of the force under his command.

He now had a foothold in Egypt, and to strengthen it he sent Stuart's and Doyle's brigades to threaten Aboukir Castle, replacing them the following day with the 2nd, the Queen's, 400 dismounted cavalry and a battalion of marines. Nevertheless, the advantage remained with the French, who held Alexandria as a strong point in territory that was familiar to them. Their troops were acclimatized, and even if previously demoralized, now had something to fight for. What Abercromby needed was a strong cavalry force that could spearhead an assault that would harass Friant back to Alexandria, about eleven miles away. Unfortunately, his cavalry was weak in numbers, poorly mounted, and no match for the French. Furthermore, his troops only had supplies for two days, while much of what was needed for the campaign was still aboard the ships. He had no choice, therefore, but to stand his ground, even though inaction would enable the French to bring up reinforcements.

The day after the landings he ordered Anstruther, accompanied by Moore, to probe the French positions.

> We took with us some cavalry, the Corsicans and the 92nd Regiment. We posted the latter about two miles in front, and proceeded a couple of miles further with the Dragoons. We then met a strong patrol of the enemy, which induced us to retire. The country which we had seen was uneven; sandy and thickly interspersed with palm and date trees. At the place where the 92nd had been posted, whilst we went forward with the cavalry, there was a small redoubt and flagstaff; and the sea and lake of Madie, running in on each side, narrowed the ground at this spot more than at any other either in front or in rear of it. Upon it being represented to Sir Ralph as a favourable point to possess, he directed me to take post upon it with the reserve. I reached it about twelve o'clock, and after posting my outposts, I went with a patrol in front until I saw the enemy's cavalry.
>
> On the 10th at daylight I advanced in front of the picquets with the Dragoons and Corsican Rangers to feel what was in my front. We very soon met the advance guard of a considerable body of cavalry, who endeavoured to push us back; but, as we were but a little way from our picquets, and as the ground was favourable to infantry, the Corsicans were directed to disperse and post themselves. By this means they forced the advance guard of the cavalry back; but instead of being satisfied with this and keeping their stations, they followed the enemy, who led them close to their main body, and then turned upon them, wounded several, and took an officer, a surgeon, and ten men prisoners.[93]

The Corsicans had demonstrated the overconfidence of raw troops, and they subsequently became much steadier. Nevertheless, this reconnaissance had enabled Moore to establish that a number of French senior officers were making preparations for what looked like an attack. Although confident that his position was secure, he took the precaution of strengthening his picquets as night fell.

The rest of the army had settled into the normal pattern of life on campaign. An hour before daylight they started the day with alarm post parade. Officers made their rounds, guards were mounted and picquets posted. Observing the effect of the cold on the troops, Abercromby ordered a half-ration of spirits for each man. Once the last of the horses had been brought ashore, the naval personnel concentrated on landing water and provisions, the heavy guns, hospital equipment and other stores considered vital. This was strenuous work and engaged about 600 men. Admiral Keith was not happy. With some justification he fretted that his manpower was dangerously depleted as he awaited the arrival of Ganteaume's fleet. He was already writing letters of exculpation to Lord Spencer for when the campaign failed.

Abercromby had problems enough without taking on Keith's concerns. As he had previously observed, to campaign successfully without transport and draught animals was impossible. Admittedly, wagons would have been of little use in the terrain, but neither could the men be expected to carry everything that was needed across loose sand under a blazing sun. Relief was to come in two forms: the first was the discovery that the previously unknown Lake Aboukir was navigable to within four miles of Alexandria; the second, the arrival of local Arabs with offers of assistance.

Cochrane immediately exploited this first discovery by assembling small boats to carry supplies. By this means, depots could be established to keep pace with the advance of the army. The French had gunboats on the lake, so Cochrane armed twelve of the flatboats with cannon. It is also worth noting that, despite Keith's concerns, the sailors were toiling willingly under great physical stress. While the admiral remained aboard *Foudroyant*, ready for conflict with Ganteaume, Sir Sidney Smith commanded ashore. A quixotic man, he was nevertheless an inspiration to the sailors. He took the credit for pointing out that digging around the roots of the palms would reveal fresh water, thus solving one of the most crucial supply problems.[94]

The French had threatened to kill any Arab who assisted the British but this did not deter them. Abercromby had already issued orders that the locals should be treated with forbearance and humanity, dealt with fairly, paid promptly, and that their habits and religion should be respected. They were urged now to bring in supplies and within a few days Mr Baldwin had established a market. On 11 March Abercromby informed Moore that with the problem of supply now solved the advance could continue. That evening three days' rations were issued, along with orders for the march. Reinforcements had arrived two days before, when seven companies of the 2/27th, recovered from their long convalescence, arrived from Lisbon. Also, the last of the Greek horse transports had finally appeared.

At 8 a.m. on 12 March, after the main force had been brought forward to join Moore, Abercromby began a cautious advance. He had learnt from a reconnaissance officer's report that reinforcements had been moving into Alexandria. In addition, the terrain was a challenge for the soldiers, as was hauling the guns in harness for the sailors. Private Nichol remembered that 'Our march was slow and often interrupted; the ground being uneven and the sand very deep, parties were frequently sent to assist the seamen with the guns.'[95] It was very much a case of two steps forward, one step back.

The troops marched in two parallel columns, each headed by half of the Reserve, which was protected by skirmishers, a tactic Abercromby had learnt from the French in Flanders. Recognizing that the Corsican Rangers and the light companies of the Reserve needed relieving after their days of outpost duty, Abercromby replaced them with the 90th and 92nd. After about five miles the head of the columns came into contact with French picquets and vedettes, and then the 22nd Chasseurs à Cheval, which brought about some sharp skirmishing before the French withdrew. By 1.30 p.m. Moore had reached the Mandora Tower, which he climbed in order to ascertain the situation ahead. He could clearly see advancing infantry. The order was immediately given for the whole force to deploy into two lines and move forward to occupy ground more favourable to a defensive position. This deployment was performed in textbook order (according to Dundas's *Principles*) and the troops then advanced without losing cohesion, despite the need to avoid the obstacles that impeded their progress.

The French had taken position on a ridge that extended almost across from the dry bed of Lake Mareotis, bordered by the equally dry Alexandria Canal on their right to the sea on their left, where their position was strengthened by the ruins of Caesar's Camp, as it was known locally. They were about a mile and a half from the British position, protecting a dyke on the route by which Menou was expected to approach Alexandria. Despite some skirmishing, it was too late for the commencement of any serious action. Abercromby appreciated, however, that on the morrow his army would be put to the test.

He had already decided to strengthen his force by sending for the battalion companies of the 2nd and the battalion of marines from the castle. This necessitated 'a long and very harassing march during the night, impeded as they were by a heavy and uncertain road, through a desert of sand, [after which] they at length reached the point of their destination. The marines, though unaccustomed to long marches, bore up with their usual firmness against the fatigues of the night.'[96] Also, to make sure no re-alignment or sudden movement of the French could pass unnoticed, Abercromby ordered Moore, out of turn, to assume outpost duty and cover the front of the army with the 90th and 92nd.

At daybreak the order was given to pile knapsacks. The men received a tot of rum. Then at 6.30 a.m. on Friday 13 March, ninety minutes later than planned, the army moved into action. Abercromby reasoned that the right was the most vulnerable part of the French line, therefore his left, under Hutchinson, was ordered to skirt the head of Lake Aboukir and manoeuvre towards the canal and Lake Mareotis. These were the untested troops of Cavan, Doyle and Stuart's brigades who had comprised the second assault line, but they would be headed by the 92nd, who had already been blooded. They were to advance in column of manoeuvre, one company wide, with 120 cavalrymen in their rear. Abercromby had command of Ludlow, Coote and Cradock's brigades, with the 90th at their head. They would advance against the French centre and left, while Moore, with the Reserve would advance in open column, thus protecting Abercromby's division. The Reserve would be protected by the Corsican Rangers in skirmish order. At this point the guns were still in the rear as the sailors struggled to bring them up through the sand. This made the columns particularly vulnerable to enemy artillery.

General Lanusse, who had assumed command from Friant upon his arrival in Alexandria three days before, had a force of nearly 5,000 men, no match in numbers for the British because Menou was still holding back troops in Cairo to deal with the attack that by now probably only he believed in. But Lanusse enjoyed the advantage in cavalry and artillery and was determined to exploit it. Also, unlike his opponent, he knew that his force was made up of experienced veterans. He had also prepared two further defensive positions, the first on the Heights of Nicopolis, a strong ridge of sand hills behind their front line, the second under the walls of Alexandria itself. There seems to have been some disagreement within the French command about how to proceed. More cautious voices advocated a withdrawal but Lanusse was determined to fight, if for no better reason than he needed Menou and his troops. If the dyke were lost, they would have to pursue a long and circuitous route from Cairo. He also instinctively favoured action. He had been with Bonaparte in Italy and had been imbued with his leader's readiness to take risks. And, after all, the inferiority of the British troops was well known, which meant the success of the landings must be regarded as a fluke.

Although most of the British force was hidden by folds in the ground, Lanusse could clearly see Hutchinson's advance on the left, and he seems to have located the extreme right since he decided to check it with a demi-brigade. He also posted two battalions to cover Caesar's Camp. To deal with the British left he advanced the 3rd Dragoons and the 22nd Chasseurs à Cheval, 400 men on good horses. The chasseurs emerged from the palms and caught the 90th, who had become detached from the following column, as they were deploying from column into line. Colonel Victor de Fay de la Latour-Maubourg, in command of the chasseurs, gave the order to charge. The 90th quickly formed themselves into a solid body, six to eight deep, holding their fire until the cavalry were close enough to suffer its full effect. The volley when it came was devastating, wounding Latour-Maubourg and bringing down large numbers of men and horses. The rest withdrew in a state of temporary confusion. They quickly re-formed, however, and moved to the right to attack the rest of Cradock's brigade as it deployed. They encountered the 8th and 18th, men who had commenced their training under Abercromby on Minorca. They had obviously learnt the lessons well as they soon put the French to flight.

Meanwhile, the 92nd had come under attack from 600 infantry of the 61st Demi-Brigade.

> Our situation was one of great danger. The enemy in front was advancing in a line formed like the blade of a scythe, the curved point towards the lake and that part was cavalry, said to be the dromedary corps. It seemed as if they meant to turn our left and get into our rear, while they attacked us in front, and, getting round our right, they would thus have surrounded us and made us prisoners or have destroyed us at once as we were not above 500 strong and every minute were getting fewer. The enemy had some fieldpieces in front which were making sad havoc among us, every shot sweeping down some of our men. Our commanding officer ordered us not to fire but to stand firm until we could see their feet as they advanced from the hollow in front of us. When the order to fire was given, like magic it dispelled the gloom from our countenances and everyone did his duty manfully.[97]

Another private soldier recorded that he had fired twenty-two rounds during this attack. Two British guns were brought up to counteract the French artillery, but had insufficient ammunition to provide more than token assistance. The marines also came up but, not having been trained by Abercromby, their advance was disordered and achieved little apart from inflicting some friendly-fire casualties. More effective were some of Dillon's Regiment, from Stuart's brigade. The position was held. The French were beaten back with the loss of two guns because so many of their gunners had been taken out. The cost to the 92nd was heavy, though. Colonel Erskine, in command, was mortally wounded, twelve other officers were also wounded, three of them mortally, and about 150 men in the ranks were either killed or wounded. Private Nichol was left wondering how anyone had survived.

The fighting had now extended to the columns behind the leading battalions: 'my regiment, leading the brigade, received a smart salutation from the enemy's light artillery. We observed at the line of hills a brigade of six guns, supported by cavalry. These guns occasioned us some loss, but they did not think proper to relinquish their strong commanding position; and as the brigade advanced, they fell back, still keeping up a sharp fire.'[98]

As the action became general, the Reserve remained in column, as did Doyle's 4th Brigade on the extreme left. The 92nd were ordered to lie down, but the 90th remained in the fight. The French were being driven back, but only slowly. They contested every yard of ground, while their horse artillery, the manoeuvrability of which contrasted painfully with the horseless British guns, inflicted damage every time there was a halt in the British progress. Their left, though, was vulnerable to the steady advance of Moore and Cradock's men. The pressure eventually told and the French were forced to retire to their original position. They had lost strict order during their withdrawal and failed to take up defensive positions, particularly as Hutchinson now outflanked them on the right. This was the moment when British cavalry would have been able to drive them into chaotic retreat, but Abercromby possessed no such cavalry. Consequently, the French

> superiority in cavalry prevented our deriving that benefit from the defeat from his army which we might otherwise have done. His artillery was powerful; ours as nothing; for, as it had to be dragged by men through a sandy country, it could not keep pace with the infantry. We were therefore destroyed by his artillery without the power of retaliation. But the undaunted spirit of the troops made them constantly advance in spite of every loss, so that we

gained ground, which is the great object in action. We drove the enemy back, though with loss superior to his. Every attempt the enemy made, either with their infantry or cavalry, was defeated, and at last the whole retired under cover of their artillery.[99]

Thanks to shortcomings that were not of his making, Abercromby could not claim the crushing victory he might have wanted, but once again he took pride in the achievements of his troops.

The French retired, protected by their guns, and occupied their second position, on the Heights of Nicopolis. Moore and Craddock then halted their advance but Dillon's Regiment charged and took two guns on the canal. Baldwin had informed Abercromby that once they were beyond the ridge held by the French there would be nothing else to prevent an attack on Alexandria. When Moore reached the ridge and looked ahead, however, he realized that the new French position had previously been prepared for defence. Although the whole British force had been given the order to advance, when the next brigade commander, Cradock, arrived, Moore urged him to halt his troops until he had consulted with Abercromby.

Abercromby believed from what he could see that there was a chance to drive the French back into the city. This misjudgement might have been caused by his myopia, but his horse had just been shot under him and he may have been out of position. When he realized what lay ahead and that a general, probably costly, attack would be required to dislodge the French he called a general halt and consulted with Moore and Hutchinson. His objective now was to turn the French flanks. To achieve this, Hutchinson would need to attack their right with the 3rd, 4th and 5th Brigades while the Reserve, under Moore, attacked the left with the support of the Guards brigade. The remaining troops were to sit down where they had halted.

Hutchinson needed to make a long detour by a bridge south of the French position, across the canal and then along the edge of Lake Mareotis, where care was needed because the salt beds, although dry, did not appear to be solid underfoot. This march brought him to the right of the French position, close to another bridge on which a single gun was posted. This gun was taken by the 44th, but the rest of the column came under heavy fire from the Heights. Hutchinson halted to assess the situation. He could see that the French occupied a strong position, with good artillery support, and appreciated that any further British advance would occasion heavy losses. He sent this information to Abercromby, adding that they would only be able to hold the position with extensive entrenchment. There was also uncertainty about what lay beyond the Heights. Despite Baldwin's insistence that if they could take the Heights they would command the town, the Arabs had reported that the distance was considerable and the area in front of Alexandria was strongly fortified. Abercromby sent Hope to reconnoitre and then followed with Anstruther to take a look for himself. He decided that the Arabs were probably right. Furthermore, it was now late in the day. Therefore, although 'Our army, in the highest spirits, and elated by its recent success, was impatient to proceed . . . Sir Ralph Abercromby, perceiving, that, if we drove the French from the heights, we could not retain them, as they appeared on reconnoitring, to be commanded by forts Cafarelli and Cretin, deemed it improper to make an attempt, which must have been attended with a useless waste of blood.'[100]

By 4 p.m. the order had been given to withdraw to Caesar's Camp and the ridge that had been the original French position, a decision that was greeted with general relief. While Hutchinson advanced, the rest of the troops had been taking considerable losses as the chosen targets of the French gunners.

In the day's actions the French lost about 500 killed but British losses were more severe: 1,300 killed and wounded, including 79 officers and sailors in the supporting gunboats. Not surprisingly, the heaviest losses were taken by the 90th and the 92nd, and both regiments were later rewarded for their excellent conduct by adding Mandora to their battle honours. Walsh ascribed the heavier British losses to the advantage enjoyed by the French in cavalry and artillery, 600 of the former and forty, mainly curricle, guns.

General Bertrand subsequently criticised Abercromby for his miscalculation. Fortescue, sharing this view, wrote of the later stages of the action, when the initiative was with the British, that it 'does not show Abercromby at his best. Either he should have halted the army after carrying the first position of the French, until he had made up his mind whether or not to assault the position upon the Heights of Nicopolis; or, having brought his troops into the plain within range of the French cannon, he should have made his attack upon the second position forthwith.'[101] He does concede, in agreement with Walsh, that any advance was inevitably hampered by the lack of cavalry and artillery, and he also understood why Abercromby was anxious to sustain the forward momentum of the advance. Mackesy however, pointed out that 'The advance from the ridge had been made in the heat of a pursuit; it would have been discouraging for the eager and elated troops to retire just before launching a fresh attack; and Abercromby did not foresee how long the next phase of the battle would take to organize.'[102] Moore came to the conclusion that 'The fault, if any, which we committed was the advancing beyond the position we afterwards took up before we had come to a determination to attack the heights. Halting to deliberate in the plain exposed us to the guns of the heights, and, when the attack was deemed imprudent, obliged us to a retrograde movement, which was mortifying to troops who had displayed such spirit, and who had been successful.' He believed that if they had persisted in a forward movement they could have driven the enemy from his position, but 'without cannon, ammunition, provisions, or the means of entrenching ourselves, I doubt if we could have held it. I therefore think we should have been satisfied with our first success, and remained upon the ground in which we first halted.'[103] If Abercromby looked for consolation, it lay in the excellent performance of the troops. At no point had they failed him.

At this point, Abercromby wrote what proved to be his last despatch to Dundas, in which he summed up the progress of the campaign so far. He started by explaining why Dundas's expectation that the army would be in Egypt by December had not been realized.

> Although it was not originally my intention to have Commenced the operations of the British Army in Egypt on the side of Alexandria, yet circumstances . . . induced me to change my opinion. We were much longer delayed on the coast of Asia Minor than we had at first any reason to appreciate, and we were ultimately obliged to sail from Marmorice in a very imperfect State of preparations. I am fully sensible of the of the exertions of His Majesty's Ambassador at the Ottoman Court as well as of the Quarter Master General and the other Officers who were sent forward to provide for the troops of the Army. Our delays originated from three Causes. In a considerable time previous to our Sailing the weather was extremely boisterous and the Winds contrary . . .

He then focused on the landings.

> . . . On the 2nd the Fleet anchored in Aboukir Bay. Until the 7th the Sea ran high, and no disembarkation could be effected: on that day, every arrangement was Completed, and on the 8th the troops forming the first Division, Consisting of the Reserve under the Command of Major General Moore, the Brigade of Guards under the Honorable Major General Ludlow; and part of the first Brigade under the Command of Major General Coote, got into the Boats

early in the Morning. They had in general from five to six miles to row, and did not arrive at the point of landing till ten o'clock. The point of Disembarkation was narrow, and a Hill which Commanded the whole seemed almost inaccessible. The enemy were fully aware of our intention, were in Force, and had every advantage on their side. The Troops however, notwithstanding their being exposed to a very severe Cannonade, and under the Fire of Grape, made good their landing, ascended the Hill with an intrepidity scarcely to be parallel'd, and forced the Enemy to retire, leaving behind him seven Pieces of Artillery and a number of Horses. The Troops that ascended the Hill were the 23rd Regiment and the four flank companies of the 40th under the Command of Colonel Spencer whose coolness and good Conduct Major General Moore has mentioned to me in the highest terms of approbation. It is impossible to pass over the good order in which the 28th Regiment and the 42nd landed under the Command of Brigadier General Oakes who is attached to the Reserve under Major General Moore; and the Troops in general lost not a moment in remedying any little disorder, which became scarcely unavoidable in a landing under such Circumstances. The disembarkation of the Army Continued on that, and the following day. The Troops which landed on the 8th advanced three miles the same day, and on the 12th the whole army moved forward, and came within sight of the Enemy, who was formed on an advantageous Ridge, with his Right to the Canal of Alexandria, and his left towards the Sea.

It was determined to attack them on the Morning of the 13th, and in Consequence, the Army marched in two lines by the left, with an intention to turn their right flank.

The Troops had not been long in motion before the Enemy descended from the Heights on which they were formed, and attacked the leading Brigades of both Lines, which were Commanded by Major General Cradock and Major General the Earl of Cavan. The 90th Regiment formed the advanced guard of the front Line, and the 92nd that of the Second; Both Battalions suffered considerably, and behaved in such a Manner as to merit the praise not only due to Courage but to discipline. Major General Cradock formed his Brigade to meet the attack made by the Enemy, and the Troops changed their Position with a quickness and precision which did them the greatest Honor. The remainder of the Army followed so good an example and were immediately in a Situation not only to face, but to repel the Enemy. The Reserve under the Command of Major General Moore which was on the Right, on the change of Position of the Army, moved on in Column, and Covered the Right flank. The Army Continued to advance pushing the Enemy with the greatest vigour and ultimately forcing them, to put themselves under the protection of the fortified Heights which form the principal defence of Alexandria.

It was intended to have attacked then in this their last Position for which purpose the Reserve under the Command of Major General Moore, which had Remained in Column during the whole of the day was brought forward, and the Second Line under the Command of Major General Hutchinson, marched to the Left across a part of the Lake Mareotis, with a view to attack the Enemy on both Flanks, but on Reconnoitring their Position, and on finding, that, we were not prepared to occupy it, after it should be Carried; Prudence required that the Troops who had behaved so bravely, and who were still willing to attempt any thing however arduous, should not be exposed to a certain loss, when the extent of the advantage could not be ascertained. They were therefore withdrawn, and now occupy a Position with their Right to the Sea and their left to the Canal of Alexandria and Lake Mareotis, about a league from the Town of Alexandria.

I have the greatest satisfaction in saying that the Conduct of the British and Foreign Troops under my Command is deserving of the highest praise, their Courage, and their discipline, have been equally conspicuous.

To all the General Officers I am indebted for their Zeal and Intelligence.

From the Honble Brigadier General Hope Adjutant General. And Lt Col. Anstruther Quarter Master General, I have received every testimony of Zeal, and the Most able Assistance in the Operations of the Army, and to the other Officers of the General Staff I feel obligations.

On the 8th the Arrangements made by Lord Keith were Such as to enable us to land at once a Body of Six Thousand Men. The Honorable Captain Cochrane, and those other Captains and Officers of the Royal Navy who were entrusted with the disembarkation, not only of the Troops, but of the Artillery, Ammunition, Provisions, and Stores of all kinds, have exerted themselves in such a Manner, as to claim the warmest acknowledgements of the whole Army.

Sir Sidney Smith and the other Captains and Officers under his Command who landed with the Army, have been indefatigable in their in their exertions in forwarding the Service on which they are Employed.

The Enemy having left a small Garrison in Aboukir Castle it has been necessary to bring up a few Pieces of Heavy Artillery and there is reason to believe it will speedily Surrender.

Majors McKerris and Fletcher of the Royal Engineers who went down in the Penelope Frigate, to Survey the Coast of Egypt a short time before we sailed from Marmorice, were unfortunately surprised in a small Boat in Aboukir Bay, the former was killed and the latter taken prisoner.

Our Communication with the Fleet is at present kept up by means of the Lake of Aboukir. Hitherto we have been fortunate enough to find water sufficient for the Safety of the Army, and we begin to obtain some supplies from the Country . . .[104]

Abercromby had never doubted the courage of British troops. Now he could enjoy the satisfaction of having instilled the discipline that had turned them into an effective fighting force. By the time Dundas wrote a reply, he knew that his friend was dead, and he addressed the letter to General Hutchinson.

I have it in command from His Majesty, to convey to you His entire satisfaction with the gallantry, the discipline and the conduct, which the Army now under your command have manifested in so distinguished a manner in effecting their landing, and in all their subsequent operations; and I am particularly directed by His Majesty, to express the deep regret with which he laments the loss of that able Commander, Sir Ralph Abercromby, who with so much ability directed those operations, and whose life has been so nobly devoted to the Service of his King and Country.[105]

This is to look ahead, however. Having discovered that Lake Aboukir was navigable to the canal, the next task was to strengthen their position. His forces were now four miles from Alexandria, with the sea and Caesar's Camp (which the British called the Roman ruins) on their right, and the lake and canal on their left. Their frontage was about one and a half miles.

The ground in the right and centre of their position was an irregular ridge of sand hills, sloping down to the plain that separated the two forces. The British were encamped in two lines with cavalry in between. The reserve was the furthest forward, separated from the Guards brigade by the declivity of the Alexandria to Aboukir road. There were ruined buildings at Caesar's Camp behind the reserve, tall enough in places to serve as firing parapets.

While the heavy artillery, siege equipment and supplies were being landed and brought forward, there was time to strengthen the position by constructing two redoubts at the canal and a flèche in front of the reserve. Caesar's Camp, where Moore had organized a strong defence, was further fortified by two redoubts on the forward slope. As a result of these entrenchments, and the positioning of two 24-pounders and thirty-four field guns, the British deployment now commanded the plain, particularly towards the south. The troops were posted to take advantage of this: the Guards and Coote's Brigade were the first line of defence, with Cradock in echelon at the head of Lake Aboukir; Stuart, Doyle, Finch and Cavan were in the second line, from left to right.

Needless to say, these defensive measures, including the hauling the guns into position once they had been brought ashore, as well as burying the dead and digging for water, put the men under considerable strain, which led to increased sickness. Even when the tents were landed, there were not enough to go round and in some battalions thirty-nine men were crowded into a tent designed for fifteen. This did little to dent morale, which was still high after Mandora. On a more positive note, though, for Abercromby there was a gift from Constantinople of some good horses which he gave to his general officers, while for the men Mr Baldwin's market was selling fresh food at fixed prices. The market was roped off to remind the troops that they should respect the Arabs, although in the event there were no problems. Indeed, the behaviour of the troops continued to be exemplary, marking what Moore considered a turning point. Their morale was high and their behaviour was soldierly. It was now generally agreed that all the training, in accordance with David Dundas's *Principles*, was proving its worth. Abercromby took particular pleasure in writing both to Dundas and to the Duke of York, who, as Commander-in-Chief, had imposed the manual on the regimental colonels, to report the effectiveness of the drill, which brought order and discipline without impairing the natural courage of British troops.

The initial French response to this overt British determination to hold their position was an attempt to drive in the vedettes, which led to skirmishing and casualties. Abercromby wrote to the French command, expressing 'a wish not to aggravate the calamities of war by any acts which, without benefit to the general cause, tended only to distress individuals. He received a polite answer from General Friant, entering fully into Sir Ralph's sentiments'[106] and there were no more attacks.

On 18 March the castle at Aboukir surrendered after it had been reduced to little more than a heap of rubble by a breaching battery that had quickly destroyed its defences. It was an honourable surrender, and the French officers were allowed to keep their swords, although not the guns that had been found in the ruins. The prisoners were then embarked for France. On the same day the Arabs reported that General Menou had left Cairo with a large force. This concerned Abercromby because he still had no precise knowledge of the enemy's strength.

Early in the afternoon a strong French cavalry patrol was seen near the canal on the British left, obviously intent on stopping the Arabs from bringing in provisions, even killing some of them as a deterrent to the others. In response, the cavalry piquets were ordered out with brigade support. The officer in command, Colonel Archdell of the 12th Light Dragoons, although unfamiliar with the ground, gave the order to his own troops and the 26th Light Dragoons to charge. They went off

> at full speed along the canal [and] came upon the enemy, who waited to receive them. Our horse charged right through theirs, and made several prisoners; but scarcely had they effected this, when the infantry, concealed behind the parapet of an old redoubt, opened a destructive fire, taking them in flank; and the French cavalry, then wheeling about, charged our people, and took several prisoners in their turn. A company of the Minorca regiment, under the command of Captain McKinnon, hastened to the support of our cavalry, but were not able to come up soon enough to be of any assistance.[107]

The losses were considerable: thirty-three men killed, wounded or taken prisoner and forty horses lost. Abercromby immediately issued a general order censuring the cavalry: '. . . that by thus undertaking enterprises without object and without use, they risked the lives of valuable men, and exposed themselves to failure'.[108]

Abercromby was now contemplating his next move. He considered a night attack on the Heights of Nicopolis but realized that even if such an attack were successful it would not guarantee the fall of Alexandria. Failure, on the other hand, would lead to nothing less than re-embarkation and an end to the campaign. At this point there was widespread pessimism among the senior officers, particularly General Hutchinson, who would assume command if anything happened to Abercromby. John Hope considered Abercromby's presence vital to the success of the expedition; but he had served with Abercromby often enough to know that he would always be in the thick of any fight, where he seemed to become more composed, clearer thinking but dangerously vulnerable. Yet it was what the men expected of him, and made him particularly popular with the Irish troops, who themselves revelled in a fight.

Menou had wasted time seeking advice on how to respond to the arrival of the British and had then made a slow advance, but French spirits were high: '. . . the common danger made us forget [Menou's] conduct. The soldiers wished to show that he might count upon their zeal and bravery, if, on his part, he would show some firmness and military talent.'[109] On 20 March it became clear that Menou had found a way across Lake Mareotis and reached Alexandria. Sir Sidney Smith had received a letter from one of his Arab contacts that Menou intended a night attack. Although this report was received with some scepticism, Abercromby had already issued a general order that the troops were to be under arms from an hour before daybreak, having slept with their accoutrements in expectation of a French attack.

The same day, Abercromby confided in Moore that their task was difficult but

> that as soon as the heavy cannon was brought up and entrenching tools forwarded, he thought it incumbent on us to make an effort. His plan was to endeavour in the night to push forward the artillery, and form the troops under such cover as he could find, and at daylight advance to the attack of both their flanks. If we failed, we could still return to our present position, and maintain it until another was prepared in our rear to favour a retreat, and finally our re-embarkation. He regretted the throwing away of so fine an army, and added that he believed nobody would envy him his situation.[110]

The disposition of the British troops, essentially defensive, remained much as it had been since Mandora. Moore's position on the right, strengthened by the ruins of Caesar's Camp and the redoubts that had been constructed, was further protected by a flotilla of gunboats at anchor under Captain Maitland. The Guards and Coote's brigade still formed the centre, with a strong battery and a signal station between them while Cradock's brigade occupied the ground towards the canal. In the second line, Cavan's brigade was behind Cradock's with responsibility for repelling the French should they attempt an approach across Lake Mareotis. Stuart was positioned to cover the gap between the Guards and the Reserve, and would move forward in the event of an enemy attack. This left Doyle's brigade, in the centre of the second line, as the only reserve force that could be called up to intervene wherever required, along with the 12th and 26th Light Dragoons, about 500 strong although only 120 were mounted. The rest of the cavalry, one troop of the 11th Light Dragoons and Hompesch's Hussars, were with Moore, most of them dismounted. A return of 18 March suggests that the total number of men present and fit for action was something just under 13,000. Opposed to them was a similar number of French, including Menou's newly-arrived force comprising troops he called in before he left Cairo.

Menou knew that General Baird was on his way to the Red Sea with an army from India. He was also aware that a Turkish force was advancing from Constantinople. This double threat gave him no choice but to take out Abercromby's army before either of the other forces approached Cairo. He confidently believed that he held the initiative, a judgement based on what he supposed to be Abercromby's inaction at den Helder and Cadiz. Nor had his opinion of the British troops improved, despite the successful landings and the action at Mandora.

Ironically, both commanders were in much the same position. Abercromby felt that he could not afford to delay, particularly as the fleet might come under attack from Ganteaume at any time. He needed to take the Heights and uncover Alexandria. Menou was equally convinced of the urgent need to send the British back to their boats. While the Scot anticipated a hard struggle which would put his army seriously at risk, the Frenchman expected to meet little opposition as he swept the enemy out of Egypt, after which there would be no point in either Baird or the Turks driving home their attacks. Furthermore, his fiercest critics, Lanusse and Reynier, the latter having disobeyed orders to get into the action, were pressing for an attack and Menou did not have the strength of character to resist. On 20 March he ordered a pre-dawn attack for the following day.

The Final Battle

A few rockets were fired during the night, but that had happened frequently enough not to alarm the British picquets. By 3 a.m. on 21 March, the French were moving into column. They then marched silently, following their proposed lines of attack while the British slept on.

The plan of battle adopted by the French seems to have been developed by General Lanusse. The impetus would come in an attack on the Reserve by Lanusse's own infantry division, 2,700 strong. Rampon with 2,000 men and Reynier with 3,700 would attack the British centre as soon as Lanusse had engaged successfully with the Reserve. Reynier would also check the British left with a false attack and send 300 cavalry to close the road to Alexandria between Lakes Aboukir and Mareotis. The rest of the cavalry, about 900 strong, was to function as a reserve under General Roize. The overall objective of the plan was simple, to drive the British into Lake Aboukir. This was confirmed by Menou's orders which were later found in General Roize's pocket. They made clear that there was to be a false attack on the British left while the real attack would be on the right and centre, thus driving the British into Lake Aboukir. Also, no quarter was to be given, an order that seemed to resurrect the ghost of Robespierre. The purpose of an attack before daybreak was not only to take the British by surprise but also to prevent the British artillery and gunboats from firing effectively in the dark or early-morning half-light.[111]

Moore later described what happened in his journal.

I was Major-General of the day on the 20th. After visiting the picquets I remained with the left picquet of the reserve until four in the morning of the 21st. The enemy had been perfectly quiet during the night. Nothing had been observed from them but some rockets, which it was not uncommon for them to throw. Imagining everything to be quiet I left orders with the field officer to retire his posts at daylight, and I rode towards the left to give similar orders to the other picquets as I went along. When I reached the left picquet of the Guards I heard a fire of musketry on the left; but everything continuing so quiet on the right, I, from the style of the firing, suspected it was a false alarm. I had observed a want of intelligence and confusion the evening before in the officer who commanded the picquets in that quarter. This confirmed my suspicion. I was, however, trotting towards the left when a firing commenced from the picquets of the reserve. I immediately turned to my aide-de-camp, Captain Sewell, and said, 'This is the real attack, let us gallop to the redoubt.' I met as I returned all the picquets falling back, and by the time I reached the redoubt in which the 28th were posted,

I found it warmly attacked. The day had not yet broken, and the darkness was made greater by the smoke of the guns and small arms.[112]

The 'false alarm' that Moore had heard on the left was the beginning of Reynier's false attack when a dismounted dromedary corps had surprised an advanced field-work, taking a gun and twenty men, but the French were then driven off by sharp musketry from the flèche, although they successfully carried off their wounded, and three officers, a sergeant and ten rank-and-file as prisoners. The distant firing caused Stuart to move to his left towards the point of attack. Neither he nor anyone else could see clearly as the day broke mistily. Abercromby believed it was an affair of outposts. He was not disabused until a sentry in the reserve peered into the gloom, saw French troops stealing towards him, and fired his musket. Almost immediately there was the thunder of guns opening fire. Moments before Abercromby had watched the 92nd, much reduced by the effects of battle and sickness, marching off to Aboukir. Now, as he prepared to gallop towards the right to assess the situation, he granted their wish to be sent into action. Stuart had also recognized the significance of the guns and redirected his troops to the right.

Moore again:

My arrangements, in case of our being attacked, had been settled beforehand. I had agreed with Brigadier-General Oakes that the redoubt and old ruins in front of the right of the army, in which I had posted the 28th and 58th Regiments, must be supported, and was the ground for the reserve to fight upon. In fact, if carried by the enemy, it would have been impossible for our army to remain in their position. The general orders were for the troops to stand to their arms an hour before daylight, and fortunately they had fallen in before the attack commenced.[113]

The 28th under Henry Paget were holding the redoubt in front of the ruins with two 24-pounder guns and some field guns. Two companies had been detached to protect the rear of the redoubt, which was open to attack. About 200 yards further back were the ruins that commanded the ground between the alarm post of the 28th and the sea, and which were well covered against artillery fire. Initially they were held by the 58th, but Moore now brought up reinforcements from the Reserve. The 23rd were positioned to the front of the building, on the left of the 58th, and looking to the rear of the 28th in a position where they could check any advance between the Guards brigade and the left of the 28th. Close to the 23rd and in further support were the four flank companies of the 40th. The 42nd were further back, with orders from Moore to advance at the first alarm and form on the left of the 28th, with their right to the ditch of the wall which sheltered the battalion. By this stage casualties were being taken, including Paget, who was shot in the neck and believed himself killed, although he recovered sufficiently to be put upon his horse.

From the French point of view, although Reynier's diversionary attack had been frustrated, on the right everything was proceeding according to Lanusse's plan. The French had advanced in two columns, Valentin's brigade along the shore and Silly's directly towards the redoubt, taking the flèche in front of the redoubt. They then came close to the ditch of the redoubt, where they were held by the fire of the 28th. Meeting opposition, they moved to their right and passed to the left of the 28th. They then approached the front of the building, threatening the 23rd. Valentin, at the same time, swung left so that his right battalion advanced on the north-west front of the redoubt while the left battalion aimed for the angle between the redoubt and the ruins. So far, so good but the right battalion now came under artillery fire as the British guns poured canister into them. General Lanusse rode forward and tried to rally his men but was mortally wounded. At this point both battalions broke and retreated.

General Rampon had also advanced as instructed, but his left brigade had moved too far to the left in the dark and now collided with Silly's men, who had diverted to the right. Nevertheless, his right brigade was able to ascend towards Caesar's Camp at the end of the ridge, unnoticed until they reached the back of the redoubt and the ruins. At this point the 42nd moved forward, the 28th faced about and the fire of the two battalions drove the French into the ruins. The 23rd and the 58th added to the musket fire, causing a rout from which 'not a man escaped without being killed, wounded, or taken prisoner'.[114]

Moore now reformed the 42nd and brought them back to the left side of the redoubt where they encountered and attacked Silly's rear battalion. Supported by the 28th, the 42nd put the French to flight, pursuing them for some distance, although Moore was shot in the leg. He also recorded that he met Abercromby at this point in the battle and was able to inform him of events at the ruins.

Day was dawning as Menou sent forward his cavalry, 1,000 strong in column in two ranks. The first rank advanced rapidly towards the left of the redoubt and overran the pursuers of Silly's defeated battalion but then stumbled into holes which the 28th had dug as shelter while they waited for the arrival of tents. The 42nd, who had quickly rallied, were able to drive them back, supported by General Stuart's regiments, which had been ordered forward from the 2nd line to support the reserve.

By this time Silly's leading brigade was at the northern face of the ridge where the attempt was made to rally the survivors of Valentin's brigade. These troops now came under fire from the British gunboats and from the 58th, who had waited until the French were within sixty yards before firing. Once again the French retreated in disorder.

Rampon, meanwhile, had rallied his division and with some support from Reynier was advancing against the Guards, but was driven off by steady musketry. Rampon then tried to turn their left flank but Ludlow threw back some companies of the 3rd Guards to counteract the attack, although it also required the intervention of the Royals, from Coote's brigade, to relieve the pressure on Ludlow's men. Thwarted twice, Rampon now withdrew.

With the battle seemingly going against him, Menou sent his second line of cavalry forward under General Roize, supported by part of Reynier's division. Roize could see the hopelessness of this last desperate throw and needed three direct orders before he obeyed. The cavalry advanced up the south slope of Caesar's Camp, then turned towards the centre of the ridge. 'Upon the left the 42nd and 28th repulsed what was in their front, but were again charged by a large body of cavalry, who penetrated, got into the redoubt and behind us.' As was his wont, Abercromby was in the thick of the action. 'Sir Ralph was actually taken by a French dragoon, but a soldier of the 42nd shot the man. I was obliged to put spurs to my horse to get clear, and I galloped to the ruins to bring up from thence some of the troops which I knew were formed and in good order.' The cavalry now directed their attack on the empty space of the redoubt, coming upon the 28th from front rear. Upon an order from Colonel Chambers, 'Rear rank 28th! Right about face,' the rear rank turned and fired a devastating volley which effectively finished the cavalry threat. The 23rd, well protected behind the building, also fired on the cavalry, forcing them to retire, not without leaving behind a large number of casualties, men and horses.[115]

Stuart's Foreign Brigade had already been ordered into the empty ground between the left of the reserve and the Guards brigade. They now became the target of this final, desperate cavalry attack but they opened line and let the cavalry through. Then they faced about, and fired a telling volley that prevented the cavalry from making an easy retreat. Roize, who had tried to persuade Menou to accept defeat and withdraw, fell in what he had recognized as a hopeless effort. Reynier was also of the opinion that Menou should either order a retreat or let him bring his troops, the last French reserve, into the fight. Menou, hovering behind the French lines, refused to take a decision either way. The French guns continued to have a galling effect on the British troops, who were almost out of ammunition, as were the British guns. Finally, the point was reached when 'Our artillery could not return a shot, and had their infantry again advanced we must have repelled them with the bayonet. Our fellows would have done it; I never saw men more determined to do their duty; but the French had suffered so severely that they could not get their men to make another attempt.'[116] The struggle descended to the ridiculous when the French resorted to throwing stones at the 28th, and the British retaliated by throwing the stones back. Finally the two companies of the 40th were sent forward to mop up the stone-throwing gentlemen and some skirmishers who still threatened. The French accepted that their day was done. The withdrawal seems to have been underway by half past nine. There were no cavalry to harass the retreating troops but the British guns, having at long last received fresh supplies of ammunition, were able to inflict further casualties. By ten o'clock, though, all firing had ceased, a little under four hours after the first attack was launched.

Thus came to an end a 'hard and well-fought' battle between two armies of roughly equal strength. Neither commander deployed all his troops; neither Reynier on the French side nor Cavan, Doyle and Craddock on the British played any crucial part in the action. Menou used more of his army than Abercromby, but Abercromby held by far the stronger position.[117] The fierceness of the struggle had inevitably claimed casualties; the British suffered 1,430, 243 of them killed in action. Inevitably, the battalions involved in the struggle around Caesar's Camp and the redoubt, including Stuart's Foreign Brigade, took the heaviest losses, approaching 90 per cent of the total. Even there it was the most exposed battalions that suffered most severely, the redoubt and the ruins offering some protection for the others. The number of French casualties counted on the battlefield was 1,700, of which over a thousand were fatalities. The French also lost Generals Roize and Lanusse. On the British side, Moore and Oakes both suffered leg injuries, but were able to stay on the battlefield.

According to his son, Abercromby knew that the safety of the army, the fate of Egypt and the chance of an honourable peace all depended on the outcome of the action. He had brought the discipline of the army 'nearly to perfection'.[118] Moore commented that Abercromby always exposed himself to danger and never more so than on this occasion. He saw him, although it was still dark, close to the rear of the 42nd 'without any of his family', they no doubt having been sent on missions to other parts of the battlefield. He was then joined by Hope. During the second cavalry charge the British were temporarily in total disorder. Moore waved Abercromby back but he was surrounded by dragoons. 'He received a cut from a sabre on the breast, which passed through his clothes, but only grazed the flesh. He must have been taken or killed if a soldier had not shot the hussar [dragoon].'[119]

It is not known for sure when he received his fatal wound but Walsh believed it was during the confusion of the second cavalry charge that 'the gallant veteran, Sir Ralph Abercromby, received the unfortunate wound, which deprived the army of a distinguished and beloved commander. It is impossible to ascertain the exact moment, as he never complained, or revealed the circumstance of his being wounded to anyone till it was perceived by those about him. No entreaty could even then prevail upon him to leave the field, till convinced by his own eyes of the enemy's retreat.'[120] John Abercromby had seen his father at daybreak, in the rear of the reserve after the first French attack. At this point he was giving orders for troop movements. He did not see him again until the end of the battle in a small gun emplacement, where the guns were still firing, in the centre of the line. Abercromby's clothes had been cut and there were some bloodstains.

> He asked if he was wounded, and he answered, 'Yes, by a spent ball, but it gives me no uneasiness.' But he added that he felt considerable pain in his breast from a French dragoon who rode against him, when the cavalry broke in on the right.
> General Ludlow and Colonel Abercromby urged in the strongest manner that his wound should be examined, but he persevered in refusing, assigning as his reason, that there were many poor fellows worse wounded than he was, and that the surgeons were more usefully employed in attending to them.[121]

Abercromby now dismounted and seemed to walk easily as he watched the French movements in the final stages of the battle. Half an hour later, though, he felt faint and sat with his back against a parapet of the redoubt. Ludlow sent for a surgeon attached to the Guards but only found a mate, who inspected the wound and established that the ball had entered Abercromby's thigh. He was urged to leave the field but he insisted that he would wait until the firing ceased. When the action was over he was carried to Colonel

Abercromby's tent. Here the wound was inspected by a surgeon of the Guards, who said that the ball was not where it might have been expected and ordered that he should be taken on board ship. He was placed on a bier and an officer (John Macdonald of the 89th, later general and adjutant general) took a soldier's blanket to make a pillow. Told by Macdonald that it was only a soldier's blanket, Abercromby objected, 'Only a soldier's blanket! A soldier's blanket is of great consequence, and you must send me the name of the soldier to whom it belongs, that it may be returned to him.'[122] (This was later done.) As he was carried past the men, there were cries of 'God bless your honour' and similar sentiments. Abercromby now instructed his son to join General Hutchinson and do his duty. He himself was taken to Keith's flagship, the *Foudroyant*.

On the 24th Abercromby's second-in-command published the following general order.

> Major-General Hely Hutchinson has received directions from his Excellency the Commander in Chief, to thank the whole of the troops for their conspicuous and brilliant conduct in the action of the 21st instant; a conduct which has dismayed an insolent enemy, has raised the glory of their country, and established their reputation for ever . . .
>
> Major General Hutchinson has sincerely to regret that a wound, though not dangerous, has deprived the army, for a moment, on the presence of the Commander in Chief, who, in all the different actions, was ever the first to lead them to danger and glory. The army will judge of the feelings of Major General Hutchinson by their own: it will, however, considerably diminish their regret, when they are informed that the superintending care of the Commander in Chief still watches over them; and that the most sanguine hopes are entertained that he will be restored to perfect health, and resume those functions which he has already exercised in a manner that entitles him to the gratitude of his country, and to the admiration of the gallant men whom he has the good fortune to command . . .[123]

The ball's trajectory was upwards, and it had lodged in the thigh bone which made extraction impossible. Yet, although the ball could not be extracted from the wound, it was expected that Abercromby would recover. On the same day that Hutchinson issued his general order, Moore, himself incapacitated by his leg wound, was informed that 'Sir Ralph is . . . much better this day;

the ball is not extracted but he is tolerably free from fever.' Five days later, though, Moore wrote in his journal: 'Sir Ralph was seldom free from fever, got no sleep but from opium, and had occasional delirium; for some days past the surgeons have had little hope of his recovery. I received a note this morning from his son, which informed that he had expired last night at 11 o'clock without pain.'[124]

Chapter 6

The Do-Something General

Abercromby was buried in Malta, under the bastion that still bears his name. The troops he had nurtured, commanded by men who were, in effect, his pupils, marched on to further victory. Cairo was taken. Alexandria was besieged. Finally, on 2 September 1801, Menou surrendered. Britain gave up much by the terms of the Peace of Amiens which the new British government had been negotiating even while the army campaigned against the French, but Bonaparte's determination to hold Egypt and threaten India had been frustrated by the first British force of the Revolutionary War that had proved a match for the battle-hardened Army of the Orient. The peace would soon break down. New coalitions would be formed. And many of the officers and other ranks who went on to win glory in the Iberian Peninsula and at Waterloo had learnt their soldiering under Sir Ralph Abercromby.

Walsh expressed the thoughts of most of those men in his journal.

> A man who has served his country in every quarter of the globe; who, as a commander, devotes to his troops an attention almost parental; as a soldier, shares in all their hardships and all their dangers; who, at an age when he might retire from the field crowned with glory, comes forth, at the call of his country, a veteran in experience, youthful in ardour; whose life is a public blessing, his death a universal misfortune; is beyond the hacknied phrase of panegyric. Such a man was Sir Ralph Abercromby. Dead to his country, his name will ever live in her recollection. Through his exertions, seconded by the cooperation of those he commanded, a nation, long oppressed by a sanguinary war, caught the first glimpse of an honourable *peace*; and while a grateful people bent over the grave of a departed hero, they beheld the yet timid olive, sheltering itself in the laurels which encircled his tomb.[1]

For Moore, the sense of loss was more personal.

Sir Ralph was a truly upright, honourable, judicious man; his great sagacity, which had been pointed all his life to military matters, made him an excellent officer . . . It was impossible, knowing him as I did, not to have the greatest respect and friendship for him; he had ever treated me with marked kindness. The only consolation I feel is, that his death has been nearly that which he himself wished, that his country, grateful to his memory, will hand down his name to posterity with the admiration it deserves.[2]

Even in a formal communication, his answer to the resolution of thanks received from the House of Commons, Hutchinson could not resist striking a personal note. 'I cannot concluded without expressing a sentiment of regret, that it has fallen to my lot to answer your resolutions, and not him who so nobly lead the way, and whose conduct, talents and example, so greatly contributed to the success of those there brilliant days.'[3]

Equally distraught at Abercromby's death was Henry Dundas. News of the successful landings did not reach him until early April, by which time he was out of office, having followed Pitt in resigning when the King refused to countenance Catholic emancipation. He wrote to the new Prime Minister, Addington: 'I have lost many nights sleep in anxiety respecting the expedition to Egypt, and it is therefore singular, that when the chief part of that anxiety is removed by the news of yesterday, the same subject should from gaiety of heart keep me more awake than it has ever done before.'[4]

The news of Abercromby's death did not take so long to arrive, prompting Dundas to write to Pitt:

I am almost ashamed to own that I mourn for Sir Ralph Abercromby, but unreasonable as it is, I find it impossible as yet to resist the effects of that affection, which insensibly every moment forces itself upon me. Our friendship was early, and has been unremitted. Our domestic interests are twinned together. I flattered myself that after closing our political and military service, we might for some years have lived in happy society together, surrounded by our families, anticipating the happiness and growing prosperity of those who were to come after us. These dreams must now pass away, but you cannot be surprised if I find it difficult at once to banish the delusion. Neither can I disguise from you, that all these feelings of a private character are at this moment cruelly aggravated by reflections of a more public nature. When I persevered in this expedition, under many discouraging circumstances, my chief confidence rested on the thorough knowledge I had of the union of enterprise and judgement which marked the military character of the General from his first outset as a soldier.[5]

Another contemporary whose regard for Abercromby was based on personal acquaintance was Henry Bunbury. He ended his account of the Battle of Alexandria with another eulogy, to follow the estimation he made during the expedition to north Holland.

> Wherever he had served, and his had been a long career, he had been respected and beloved. There was an absence of selfishness in Abercromby, a liberality of feeling, and an independence of spirit which entitled him to the highest respect as a gentleman; while his justice, his intrepidity, and experience assured to him as a commander, the attachment and confidence of his troops. To fall in the moment of victory, and to know when dying that his victory was complete, was what the gallant veteran himself would have desired; but on the officers and soldiers who had toiled, and bled, and conquered under his leading, the tidings of his death fell like a chilling cloud.[6]

The King had been a firm advocate of Abercromby ever since the Flanders campaign. Obviously aware of this, Lord Hobart, the Minister for War and the Colonies in Addington's government, felt constrained to write to the King on 15 May, almost as soon as the news of Abercromby's death had reached London:

> The loss which your Majesty's service has sustain'd by the death of that excellent and gallant Officer General Abercrombie cannot but be most sincerely felt both by his country and his friends. They will however derive no small consolation from the reflection that, directed by his experience and talents, and animated by the example of that intrepidity and coolness for which he has at all times been so conspicuous, the gallantry and conduct of the British troops has never been more distinguish'd than in the several actions which have taken place under his command in Egypt.[7]

For Burne, Abercromby was 'the give-up general', but this was not how he was perceived in his own time, as Hobart's comments demonstrate.

When Gifford compiled his *History of the Wars Occasioned by the French Revolution* in 1817, there were other heroes to praise, most notably Moore and Wellington. This did not prevent him from writing an extended eulogy of the earlier general, whose memory still lived on.

> On the 28th March brave Gen. Abercromby breathed his last. His death was first made known to the army the next morning. For his cure he had undergone the most painful operations with great firmness; but as the ball could not be extracted, a mortification ensued. This eminent man had also served his country in a legislative capacity. In the year 1774 he was elected to represent the county of Kinross in parliament, and continued a member of the house of commons until the next annual election in 1780. His chief talents however were of the martial kind. In his military character he was strictly uniform and regular, preserving the best order and discipline possible throughout all ranks under his command. In action he possessed the intrepidity, coolness and presence of mind requisite; and characteristic of the British nation. In his private character he was modest and unassuming; in all his transactions disinterested and upright, and in his morals circumspect, and unstained by licentious vices. In company he was naturally reserved, and in promiscuous or mixed company extremely silent; yet perfectly easy of access, and free from haughtiness. In his domestic relations he was unimpeachable, and fulfilled the several duties of a son, brother, husband, father, and friend, with that rectitude inseparable to a character of his magnanimity.[8]

Another aspect of Abercromby was brought out in a brief account of his life. 'It was part indeed, not only of the military skill, but of the humanity in the character of Sir Ralph Abercrombie, that he never, uselessly had recourse to violence; that he valued even the blood of his enemies, and never from any punctilio of false honour, or imagined laws of war, sought that from arms, which he could in any way accomplish by treaty.'[9] The same humanity had been evident as he brought the sick to safety in 1795, as he made the comfort of his men his first priority; and the same humanity had earned him the love of those who served under him.

Since 1817 Abercromby's reputation has diminished as the failures of the Revolutionary Wars have been eclipsed by the victories of the Napoleonic. He was not a battlefield commander in the mould of Marlborough or

Wellington, and his tendency to be in the thick of the action sometimes detracted from his overall control; but he certainly possessed courage and integrity. He led from the front and his men willingly followed. Indeed, it was this aspect of Abercromby that John Colborne remembered from the time he had served under him in North Holland:

> During the course of the battle [Bergen] General Abercromby came galloping among our artillery, exclaiming, 'Now, fire one more round.'
>
> The officer in command said, 'We have no ammunition left.'
>
> 'The first time I have ever seen the artillery ill served.' Said the General, in vexation, and then, turning to the 20th, 'Now are there not forty or fifty of you who will charge with me into the village and drive the French back?' Immediately the whole regiment rushed forward, and a good many militia with them, who had only just come from England and had not had time to change their militia uniforms. Sir Ralph, recognizing this, called out, 'Come along! You are as safe here as you were in Norfolk!'[10]

Furthermore, as his career demonstrated, culminating in Egypt, he was a peerless trainer of men at a time when such a figure was critically necessary. In those vital months on Minorca and at Marmoris Bay his efforts produced an army that not only fought with the intrepidity and determination that he so highly valued but also behaved with the discipline and respect that brings about success on the battlefield. Others might have done more with them once they were there; but few had the talent to get them there in such good order. He had also learnt much from the logistic shortcomings of his previous campaigns. At the heart of his command was the welfare of his troops, first demonstrated during the horrendous winter retreat of 1795. And it earned him their love. Burne considered him a defeatist. There certainly was a streak of pessimism that he shared with Moore; and he was consistently pragmatic in response to Grenville's grandiose schemes. Above all, though, he was a *gentleman*, with everything that word denoted.

> ...Abercromby's army admired his courage, high moral character, and judgement. Above all, he had brought them victory. After eight years of disappointment, he had given the British army the smell of success against good French troops. 'It has happened

to no other general during this war to beat the French in three successive actions', Moore reminded his father. Abercromby was 'the best man, and the best soldier, who has appeared amongst us this war.'[11]

As the Duke of York wrote in his general order: 'the splendour of his actions in the field, and the heroism of his death, are worthy of the imitation of all, who desire like him, a life of honour and a death of glory.'

Tables

Table 1
November 1795 Return: Troops under Abercromby's Command

1st Brigade	14th, 27th, 28th, 57th
2nd Brigade	3rd, 19th, 31st, 33rd
3rd Brigade	8th, 37th, 44th, 55th
4th Brigade	38th, 48th, 53rd, 63rd
5th Brigade	2nd, 10th, 25th, 29th, 88th
6th Brigade	Composite Grenadier Battn, 42nd
Cavalry	26th Light Dragoons
Artillery	Royal Irish Artillery
Hospital Corps	
Total	641 officers
	17,792 NCOs and men

Table 2
April 1796 Return: Abercromby's Force on St Lucia

1st Brigade	Major General Campbell	14th, 27th, 28th, 44th, 48th
2nd Brigade	Major General Morshead	42nd, 53rd, 55th, composite battn.
Foreign Regts	Brigadier General Perryn	York Fusiliers, York Rangers
Reserve	Lieutenant Colonel Macdonald	26th Light Dragoons, Grenadier Battn.
Light Infantry		Lowenstein Chasseurs, Black Native Troops
Total	434 officers, 9,150 NCOs and men	
700 artillerymen and 70 engineer officers subsequently joined		

Table 3
Troops under Abercromby's command, 4 August 1799

1st Brigade	Major General D'Oyley	Grenadiers of the Guards, 3/1st Guards
2nd Brigade	Major General Burrard	1st battn Coldstream Guards, 1/3rd Guards
3rd Brigade	Major General Coote	2nd, 27th, 29th, 69th, 85th
4th Brigade	Major General Moore	2/1st, 25th, 49th, 79th, 92nd
Reserve	Colonel Macdonald	23rd 55th

Total 479 officers, 11,829 NCOs and men (including 753 sick)
Also present: 18th Light Dragoons (13 officers, 208 NCOs and men
Royal Artillery (26 officers, 417 NCOs and men, 157 drivers)

Table 4
March 1801: Troops under General Abercromby's Command

Major General Ludlow	1/Coldstream, 1/3rd Guards	1,813	1,578
Major General Coote	1st, 1/54th 2/54th, 92nd	2,535	2,129
Major General Cradock	8th, 13th, 18th, 90th	2,483	2,135
Major General Lord Cavan	50th, 79th	1,247	1,081
Brigadier General Doyle	2nd*, 30th, 44th, 89th	1,719	1,583
Brigadier General Stuart	Stuart's (Minorca), De Roll's, Dillon's	2,113	1,987
Major General Moore Brigadier General Oakes	23rd, 28th, 42nd, 58th, Corsican Rangers, 40th (flank companies)	2,954	2,726
Brigadier General Finch	11th Lt Dragoons, 12th Lt Dragoons, 26th Lt Dragoons, Hompesch's Hussars	1,063	1,034
Brigadier General Lawson	13th, 14th, 26th, 28th, 55th, 69th, 70th, 71st companies	656 627	

Note: the first set of figures are the total strength, the second omit sick, present and absent. In addition there was a staff corps of 82.
* The 2nd (Queen's) subsequently transferred to Cavan's brigade to replace the 1/27th and 2/27th who had been left sick at Gibraltar and Malta

Endnotes

Introduction

1. Dunfermline, p. 33.
2. Ibid., p. 16.
3. Ibid., p. 25.
4. Melville MSS 08/04/89.
5. As, published in *The Universal Magazine of Knowledge and Pleasure* 1801.
6. Burne, pp. 270–1, 285.
7. Dunfermline, p. 1.
8. Fortescue Volume IV, p. 844.

Chapter 1: The War of the First Coalition

1. Banning, pp. 37ff.
2. The *Déclaration* was influenced by John Locke's ideas on natural rights and civic equality in his *Second Treatise of Government* 1690.
3. Dunfermline, pp. 32–3.
4. Harvey, pp. 71–2.
5. Cornwallis, *Correspondence*, Vol. III, p. 270.
6. Ward & Gooch Vol. I, p. 219.
7. Fulford, p. 64.
8. Hathaway Vol. II, p. 36
9. HO 102/6 24 November 1792.
10. Dunfermline, p. 34.
11. Burke, p. 181.
12. Alison Vol. II, p. 415, and see Farrer, pp. 13–20 for a more detailed account of the sabre-rattling indulged in by both Britain and France.
13. Bunbury, pp. xv, xxi.
14. Jupp, p. 152.
15. Dunfermline, p. 39.
16. Ibid., p. 33.
17. Ibid., p. 31.
18. Calvert, p. 28.

19. Alison Vol. IV, p. 22.
20. Auckland Vol. III, p. 12.
21. WO1/166, 15 March 1793.
22. WO1/166, 21 March 1793.
23. WO1/166 1 April 1793.
24. Fortescue Vol. IV, pp. 80–1.
25. Calvert, p. 52.
26. Ibid., pp. 67–8.
27. Dunfermline, pp. 39–40.
28. Fortescue Vol. IV, p. 86.
29. Dropmore Papers Vol. V, p. 147.
30. Auckland Vol. III, pp. 106–7.
31. Fortescue Vol. IV, p. 96.
32. Calvert, pp. 76–7.
33. Brown, p. 54.
34. Aspinall Vol. II, p. 66.
35. Roider, pp. 131–6.
36. Quoted in Fremont-Barnes, pp. 29–30.
37. Brown, p. 70.
38. Fortescue Vol. IV, p. 132.
39. Calvert, p. 121.
40. Ibid., pp. 126 and 130–1.
41. Ibid., p. 147.
42. Fortescue Vol. IV, p. 146.
43. Brown, pp. 82–3.
44. Aspinall Vol. II, p. 134.
45. Ibid., p. 133.
46. Auckland Vol. IV, pp. 144–5.
47. Brown, p. 101.
48. Cantlie, p. 211.
49. Ibid., p. 178.
50. Rothenburg, p. 39.
51. Ibid., p. 40.
52. Calvert, p. 187.
53. Schama, p. 164.
54. Ibid.
55. WO 1/168 11 April 1794.
56. Burne, pp. 119–20.

57. Jones, p. 8.
58. Calvert, p. 203.
59. Ibid., p. 206.
60. M. Glover, p. 31.
61. Gifford, pp. 48–9.
62. Dunfermline, p. 49.
63. Brown, p. 132.
64. Ibid., p. 141.
65. Ibid., pp. 142–3
66. Fortescue IV, p. 270.
67. Roider, p. 152.
68. Calvert, p. 217.
69. Jones, p. 41.
70. Calvert, pp. 228–9
71. Burne, p. 157.
72. Ibid., pp. 158–9.
73. Douglas, p. 43.
74. Calvert, p. 256.
75. Burne, p. 153.
76. Hussey Vivian, p. 17.
77. Ibid., p. 19.
78. Calvert, p. 269.
79. Ibid., p. 277.
80. Ibid., p. 301.
81. Rothenburg, p. 43.
82. Auckland III, p. 225.
83. Calvert, p. 325.
84. Jones, p. 120.
85. Wills, pp. 21–3.
86. Fortescue IV, p. 305.
87. WO1/168, 17 September 1794.
88. Burne, pp. 179–81.
89. Calvert, pp. 356 and 361.
90. Ward & Gooch I, p. 253.
91. Roider, p. 167.
92. Auckland III, pp. 268–71 and 275.
93. Jones, p. 144.
94. Aspinall II, pp. 272–4.

95.   Harcourt V, p. 560.
96.   Brown, pp. 220–1.
97.   Blanco, pp. 31–2.
98.   Hussey Vivian, p. 31.
99.   Brown, p. 223
100. Jones, pp. 175–6.
101. E. Walsh, p. 11.
102. *Royal Military Panorama* Dec.1813, p. 6.
103. Schama, p. 199.
104. Fitchett Vol I, p. 64.
105. Stanhope, p. 182.
106. Dunfermline, pp. 52–3.
107. Aspinall, p. 355.

Chapter 2: War in the West Indies

1.   M. Duffy, Preface.
2.   Fortescue Vol. IV, p. 79.
3.   Aspinall Vol. II, p. 368.
4.   WO 1/31 22 December 1794.
5.   Duffy, p. 164.
6.   NLS MS 3835 fo.121.
7.   Aspinall II, p. 381
8.   Condon, p. 57.
9.   Boult, p. 26.
10.   Cantlie, pp. 241–2.
11.   CO 318/18 2 November 1795.
12.   Condon, pp. 164–5.
13.   Fortescue, p. 478.
14.   Morris, p. 66.
15.   M. Howard, p. 92.
16.   Spencer Papers Vol. I, pp. 51–2.
17.   Pinckard Vol. I, pp. 102–4.
18.   Boult Chapter 6.
19.   Cornwallis-West, p. 306.
20.   Dunfermline, p. 55.
21.   Burne, p. 238.
22.   Moore Vol. I, p. 193.
23.   Fortescue Vol. IV, p. 485.

24. Howard, p. 96.
25. Moore Vol. I, p. 196.
26. See Table 2 for Abercromby's force on St Lucia.
27. WO 1/85 2 April 1796.
28. Moore Vol. I, p. 200.
29. Ibid., p. 203.
30. Ibid., p. 205.
31. WO 1/85 2 May 1796.
32. Moore Vol. I, p. 206.
33. WO 1/85 4 May 1796
34. Moore Vol. I, p. 207.
35. Duffy, p. 227 and BL Add, MS 37876 2, 4.
36. Moore Vol. I, p. 208.
37. Ibid., p. 210.
38. Duffy, pp. 231–2.
39. Fortescue Vol. IV, p. 491.
40. Moore Vol. I, p. 213.
41. Ibid., p. 214.
42. WO 1/85 26 May 1793.
43. Moore Vol. I, p. 219.
44. A Collection of State Papers V, pp. 40–1.
45. Moore Vol. I, pp. 219–20.
46. WO 1/85 21 June 1796.
47. Moore Vol. I, p. 233.
48. Ibid., p. 245.
49. *The Universal Politician*, p. 251.
50. NAM 2001–10–611.
51. Duffy, p. 270.
52. WO 1/86 16 January and 13 March 1797.
53. Details of troops – Fortescue Vol. IV, p. 539.
54. WO 1/86 20 February 1797.
55. SRO TD 73/25/1032.
56. WO 1/86 28 February 1797.
57. Howard, Robert, pp. 8–9.
58. His infantry comprised the 14th, 42nd, 53rd, 3/60th and 87th, with a detachment from the Tobago Negro Corps, supported by detachments from the 26th Light Dragoons, Artillery and Engineers.
59. Dunfermline, pp. 58–9.

60. Moore Vol. I, p. 250.
61. Dunfermline, pp. 59–60.
62. Moore Vol. I, p. 254.
63. Aspinall Vol. III, p. 515.
64. Buckley, p. 271.
65. Dunfermline, pp. 311–16.

Chapter 3: Ireland – a Poisoned Chalice

1. Leckie Vol. IV, p. 140.
2. Philpen, p. 194.
3. Auckland Vol. IV, p. 202.
4. Leckie Vol. IV, p. 117.
5. Moore Vol. I, p. 275.
6. HO100/69.
7. Barrington Vol. II, p. 275.
8. Musgrave, p. 178.
9. Grattan, p. 36.
10. Leckie Vol IV, pp. 197–8.
11. Packenham, p. 53.
12. Moore Vol. I, p. 270.
13. Quoted in Packenham, p. 52.
14. Moore Vol. I, p. 271.
15. HO30/66.
16. Moore Vol. I, p. 271.
17. Dunfermline, pp. 77–8.
18. Lecky Vol. IV, pp. 199–200.
19. Dunfermline, pp. 84–5.
20. Ibid., pp. 85–6.
21. Barrington Vol. II, p. 255.
22. Dunfermline, p. 86.
23. Ibid., pp. 92–3.
24. Ibid., pp. 91–2.
25. Ibid., pp. 90–1.
26. Ibid., p. 94.
27. Ibid., pp. 95–6.
28. Auckland Vol. IV, pp. 394–5.
29. Fortescue IV, p. 573.
30. Dunfermline, pp. 112–14.

31. Ibid., p. 98.
32. HO100/72.
33. Moore Vol. I, pp. 283–5.
34. BL Add. MSS 33105.
35. Dunfermline, pp. 101–2.
36. Ibid., pp. 116–17.
37. Auckland Vol. IV, pp. 396–7.
38. Dunfermline, pp. 103–4.
39. Ibid., pp. 106–7.
40. Ibid., pp. 108–10.
41. Ibid., pp. 125–7.
42. BM Add. MSS 37308.
43. Dunfermline, pp. 127–8.
44. Moore Vol. I, pp. 286–8.
45. Dunfermline, p. 134.
46. Ibid., pp. 128–30.
47. Holland, p. 101 and pp. 111–112.
48. Dunfermline, pp. 135–6.
49. Madden, p. 305.
50. Cookson, p. 55.

Chapter 4: The War of the Second Coalition

1. Morton Eden to Grenville 1/04/97; Roider, pp. 237–8.
2. Blanning, pp. 176–7.
3. Mackesy, *Overthrow*, p. 4.
4. Blanning, pp. 177–8.
5. Roider, p. 292.
6. Stowe Papers, Box 310, 5 April 1799.
7. R. Glover, p. 4.
8. Ibid., p. 25.
9. Dunfermline, pp. 144–5.
10. The 4th, 5th, 9th, 17th, 20th, 31st, 35th, 40th, 42nd, 46th, 52nd, 62nd, 63rd, and 82nd were the nominated regiments; of these the 4th, 5th, 9th, 20th, 31st, 35th, 40th and 63rd went to den Helder.
11. Fortescue Vol. IV, p. 642.
12. Bunbury, p. 25.
13. Jackson, p. 19.
14. Schama, p. 247.

15. Ibid., p. 277.
16. Ibid.
17. Ibid., pp. 319–20.
18. Ibid., pp. 389–90.
19. Dunfermline, p. 149.
20. Mathieson, p. 266.
21. Moore Vol. I, p. 339.
22. Surtees, pp. 3–4.
23. Dunfermline, pp. 140–1.
24. Cantlie, p. 261.
25. WO 1/179 3r August 1799.
26. Dropmore Vol. V, p. 207.
27. Moore Vol. I, p. 340.
28. Dunfermline, p. 162.
29. See Table 3 for the advance force under Abercromby.
30. Mackesy. *Overthrow*, p. 180.
31. E. Walsh, p. 21.
32. Moore Vol. I, p. 341.
33. WO 1/179 14 August 1799.
34. E. Walsh, p. 25.
35. Moore Vol. I, pp. 341–2.
36. WO 1/179 28 August 1799.
37. Ibid.
38. Ibid.
39. Moore Vol. I, p. 242.
40. Maule, p. 8.
41. Bunbury, p. 3.
42. WO 1/179 28 August 1799.
43. Jackson, p. 23.
44. Moore Vol. I, p. 343.
45. WO 1/179 September 1799.
46. Dunfermline, p. 174.
47. Jackson, p. 21.
48. Moore Vol. I, pp. 344–5.
49. Jomini Vol. XII, p. 157.
50. Dropmore Vol. V, p. 388.
51. Mathieson, p. 269.
52. Moore Vol. I, p. 345.

53. Jackson, p. 22.
54. Alison Vol. VII, p. 46.
55. Moore Vol. I, p. 347
56. Bunbury, pp. 7–8.
57. Dunfermline, pp. 181–2.
58. Fortescue Vol. IV, p. 665.
59. Bunbury, p. 15.
60. Ibid., pp. 28–9.
61. E. Walsh, p. 45.
62. Fortescue Vol. IV, p. 668
63. WO 1/180 11 September 1799.
64. Surtees, pp. 10–12.
65. Ibid., p. 12.
66. Jackson, p. 25.
67. WO 1/180 20 September 1799.
68. Bunbury, pp. 13–15.
69. Moore Vol. I, p. 350.
70. Jackson, p. 26.
71. Jomini Vol. XII, p. 168.
72. Burne, p. 268.
73. Mackesy, p. 274.
74. Hussey Vivian, p. 51.
75. Bunbury, p. 15.
76. Jackson, p. 28.
77. Dunfermline, pp. 203–4.
78. Burne, p. 275.
79. Bunbury, p. 17.
80. Burne, pp. 276–7.
81. E. Walsh, p. 67.
82. Bunbury, p. 18.
83. E. Walsh, p. 67.
84. Ibid., p. 68.
85. Jackson, p. 29.
86. Fortescue Vol. IV, p. 693.
87. WO 1/179 6 September 1799.
88. Bunbury, p. 21.
89. Fortescue Vol. IV, p. 699.
90. E. Walsh, p. 80.

91. Bunbury, pp. 22–3.

92. E. Walsh, p. 86.

93. Mackesy, *Overthrow*, pp. 302 and 305.

94. Dunfermline, pp. 198–9.

95. Ibid., pp. 200–1.

96. Ibid., pp. 202–3.

97. Ibid., pp. 204–5.

98. Ibid., pp. 207–8.

99. Holland, p. 152.

100. See Ball, pp. 158–63 for further contemporary opinions.

101. Bunbury, p. 27.

102. Ibid., p. 28.

103. Dunfermline, p. 212.

104. Their forebear was an iconic hero of the Dutch rising against the Spanish in the sixteenth century.

105. Dunfermline, p. 213.

106. Ibid., p. 214.

107. Ibid.

108. Ibid., pp. 214–15.

109. Mackesy, *Overthrow*, pp. 314–15.

110. Ibid., p. 319.

111. Mathieson, pp. 273–4.

Chapter 5: The Last Campaign

1. Mackesy, *War*, pp. 8–9.

2. Wickham II, p. 258.

3. Mackesy, War, Chapter 2.

4. Fry, p. 225.

5. Alison Vol. VII, p. 150.

6. Bourrienne Vol. III, p. 214.

7. Alison Vol. IV, pp. 140 and 147; also, pp. 134–49 for the full debate.

8. Dunfermline, p. 208.

9. Hope of Lufness 20 November 1799.

10. Aspinall, pp. 318–22.

11. J.H. Rose, pp. 266–8 and 271

12. Aspinall, pp. 337–8.

13. Dropmore Vol. VI, p. 233.

14. Keith Vol. II, pp. 110–11.

15. Dropmore Vol. VI, p. 233.

16. Jackson, p. 45.
17. Anderson, p. 19.
18. Jackson, p. 46.
19. Anderson, p. 33.
20. *Life of Lord Lynedoch*, p. 201.
21. Anderson, p. 40.
22. Ibid., pp. 41–2.
23. Ibid., pp. 42–9.
24. Aspinall, pp. 382–4.
25. Ibid., pp. 385–7.
26. Dundas, however, had been trying to resign virtually from the moment he was made Secretary for War.
27. The situation would finally be resolved by the Battle of Copenhagen on 2 April 1801.
28. Stathern, p. 409.
29. Ibid., p. 409.
30. Mackesy, *Egypt*, p. 39.
31. Moore Vol. I, pp. 377–8.
32. Ibid., p. 379.
33. Bunbury, p. 48.
34. Moore Vol. I, p. 374.
35. Ibid., pp. 275–6.
36. Bunbury, pp. 50–1.
37. Anderson, p. 80.
38. Fry, pp. 225–6 outlines Dundas' plan.
39. Dunfermline, p. 253.
40. Ibid., pp. 245–6.
41. Ibid., pp. 251–2.
42. T. Walsh, p. 2.
43. Cantlie, p. 265.
44. Maule, p. 46.
45. Ibid., pp. 47–8.
46. Dunfermline, p. 258.
47. Anderson, p. 104.
48. Jackson, p. 58
49. Moore, I, pp. 385–7
50. Ibid., p. 388.
51. Anderson, pp. 105–6.
52. Maule, p. 50.

53. Ibid., pp. 57–8.
54. Nichol, p. 21.
55. T. Walsh, p. 45.
56. Moore Vol. I, p. 395.
57. T. Walsh, p. 54.
58. Ibid., p. 50.
59. Dunfermline, pp. 267–8.
60. Ibid., p. 268.
61. Moore Vol. I, p. 398.
62. Ibid., pp. 397–8.
63. T. Walsh, pp. 48–9.
64. Anderson, p. 192.
65. Mackesy, *Egypt*, p. 35.
66. Moore Vol. II, pp. 3–4.
67. Ibid., p. 399.
68. Mackesy, *Egypt*, pp. 47–8.
69. Nichol, p. 21.
70. T. Walsh, p. 52.
71. See Table 4 for Abercromby's force, March 1801 return.
72. Dunfermline, pp. 273–4.
73. Maule, p. 70.
74. Nichol, p. 23.
75. T. Walsh, p. 69.
76. Moore Vol. I, p. 401.
77. Maule, p. 76.
78. Ibid., pp. 76–7.
79. T. Walsh, p. 72.
80. Moore Vol. II, pp. 1–2.
81. T. Walsh, p. 75.
82. Moore Vol. II, p. 3.
83. Mackesy, *Egypt*, p. 71
84. T. Walsh, p. 77.
85. Nichol, p. 26.
86. *The Gloucester Journal*, Monday, 11 May 1801.
87. Moore Vol. II, pp. 3–4.
88. Maule, pp. 78–9.
89. Dunfermline, pp. 280–1 footnote.
90. Robertson, p. 7.
91. Mackesy, *Egypt*, p. 80.

92. Ibid., p. 76.
93. Moore Vol. II, p. 5.
94. It is equally likely that the idea was Abercromby's, based on his reading of Caesar's *Commentaries*.
95. Nichol, p. 29.
96. Maule, pp. 82–3.
97. Nichol, p. 30.
98. Maule, pp. 84–5.
99. Moore Vol. II, p. 9.
100. Walsh, p. 90.
101. Fortescue Vol. IV, p. 829.
102. Mackesy, p. 97.
103. Moore Vol. II, pp. 9–10.
104. WO 1/345 16 March 1801.
105. WO 1/345 9 May 1801.
106. Moore Vol. II, p. 10.
107. Walsh, p. 95.
108. Dunfermline, p. 290.
109. Douglas, p. 129.
110. Moore Vol. II, p. 12.
111. Ibid., pp. 12–13
112. Ibid., p. 13.
113. Dunfermline, p. 293.
114. Moore Vol. II, p. 15.
115. Ibid., p. 15.
116. Ibid., p. 16.
117. Fortescue Vol. IV, p. 839.
118. Dunfermline, p. 297.
119. Ibid., pp. 297–8.
120. Walsh, pp. 103–4.
121. Dunfermline, pp. 298–9.
122. Ibid., pp. 299–300.
123. Anderson, pp. 269–71.
124. Moore Vol. II, pp. 17–18.

Chapter 6: The Do-Something General

1. T. Walsh, pp. 111–12.
2. Moore Vol. II, p. 18.
3. Army Service and Commission Book II, p. 3.

4. Mathieson, p. 307.
5. Ibid., pp. 307–8.
6. Bunbury, p. 76.
7. Aspinall Vol. III, pp. 538–9.
8. Gifford Vol. I, p. 329.
9. *Royal Military Chronicle* III, p. 386.
10. Colborne, p. 20.
11. Mackesy, p. 142.

Bibliography

Primary Sources:

The British Library
Add MSS 33105
Add MSS 37308

The National Archives
CO 318 Original correspondence West Indies before 1782
HO 30 State Papers Ireland
HO 100 Ireland: Home Office correspondence
WO 1 War office and predecessors: In-letters and Miscellaneous

The National Army Museum
2001-10-611

The National Library of Scotland
MS 3835 fo.121

The National Records of Scotland
Hope of Lufness Papers
Melville Correspondence and Papers

The Stowe Papers
Collection of State Papers, relative to the war against France, A, London 1797.
Universal Politician and Periodical Reporter of the most interesting occurrences…for July and August 1798

Periodicals
The Royal Military Chronicle
Royal Military Panorama or Officers' Companion
The World

Anderson, Aeneas, *Journal of the Forces under the Command of Sir Ralph Abercromby in the Mediterranean and Egypt*, London 1802.

Aspinall, A. (ed.), *The Later Correspondence of George III Vols II & III*, Cambridge at the University Press 1963.

Auckland, William Lord, *The Journal and Correspondence of William, Lord Auckland*, London 1862.

Baines, Edward, *History of the Wars of the French Revolution*, London 1817.

Baldwin, George, *Political Recollections Relative to Egypt . . . with a Narrative of the Ever-Memorable British Campaign in the Spring of 1801*, London 1802.

Barrington, Jonah, *Historic Memoirs of Ireland, Comprising Secret Records of the National Convention, the Rebellion, and the Union*, London 1809.

Bourrienne, Louis Antoine de Fauvelet, *Mémoires de Napoléon Bonaparte*, Paris 1829.

Brown, Robert, *History of the Campaigns in the Years 1793, 1794, 1795*, Stockdale 1795.

Bunbury, Sir Henry, *Narratives of Some Passages of the Great War with France 1799-1810*, London 1927.

Burke, Edmund, *Reflections on the Revolution in France*, London 1790.

Calvert, Sir Henry (ed. Sir H. Verney), *The Journals and Correspondence of General Sir Henry Calvert*, Hurst & Blackett 1853.

Colborne, John (ed. G.C. Moore Smith), *Colborne: a Singular Talent for War*, Leonaur Ltd 2007.

Cornwallis, Lord, (ed. Charles Ross), *Correspondence of Charles, 1st Marquis Cornwallis*, John Murray 1859.

Dundas, David, *Principles of Military Movements Chiefly Applied to Infantry*, London 1788.

Fortescue, The Hon. J.W., *Report on the Manuscripts of J.B. Fortescue Esq., preserved at Dropmore*, Historical Manuscripts Commission 1905–1908.

Gifford, C.H., *History of the Wars Occasioned by the French Revolution from the Commencement of Hostilities in 1792, to the End of the Year 1816*, London 1817.

Grattan, Henry, *Mr Grattan's Address to his Fellow-Citizens*, Dublin 1797.

Harcourt, F.W. (ed.), *The Harcourt Papers*, Jas Parker & Co., Oxford 1880.

Hathaway, W.S. (ed.), *The Speeches of the Right Honourable William Pitt in the House of Commons*, Longman, London 1806.

Holland, Lord, *Memoirs of the Whig Party during my Time*, Longman, Brown, Green and Longmans 1852.

Jackson, Major Alexander Cosby, *Memoirs*, unpublished.

Jomini, Henri, *Histoire Critique et Militaire des Guerres de la Révolution*, Brussels 1838.

Jones, Captain L.T., *Historical Journal of the British Campaign on the Continent in the Year 1794, with the Retreat through Holland, in the Year 1795*, Birmingham 1797.

Keith, Admiral (ed. Christopher Lloyd), *The Keith Papers*, Naval Record Society 1927.

Le Marchant, Denis, *Memoirs of the Late Major-General Le Marchant*, The Naval and Military Press 2006.

Maule, Major Francis, *Memoirs of the Principal Events of the Campaigns of North Holland and Egypt*, London 1816.

Moiret, Joseph-Marie (trans. Rosemary Brindle), *Memoirs of Napoleon's Egyptian Expedition 1798-1801*, Greenhill Books 2001.

Moore, Sir John, (ed. J.F. Maurice), *The Diary of Sir John Moore*, Edward Arnold 1904.

Musgrave, Sir Richard, *Memoirs of the Different Rebellions in Ireland*, Dublin 1802.

Nichol, Daniel, 'The Unpublished Diary of Sergeant Daniel Nichol', in Low. Bruce, *With Napoleon at Waterloo*, London 1911.

Officer of the Guards, *An Accurate an Impartial Narrative of the War*, London 1796.

Paine, Thomas, *The Rights of Man*, London 1791.

Pinckard, George, *Notes on the West Indies: written during the Expedition of the Late General Sir Ralph Abercromby*, London 1806.

Robertson, David, *Journal of Sergeant D. Robertson, Late 92nd Foot*, Perth 1842.

Spencer, George Lord (ed. J.S. Corbett & H.W. Richmond), *The Private Papers of George, 2nd Earl Spencer, 1794-1801*, Navy Records Society 1913–1924.

Stanhope, Philip Henry, Lord, *Notes of Conversations with the Duke of Wellington*, London 1888.

Surtees, William, *Twenty-Five Years in the Rifle Brigade*, Edinburgh 1833/ Greenhill Books 1996.

Thiébault, Paul (translated by Arthur John Butler), *The Memoirs of Baron Thiébault*, London 1896.

Walsh, Edward, *A Narrative of the Expedition to Holland in the Autumn of the Year 1799*, London 1800.

Walsh, Thomas, *Journal of the Campaign in Egypt*, London 1803.

Wickham, William (ed. W. Wickham), *The Correspondence of William Wickham from the Year 1794*, London 1870.

Windham, William (ed. Mrs Henry Baring), *The Diary of the Right Hon. William Windham*, London 1866.

_____, (ed. Lord Rosebery), *The Windham Papers*, Herbert Jenkins Ltd 1913.

Secondary Sources

Alison, Archibald, *History of Europe from the Commencement of the French Revolution to the Restoration of the Bourbons*, Blackwood and Sons 1847.

Anglesey, the Marquess of, *One Leg: the life and Letters of Henry William Paget, 1st Marquess of Anglesey, K.G. 1768-1854*, Leo Cooper 1961.

Arnold, James R., *Marengo & Hohenlinden: Napoleon's Rise to Power*, Pen & Sword 2005.

Asprey, Robert, *The Rise and Fall of Napoleon*, Little, Brown and Company 2000.

Ball, Philip, *A Waste of Blood and Treasure; the 1799 Anglo-Russian Invasion of the Netherlands*, Pen & Sword 2017.

Bartlett, Keith John, *The Development of the British Army during the Wars with France 1793-1815*, Ph.D Thesis, 1998.

Bartlett, Thomas and Jeffery, Keith (eds), *A Military History of Ireland*, Cambridge University Press 1996.

Bew, John, *Castlereagh: the Biography of a Statesman*, Quercus 2011.

Bew, Paul, *Ireland: the Politics of Enmity 1789-2006*, O.U.P. 2007.

Blanco, Richard L., *Wellington's Surgeon General: Sir James McGrigor*, Duke University Press 1974.

Blanning, T.C.W., *The Origins of the French Revolutionary Wars*, Longman 1986.

_____, *The Pursuit of Glory: Europe 1648-1815*, Viking 2007.

Boult, Edwina, *Christian's Fleet: a Dorset Shipping Tragedy*, Tempus 2003.

Bruce, R., Dickie, I., Kiley, K., Pavkovic, M., and Schneid, F., *Fighting Techniques of the Napoleonic Age 1792-1815*, Amber Books 2008.

Buckley, Roger Norman, *The British Army in the West Indies*, University Press of Florida 1998.

Burne, Alfred H., *The Noble Duke of York*, Staples Press 1941.

Cantlie, Lt.Gen. Sir Neil, *A History of the Army Medical Department*, Longmans Group Ltd 1973.

Cobb, Richard and Jones, Colin (eds), *The French Revolution: Voices from a Momentous Epoch 1789-1795*, Simon & Schuster 1988.

Condon, Mary Ellen, *The Administration of the Transport Service during the War against Revolutionary France 1793-1802*, Ph.D thesis, University College, London 1968.

Connolly, S.J., *Divided Kingdom: Ireland 1630-1800*, Oxford University Press 2008.

Cookson, J.E., *The British Armed Nation 1793-1815*, Clarendon Press 1997.

Cornwallis-West, G., *The Life and Letters of Admiral Cornwallis*, London 1927.

Day, Roger, *Sir John Moore: 'Not a Drum was Heard'*, Leo Cooper 2001.

Delavoye, Alex M., *Life of Thomas Graham Lord Lynedoch*, London 1880.

Dodge, Theodore A., *Warfare in the Age of Napoleon*, Riverside 1907; Leonaur 2011.

Douglas, R.B., *From Valmy to Waterloo: Extracts from the Diary of Captain Charles François*, London 1906.

Duffy, Michael, *Soldiers, Sugar, and Seapower: the British Expeditions to the West Indies and the War against Revolutionary France*, Clarendon Press, 1987.

Dunfermline, James Lord, *Lieutenant-General Sir Ralph Abercromby, A Memoir*, 1861; Naval and Military Press Ltd reprint.

Ellis, A.B., *The First West India Regiment*, Chapman & Hall 1885.

Esdaile, Charles, *Napoleon's Wars*, Penguin Books 2008.

Fitchett, W.H., *How England Saved Europe*, London 1899.

Fortescue, The Hon. J.W., *A History of the British Army*, Macmillan 1906.

Fremont-Barnes, Gregory, *The French Revolutionary Wars*, Osprey 2001.

Furber, Holden, *Henry Dundas, First Viscount Melville, 1741-1811*, Oxford University Press 1931.

Fry, Michael, *The Dundas Despotism*, Edinburgh University Press 1992.

Gardyne, Lt-Col C. Greenhill, *The Life of a Regiment: The History of the Gordon Highlanders from its Formation in 1794 to 1816*, London 1901.

Garnham, Neal, *The Militia in Eighteenth Century Ireland: In Defence of the Protestant Interest*, The Boydell Press 2012.

Glover, Michael, *Warfare in the Age of Bonaparte*, Guild Publishing 1980.

Glover, Richard, *Peninsular Preparation: the Reform of the British Army 1795-1809*, Cambridge University Press 1970.

Gould, Robert W., *Mercenaries of the Napoleonic Wars*, Tom Donovan 1995.

Graves, Donald E., *Fix Bayonets: a Royal Welch Fusilier at War 1796-1815*, Spellmount 2007.

Groves, Major J. Percy, *Some Notable Generals and their Notable Battles*, London 1893.

Guy, Alan J. (ed.), *The Road to Waterloo*, National Army Museum 1990.

Hague, William, *William Pitt the Younger*, Harper Collins 2004.

Harvey, Robert, *The War of Wars: the Epic Struggle between Britain and France 1793-1815*, Constable & Robinson Ltd 2006.

Hill, Joanna, *Wellington's Right Hand Man: Rowland, Viscount Hill*, The History Press 2011.

Holland Rose, J., *William Pitt and the Great War*, G. Bell & Sons 1912.

Howard, Martin, *Death before Glory! The British Soldier in the West Indies in the French Revolutionary & Napoleonic Wars*, Pen & Sword 2015.

Howard, Robert, *Wellington's Welsh General: A Life of Sir Thomas Picton*, Aurum Press 1996.

Jacob, Rosamund, *The Rise of the United Irishmen 1791-94*, Harrap & Co. Ltd 1937.

Joseph, Edward Lanzon, *History of Trinidad*, Routledge 1970.

Jupp, Peter, *Lord Grenville*, Clarendon Press 1985.

Knight, Roger, *Britain against Napoleon: the Organization of Victory 1793-1815*, Penguin Books 2014.

Lecky, William Edward Hartpole, *A History of Ireland in the Eighteenth Century*, Longmans, Green 1892–1896; Cambridge University Press reprint 2010.

Longford, Elizabeth, *Wellington: the Years of the Sword*, Weidenfeld and Nicholson 1969.

Macdonald, Janet, *Sir John Moore: the Making of a Controversial Hero*, Pen & Sword 2016.

Mackesy, Piers, *The Strategy of Overthrow 1798-1799*, Longman 1974.

_____, *War without Victory: the Downfall of Pitt 1799-1802*, Clarendon Press 1984.

_____, *British Victory in Egypt: the End of Napoleon's Conquest*, Routledge 1995.

Madden, Richard Robert, *The United Irishmen, their Lives and Times*, James Duffy, Dublin 1854.

Mahan, A.T., *The Influence of Sea Power upon the French Revolution and Empire*, 1892; Forgotten Books 2012.

Mallinson, Allan, *The Making of the British Army: From the English Civil War to the War on Terror*, Bantam Press 2009.

Martin, Yves, *The French Army of the Orient 1798-1801: Napoleon's Beloved 'Egyptians'*, Helion & Company 2017.

Mathieson, C., *The Life of Henry Dundas, 1st Viscount Melville*, Constable & Co. 1933.

McAnally, Henry, *The Irish Militia 1793-1816*, Eyre and Spottiswood 1949.

McPhee, Peter, *Liberty or Death: the French Revolution*, Yale University Press 2016.

Morewood, John, *Waterloo General*, Pen & Sword 2016.

Morris, Roger, *The Foundations of British Maritime Ascendancy 1755-1815*, Cambridge University Press 2011.

Myatt, Frederick, *Peninsular General: Sir Thomas Picton 1758-1815*, David & Charles 1980.

Packenham, Thomas, *The Year of Liberty: the Great Irish Rebellion of 1798*, Weidenfeld & Nicolson, revised edition 1997.

Philpin, C.H.E. (ed.), *Nationalism and Popular Protest in Ireland*, Cambridge University Press 1987.

Reiter, Jacqueline, *The Late Lord: the Life of John Pitt, 2nd Earl of Chatham*, Pen & Sword 2017.

Rodger, A.B., *The War of the Second Coalition 1798-1801: a Strategic Commentary*, Clarendon Press 1964.

Roider, Karl A., *Baron Thugut and the Austrian Response to the French Revolution*, Princeton University Press 1987.

Rose, J. Holland, *Pitt and Napoleon: Essays and Letters*, G. Bell & Sons 1912.

_____, *William Pitt and the Great War*, G. Bell & Sons 1912.

Rosebery, Lord, *Pitt*, London 1891.

Rothenburg, Gunther E., *The Art of Warfare in the Age of Napoleon*, Batsford 1978.

_____, *Napoleon's Great Adversaries: The Archduke Charles and the Austrian Army 1792-1814*, Batsford 1982.

Schama, Simon, *Patriots & Liberators: Revolution in the Netherlands 1780-1813*, Collins 1977.

Shankland, Peter, *Beware of Heroes: Admiral Sir Sidney Smith's War against Napoleon*, William Kimber 1975.

Smyth, Jim, *The Men of No Property: Irish Radicals and Popular Politics of the Late Eighteenth Century*, Palgrave Macmillan 1998.

Stathern, Paul, *Napoleon in Egypt: 'The Greatest Glory'*, Jonathan Cape 2007.

Tillyard, Stella, *Citizen Lord*, Farrar Strauss & Giroux 1998.

Vivian, Claud, *Hussey Vivian: Wellington's Hussar General*, Leonaur 2010.

Ward, Sir A.W. and Gooch, G.P. (eds), *The Cambridge History of British Foreign Policy 1783-1919*, Cambridge University Press 1922.

Wills, Garry David, *Wellington's First Battle: Combat for Boxtel, 15th September 1794*, Caseshot Publishing 2011.

Winterbottom, Derek, *The Grand Old Duke of York*, Pen & Sword 2016.

Index